C-1739   CAREER EXAMINATION SERIES

This is your
PASSBOOK for...

Police Officer, New York Police Dept. (NYPD)

Test Preparation Study Guide
Questions & Answers

COPYRIGHT NOTICE

This book is SOLELY intended for, is sold ONLY to, and its use is RESTRICTED to individual, bona fide applicants or candidates who qualify by virtue of having seriously filed applications for appropriate license, certificate, professional and/or promotional advancement, higher school matriculation, scholarship, or other legitimate requirements of education and/or governmental authorities.

This book is NOT intended for use, class instruction, tutoring, training, duplication, copying, reprinting, excerption, or adaptation, etc., by:

1) Other publishers
2) Proprietors and/or Instructors of "Coaching" and/or Preparatory Courses
3) Personnel and/or Training Divisions of commercial, industrial, and governmental organizations
4) Schools, colleges, or universities and/or their departments and staffs, including teachers and other personnel
5) Testing Agencies or Bureaus
6) Study groups which seek by the purchase of a single volume to copy and/or duplicate and/or adapt this material for use by the group as a whole without having purchased individual volumes for each of the members of the group
7) Et al.

Such persons would be in violation of appropriate Federal and State statutes.

PROVISION OF LICENSING AGREEMENTS – Recognized educational, commercial, industrial, and governmental institutions and organizations, and others legitimately engaged in educational pursuits, including training, testing, and measurement activities, may address request for a licensing agreement to the copyright owners, who will determine whether, and under what conditions, including fees and charges, the materials in this book may be used them. In other words, a licensing facility exists for the legitimate use of the material in this book on other than an individual basis. However, it is asseverated and affirmed here that the material in this book CANNOT be used without the receipt of the express permission of such a licensing agreement from the Publishers. Inquiries re licensing should be addressed to the company, attention rights and permissions department.

All rights reserved, including the right of reproduction in whole or in part, in any form or by any means, electronic or mechanical, including photocopying, recording, or by any information storage and retrieval system, without permission in writing from the Publisher.

Copyright © 2024 by
National Learning Corporation

212 Michael Drive, Syosset, NY 11791
(516) 921-8888 • www.passbooks.com
E-mail: info@passbooks.com

PUBLISHED IN THE UNITED STATES OF AMERICA

PASSBOOK® SERIES

THE *PASSBOOK® SERIES* has been created to prepare applicants and candidates for the ultimate academic battlefield – the examination room.

At some time in our lives, each and every one of us may be required to take an examination – for validation, matriculation, admission, qualification, registration, certification, or licensure.

Based on the assumption that every applicant or candidate has met the basic formal educational standards, has taken the required number of courses, and read the necessary texts, the *PASSBOOK® SERIES* furnishes the one special preparation which may assure passing with confidence, instead of failing with insecurity. Examination questions – together with answers – are furnished as the basic vehicle for study so that the mysteries of the examination and its compounding difficulties may be eliminated or diminished by a sure method.

This book is meant to help you pass your examination provided that you qualify and are serious in your objective.

The entire field is reviewed through the huge store of content information which is succinctly presented through a provocative and challenging approach – the question-and-answer method.

A climate of success is established by furnishing the correct answers at the end of each test.

You soon learn to recognize types of questions, forms of questions, and patterns of questioning. You may even begin to anticipate expected outcomes.

You perceive that many questions are repeated or adapted so that you can gain acute insights, which may enable you to score many sure points.

You learn how to confront new questions, or types of questions, and to attack them confidently and work out the correct answers.

You note objectives and emphases, and recognize pitfalls and dangers, so that you may make positive educational adjustments.

Moreover, you are kept fully informed in relation to new concepts, methods, practices, and directions in the field.

You discover that you are actually taking the examination all the time: you are preparing for the examination by "taking" an examination, not by reading extraneous and/or supererogatory textbooks.

In short, this PASSBOOK®, used directedly, should be an important factor in helping you to pass your test.

POLICE OFFICER, NYPD

DUTIES
Police Officers perform general police duties and related work in the New York City Police Department. They patrol an assigned area on foot or in a vehicle; apprehend crime suspects; intervene in various situations involving crimes in progress, aided cases, complaints, emotionally disturbed persons, etc.; respond to and investigate vehicular accidents; investigate specific offenses; interact with prisoners; operate and maintain patrol vehicles; issue summonses; obtain information regarding incidents by interviewing witnesses, victims and/or complainants; safeguard and voucher found, seized or recovered property; provide information to the public; handle situations involving maltreated, abused or missing children; interact with juveniles; prepare forms and reports; testify in court; and perform related work.

Some of the physical activities performed by Police Officers and environmental conditions experienced are: working outdoors in all kinds of weather; walking and/or standing in an assigned area during a tour; driving or sitting in a patrol car during a tour while remaining alert; running after a fleeing suspect; climbing up stairs; carrying an injured adult with assistance; gripping persons to prevent escape; restraining a suspect by use of handcuffs; detecting odors such as those caused by smoke or gas leaks; engaging in hand-to-hand struggles to subdue a suspect resisting arrest; being physically active for prolonged periods of time; understanding verbal communication over the radio with background noise; reading and writing under low-light conditions; carrying or wearing heavy equipment and wearing a bullet-resistant vest.

SCOPE OF THE EXAMINATION
The written test will cover knowledge, skills and/or abilities in such areas as:

1. Written comprehension;
2. Written expression;
3. Memorization;
4. Problem sensitivity;
5. Inductive and deductive reasoning;
6. Information ordering;
7. Spatial orientation; and
8. Visualization.

HOW TO TAKE A TEST

I. YOU MUST PASS AN EXAMINATION

A. WHAT EVERY CANDIDATE SHOULD KNOW

Examination applicants often ask us for help in preparing for the written test. What can I study in advance? What kinds of questions will be asked? How will the test be given? How will the papers be graded?

As an applicant for a civil service examination, you may be wondering about some of these things. Our purpose here is to suggest effective methods of advance study and to describe civil service examinations.

Your chances for success on this examination can be increased if you know how to prepare. Those "pre-examination jitters" can be reduced if you know what to expect. You can even experience an adventure in good citizenship if you know why civil service exams are given.

B. WHY ARE CIVIL SERVICE EXAMINATIONS GIVEN?

Civil service examinations are important to you in two ways. As a citizen, you want public jobs filled by employees who know how to do their work. As a job seeker, you want a fair chance to compete for that job on an equal footing with other candidates. The best-known means of accomplishing this two-fold goal is the competitive examination.

Exams are widely publicized throughout the nation. They may be administered for jobs in federal, state, city, municipal, town or village governments or agencies.

Any citizen may apply, with some limitations, such as the age or residence of applicants. Your experience and education may be reviewed to see whether you meet the requirements for the particular examination. When these requirements exist, they are reasonable and applied consistently to all applicants. Thus, a competitive examination may cause you some uneasiness now, but it is your privilege and safeguard.

C. HOW ARE CIVIL SERVICE EXAMS DEVELOPED?

Examinations are carefully written by trained technicians who are specialists in the field known as "psychological measurement," in consultation with recognized authorities in the field of work that the test will cover. These experts recommend the subject matter areas or skills to be tested; only those knowledges or skills important to your success on the job are included. The most reliable books and source materials available are used as references. Together, the experts and technicians judge the difficulty level of the questions.

Test technicians know how to phrase questions so that the problem is clearly stated. Their ethics do not permit "trick" or "catch" questions. Questions may have been tried out on sample groups, or subjected to statistical analysis, to determine their usefulness.

Written tests are often used in combination with performance tests, ratings of training and experience, and oral interviews. All of these measures combine to form the best-known means of finding the right person for the right job.

II. HOW TO PASS THE WRITTEN TEST

A. NATURE OF THE EXAMINATION

To prepare intelligently for civil service examinations, you should know how they differ from school examinations you have taken. In school you were assigned certain definite pages to read or subjects to cover. The examination questions were quite detailed and usually emphasized memory. Civil service exams, on the other hand, try to discover your present ability to perform the duties of a position, plus your potentiality to learn these duties. In other words, a civil service exam attempts to predict how successful you will be. Questions cover such a broad area that they cannot be as minute and detailed as school exam questions.

In the public service similar kinds of work, or positions, are grouped together in one "class." This process is known as *position-classification*. All the positions in a class are paid according to the salary range for that class. One class title covers all of these positions, and they are all tested by the same examination.

B. FOUR BASIC STEPS

1) Study the announcement

How, then, can you know what subjects to study? Our best answer is: "Learn as much as possible about the class of positions for which you've applied." The exam will test the knowledge, skills and abilities needed to do the work.

Your most valuable source of information about the position you want is the official exam announcement. This announcement lists the training and experience qualifications. Check these standards and apply only if you come reasonably close to meeting them.

The brief description of the position in the examination announcement offers some clues to the subjects which will be tested. Think about the job itself. Review the duties in your mind. Can you perform them, or are there some in which you are rusty? Fill in the blank spots in your preparation.

Many jurisdictions preview the written test in the exam announcement by including a section called "Knowledge and Abilities Required," "Scope of the Examination," or some similar heading. Here you will find out specifically what fields will be tested.

2) Review your own background

Once you learn in general what the position is all about, and what you need to know to do the work, ask yourself which subjects you already know fairly well and which need improvement. You may wonder whether to concentrate on improving your strong areas or on building some background in your fields of weakness. When the announcement has specified "some knowledge" or "considerable knowledge," or has used adjectives like "beginning principles of..." or "advanced ... methods," you can get a clue as to the number and difficulty of questions to be asked in any given field. More questions, and hence broader coverage, would be included for those subjects which are more important in the work. Now weigh your strengths and weaknesses against the job requirements and prepare accordingly.

3) Determine the level of the position

Another way to tell how intensively you should prepare is to understand the level of the job for which you are applying. Is it the entering level? In other words, is this the position in which beginners in a field of work are hired? Or is it an intermediate or advanced level? Sometimes this is indicated by such words as "Junior" or "Senior" in the class title. Other jurisdictions use Roman numerals to designate the level – Clerk I, Clerk II, for example. The word "Supervisor" sometimes appears in the title. If the level is not indicated by the title, check the description of duties. Will you be working under very close supervision, or will you have responsibility for independent decisions in this work?

4) Choose appropriate study materials

Now that you know the subjects to be examined and the relative amount of each subject to be covered, you can choose suitable study materials. For beginning level jobs, or even advanced ones, if you have a pronounced weakness in some aspect of your training, read a modern, standard textbook in that field. Be sure it is up to date and has general coverage. Such books are normally available at your library, and the librarian will be glad to help you locate one. For entry-level positions, questions of appropriate difficulty are chosen -- neither highly advanced questions, nor those too simple. Such questions require careful thought but not advanced training.

If the position for which you are applying is technical or advanced, you will read more advanced, specialized material. If you are already familiar with the basic principles of your field, elementary textbooks would waste your time. Concentrate on advanced textbooks and technical periodicals. Think through the concepts and review difficult problems in your field.

These are all general sources. You can get more ideas on your own initiative, following these leads. For example, training manuals and publications of the government agency which employs workers in your field can be useful, particularly for technical and professional positions. A letter or visit to the government department involved may result in more specific study suggestions, and certainly will provide you with a more definite idea of the exact nature of the position you are seeking.

III. KINDS OF TESTS

Tests are used for purposes other than measuring knowledge and ability to perform specified duties. For some positions, it is equally important to test ability to make adjustments to new situations or to profit from training. In others, basic mental abilities not dependent on information are essential. Questions which test these things may not appear as pertinent to the duties of the position as those which test for knowledge and information. Yet they are often highly important parts of a fair examination. For very general questions, it is almost impossible to help you direct your study efforts. What we can do is to point out some of the more common of these general abilities needed in public service positions and describe some typical questions.

1) General information

Broad, general information has been found useful for predicting job success in some kinds of work. This is tested in a variety of ways, from vocabulary lists to questions about current events. Basic background in some field of work, such as sociology or economics, may be sampled in a group of questions. Often these are principles which have become familiar to most persons through exposure rather than through formal training. It is difficult to advise you how to study for these questions; being alert to the world around you is our best suggestion.

2) Verbal ability

An example of an ability needed in many positions is verbal or language ability. Verbal ability is, in brief, the ability to use and understand words. Vocabulary and grammar tests are typical measures of this ability. Reading comprehension or paragraph interpretation questions are common in many kinds of civil service tests. You are given a paragraph of written material and asked to find its central meaning.

3) Numerical ability

Number skills can be tested by the familiar arithmetic problem, by checking paired lists of numbers to see which are alike and which are different, or by interpreting charts and graphs. In the latter test, a graph may be printed in the test booklet which you are asked to use as the basis for answering questions.

4) Observation

A popular test for law-enforcement positions is the observation test. A picture is shown to you for several minutes, then taken away. Questions about the picture test your ability to observe both details and larger elements.

5) Following directions

In many positions in the public service, the employee must be able to carry out written instructions dependably and accurately. You may be given a chart with several columns, each column listing a variety of information. The questions require you to carry out directions involving the information given in the chart.

6) Skills and aptitudes

Performance tests effectively measure some manual skills and aptitudes. When the skill is one in which you are trained, such as typing or shorthand, you can practice. These tests are often very much like those given in business school or high school courses. For many of the other skills and aptitudes, however, no short-time preparation can be made. Skills and abilities natural to you or that you have developed throughout your lifetime are being tested.

Many of the general questions just described provide all the data needed to answer the questions and ask you to use your reasoning ability to find the answers. Your best preparation for these tests, as well as for tests of facts and ideas, is to be at your physical and mental best. You, no doubt, have your own methods of getting into an exam-taking mood and keeping "in shape." The next section lists some ideas on this subject.

IV. KINDS OF QUESTIONS

Only rarely is the "essay" question, which you answer in narrative form, used in civil service tests. Civil service tests are usually of the short-answer type. Full instructions for answering these questions will be given to you at the examination. But in case this is your first experience with short-answer questions and separate answer sheets, here is what you need to know:

1) Multiple-choice Questions

Most popular of the short-answer questions is the "multiple choice" or "best answer" question. It can be used, for example, to test for factual knowledge, ability to solve problems or judgment in meeting situations found at work.

A multiple-choice question is normally one of three types—
- It can begin with an incomplete statement followed by several possible endings. You are to find the one ending which *best* completes the statement, although some of the others may not be entirely wrong.
- It can also be a complete statement in the form of a question which is answered by choosing one of the statements listed.

- It can be in the form of a problem – again you select the best answer.

Here is an example of a multiple-choice question with a discussion which should give you some clues as to the method for choosing the right answer:

When an employee has a complaint about his assignment, the action which will *best* help him overcome his difficulty is to
- A. discuss his difficulty with his coworkers
- B. take the problem to the head of the organization
- C. take the problem to the person who gave him the assignment
- D. say nothing to anyone about his complaint

In answering this question, you should study each of the choices to find which is best. Consider choice "A" – Certainly an employee may discuss his complaint with fellow employees, but no change or improvement can result, and the complaint remains unresolved. Choice "B" is a poor choice since the head of the organization probably does not know what assignment you have been given, and taking your problem to him is known as "going over the head" of the supervisor. The supervisor, or person who made the assignment, is the person who can clarify it or correct any injustice. Choice "C" is, therefore, correct. To say nothing, as in choice "D," is unwise. Supervisors have and interest in knowing the problems employees are facing, and the employee is seeking a solution to his problem.

2) True/False Questions

The "true/false" or "right/wrong" form of question is sometimes used. Here a complete statement is given. Your job is to decide whether the statement is right or wrong.

SAMPLE: A roaming cell-phone call to a nearby city costs less than a non-roaming call to a distant city.

This statement is wrong, or false, since roaming calls are more expensive.

This is not a complete list of all possible question forms, although most of the others are variations of these common types. You will always get complete directions for answering questions. Be sure you understand *how* to mark your answers – ask questions until you do.

V. RECORDING YOUR ANSWERS

Computer terminals are used more and more today for many different kinds of exams.

For an examination with very few applicants, you may be told to record your answers in the test booklet itself. Separate answer sheets are much more common. If this separate answer sheet is to be scored by machine – and this is often the case – it is highly important that you mark your answers correctly in order to get credit.

An electronic scoring machine is often used in civil service offices because of the speed with which papers can be scored. Machine-scored answer sheets must be marked with a pencil, which will be given to you. This pencil has a high graphite content which responds to the electronic scoring machine. As a matter of fact, stray dots may register as answers, so do not let your pencil rest on the answer sheet while you are pondering the correct answer. Also, if your pencil lead breaks or is otherwise defective, ask for another.

Since the answer sheet will be dropped in a slot in the scoring machine, be careful not to bend the corners or get the paper crumpled.

The answer sheet normally has five vertical columns of numbers, with 30 numbers to a column. These numbers correspond to the question numbers in your test booklet. After each number, going across the page are four or five pairs of dotted lines. These short dotted lines have small letters or numbers above them. The first two pairs may also have a "T" or "F" above the letters. This indicates that the first two pairs only are to be used if the questions are of the true-false type. If the questions are multiple choice, disregard the "T" and "F" and pay attention only to the small letters or numbers.

Answer your questions in the manner of the sample that follows:

32. The largest city in the United States is
 A. Washington, D.C.
 B. New York City
 C. Chicago
 D. Detroit
 E. San Francisco

1) Choose the answer you think is best. (New York City is the largest, so "B" is correct.)
2) Find the row of dotted lines numbered the same as the question you are answering. (Find row number 32)
3) Find the pair of dotted lines corresponding to the answer. (Find the pair of lines under the mark "B.")
4) Make a solid black mark between the dotted lines.

VI. BEFORE THE TEST

Common sense will help you find procedures to follow to get ready for an examination. Too many of us, however, overlook these sensible measures. Indeed, nervousness and fatigue have been found to be the most serious reasons why applicants fail to do their best on civil service tests. Here is a list of reminders:

- Begin your preparation early – Don't wait until the last minute to go scurrying around for books and materials or to find out what the position is all about.
- Prepare continuously – An hour a night for a week is better than an all-night cram session. This has been definitely established. What is more, a night a week for a month will return better dividends than crowding your study into a shorter period of time.
- Locate the place of the exam – You have been sent a notice telling you when and where to report for the examination. If the location is in a different town or otherwise unfamiliar to you, it would be well to inquire the best route and learn something about the building.
- Relax the night before the test – Allow your mind to rest. Do not study at all that night. Plan some mild recreation or diversion; then go to bed early and get a good night's sleep.
- Get up early enough to make a leisurely trip to the place for the test – This way unforeseen events, traffic snarls, unfamiliar buildings, etc. will not upset you.
- Dress comfortably – A written test is not a fashion show. You will be known by number and not by name, so wear something comfortable.

- Leave excess paraphernalia at home – Shopping bags and odd bundles will get in your way. You need bring only the items mentioned in the official notice you received; usually everything you need is provided. Do not bring reference books to the exam. They will only confuse those last minutes and be taken away from you when in the test room.
- Arrive somewhat ahead of time – If because of transportation schedules you must get there very early, bring a newspaper or magazine to take your mind off yourself while waiting.
- Locate the examination room – When you have found the proper room, you will be directed to the seat or part of the room where you will sit. Sometimes you are given a sheet of instructions to read while you are waiting. Do not fill out any forms until you are told to do so; just read them and be prepared.
- Relax and prepare to listen to the instructions
- If you have any physical problem that may keep you from doing your best, be sure to tell the test administrator. If you are sick or in poor health, you really cannot do your best on the exam. You can come back and take the test some other time.

VII. AT THE TEST

The day of the test is here and you have the test booklet in your hand. The temptation to get going is very strong. Caution! There is more to success than knowing the right answers. You must know how to identify your papers and understand variations in the type of short-answer question used in this particular examination. Follow these suggestions for maximum results from your efforts:

1) Cooperate with the monitor

The test administrator has a duty to create a situation in which you can be as much at ease as possible. He will give instructions, tell you when to begin, check to see that you are marking your answer sheet correctly, and so on. He is not there to guard you, although he will see that your competitors do not take unfair advantage. He wants to help you do your best.

2) Listen to all instructions

Don't jump the gun! Wait until you understand all directions. In most civil service tests you get more time than you need to answer the questions. So don't be in a hurry. Read each word of instructions until you clearly understand the meaning. Study the examples, listen to all announcements and follow directions. Ask questions if you do not understand what to do.

3) Identify your papers

Civil service exams are usually identified by number only. You will be assigned a number; you must not put your name on your test papers. Be sure to copy your number correctly. Since more than one exam may be given, copy your exact examination title.

4) Plan your time

Unless you are told that a test is a "speed" or "rate of work" test, speed itself is usually not important. Time enough to answer all the questions will be provided, but this does not mean that you have all day. An overall time limit has been set. Divide the total time (in minutes) by the number of questions to determine the approximate time you have for each question.

5) Do not linger over difficult questions

If you come across a difficult question, mark it with a paper clip (useful to have along) and come back to it when you have been through the booklet. One caution if you do this – be sure to skip a number on your answer sheet as well. Check often to be sure that you have not lost your place and that you are marking in the row numbered the same as the question you are answering.

6) Read the questions

Be sure you know what the question asks! Many capable people are unsuccessful because they failed to *read* the questions correctly.

7) Answer all questions

Unless you have been instructed that a penalty will be deducted for incorrect answers, it is better to guess than to omit a question.

8) Speed tests

It is often better NOT to guess on speed tests. It has been found that on timed tests people are tempted to spend the last few seconds before time is called in marking answers at random – without even reading them – in the hope of picking up a few extra points. To discourage this practice, the instructions may warn you that your score will be "corrected" for guessing. That is, a penalty will be applied. The incorrect answers will be deducted from the correct ones, or some other penalty formula will be used.

9) Review your answers

If you finish before time is called, go back to the questions you guessed or omitted to give them further thought. Review other answers if you have time.

10) Return your test materials

If you are ready to leave before others have finished or time is called, take ALL your materials to the monitor and leave quietly. Never take any test material with you. The monitor can discover whose papers are not complete, and taking a test booklet may be grounds for disqualification.

VIII. EXAMINATION TECHNIQUES

1) Read the general instructions carefully. These are usually printed on the first page of the exam booklet. As a rule, these instructions refer to the timing of the examination; the fact that you should not start work until the signal and must stop work at a signal, etc. If there are any *special* instructions, such as a choice of questions to be answered, make sure that you note this instruction carefully.

2) When you are ready to start work on the examination, that is as soon as the signal has been given, read the instructions to each question booklet, underline any key words or phrases, such as *least, best, outline, describe* and the like. In this way you will tend to answer as requested rather than discover on reviewing your paper that you *listed without describing*, that you selected the *worst* choice rather than the *best* choice, etc.

3) If the examination is of the objective or multiple-choice type – that is, each question will also give a series of possible answers: A, B, C or D, and you are called upon to select the best answer and write the letter next to that answer on your answer paper – it is advisable to start answering each question in turn. There may be anywhere from 50 to 100 such questions in the three or four hours allotted and you can see how much time would be taken if you read through all the questions before beginning to answer any. Furthermore, if you come across a question or group of questions which you know would be difficult to answer, it would undoubtedly affect your handling of all the other questions.

4) If the examination is of the essay type and contains but a few questions, it is a moot point as to whether you should read all the questions before starting to answer any one. Of course, if you are given a choice – say five out of seven and the like – then it is essential to read all the questions so you can eliminate the two that are most difficult. If, however, you are asked to answer all the questions, there may be danger in trying to answer the easiest one first because you may find that you will spend too much time on it. The best technique is to answer the first question, then proceed to the second, etc.

5) Time your answers. Before the exam begins, write down the time it started, then add the time allowed for the examination and write down the time it must be completed, then divide the time available somewhat as follows:
    - If 3-1/2 hours are allowed, that would be 210 minutes. If you have 80 objective-type questions, that would be an average of 2-1/2 minutes per question. Allow yourself no more than 2 minutes per question, or a total of 160 minutes, which will permit about 50 minutes to review.
    - If for the time allotment of 210 minutes there are 7 essay questions to answer, that would average about 30 minutes a question. Give yourself only 25 minutes per question so that you have about 35 minutes to review.

6) The most important instruction is to *read each question* and make sure you know what is wanted. The second most important instruction is to *time yourself properly* so that you answer every question. The third most important instruction is to *answer every question*. Guess if you have to but include something for each question. Remember that you will receive no credit for a blank and will probably receive some credit if you write something in answer to an essay question. If you guess a letter – say "B" for a multiple-choice question – you may have guessed right. If you leave a blank as an answer to a multiple-choice question, the examiners may respect your feelings but it will not add a point to your score. Some exams may penalize you for wrong answers, so in such cases *only*, you may not want to guess unless you have some basis for your answer.

7) Suggestions
    a. Objective-type questions
        1. Examine the question booklet for proper sequence of pages and questions
        2. Read all instructions carefully
        3. Skip any question which seems too difficult; return to it after all other questions have been answered
        4. Apportion your time properly; do not spend too much time on any single question or group of questions

5. Note and underline key words – *all, most, fewest, least, best, worst, same, opposite*, etc.
6. Pay particular attention to negatives
7. Note unusual option, e.g., unduly long, short, complex, different or similar in content to the body of the question
8. Observe the use of "hedging" words – *probably, may, most likely*, etc.
9. Make sure that your answer is put next to the same number as the question
10. Do not second-guess unless you have good reason to believe the second answer is definitely more correct
11. Cross out original answer if you decide another answer is more accurate; do not erase until you are ready to hand your paper in
12. Answer all questions; guess unless instructed otherwise
13. Leave time for review

  b. Essay questions
    1. Read each question carefully
    2. Determine exactly what is wanted. Underline key words or phrases.
    3. Decide on outline or paragraph answer
    4. Include many different points and elements unless asked to develop any one or two points or elements
    5. Show impartiality by giving pros and cons unless directed to select one side only
    6. Make and write down any assumptions you find necessary to answer the questions
    7. Watch your English, grammar, punctuation and choice of words
    8. Time your answers; don't crowd material

8) Answering the essay question

Most essay questions can be answered by framing the specific response around several key words or ideas. Here are a few such key words or ideas:

M's: manpower, materials, methods, money, management
P's: purpose, program, policy, plan, procedure, practice, problems, pitfalls, personnel, public relations

  a. Six basic steps in handling problems:
    1. Preliminary plan and background development
    2. Collect information, data and facts
    3. Analyze and interpret information, data and facts
    4. Analyze and develop solutions as well as make recommendations
    5. Prepare report and sell recommendations
    6. Install recommendations and follow up effectiveness

  b. Pitfalls to avoid
    1. *Taking things for granted* – A statement of the situation does not necessarily imply that each of the elements is necessarily true; for example, a complaint may be invalid and biased so that all that can be taken for granted is that a complaint has been registered

2. *Considering only one side of a situation* – Wherever possible, indicate several alternatives and then point out the reasons you selected the best one
3. *Failing to indicate follow up* – Whenever your answer indicates action on your part, make certain that you will take proper follow-up action to see how successful your recommendations, procedures or actions turn out to be
4. *Taking too long in answering any single question* – Remember to time your answers properly

IX. AFTER THE TEST

Scoring procedures differ in detail among civil service jurisdictions although the general principles are the same. Whether the papers are hand-scored or graded by machine we have described, they are nearly always graded by number. That is, the person who marks the paper knows only the number – never the name – of the applicant. Not until all the papers have been graded will they be matched with names. If other tests, such as training and experience or oral interview ratings have been given, scores will be combined. Different parts of the examination usually have different weights. For example, the written test might count 60 percent of the final grade, and a rating of training and experience 40 percent. In many jurisdictions, veterans will have a certain number of points added to their grades.

After the final grade has been determined, the names are placed in grade order and an eligible list is established. There are various methods for resolving ties between those who get the same final grade – probably the most common is to place first the name of the person whose application was received first. Job offers are made from the eligible list in the order the names appear on it. You will be notified of your grade and your rank as soon as all these computations have been made. This will be done as rapidly as possible.

People who are found to meet the requirements in the announcement are called "eligibles." Their names are put on a list of eligible candidates. An eligible's chances of getting a job depend on how high he stands on this list and how fast agencies are filling jobs from the list.

When a job is to be filled from a list of eligibles, the agency asks for the names of people on the list of eligibles for that job. When the civil service commission receives this request, it sends to the agency the names of the three people highest on this list. Or, if the job to be filled has specialized requirements, the office sends the agency the names of the top three persons who meet these requirements from the general list.

The appointing officer makes a choice from among the three people whose names were sent to him. If the selected person accepts the appointment, the names of the others are put back on the list to be considered for future openings.

That is the rule in hiring from all kinds of eligible lists, whether they are for typist, carpenter, chemist, or something else. For every vacancy, the appointing officer has his choice of any one of the top three eligibles on the list. This explains why the person whose name is on top of the list sometimes does not get an appointment when some of the persons lower on the list do. If the appointing officer chooses the second or third eligible, the No. 1 eligible does not get a job at once, but stays on the list until he is appointed or the list is terminated.

X. HOW TO PASS THE INTERVIEW TEST

The examination for which you applied requires an oral interview test. You have already taken the written test and you are now being called for the interview test – the final part of the formal examination.

You may think that it is not possible to prepare for an interview test and that there are no procedures to follow during an interview. Our purpose is to point out some things you can do in advance that will help you and some good rules to follow and pitfalls to avoid while you are being interviewed.

What is an interview supposed to test?

The written examination is designed to test the technical knowledge and competence of the candidate; the oral is designed to evaluate intangible qualities, not readily measured otherwise, and to establish a list showing the relative fitness of each candidate – as measured against his competitors – for the position sought. Scoring is not on the basis of "right" and "wrong," but on a sliding scale of values ranging from "not passable" to "outstanding." As a matter of fact, it is possible to achieve a relatively low score without a single "incorrect" answer because of evident weakness in the qualities being measured.

Occasionally, an examination may consist entirely of an oral test – either an individual or a group oral. In such cases, information is sought concerning the technical knowledges and abilities of the candidate, since there has been no written examination for this purpose. More commonly, however, an oral test is used to supplement a written examination.

Who conducts interviews?

The composition of oral boards varies among different jurisdictions. In nearly all, a representative of the personnel department serves as chairman. One of the members of the board may be a representative of the department in which the candidate would work. In some cases, "outside experts" are used, and, frequently, a businessman or some other representative of the general public is asked to serve. Labor and management or other special groups may be represented. The aim is to secure the services of experts in the appropriate field.

However the board is composed, it is a good idea (and not at all improper or unethical) to ascertain in advance of the interview who the members are and what groups they represent. When you are introduced to them, you will have some idea of their backgrounds and interests, and at least you will not stutter and stammer over their names.

What should be done before the interview?

While knowledge about the board members is useful and takes some of the surprise element out of the interview, there is other preparation which is more substantive. It *is* possible to prepare for an oral interview – in several ways:

1) Keep a copy of your application and review it carefully before the interview

This may be the only document before the oral board, and the starting point of the interview. Know what education and experience you have listed there, and the sequence and dates of all of it. Sometimes the board will ask you to review the highlights of your experience for them; you should not have to hem and haw doing it.

2) Study the class specification and the examination announcement

Usually, the oral board has one or both of these to guide them. The qualities, characteristics or knowledges required by the position sought are stated in these documents. They offer valuable clues as to the nature of the oral interview. For example, if the job involves supervisory responsibilities, the announcement will usually indicate that knowledge of modern supervisory methods and the qualifications of the candidate as a supervisor will be tested. If so, you can expect such questions, frequently in the form of a hypothetical situation which you are expected to solve. NEVER go into an oral without knowledge of the duties and responsibilities of the job you seek.

3) Think through each qualification required

Try to visualize the kind of questions you would ask if you were a board member. How well could you answer them? Try especially to appraise your own knowledge and background in each area, *measured against the job sought*, and identify any areas in which you are weak. Be critical and realistic – do not flatter yourself.

4) Do some general reading in areas in which you feel you may be weak

For example, if the job involves supervision and your past experience has NOT, some general reading in supervisory methods and practices, particularly in the field of human relations, might be useful. Do NOT study agency procedures or detailed manuals. The oral board will be testing your understanding and capacity, not your memory.

5) Get a good night's sleep and watch your general health and mental attitude

You will want a clear head at the interview. Take care of a cold or any other minor ailment, and of course, no hangovers.

What should be done on the day of the interview?

Now comes the day of the interview itself. Give yourself plenty of time to get there. Plan to arrive somewhat ahead of the scheduled time, particularly if your appointment is in the fore part of the day. If a previous candidate fails to appear, the board might be ready for you a bit early. By early afternoon an oral board is almost invariably behind schedule if there are many candidates, and you may have to wait. Take along a book or magazine to read, or your application to review, but leave any extraneous material in the waiting room when you go in for your interview. In any event, relax and compose yourself.

The matter of dress is important. The board is forming impressions about you – from your experience, your manners, your attitude, and your appearance. Give your personal appearance careful attention. Dress your best, but not your flashiest. Choose conservative, appropriate clothing, and be sure it is immaculate. This is a business interview, and your appearance should indicate that you regard it as such. Besides, being well groomed and properly dressed will help boost your confidence.

Sooner or later, someone will call your name and escort you into the interview room. *This is it.* From here on you are on your own. It is too late for any more preparation. But remember, you asked for this opportunity to prove your fitness, and you are here because your request was granted.

What happens when you go in?

The usual sequence of events will be as follows: The clerk (who is often the board stenographer) will introduce you to the chairman of the oral board, who will introduce you to the other members of the board. Acknowledge the introductions before you sit down. Do not be surprised if you find a microphone facing you or a stenotypist sitting by. Oral interviews are usually recorded in the event of an appeal or other review.

Usually the chairman of the board will open the interview by reviewing the highlights of your education and work experience from your application – primarily for the benefit of the other members of the board, as well as to get the material into the record. Do not interrupt or comment unless there is an error or significant misinterpretation; if that is the case, do not hesitate. But do not quibble about insignificant matters. Also, he will usually ask you some question about your education, experience or your present job – partly to get you to start talking and to establish the interviewing "rapport." He may start the actual questioning, or turn it over to one of the other members. Frequently, each member undertakes the questioning on a particular area, one in which he is perhaps most competent, so you can expect each member to participate in the examination. Because time is limited, you may also expect some rather abrupt switches in the direction the questioning takes, so do not be upset by it. Normally, a board member will not pursue a single line of questioning unless he discovers a particular strength or weakness.

After each member has participated, the chairman will usually ask whether any member has any further questions, then will ask you if you have anything you wish to add. Unless you are expecting this question, it may floor you. Worse, it may start you off on an extended, extemporaneous speech. The board is not usually seeking more information. The question is principally to offer you a last opportunity to present further qualifications or to indicate that you have nothing to add. So, if you feel that a significant qualification or characteristic has been overlooked, it is proper to point it out in a sentence or so. Do not compliment the board on the thoroughness of their examination – they have been sketchy, and you know it. If you wish, merely say, "No thank you, I have nothing further to add." This is a point where you can "talk yourself out" of a good impression or fail to present an important bit of information. Remember, *you close the interview yourself.*

The chairman will then say, "That is all, Mr. _____, thank you." Do not be startled; the interview is over, and quicker than you think. Thank him, gather your belongings and take your leave. Save your sigh of relief for the other side of the door.

How to put your best foot forward
Throughout this entire process, you may feel that the board individually and collectively is trying to pierce your defenses, seek out your hidden weaknesses and embarrass and confuse you. Actually, this is not true. They are obliged to make an appraisal of your qualifications for the job you are seeking, and they want to see you in your best light. Remember, they must interview all candidates and a non-cooperative candidate may become a failure in spite of their best efforts to bring out his qualifications. Here are 15 suggestions that will help you:

1) Be natural – Keep your attitude confident, not cocky
If you are not confident that you can do the job, do not expect the board to be. Do not apologize for your weaknesses, try to bring out your strong points. The board is interested in a positive, not negative, presentation. Cockiness will antagonize any board member and make him wonder if you are covering up a weakness by a false show of strength.

2) Get comfortable, but don't lounge or sprawl
Sit erectly but not stiffly. A careless posture may lead the board to conclude that you are careless in other things, or at least that you are not impressed by the importance of the occasion. Either conclusion is natural, even if incorrect. Do not fuss with your clothing, a pencil or an ashtray. Your hands may occasionally be useful to emphasize a point; do not let them become a point of distraction.

3) Do not wisecrack or make small talk
This is a serious situation, and your attitude should show that you consider it as such. Further, the time of the board is limited – they do not want to waste it, and neither should you.

4) Do not exaggerate your experience or abilities

In the first place, from information in the application or other interviews and sources, the board may know more about you than you think. Secondly, you probably will not get away with it. An experienced board is rather adept at spotting such a situation, so do not take the chance.

5) If you know a board member, do not make a point of it, yet do not hide it

Certainly you are not fooling him, and probably not the other members of the board. Do not try to take advantage of your acquaintanceship – it will probably do you little good.

6) Do not dominate the interview

Let the board do that. They will give you the clues – do not assume that you have to do all the talking. Realize that the board has a number of questions to ask you, and do not try to take up all the interview time by showing off your extensive knowledge of the answer to the first one.

7) Be attentive

You only have 20 minutes or so, and you should keep your attention at its sharpest throughout. When a member is addressing a problem or question to you, give him your undivided attention. Address your reply principally to him, but do not exclude the other board members.

8) Do not interrupt

A board member may be stating a problem for you to analyze. He will ask you a question when the time comes. Let him state the problem, and wait for the question.

9) Make sure you understand the question

Do not try to answer until you are sure what the question is. If it is not clear, restate it in your own words or ask the board member to clarify it for you. However, do not haggle about minor elements.

10) Reply promptly but not hastily

A common entry on oral board rating sheets is "candidate responded readily," or "candidate hesitated in replies." Respond as promptly and quickly as you can, but do not jump to a hasty, ill-considered answer.

11) Do not be peremptory in your answers

A brief answer is proper – but do not fire your answer back. That is a losing game from your point of view. The board member can probably ask questions much faster than you can answer them.

12) Do not try to create the answer you think the board member wants

He is interested in what kind of mind you have and how it works – not in playing games. Furthermore, he can usually spot this practice and will actually grade you down on it.

13) Do not switch sides in your reply merely to agree with a board member

Frequently, a member will take a contrary position merely to draw you out and to see if you are willing and able to defend your point of view. Do not start a debate, yet do not surrender a good position. If a position is worth taking, it is worth defending.

14) Do not be afraid to admit an error in judgment if you are shown to be wrong

The board knows that you are forced to reply without any opportunity for careful consideration. Your answer may be demonstrably wrong. If so, admit it and get on with the interview.

15) Do not dwell at length on your present job

The opening question may relate to your present assignment. Answer the question but do not go into an extended discussion. You are being examined for a *new* job, not your present one. As a matter of fact, try to phrase ALL your answers in terms of the job for which you are being examined.

Basis of Rating

Probably you will forget most of these "do's" and "don'ts" when you walk into the oral interview room. Even remembering them all will not ensure you a passing grade. Perhaps you did not have the qualifications in the first place. But remembering them will help you to put your best foot forward, without treading on the toes of the board members.

Rumor and popular opinion to the contrary notwithstanding, an oral board wants you to make the best appearance possible. They know you are under pressure – but they also want to see how you respond to it as a guide to what your reaction would be under the pressures of the job you seek. They will be influenced by the degree of poise you display, the personal traits you show and the manner in which you respond.

ABOUT THIS BOOK

This book contains tests divided into Examination Sections. Go through each test, answering every question in the margin. We have also attached a sample answer sheet at the back of the book that can be removed and used. At the end of each test look at the answer key and check your answers. On the ones you got wrong, look at the right answer choice and learn. Do not fill in the answers first. Do not memorize the questions and answers, but understand the answer and principles involved. On your test, the questions will likely be different from the samples. Questions are changed and new ones added. If you understand these past questions you should have success with any changes that arise. Tests may consist of several types of questions. We have additional books on each subject should more study be advisable or necessary for you. Finally, the more you study, the better prepared you will be. This book is intended to be the last thing you study before you walk into the examination room. Prior study of relevant texts is also recommended. NLC publishes some of these in our Fundamental Series. Knowledge and good sense are important factors in passing your exam. Good luck also helps. So now study this Passbook, absorb the material contained within and take that knowledge into the examination. Then do your best to pass that exam.

EXAMINATION SECTION

EXAMINATION SECTION
TEST 1

DIRECTIONS: Each question or incomplete statement is followed by several suggested answers or completions. Select the one that BEST answers the question or completes the statement. *PRINT THE LETTER OF THE CORRECT ANSWER IN THE SPACE AT THE RIGHT.*

Questions 1-11.

DIRECTIONS: Questions 1 through 11 are to be answered on the basis of the two Memory Scenes shown on the following pages. Memory Scene 1 is on Pages 2 and 3. Memory Scene 2 is on Pages 4 and 5. You are to study Scene 1 carefully and try to remember as many details on the scene as you can. You should pay equal attention both to objects and to people shown in the scene. Then turn to Questions 1 through 6 which follow and answer these questions based upon what you remember from Scene 1. Do not turn back to Scene 1 while answering the questions. After you complete Questions 1 through 6, study Memory Scene 2. Then turn to Questions 7 through 11 and answer them based on Scene 2.

SCENE 1

SCENE 2

Questions 1-6.

DIRECTIONS: Questions 1 through 6 are to be answered SOLELY on the basis of Memory Scene 1.

1. Which one of the following vehicles is parked on Elm Road? A(n)

   A. police car
   B. ambulance
   C. tow truck
   D. fire truck

2. What are the words printed on the side of the bus? _____ Bus.

   A. Northside   B. Southside   C. Eastside   D. Westside

3. The man with the gun is wearing a

   A. white shirt with black stripes
   B. tee shirt with the words SPOT NEWS
   C. sweat shirt with the word ACE
   D. white shirt with black dots

4. The taxi which is being repaired is parked in a _____ Zone.

   A. No Standing
   B. No Parking
   C. Towaway
   D. Authorized Vehicles Only

5. The license plate number of the vehicle which is CLOSEST to the person lying on the street is

   A. G498   B. 8K46   C. 302L   D. 31S4

6. The person in the second floor window is directly above

   A. Uncle Dan's Lunch
   B. Mandley Discount Clothing Outlet
   C. Cafeteria Europa
   D. M & P Music World

Questions 7-11.

DIRECTIONS: Questions 7 through 11 are to be answered SOLELY on the basis of Memory Scene 2.

7. The robbery at knifepoint is occurring on

   A. the corner of Brady Avenue and E. 7th Street
   B. Brady Avenue in front of Mario's Pizza Hole
   C. the corner of Brady Avenue and W. 7th Street
   D. Brady Avenue in front of Sparta Senior Center

8. The street musician is standing CLOSEST to

   A. Crane Hotel
   B. the subway entrance
   C. Mario's Pizza Hole
   D. Blair Savings Bank

9. The youth holding the knife is wearing a _____ cap, shirt, and _____ pants. 9._____

   A. black ski; plaid; white
   B. white ski; plaid; black
   C. black baseball; white; plaid
   D. white baseball; white; black

10. Which one of the following BEST describes the person holding the gun? 10._____

    A. White male, white pants, and a plaid shirt
    B. Asian male, black pants, and a heart-print shirt
    C. White male, plaid pants, and a black jacket
    D. Black male, black pants, and a white jacket

11. What is the number on the shirt of the man running towards the subway? 11._____

    A. 49   B. 54   C. 45   D. 94

Questions 12-14.

DIRECTIONS: Questions 12 through 14 are to be answered SOLELY on the basis of the following passage.

At 11:30 P.M., while parked in front of 945 Howard Street, Police Officers Abbott and Johnson received a radio call of a family dispute at 779 Seward Street, Apartment 1928. The radio dispatcher informed the Officers that the call came from Mrs. Debra Lacoste who lives in Apartment 1930. The Officers arrived at the location and heard yelling and screaming. When the Officers knocked on the door, a woman crying hysterically opened the door. The woman, Gloria Ross, informed the Officers that her husband, Sam Ross, was in her apartment. She said he was drunk, had yelled at her, and had made threats to hurt her if she did not let him see his children. Mrs. Ross then presented a letter to Officer Abbott, which he recognized as being an Order of Protection issued by Family Court. The Order of Protection stated that Mr. Ross was not to be seen anywhere near his wife, including her residence and place of employment. Furthermore, the Order stated that he had no right to see the children or to yell at his wife or use obscene language in his wife's presence. Mrs. Ross told the Officer that she wanted her husband arrested for violating the Order of Protection. Officer Johnson quickly read the Order of Protection and informed Officer Abbott that the Order was valid. Officer Abbott ordered Sam Ross to turn around with his hands behind his back, and Officer Abbott handcuffed him and placed him under arrest.

12. Which of the following persons FIRST made the authorities aware of the family dispute? 12._____

    A. A neighbor   B. The victim
    C. A Police Officer   D. The suspect

13. The Police Officers responded to a report of a disturbance at _____ Street, Apartment _____. 13._____

    A. 945 Howard; 1928   B. 779 Seward; 1930
    C. 779 Seward; 1928   D. 945 Howard; 1930

14. Which of the following actions caused Mr. Ross to be arrested? 14._____
    He

    A. called his children on the telephone
    B. tried to visit his children

C. waited for his wife in front of her job
D. yelled at his children

Question 15.

DIRECTIONS: Question 15 is to be answered SOLELY on the basis of the following information.

Sexual Abuse 3rd Degree - occurs when a person intentionally subjects an individual to sexual contact without the individual's consent.

15. Which one of the following situations is the BEST example of Sexual Abuse in the 3rd Degree?   15.____

   A. Joe is riding a crowded train and bumps into JoAnn when the train comes to a sudden stop.
   B. When Jean carelessly steps on Bob's toe, Bob curses at her and uses sexually explicit language.
   C. John is standing on a crowded train and starts rubbing himself against a woman's buttocks.
   D. Bill accidentally brushes his newspaper against a woman's chest while he is reading on a crowded train.

Question 16.

DIRECTIONS: Question 16 is to be answered SOLELY on the basis of the following information.

Police Officers are required to provide assistance to sick or injured persons. Upon arrival at the scene of a sick or injured, person, a Police Officer should do the following in the order given:

   I. Give reasonable aid to the sick or injured person.
   II. Request an ambulance or doctor, if necessary.
   III. Wait outside to direct the ambulance, or have some responsible person do so.
   IV. Make a second call in 20 minutes if ambulance does not arrive.

16. Police Officer Jones, while on patrol, is approached by John Rutherford, who informs the   16.____
Officer that his business partner, Silvio Monteleone, tripped on the 5th floor stairs outside his apartment located at 1276 Stork Lane. When Officer Jones and Rutherford arrive at the scene, the Officer finds that Silvio may have broken his right arm. At 12:20 P.M., Officer Jones radios for an ambulance to take Silvio to the hospital. While waiting, Officer Jones attempts to locate a blanket to place over Silvio, who is lying on a cold tile floor. After knocking at three apartments, Officer Jones receives a blanket from Mrs. Flores. It is now 12:35 P.M., and the ambulance has not arrived.
The NEXT step Officer Jones should take is to

   A. call his patrol supervisor
   B. send Silvio's friend John down to the street to direct the medical personnel
   C. call the ambulance a second time to request assistance
   D. radio for a patrol car to transport Silvio to the hospital

17. Sergeant Burroughs assigns Police Officer Holland to patrol the area between Webster and St. Paul Avenues. She informs Officer Holland that over the past month there has been a sharp increase in the number of burglaries. She instructs Officer Holland to pay close attention to any suspicious activities.
Which one of the following situations should Officer Holland give the MOST attention?

    A. Two young children who knock on doors and run away
    B. Two teenagers who live around the corner, sitting on the stairs of a building listening to the radio
    C. A group of elderly men sitting on a bench in front of a row of buildings
    D. Two men going from door to door asking if Mr. Jones is home

18. While on patrol, Police Officer Fuentes is approached by a woman who states that she has just been robbed. Officer Fuentes obtains the following information relating to the robbery:
    Place of Occurrence: 168 Delancey Street
    Time of Occurrence: 5 minutes earlier
    Description of Suspect: Male, White, 6 feet tall, wearing a black jacket, grey pants, and white sneakers
    Direction of Flight: Northbound on Delancey Street
    Officer Fuentes radios this information to the other Officers.
    Which one of the following expresses the above information MOST clearly and accurately?

    A. I have a robbery. The suspect is six feet tall wearing a black jacket, grey pants, and white sneakers. The robbery occurred five minutes ago at 168 Delancey Street. A White male fled northbound on Delancey Street.
    B. A robbery occurred five minutes ago at 168 Delancey Street. The suspect fled northbound on Delancey Street. He is a White male, approximately 6 feet tall, wearing a black jacket, grey pants, and white sneakers.
    C. I have a robbery. The suspect fled northbound on Delancey Street and is a male, approximately 6 feet tall, five minutes ago. Suspect is White and is wearing a black jacket, grey pants, and white sneakers. The robbery occurred at 168 Delancey Street.
    D. A robbery has occurred at 168 Delancey Street. The suspect is wearing white sneakers. He fled northbound wearing a black jacket on Delancey Street, and he is approximately 6 feet tall, wearing grey pants. The robbery took place five minutes ago with a White male.

19. Police Officer Waters was the first person at the scene of a fire which may have been the result of arson. He obtained the following information:

   Place of Occurrence: 35 John Street, Apartment 27
   Time of Occurrence: 4:00 P.M.
   Witness: Daisy Logan
   Incident: Fire (possible arson)
   Suspect: Male, White, approximately 18 years old, wearing blue jeans and a plaid shirt, running away from incident

   Officer Waters is completing a report on the incident.
   Which one of the following expresses the above information MOST clearly and accurately?

   A. At 4:00 P.M., Daisy Logan saw a White male, approximately 18 years old who was wearing blue jeans and a plaid shirt, running from the scene of a fire at 35 John Street, Apartment 27.
   B. Seeing a fire at 35 John Street, a White male approximately 18 years old, wearing blue jeans and a plaid shirt was seen running from Apartment 27 at 4:00 P.M. reported Daisy Logan.
   C. Approximately 18 years old and wearing blue jeans and a plaid shirt, Daisy Logan saw a fire and a White male running from 35 John Street, Apartment 27 at 4:00 P.M.
   D. Running from 35 John Street, Apartment 27, the scene of the fire, reported Daisy Logan at 4:00 P.M., was a White male approximately 18 years old and wearing blue jeans and a plaid shirt.

20. Police Officer Sullivan obtained the following information at the scene of a two-car accident:

   Place of Occurrence: 2971 William Street
   Drivers and Vehicles Involved: Mrs. Wilson, driver of blue 2004 Toyota Camry; Mr. Bailey, driver of white 2001 Dodge Omni
   Injuries Sustained: Mr. Bailey had a swollen right eye; Mrs. Wilson had a broken left hand

   Which one of the following expresses the above information MOST clearly and accurately?

   A. Mr. Bailey, owner of a white, 2001 Dodge Omni, at 2971 William Street, had a swollen right eye. Mrs. Wilson, with a broken left hand, is the owner of the blue 2004 Toyota Camry. They were in a car accident.
   B. Mrs. Wilson got a broken left hand and Mr. Bailey a swollen right eye at 2971 William Street. The vehicles involved in the car accident were a 2001 Dodge Omni, white, owned by Mr. Bailey, and Mrs. Wilson's blue 2004 Toyota Camry.
   C. Mrs. Wilson, the driver of the blue 2004 Toyota Camry, and Mr. Bailey, the driver of the white 2001 Dodge Omni, were involved in a car accident at 2971 William Street. Mr. Bailey sustained a swollen right eye, and Mrs. Wilson broke her left hand.

D. Mr. Bailey sustained a swollen right eye and Mrs. Wilson broke her left hand in a car accident at 2971 William Street. They owned a 2001 white Dodge Omni and a 2004 blue Toyota Camry.

Question 21.

DIRECTIONS: Question 21 is to be answered SOLELY on the basis of the following information.

When a Police Officer observes a person who is in possession of a firearm, the Officer is required to:

I. Ask the person to produce identification and the pistol license.
II. Verify the pistol license, if it is questionable, by telephoning the Police Department License Division during business hours between 9:00 A.M. and 5:00 P.M., Monday to Friday.
III. Make an Activity Log entry, including the person's name, address, date of birth, and the pistol license number and expiration date.
IV. Remove person to station house if license has expired.
V. If license is valid, return all identification and notify Desk Officer.

21. At 3:00 P.M. on September 10, 2008, Police Officer Rogers sees a man walking towards him with a gun in his waistband. The Officer stops the man and asks him for identification and his pistol license. The man gives the Officer his pistol license and driver's license. The information on the pistol license identifies the man as John Wilson, residing at 4 Auburn Street, Apt. #1B.
Mr. Wilson is 34 years old and was born on May 15, 1974. His pistol license number is 71554, and the expiration date is September 9, 2008. His driver's license indicates the same name, address, and date of birth. The Officer makes an Activity Log entry listing all of the required information obtained from Mr. Wilson, returns both licenses to him, and then notifies the Desk Officer. In this situation, the actions taken by Officer Rogers were

A. *proper*, primarily because Mr. Wilson was not a city resident
B. *improper*, primarily because the Officer did not verify the pistol license with the License Division
C. *proper*, primarily because he returned the pistol license to Mr. Wilson and notified the Desk Officer that the license was valid
D. *improper*, primarily because Mr. Wilson should have been brought to the station house

Question 22.

DIRECTIONS: Question 22 is to be answered SOLELY on the basis of the following information.

Police Officers must sometimes rely on eyewitness accounts of incidents, even though eyewitnesses may make mistakes with regard to some details.

22. Police Officer Colon responded to a report of a purse snatch on 110th Street. Upon arrival at the scene, she interviewed the complainant, Mrs. Smith, and three other witnesses who had been standing at a bus stop. The witnesses saw two men fleeing from the scene in a black car. The following are license plate numbers provided by the complainant and witnesses.
Which one of these numbers should Officer Colon consider MOST likely to be correct?

   A. P-51856   B. T-58166   C. P-51886   D. T-41685

Question 23.

DIRECTIONS: Question 23 is to be answered SOLELY on the basis of the following information.

When Police Officers receive a report of a missing person, they should do the following in the order given:

    I.   Report to the location of the complainant who reported the missing person.
    II. Interview the complainant.
    III. Obtain a physical description of the missing person and a description of the clothes worn by the missing person.
    IV. Determine where the missing person was last seen.
    V. Start a search at the location where the missing person was last seen.
    VI. Request a Patrol Supervisor to respond to the scene.

23. Police Officer Jane Anderson responds to a report of a missing 15-year-old at 187 Rockwell Avenue, Apt. 6F. The teenager's mother, the complainant, informs Officer Anderson that her son is 5'5", 140 lbs., and was wearing a red-striped shirt and black shorts.
Police Officer Anderson should NEXT

   A. search the apartment building for the teenager
   B. begin searching the neighborhood
   C. ask the mother where her son was last seen
   D. request a Patrol Supervisor to respond to the scene

Question 24.

DIRECTIONS: Question 24 is to be answered SOLELY on the basis of the following information.
Grand Larceny 4th Degree - occurs when a person steals property and:

    I.   The value of the property is more than one thousand dollars; or
    II. The property, regardless of its nature and value, is taken from the victim; or
    III. The property consists of one or more firearms

24. Which one of the following is the BEST example of Grand Larceny in the Fourth Degree? 24.____
    A. Samuel, a security guard working at Beacon's Warehouse, enters an unauthorized area and steals a clock radio.
    B. Jonathan enters Lacy's Department Store, loads $500 worth of merchandise into a large shopping bag, and leaves the store.
    C. Harry is walking down the street at night when a shabbily dressed woman pulls out a gun and tells him to put his hands up.
    D. Mildred discovers that the man who just bumped into her has stolen her wallet containing $20 in cash from her pants pocket.

25. Officer Johnson has issued a summons to a driver and has obtained the following information: 25.____

Place of Occurrence:	Corner of Foster Road and Woodrow Avenue
Time of Occurrence:	7:10 P.M.
Driver:	William Grant
Offense:	Driving through a red light
Age of Driver:	42
Address of Driver:	23 Richmond Avenue

    Officer Johnson is making an entry in his Memo Book regarding the incident.
    Which one of the following expresses the above information MOST clearly and accurately?

    A. William Grant, lives at 23 Richmond Avenue at 7:10 P.M., went through a red light. He was issued a summons at the corner of Foster Road and Woodrow Avenue. The driver is 42 years old.
    B. William Grant, age 42, who lives at 23 Richmond Avenue, was issued a summons for going through a red light at 7:10 P.M. at the corner of Foster Road and Woodrow Avenue.
    C. William Grant, age 42, was issued a summons on the corner of Foster Road and Woodrow Avenue for going through a red light. He lives at 23 Richmond Avenue at 7:10 P.M.
    D. A 42-year-old man who lives at 23 Richmond Avenue was issued a summons at 7:10 P.M. William Grant went through a red light at the corner of Foster Road and Woodrow Avenue.

KEY (CORRECT ANSWERS)

1.	B	11.	D
2.	A	12.	A
3.	D	13.	C
4.	C	14.	B
5.	B	15.	C
6.	D	16.	B
7.	A	17.	D
8.	D	18.	B
9.	C	19.	A
10.	A	20.	C

21. D
22. C
23. C
24. D
25. B

TEST 2

DIRECTIONS: Each question or incomplete statement is followed by several suggested answers or completions. Select the one that BEST answers the question or completes the statement. *PRINT THE LETTER OF THE CORRECT ANSWER IN THE SPACE AT THE RIGHT.*

1. Police Officer Frome has completed investigating a report of a stolen auto and obtained the following information:
   Date of Occurrence: October 26, 2008
   Place of Occurrence: 51st Street and 8th Avenue
   Time of Occurrence: 3:30 P.M.
   Crime: Auto Theft
   Suspect: Michael Wadsworth
   Action Taken: Suspect arrested
   Officer Frome is preparing a report on the incident.
   Which one of the following expresses the above information MOST clearly and accurately?

   A. Arrested on October 26, 2008 was a stolen auto at 51st Street and 8th Avenue at 3:30 P.M. driven by Michael Wadsworth.
   B. For driving a stolen auto at 3:30 P.M., Michael Wadsworth was arrested at 51st Street and 8th Avenue on October 26, 2008.
   C. On October 26, 2008 at 3:30 P.M., Michael Wadsworth was arrested at 51st Street and 8th Avenue for driving a stolen auto.
   D. Michael Wadsworth was arrested on October 26, 2008 at 3:30 P.M. for driving at 51st Street and 8th Avenue. The auto was stolen.

1.____

Questions 2-3.

DIRECTIONS: Questions 2 and 3 are to be answered SOLELY on the basis of the following information.

As a result of numerous interviews of complainants and witnesses of violent crimes, Officer Wells has noticed a serious rise in the number of certain crimes in his patrol area over the past three months. He has observed that most of the rapes take place on E. 98th Street between Lott Avenue and Herk Place; assaults happen on Lott Avenue between Chester Avenue and E. 98th Street; and the majority of the robberies occur on Lott Avenue between E. 98th Street and Hughes Place. The assaults take place between 1:00 A.M. and 3:00 A.M. All of the robberies happen between 1:00 A.M. and 6:00 A.M., and most of the rapes happen between 8:00 A.M. and 11:00 A.M. The rapes usually occur on Mondays and Wednesdays, the robberies on Fridays and Saturdays, and the assaults on Saturdays and Sundays.

2. Officer Wells would MOST effectively reduce the number of robberies by patrolling

   A. Lott Avenue between E. 98th Street and Hughes Place on Fridays and Saturdays between 1:00 A.M. and 8:00 A.M.
   B. Lott Avenue between E. 98th Street and Chester Avenue on Saturdays and Sundays between 1:00 A.M. and 6:00 A.M.
   C. E. 98th Street between Lott Avenue and Herk Place on Saturdays and Sundays between 1:00 A.M. and 3:00 A.M.
   D. E. 98th Street between Herk Place and Chester Avenue on Mondays and Wednesdays between 8:00 A.M. and 11:00 A.M.

2.____

15

3. Officer Wells has been informed by his supervisor that he will be assigned to a patrol each week that would allow him to concentrate on reducing the number of rapes.
What would be the MOST appropriate patrol for Officer Wells to work?

   A. Tuesday through Saturday, 8:00 P.M. to 4:00 P.M.
   B. Monday through Friday, 7:30 A.M. to 3:30 P.M.
   C. Wednesday through Sunday, noon to 8:00 P.M.
   D. Monday through Friday, 3:00 P.M. to 11:00 P.M.

4. Police Officers are required to remove potentially dangerous property from a prisoner prior to placing him in a jail cell.
Which of the following items should be removed from a prisoner?
A(n)

   A. empty wallet
   B. gold wedding ring
   C. box of cough drops
   D. pair of shoelaces

Question 5.

DIRECTIONS: Question 5 is to be answered SOLELY on the basis of the following information.

When a Police Officer makes an arrest, the Officer should do the following in the order given:
   I. Inform the prisoner of the reason for the arrest.
   II. Handcuff the prisoner's hands behind his back.
   III. Search the prisoner and the nearby area for weapons and evidence.
   IV. Advise the prisoner of his legal rights before questioning.

5. Police Officer Golden arrests Roy Owen and informs Mr. Owen that he is being arrested for the robbery of a jewelry store. While properly handcuffing the prisoner, the Officer notices a small handgun in Mr. Owen's back pants pocket. The Officer finishes handcuffing the prisoner and then removes the handgun from his pants pocket.
The Officer should NEXT

   A. inform the prisoner of his rights
   B. question the prisoner
   C. return, with the prisoner, to the jewelry store
   D. search the prisoner and the immediate area for weapons and evidence

6. Police Officer Wright has finished investigating a report of Grand Larceny and has obtained the following information:

Time of Occurrence:	Between 1:00 P.M. and 2:00 P.M.
Place of Occurrence:	In front of victim's home, 85 Montgomery Avenue
Victim:	Mr. Williams, owner of the vehicle
Crime:	Automobile broken into
Property Taken:	Stereo valued at $1,200

Officer Wright is preparing a report on the incident.
Which one of the following expresses the above information MOST clearly and accurately?

A. While parked in front of his home Mr. Williams states that between 1:00 P.M. and 2:00 P.M. an unknown person broke into his vehicle. Mr. Williams, who lives at 85 Montgomery Avenue, lost his $1,200 stereo.
B. Mr. Williams, who lives at 85 Montgomery Avenue, states that between 1:00 P.M. and 2:00 P.M. his vehicle was parked in front of his home when an unknown person broke into his car and took his stereo worth $1,200.
C. Mr. Williams was parked in front of 85 Montgomery Avenue, which is his home, when it was robbed of a $1,200 stereo. When he came out he observed between 1:00 P.M. and 2:00 P.M. that his car had been broken into by an unknown person.
D. Mr. Williams states between 1:00 P.M. and 2:00 P.M. that an unknown person broke into his car in front of his home. Mr. Williams further states that he was robbed of a $1,200 stereo at 85 Montgomery Avenue.

6.____

Questions 7-10.

DIRECTIONS: Questions 7 through 10 are to be answered SOLELY on the basis of the following passage.

Police Officers Grice and Sexton were working a 4:00 P.M. to Midnight tour of duty on Friday, December 5, when they were assigned to investigate a burglary. They were told to respond to 355 Grand Street, the 14th Floor, Apartment 1402, and to speak to the complainant, Ms. Starr. Upon arrival, Officer Sexton interviewed Ms. Starr, who stated that when she returned home from work at approximately 6:10 P.M., she was unable to unlock her door because the keyhole had been stuffed with toothpicks. After the door was opened by building maintenance, she entered her apartment and saw that her jewelry box had been emptied and was laying on the floor.

Officer Grice, who is qualified in the recovery of fingerprints, dusted the jewelry box and the front door in an attempt to recover any fingerprints that the burglar may have left. The Officers also interviewed Mrs. Caputo, who lives in Apartment 1404,; and Mr. Babbit, who lives in Apartment 1407. Both individuals stated that they neither saw nor heard anything unusual.

The next night, Saturday, December 6, Officers Grice and Sexton responded to Apartment 1514 in the same building on a call of a burglary. The complainant, Ms. Chung, stated that when she returned home from shopping she discovered that her lock had been stuffed with chewing gum and that her apartment had been burglarized. Officer Grice dusted the front door and a dresser, which had been opened, for prints.

Ten days after the last burglary, Detective Carrano, who had been assigned to investigate the burglaries, was informed by Mr. Hunt of the fingerprint identification unit that the prints recovered from both apartments belonged to Peter Remo of 355 Gravel Street, Apartment 1705. Later that evening, after obtaining an arrest warrant, Detective Carrano arrested Peter Remo for the burglaries.

7. Who lived on the same floor as Ms. Starr?

    A. Ms. Chung
    B. Peter Remo
    C. Mr. Babbit
    D. Mr. Hunt

8. Who was responsible for recovering the fingerprints that were used to identify Peter Remo?

    A. Officer Grice
    B. Mr. Hunt
    C. Detective Carrano
    D. Officer Sexton

9. When was Peter Remo arrested? December

    A. 5   B. 6   C. 15   D. 16

10. Why was Ms. Starr unable to unlock her door?

    A. She lost her keys.
    B. Chewing gum had been stuffed into the lock.
    C. Her keys had been taken from her jewelry box.
    D. The lock was stuffed with toothpicks.

Question 11.

DIRECTIONS: Question 11 is to be answered SOLELY on the basis of the following information.

Upon arriving at the scene of any offense committed between members of the same family or household, a Police Officer should do the following in the order given:

   I. Ascertain all the facts.
   II. Obtain medical assistance, if needed.
   III. Determine whether:
       (a) a family offense has been committed; or
       (b) an Order of Protection has been obtained by the complainant in order to keep the offender from entering the complainant's home or workplace.
   IV. Begin a search of the immediate area for the offender, if the offender has fled the scene.
   V. If the search produces no results, advise the complainant/victim to call the police when the offender returns.
   VI. Prepare a Complaint Report.

11. Police Officer Laura Molina responds to 285 Oak Street, Apartment 3A, in regard to a possible violent family offense. Upon arrival, Police Officer Molina is met at the apartment door by Ms. Martin. Officer Molina notices that Ms. Martin had been bleeding from a cut over her right eye. Ms. Martin tells Police Officer Molina that she and her husband had been having serious marital problems for the past six months. She saidthat just last week she had gotten an Order of Protection against her husband. However, her husband had returned to their home drunk and hit her on the head with a glass bottle. Police Officer Molina noticed broken glass on the floor in the living room. Police Officer Molina asked Ms. Martin if she needed an ambulance, but Ms. Martin told the Officer that she did not. Ms. Martin further explained that after her husband hit her, he ran out of the apartment. Ms. Martin added that he was wearing white sneakers, green army fatigue pants, and a light blue shirt. The NEXT step Police Officer Molina should take is to

    A. call an ambulance
    B. search the area for Mr. Martin
    C. prepare a Complaint Report
    D. advise Ms. Martin to call the police when her husband returns

Question 12.

DIRECTIONS: Question 12 is to be answered SOLELY on the basis of the following information.
              When handcuffing a prisoner, a Police Officer should:

    I. Handcuff person with hands behind his back.
    II. Search person for weapons, evidence, or contraband.
    III. Escort person to station house and inform the supervisor of the charges.
    IV. Remove handcuffs and place the person in a cell.

12. While on patrol, Police Officer Lewis arrests Robert Hendricks for assaulting his wife, Mrs. Hendricks. Police Officer Davis, who is also on patrol, arrives to assist Officer Lewis and observes her handcuffing the prisoner with his hands in front of his body. When Officer Lewis begins to search the prisoner for weapons, the prisoner swings his arms around and hits Officer Lewis on the side of the head. Officer Davis then steps in to subdue the prisoner. A patrol car arrives to transport the prisoner to the station house. There, Officer Lewis informs the Supervisor of the charges against the prisoner, removes the handcuffs, and places him in a cell. In this situation, Officer Lewis' actions were

    A. *improper,* primarily because she should not have removed the handcuffs from the prisoner until he was safely in his cell
    B. *proper,* primarily because she did not place the handcuffs on the legs or ankles of the prisoner
    C. *improper,* primarily because the prisoner's hands were not handcuffed behind his back
    D. *proper,* primarily because she placed the handcuffs on the prisoner in the presence of another Police Officer

Question 13.

DIRECTIONS: Question 13 is to be answered SOLELY on the basis of the following information.

Police Officers must sometimes rely on eyewitness accounts of incidents, even though eyewitnesses may make mistakes with regard to some details.

13. While crossing the street, Robert Green was struck by a delivery truck. Police Officer Luther was called to the scene and spoke with four witnesses who saw the truck that struck Mr. Green. The following are descriptions of the truck given by the witnesses. Which one of the descriptions should Officer Luther consider MOST likely to be correct?
A _____ truck, Plate _____.

   A. brown GMC; G-1843
   B. black Ford; G-1854
   C. brown Ford; G-1845
   D. brown Ford; C-1845

Question 14.

DIRECTIONS: Question 14 is to be answered SOLELY on the basis of the following information.

Police Officers may be required to safeguard the property of a deceased person who lived alone. When safeguarding the property, a Police Officer should do the following in the order given:

   I. Request a Patrol Supervisor to respond to the scene.
   II. In the presence of the Patrol Supervisor, search the body for valuables and documents concerning identity.
   III. Remove all property except clothing.
   IV. Enter in Memo Book a complete list of property removed from deceased.
   V. Complete the Property Clerk's Invoice Work Sheet indicating what property was removed.
   VI. Deliver all property and the Property Clerk's Invoice Work Sheet to the Desk Officer at the precinct.

14. Police Officer Frey responds to 220 E. 5th Street, Apt. 8M. He finds Mr. Johnson lying dead on the living room floor. The building superintendent, who had let Officer Frey into the apartment, informs Officer Frey that Mr. Johnson lived alone. The Officer radios the dispatcher and requests the Patrol Supervisor to respond to the scene. When Sergeant O'Malley, the Patrol Supervisor, arrives, he and Officer Frey search the body. They find a wallet with various personal papers and $3,200 in cash. Officer Frey removes the property.
The NEXT step Officer Frey should take is to

   A. continue searching the area around the body for any additional property
   B. deliver the property to the precinct and give it to the Desk Officer
   C. prepare the Property Clerk's Invoice Work Sheet
   D. make a Memo Book entry listing the wallet and its contents

15. On August 31st at 2:30 P.M., Police Officer Jones is assigned to a post at the West Side Shopping Mall. Captain Franks tells Officer Jones that there has been a sharp increase in shoplifting at the mall over the past three weeks. He instructs the Officer to watch closely any persons whose behavior appears to be suspicious. Officer Jones observes the following four situations.
Which person should Officer Jones watch most closely?

A. A woman who is dressed in jeans and a winter overcoat is looking at a display counter in a dress shop.
B. A woman with a large shopping bag who appears to be counting money while leaving a store
C. An old man who is pushing a stroller with a two-year-old child in the toy department of a large store
D. Two teenaged boys who are looking in the display window of an electronics store

Questions 16-17.

DIRECTIONS: Questions 16 and 17 are to be answered SOLELY on the basis of the map which appears on the next page. The flow of traffic is indicated by the arrows. If there is only one arrow shown, then traffic flows only in the direction indicated by the arrow. If there are two arrows shown, then traffic flows in both directions. You must follow the flow of traffic.

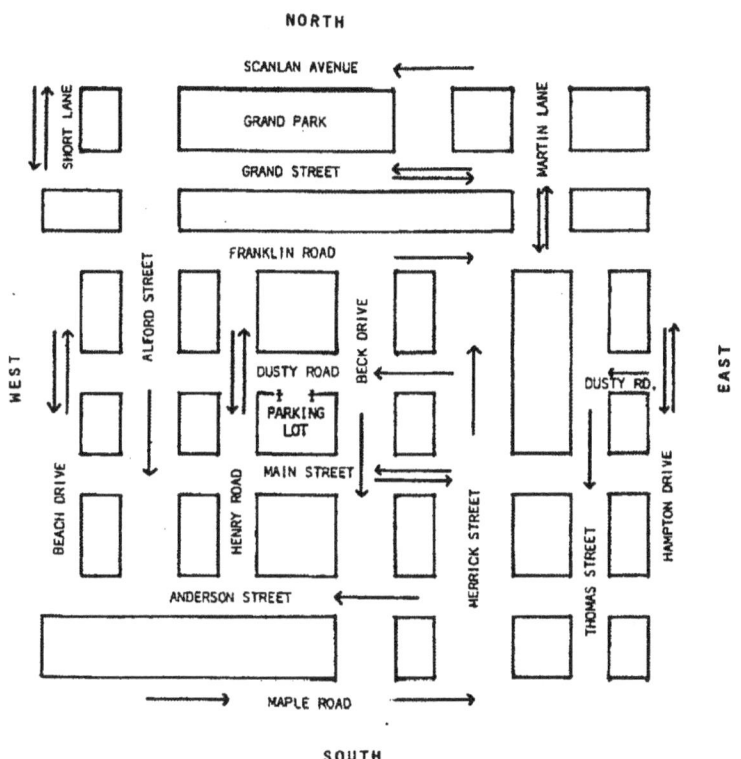

16. Police Officers Gold and Warren are at the intersection of Maple Road and Hampton Drive. The radio dispatcher has assigned them to investigate an attempted auto theft in the parking lot on Dusty Road.
Which one of the following is the SHORTEST route for the Officers to take in their patrol car to get to the entrance of the parking lot on Dusty Road, making sure to obey all traffic regulations? Travel _____ to the parking lot entrance.

    A. north on Hampton Drive, then west on Dusty Road
    B. west on Maple Road, then north on Beck Drive, then west on Dusty Road
    C. north on Hampton Drive, then west on Anderson Street, then north on Merrick Street, then west on Dusty Road
    D. west on Maple Road, then north on Merrick Street, then west on Dusty Road

17. Police Officer Gladden is in a patrol car at the intersection of Beach Drive and Anderson Street when he spots a suspicious car. Police Officer Gladden calls the radio dispatcher to determine if the vehicle was stolen. Police Officer Gladden then follows the vehicle north on Beach Drive for three blocks, then turns right and proceeds for one block and makes another right. He then follows the vehicle for two blocks, and then they both make a left turn and continue driving. Police Officer Gladden now receives a call from the dispatcher stating the car was reported stolen and signals for the vehicle to pull to the side of the road.
In what direction was Police Officer Gladden heading at the time he signaled for the other car to pull over?

    A. North   B. East   C. South   D. West

Question 18.

DIRECTIONS: Question 18 is to be answered SOLELY on the basis of the following information.

Criminal Possession of Stolen Property 3rd Degree - occurs when a person knowingly possesses stolen property in order to benefit himself or another person who does not own the property.

18. Which one of the following situations is the BEST example of Criminal Possession of Stolen Property in the 3rd Degree?

    A. Police Officers enter Mr. Hanson's home and discover a stolen television. Hanson shows the Officers a receipt for the television from what he thought was an honest dealer.
    B. While walking to work, Anne finds a diamond ring in the street and keeps it.
    C. John purchases what he believes is an expensive stolen stereo which is actually a low-priced stereo that the dealer obtained properly.
    D. Tim warns his customers that the stereos he has for sale are stolen and shouldn't be brought to authorized dealers for repairs.

19. Police Officer Fontaine obtained the following details relating to a suspicious package: 19._____

    Place of Occurrence: Case Bank, 2 Wall Street
    Time of Occurrence: 10:30 A.M.
    Date of Occurrence: October 10, 2008
    Complaint: Suspicious package in doorway
    Found By: Emergency Service Unit

    Officer Fontaine is preparing a report for department records.
    Which one of the following expresses the above information MOST clearly and accurately?

    A. At 10:30 A.M. the Emergency Service Unit reported they found a package on October 10, 2008; which appeared suspicious. This occurred in a doorway at 2 Wall Street, Case Bank.
    B. A package which appeared suspicious was in the doorway of Case Bank. The Emergency Service Unit reported this at 2 Wall Street at 10:30 A.M. on October 10, 2008 when found.
    C. On October 10, 2008 at 10:30 A.M. a suspicious package was found by the Emergency Service Unit in the doorway of Case Bank at 2 Wall Street.
    D. The Emergency Service Unit found a package at the Case Bank. It appeared suspicious at 10:30 A.M. in the doorway of 2 Wall Street on October 10, 2008.

20. Police Officer Reardon receives the following information regarding a case of child abuse: 20._____

    Victim: Joseph Mays
    Victim's Age: 10 years old
    Victim's Address: Resides with his family at 42 Columbia Street, Apartment IB
    Complainant: Victim's uncle, Kevin Mays
    Suspects: Victim's parents

    Police Officer Reardon is preparing a report to send to the Department of Social Services.
    Which one of the following expresses the above information MOST clearly and accurately?

    A. Kevin Mays reported a case of child abuse to his ten-year-old nephew, Joseph Mays, by his parents. He resides with his family at 42 Columbia Street, Apartment IB.
    B. Kevin Mays reported that his ten-year-old nephew, Joseph Mays, has been abused by the child's parents. Joseph Mays resides with his family at 42 Columbia Street, Apartment IB.
    C. Joseph Mays has been abused by his parents. Kevin Mays reported that his nephew resides with his family at 42 Columbia Street, Apartment IB. He is ten years old.
    D. Kevin Mays reported that his nephew is ten years old. Joseph Mays has been abused by his parents. He resides with his family at 42 Columbia Street, Apartment IB.

21. While on patrol, Police Officer Hawkins was approached by Harry Roland, a store owner, who found a leather bag valued at $200.00 outside his store. Officer Hawkins took the property into custody and removed the following items:
2 Solex watches, each valued at $500.00
4 14-kt. gold necklaces, each valued at $315.00
Cash $519.00
1 diamond ring, valued at $400.00
Officer Hawkins is preparing a report on the found property.
Which one of the following is the TOTAL value of the property and cash found?

   A. $1,734.00   B. $3,171.00
   C. $3,179.00   D. $3,379.00

Question 22.

DIRECTIONS: Question 22 is to be answered SOLELY on the basis of the following information.

During the month of September, three rapes were committed near Pier 21 on Westerly Avenue. The description of each of the suspects given by the victims is as follows:

Rape No. 1 - Male, White, mid-thirties, 5'8", 190 lbs., long wavy hair, wearing dark sunglasses, black jacket, green pants, black boots, moustache

Rape No. 2 - Male, White, late 20's, 5'8", slim build, moustache, closely cropped hair, brown eyes, black jacket, blue jeans, black boots

Rape No. 3 - Male, White, 35, 5'7", 180 lbs., long hair, moustache, dark glasses, blue denim jacket, blue jeans, black boots

On October 3, 2003, a fourth rape was committed. The suspect was arrested by Police Officer Jackson. The description of the suspect is as follows:

Rape No. 4 - Male, White, 30-35, 5'7", 185 lbs., long curly hair, moustache, grey jacket, blue jeans, baseball cap, white boots

22. Based on the above descriptions of the suspects in the first three rapes, Officer Jackson should consider the suspect in the fourth rape as a suspect in Rape No.

   A. 1   B. 1 and 3
   C. 2 and 3   D. 1, 2, and 3

Question 23.

DIRECTIONS: Question 23 is to be answered SOLELY on the basis of the following information.

When a warrant has been issued for the arrest of a parent who has physically abused or neglected a child, Police Officers should do the following in the order given:

   I. Respond to the location and arrest the parent(s) named in the warrant if the parent is present.

II. Remove the child from the home, even if parent named in warrant is not present and an arrest is not made.
III. Deliver the child to Family Court between the hours of 9 A.M. and 5 P.M.
IV. If Family Court is not in session, bring the child to the precinct station house and locate temporary housing.
V. If either the child or parent is not home, attempt to locate child or parent.

23. Officers Batts and Peters are informed by the Desk Officer that a warrant has been issued for the arrest of Mr. Hughes. It has been reported that Mr. Hughes has physically abused his five-year-old son, Michael. The Officers arrive at the Hughes home at 1:00 M. They find Michael at home alone. When asked where his parents are, he informs the Officers that his father went away yesterday and that his mother doesn't live with them. Michael tells the Officers that his uncle has been visiting but hasn't been home all day. The Officers return to the station house with Michael and locate temporary housing for him. What should the Officers do NEXT?

    A. Attempt to locate Michael's uncle.
    B. Take Michael to Family Court.
    C. Try to locate Michael's parents.
    D. Hold Michael in the station house until his mother is located.

23._____

Question 24.

DIRECTIONS: Question 24 is to be answered SOLELY on the basis of the following information.

Police Department policy requires that a vehicle pursuit should be ended whenever the pursuit causes a greater risk to Police Officers and the public than the danger to the community if the suspect is not caught. If the chase is ended, the Officers should attempt to obtain enough information to apprehend the suspect at a later time.

24. Officer Jordan is in her patrol car when she sees a blue Ford, license plate #7744-AEK, hit an unoccupied red Chevrolet and speed away from the scene of the accident. Officer Jordan pursues the blue Ford at 80 mph on a busy street. While in pursuit, Officer Jordan weaves in and out of traffic, causing some cars to skid and swerve. After a few blocks, the blue Ford skids and Officer Jordan's car crashes into it. Officer Jordan immediately arrests the driver of the Ford. In this situation, Officer Jordan's actions were

    A. *proper,* primarily because it is her duty to arrest criminal suspects
    B. *improper,* primarily because Officer Jordan should not have pursued the blue Ford without knowing how badly the red Chevrolet was damaged
    C. *proper,* primarily because Officer Jordan arrested the driver without causing serious injury to another person
    D. *improper,* primarily because Officer Jordan should have discontinued the pursuit and tried to arrest the suspect at another time

24._____

25. While on patrol, Police Officer Blake observes a man running from a burning abandoned building. Officer Blake radios the following information:

Place of Occurrence: 310 Hall Avenue
Time of Occurrence: 8:30 P.M.
Type of Building: Abandoned
Suspect: Male, White, about 35 years old
Crime: Arson

Officer Blake is completing a report on the incident.
Which one of the following expresses the above information MOST clearly and accurately?

- A. An abandoned building located at 310 Hall Avenue was on fire at 8:30 P.M. A White male, approximately 35 years old, was observed fleeing the scene.
- B. A White male, approximately 35 years old, at 8:30 P.M. was observed fleeing 310 Hall Avenue. The fire was set at an abandoned building.
- C. An abandoned building was set on fire. A White male, approximately 35 years old, was observed fleeing the scene at 8:30 P.M. at 310 Hall Avenue.
- D. Observed fleeing a building at 8:30 P.M. was a White male, approximately 35 years old. An abandoned building, located at 310 Hall Avenue, was set on fire.

KEY (CORRECT ANSWERS)

1. C
2. A
3. B
4. D
5. D

6. B
7. C
8. A
9. D
10. D

11. B
12. C
13. C
14. D
15. A

16. C
17. B
18. D
19. C
20. B

21. D
22. B
23. C
24. D
25. A

TEST 3

DIRECTIONS: Each question or incomplete statement is followed by several suggested answers or completions. Select the one that BEST answers the question or completes the statement. *PRINT THE LETTER OF THE CORRECT ANSWER IN THE SPACE AT THE RIGHT.*

1. Police Officers must sometimes rely on eyewitness accounts of incidents, even though eyewitnesses may make mistakes with regard to some details.
   While on patrol, Police Officer Hanson was approached by a woman who was screaming that her pocketbook had just been stolen. Officer Hanson questions four witnesses who saw the robbery. The following are descriptions of the suspect given by the witnesses.
   Which one of the descriptions should Officer Hanson consider MOST likely to be correct? Male,

   A. White, 40 years old, wearing a black hat and red sneakers
   B. Black, 25 years old, wearing a black hat and red sneakers
   C. White, 25 years old, wearing a black hat and red sneakers
   D. White, 20 years old, wearing a grey hat and maroon sneakers

   1.____

2. Police Officers may be required to transport to a hospital persons who are in need of immediate treatment when an ambulance is not immediately available.
   It would be MOST appropriate for a Police Officer to transport which one of the following individuals? A(n)

   A. elderly woman who twists her ankle while walking to the grocery store
   B. 4-year-old boy who trips and breaks his arm while walking to school with his mother
   C. man who has a heart attack and is lying unconscious in the street
   D. man who bangs his forehead in a car accident and claims he might have a broken nose

   2.____

3. Police Officer Winters responds to a call regarding a report of a missing person. The following information was obtained by the Officer:
   Time of Occurrence: 3:30 P.M.
   Place of Occurrence: Harrison Park
   Reported By: Louise Dee - daughter
   Description of Missing Person: Sharon Dee, 70 years old,
                                  5'5", brown eyes,
                                  black hair - mother
   Officer Winters is completing a report on the incident.
   Which one of the following expresses the above information MOST clearly and accurately?

   A. Mrs. Sharon Dee, reported missing by her daughter, Louise, was seen in Harrison Park. The last time she saw her was at 3:30 P.M. She is 70 years old with black hair, brown eyes, and 5'5".
   B. Louise Dee reported that her mother, Sharon Dee, is missing. Sharon Dee is 70 years old, has black hair, brown eyes, and is 5'5". She was last seen at 3:30 P.M. in Harrison Park.

   3.____

C. Louise Dee reported Sharon, her 70-year-old mother at 3:30 P.M., to be missing after being seen last at Harrison Park. Described as being 5'5", she has black hair and brown eyes.
D. At 3:30 P.M. Louise Dee's mother was last seen by her daughter in Harrison Park. She has black hair and brown eyes. Louise reported Sharon is 5'5" and 70 years old.

Questions 4-7.

DIRECTIONS: Questions 4 through 7 are to be answered SOLELY on the basis of the following passage.

While working an 8:00 A.M. to 4:00 P.M. shift on January 14, Police Officers Jones and Smith received a radio call at 1:45 P.M. to investigate a report of a man with a gun in front of 103 Lexington Avenue. Mary Holmes had called 911 from her home at 1:43 P.M. and explained that two days ago while on her way home from work, she had been threatened by a man with a gun in front of her home at 113 Lowell Street. She told the police operator that the same man was now standing in front of Harry's Lounge at 103 Lexington Avenue, drinking a beer. She described him as being 30-40 years old, 5'6", 160 lbs., wearing a gray coat, gray brim hat, and gold wire bim glasses. The Officers responded to the location and observed a male fitting the description given by Miss Holmes. The Officers approached the suspect and, while searching his right front waistband, Officer Jones found a chromeplated .38 caliber revolver licensed and registered under the name of Joseph Fitz. Miss Holmes was brought to the scene and identified the suspect as the person who had threatened her earlier. Officer Smith then placed the man, identified as Joseph Fitz, under arrest.

4. On what day did the suspect threaten Miss Holmes? January

   A. 10   B. 12   C. 14   D. 16

5. Officer Jones recovered the gun from the suspect's _____ waistband.

   A. left front   B. right rear
   C. left rear   D. right front

6. Miss Holmes stated that the suspect had threatened her in front of

   A. Harry's Lounge   B. her home
   C. a bar   D. her office

7. Joseph Fitz was arrested because he

   A. illegally possessed a weapon
   B. was drinking in a public place
   C. committed a robbery two days earlier
   D. was identified as the suspect in a previous incident

8. While on patrol, Police Officers Mertz and Gallo receive a call from the dispatcher regarding a crime in progress. When the Officers arrive, they obtain the following information:

Time of Occurrence: 2:00 P.M.
Place of Occurrence: In front of 2124 Bristol Avenue
Crime: Purse snatch
Victim: Maria Nieves
Suspect: Carlos Ortiz
Witness: Jose Perez, who apprehended the subject

The Officers are completing a report on the incident. Which one of the following expresses the above information MOST clearly and accurately?

- A. At 2:00 P.M. Jose Perez witnessed Maria Nieves. Her purse was snatched. The suspect, Carlos Ortiz, was apprehended in front of 2124 Bristol Avenue.
- B. In front of 2124 Bristol Avenue, Carlos Ortiz snatched the purse belonging to Maria Nieves. Carlos Ortiz was apprehended by a witness to the crime after Jose Perez saw the purse snatch at 2:00 P.M.
- C. At 2:00 P.M. Carlos Ortiz snatched a purse from Maria Nieves in front of 2124 Bristol Avenue. Carlos Ortiz was apprehended by Jose Perez, a witness to the crime.
- D. At 2:00 P.M. Carlos Ortiz was seen snatching the purse of Maria Nieves as seen and apprehended by Jose Perez in front of 2124 Bristol Avenue.

9. Police Officers Willis and James respond to a crime in progress and obtain the following information:

Time of Occurrence: 8:30 A.M.
Place of Occurrence: Corner of Hopkin Avenue and Amboy Place
Crime: Chain snatch
Victim: Mrs. Paula Evans
Witness: Mr. Robert Peters
Suspect: White male

Officers Willis and James are completing a report on the incident.
Which one of the following expresses the above information MOST clearly and accurately?

- A. Mrs. Paula Evans was standing on the corner of Hopkin Avenue and Amboy Place at 8:30 A.M. when a White male snatched her chain. Mr. Robert Peters witnessed the crime.
- B. At 8:30 A.M., Mr. Robert Peters witnessed Mrs. Paula Evans and a White male standing on the corner of Hopkin Avenue and Amboy Place. Her chain was snatched.
- C. At 8:30 A.M. a White male was standing on the corner of Hopkin Avenue and Amboy Place. Mrs. Paula Evans' chain was snatched and Mr. Robert Peters witnessed the crime.
- D. At 8:30 A.M. Mr. Robert Peters reported he witnessed a White male snatching Mrs. Paula Evans' chain while standing on the corner of Hopkin Avenue and Amboy Place.

Question 10.

DIRECTIONS: Question 10 is to be answered SOLELY on the basis of the following information.

When a Police Officer reasonably suspects that a person has committed, is committing, or is about to commit a crime, the Officer, in order to protect himself from being injured, should do the following in the order given:

    I. Stop the person and request identification and an explanation of the person's conduct.
    II. Frisk the person by running hands over the person's clothing if the Officer thinks his life may be in danger.
    III. Search the person by placing hands inside pockets and interior parts of the person's clothing if a frisk reveals an object which appears to be a weapon.
    IV. Prepare a Stop and Frisk Report for each person stopped if:
        (a) person was stopped by use of force; or
        (b) person was stopped and frisked or searched; or
        (c) person was stopped and arrested

10. Police Officers Darcey and Sanchez are investigating a report of a man with a gun on the corner of Boston Road and Montana Avenue. The Officers stop a man fitting the description they were given. Officer Darcey asks the man why he is in the area. Officer Darcey then asks the man for some proper identification. He then frisks the man and feels an object which seems to be an address book in the man's shirt pocket. Officer Darcey should NEXT

    A. complete a Stop and Frisk Report
    B. search the man's clothing
    C. request the man's identification and an explanation of his conduct
    D. place the man under arrest for possession of a weapon

11. *Robbery 3rd Degree* - *occurs when a person forcibly steals property.*
Which one of the following situations is the BEST example of Robbery in the Third Degree?

    A. Stephanie was riding the train to Coney Island. When the train reached her stop, she realized her briefcase was missing.
    B. June was walking north on 119 Avenue to the bus stop when Sam approached her and snatched her bag. As she struggled with the attacker, he knocked her to the ground and fled south on 119 Avenue.
    C. Clifton was riding the train to Chambers Street during rush hour when Joe brushed past him, picked his pocket, and got off at the next stop.
    D. Denise's purse was hanging on the back of her chair while she ate at a local coffee shop when Bill slit the purse strap with a razor and fled with the purse.

Question 12.

DIRECTIONS: Question 12 is to be answered SOLELY on the basis of the following information.

Police Officer Gray has been instructed by his supervisor to help search for a suspected murderer who was seen running into an abandoned building after committing the crime. The description of the suspect is as follows:

Male, White, about 38 years old, 6'5", 225 lbs., short hair, gray pants, brown sweatshirt, brown construction boots, moustache, 2" scar above right eye.

Officer Gray has also been informed that there were three other murders committed on the same block since the beginning of the year and has been given the following descriptions of the suspects:

<u>Murder No. 1</u> - Male, White, 40 years old, 6'4", 220 lbs., short black hair, black pants, brown shirt, black jacket, construction boots, moustache, scar on face.
<u>Murder No. 2</u> - Male, White, 25 years old, 6'3", 170 lbs., short afro, gray pants, brown sweatshirt, brown boots, moustache, beard.
<u>Murder No. 3</u> - Male, White, 35 years old, 6'0", 225 lbs., black hair, gray pants, brown sweatshirt, brown shoes, moustache, long sideburns.

12. Based on the above descriptions of the suspects in the three previous murders, Officer Gray should tell his supervisor that the suspect in the last murder should also be considered a suspect in Murder No.

    A. 1   B. 3   C. 1 and 2   D. 2 and 3

13. *When a Police Officer responds to the scene of an incident, the Officer may find it necessary to request the immediate assistance of another Department, such as Fire, Sanitation, etc.*
In which of the following incidents would an Officer MOST likely request the assistance of another Department?

    A. A man reports that he was robbed at gunpoint.
    B. Two teenage boys are caught spray-painting their names on a factory wall.
    C. A truck carrying a poisonous liquid overturns and spills the liquid onto a crowded street.
    D. A box of jewelry is found in the basement of an apartment house.

Question 14.

DIRECTIONS: Question 14 is to be answered SOLELY on the basis of the following information.

When a juvenile who is less than 16 years old is arrested by a Police Officer and charged with a felony, the Officer must take the following steps in the order given:

        I. Transport juvenile to Central Booking.
        II. Place juvenile in a cell separate from adult prisoners.
        III. Notify juvenile's parents of arrest.
        IV. Deliver arrest report to Central Booking Supervisor.
        V. Have juvenile fingerprinted and photographed.
        VI. Deliver juvenile to Spofford Juvenile Center for detention.

14. Police Officer Wilson arrested 15-year-old Johnny Leon after Leon was seen threatening and eventually hitting Mr. Perez over the head with an ax handle. Leon was charged with Assault 1st Degree. Officer Wilson placed Leon in the patrol wagon.
    When they arrive at Central Booking, Officer Wilson should NEXT

    A. ensure that Leon is not put in a cell with adult prisoners
    B. telephone Leon's parents
    C. have Leon fingerprinted and photographed
    D. submit arrest report to Supervisor at Central Booking

Question 15.

DIRECTIONS: Question 15 is to be answered SOLELY on the basis of the following information.

When evidence is required for presentation in court, a Police Officer must:

   I. Request evidence from the Officer assigned to the Property Clerk facility where it is stored.
   II. Give the Officer the Property Clerk's Index Number.
   III. Present shield and identification card.
   IV. Sign a receipt for evidence.

15. Police Officer Dana is informed that she is scheduled to testify in court about a narcotics arrest she made four months ago. The case involves evidence stored at the Property Clerk's Office. Since Officer Dana was scheduled to work on patrol that day, she appears at the Property Clerk's Office in full police uniform. She requests the evidence from Officer Baskin, who is assigned to the Property Clerk's Office, and gives the Clerk the correct Property Clerk's Index Number. Officer Dana presents her shield to Officer Baskin and signs a receipt for the evidence. She then proceeds to court. Officer Dana's actions in this situation were

    A. *proper,* primarily because she was scheduled to work patrol that day
    B. *improper,* primarily because a patrol supervisor should have been present to witness the transfer of property
    C. *proper,* primarily because the evidence was critical to the case
    D. *improper,* primarily because she did not show proper identification to Officer Baskin

16. Police Officers Cleveland and Logan responded to an assault that had recently occurred. The following information was obtained at the scene:
    Place of Occurrence: Broadway and Roosevelt Avenue
    Time of Occurrence: 1:00 A.M.
    Crime: Attempted robbery, assault
    Victim: Chuck Brown, suffered a broken tooth
    Suspect: Lewis Brown, victim's brother
    Officer Logan is completing a report on the incident.
    Which one of the following expresses the above information MOST clearly and accurately?

A. Lewis Brown assaulted his brother Chuck on the corner of Broadway and Roosevelt Avenue. Chuck Brown reported his broken tooth during the attempted robbery at 1:00 A.M.
B. Chuck Brown had his tooth broken when he was assaulted at 1:00 A.M. on the corner of Broadway and Roosevelt Avenue by his brother, Lewis Brown, while Lewis was attempting to rob him.
C. An attempt at 1:00 A.M. to rob Chuck Brown turned into an assault at the corner of Broadway and Roosevelt Avenue when his brother Lewis broke his tooth.
D. At 1:00 A.M. Chuck Brown reported that he was assaulted during his brother's attempt to rob him. Lewis Brown broke his tooth. The incident occurred on the corner of Broadway and Roosevelt Avenue.

17. Police Officer Mannix has just completed an investigation regarding a hit-and-run accident which resulted in a pedestrian being injured. Officer Mannix has obtained the following information:

    Make and Model of Car: Pontiac, Trans Am
    Year and Color of Car: 2006, white
    Driver of Car: Male, Black
    Place of Occurrence: Corner of E. 15th Street and 8th Avenue
    Time of Occurrence: 1:00 P.M.

    Officer Mannix is completing a report on the accident. Which one of the following expresses the above information MOST clearly and accurately?

    A. At 1:00 P.M., at the corner of E. 15th Street and 8th Avenue, a Black male driving a white 2006 Pontiac Trans Am was observed leaving the scene of an accident after injuring a pedestrian with the vehicle.
    B. On the corner of E. 15th Street and 8th Avenue, a white Pontiac, driven by a Black male, a 2006 Trans Am injured a pedestrian and left the scene of the accident at 1:00 P.M.
    C. A Black male driving a white 2006 Pontiac Trans Am, injured a pedestrian and left with the car while driving on the corner of E. 15th Street and 8th Avenue at 1:00 P.M.
    D. At the corner of E. 15th Street and 8th Avenue, a pedestrian was injured by a Black male. He fled in his white 2006 Pontiac Trans Am at 1:00 P.M.

17.____

Questions 18-19.

DIRECTIONS: Questions 18 and 19 are to be answered SOLELY on the basis of the following information.

Police Officer Jones has been made aware by merchants on her post that an increase of crimes have been occurring in her area. All of the assaults seem to take place on Pitt Avenue between Van Syck Street and Stone Street. Most of the robberies take place on Pitt Avenue between Amboy Place and Herzl Street. All of the larcenies take place on Amboy Place between Pitt Avenue and East Avenue. The robberies usually occur on Fridays and Saturdays; the larcenies occur on Sundays and Mondays; and the assaults occur on Wednesdays and Thursdays. Most of the larcenies occur between 4:00 P.M. and 8:00 P.M.; all of the robberies occur between 1:00 P.M. and 3:00 P.M.; and the assaults occur between 1:00 A.M. and 4:00 A.M.

18. In order to reduce the number of larcenies, Officer Jones should inform the merchants that she will INCREASE patrol on

    A. Pitt Avenue between Amboy Place and Herzl Street on Sundays and Mondays between 4:00 P.M. and 8:00 P.M.
    B. Amboy Place between Pitt Avenue and East Avenue on Mondays and Tuesdays between 3:00 A.M. and 8:00 A.M.
    C. Amboy Place between East Avenue and Pitt Avenue on Sundays and Mondays between 3:00 P.M. and 10:00 P.M.
    D. Herzl Street between Amboy Place and Pitt Avenue on Wednesdays and Thursdays between 1:00 A.M. and 9:00 A.M.

19. Officer Jones would be MOST effective in reducing the number of robberies if she patrolled from

    A. 10:00 A.M. to 6:00 P.M., Monday through Friday
    B. 1:00 P.M. to 9:00 P.M., Saturday through Wednesday
    C. 1:00 A.M. to 9:00 A.M., Wednesday through Sunday
    D. 8:00 A.M. to 4:00 P.M., Tuesday through Saturday

20. Under certain circumstances, Police Officers are required to request the assistance and advice of a supervisor. Which one of the following situations would MOST likely require a supervisor?

    A. Two men are verbally arguing over a parking space.
    B. Several teenagers are listening and dancing to loud music in the schoolyard.
    C. A woman threatens to jump from the twelfth floor of a building.
    D. A man complains that his next door neighbor smokes marijuana in the building hallways.

KEY (CORRECT ANSWERS)

1. C
2. C
3. B
4. B
5. D

6. B
7. D
8. C
9. A
10. A

11. B
12. A
13. C
14. A
15. D

16. B
17. A
18. C
19. D
20. C

EXAMINATION SECTION
TEST 1

DIRECTIONS: Each question or incomplete statement is followed by several suggested answers or completions. Select the one that BEST answers the question or completes the statement. *PRINT THE LETTER OF THE CORRECT ANSWER IN THE SPACE AT THE RIGHT.*

1. <u>Reckless Endangerment 1st Degree</u> - *occurs when, under circumstances which clearly show a total disregard for human life, a person acts in a manner which creates a grave risk of death to another person.*
   Which one of the following is the BEST example of Reckless Endangerment in the First Degree?

   A. James, while attending a football game where his favorite team is losing, fires a rifle into the stands to get the crowd to stop cheering for the opposing team.
   B. A woman threatens to kill herself if her husband is not immediately released from prison.
   C. A motorist whose gas pedal is stuck hits a woman who is pushing a baby carriage down the block, causing her death.
   D. A person continues to throw garbage out of his second floor window into an empty lot, even after he is warned he could injure someone.

Question 2.

DIRECTIONS: Question 2 is to be answered SOLELY on the basis of the following information.

When a Police Officer recovers a stolen vehicle, the following should be done in the order given:
   I. Make a Memo Book entry describing the vehicle and where the vehicle was found.
   II. Notify the Desk Officer.
   III. Prepare a Property Clerk's Invoice.
   IV. Notify the owner, if known.

2. While on patrol, Police Officer Vasquez notices an unoccupied vehicle with lit headlights on the corner of 101st and Kane Avenue. She recalls seeing that same vehicle parked in the same place with its engine running one hour earlier. Officer Vasquez requests the radio dispatcher to run a check on the vehicle's Florida license plate ZBF293. She is informed that the vehicle is registered to Ms. Patti Tucci of Miami Beach. Officer Vasquez notices that the steering column of the vehicle has been broken. Officer Vasquez suspects that the vehicle has been stolen.
   Officer Vasquez should NEXT

   A. notify the owner of the vehicle
   B. record all details related to the vehicle in her Memo Book
   C. prepare a Property Clerk's Invoice
   D. call the Desk Officer

Questions 3-6.

DIRECTIONS: Questions 3 through 6 are to be answered SOLELY on the basis of the following passage.

On April 6, at 5:25 A.M., while patrolling the #8 train southbound to Brooklyn, Transit Police Officer O'Rourke noticed a young woman at the end of the car who appeared to be ill. Officer O'Rourke approached the woman and asked her if she was feeling all right. The woman was crying and began speaking incoherently. Officer O'Rourke escorted the woman off the train at the next southbound #8 platform in order to obtain information from her. After speaking with her for fifteen minutes, Officer O'Rourke learned that her name was Carol Rivers and that she had been assaulted and sexually molested while waiting for the southbound #8 train about a half hour before meeting the Officer. Miss Rivers described the suspect as a White male, in his forties, with gray hair, glasses, a red shirt, black pants, and a brown hat. The suspect fled on a northbound #8 train with the victim's pocketbook. Officer O'Rourke then radioed for an ambulance to respond to the location to assist Miss Rivers.

The next day at approximately 5:30 A.M., while Officer O'Rourke was standing on the subway platform waiting to board the uptown #7 train to Queens, he noticed an individual coming down the steps from the southbound platform. The man was in his forties, with gray hair, dark glasses, and the same clothing described by Miss Rivers the day before, except for his shirt, which was white. Officer O'Rourke, believing the man to be the same perpetrator, decided to follow him in order to observe the suspect's actions. The man was walking alongside a woman on the northbound platform and attempted to snatch her pocketbook. The woman held onto her purse, and started to yell for the police. The man immediately released his hold on the pocketbook and ran down the platform onto an awaiting #7 train to Manhattan. Officer O'Rourke pursued the man onto the train and subsequently placed him under arrest two stations later.

3. Officer O'Rourke requested that the ambulance respond to the subway platform of the _____ train.

   A. northbound #8 B. uptown #7
   C. downtown #7   D. southbound #8

4. At approximately what time was Miss Rivers assaulted? _____ A.M.

   A. 4:55   B. 5:10   C. 5:25   D. 5:40

5. The suspect arrested by Officer O'Rourke was wearing a _____ shirt and _____ pants.

   A. red; blue   B. white; black
   C. red; black   D. white; red

6. On April 7, Officer O'Rourke boarded a train to

   A. Manhattan   B. Queens
   C. the Bronx   D. Brooklyn

7. Police Officer Brown has responded to a domestic dispute and has obtained the following information:

Time of Complaint:	3:20 P.M.
Complainant:	Mrs. Jenny Shawn
Address of Complainant:	39 Waring Place
Complaint:	Husband and wife screaming, and threatening each other with knives
People Involved:	Mr. and Mrs. George Roberts

Officer Brown is completing a report on the incident. Which one of the following expresses the above information MOST clearly and accurately?

    A. At 39 Waring Place Mrs. Jenny Shawn called the police because Mr. and Mrs. George Roberts were screaming and threatening each other with knives at 3:20 P.M.
    B. At 3:20 P.M. Mrs. Jenny Shawn reported Mr. and Mrs. George Roberts to the police. At 39 Waring Place, they were screaming and threatening each other with knives.
    C. Mrs. Jenny Shawn reported to the police of 39 Waring Place at 3:20 P.M., that Mr. and Mrs. George Roberts were screaming and threatening each other with knives.
    D. At 3:20 P.M. Mrs. Jenny Shawn, of 39 Waring Place, called the police because Mr. and Mrs. George Roberts were screaming and threatening each other with knives.

8. While on patrol, Police Officer Beckman witnesses the following incident:

Incident:	Person hit by brick that was thrown from 12th floor of a building
Place of Incident:	In front of 227 20th Street
Time of Incident:	11:21 A.M.
Victim:	Mr. George Manson, Injured
Suspect:	Mr. Brian Mor

Officer Beckman is completing a report regarding this incident.
Which one of the following expresses the above information MOST clearly and accurately?

    A. At 11:21 A.M., in front of 227 20th Street a brick was thrown. Mr. George Manson was walking and injured by Mr. Brian Mor on the 12th floor of a building.
    B. A brick was thrown from the 12th floor of a building in front of 227 20th Street. Mr. George Manson was walking at 11:21 A.M. and was injured by Mr. Brian Mor.
    C. Mr. Brian Mor threw a brick in front of 227 20th Street. At 11:21 A.M., Mr. George Manson was injured when walking from the 12th floor of a building.
    D. At 11:21 A.M., Mr. George Manson was walking in front of 227 20th Street. He was injured by a brick that Mr. Brian Mor threw from the 12th floor of a building.

Question 9.

DIRECTIONS: Question 9 is to be answered SOLELY on the basis of the following information.

When a Police Officer investigates a complaint of a rape or an attempted rape, the Officer should do the following in the order given:

    I. Interview the complainant and witnesses and attempt to obtain the facts.

II. Search for and remove any evidence from the location of the complaint.
III. Notify the Sex Crime Squad if the victim was raped.
IV. Prepare a Complaint Report Worksheet.
V. Notify supervisor upon completion of investigation.

9. Police Officers King and Ross respond to 110-30 11th Avenue. Upon arriving at the location, they find Mary Jones and Sam Dean sitting on the front steps of the building. Mr. Dean informs the Officers that as he was walking home he heard screams, ran into an alley, and discovered a man threatening Mary Jones with a knife. Mr. Dean ran towards the man, who dropped his knife and ran away. Mary Jones confirms what Mr. Dean told the Officers and added that when the man threatened her with a knife, he said he was going to rape her. She said that if Mr. Dean hadn't chased the man away, she would have been raped. The NEXT step that Officers King and Ross should take is to

   A. prepare a Complaint Report Worksheet
   B. interview Mr. Dean
   C. search for the knife
   D. call the Sex Crime Squad

10. Police Officer Selma is assigned to patrol Blum and Tan Streets in order to reduce the sale of drugs. Officer Selma is informed that drugs are being sold at 416 Blum Street in Apt. 1A and at 428 Tan Street in Apt. IB. Most of the drug sales in Apt. 1A occur between 10:30 A.M. and 4:00 P.M. Most of the drug sales in Apt. IB take place from 5:00 P.M. to 8:00 P.M. Officer Selma is also informed that most of the drug sales are taking place on Thursdays and Sundays on Tan Street and Wednesdays and Fridays on Blum Street. Officer Selma would MOST likely reduce the number of drug sales taking place in Apt. 1A by patrolling in the area of _____ Street.

   A. 428 Tan; 9:00 A.M. to 5:00 P.M.
   B. 416 Blum; 9:00 A.M. to 5:00 P.M.
   C. 428 Tan; 3:00 P.M. to 11:00 P.M.
   D. 416 Blum; 3:00 P.M. to 11:00 P.M.

Question 11.

DIRECTIONS: Question 11 is to be answered SOLELY on the basis of the following information.

When a Police Officer stops a vehicle and discovers that the operator is driving with a suspended license, the Officer should

I. Take away the driver's license.
II. Give the operator of the vehicle a receipt for the license.
III. If the operator has two or more unrelated suspensions, or if the driver's license has been revoked for any reason, arrest the motorist.
IV. Do not mark or mutilate the license in any manner.
V. Have the violator's vehicle parked in a legal parking area until removed by a licensed operator.

11. Police Officers Wells and Cortese, while on patrol, observed the driver of a blue Firebird make an illegal U-turn at an intersection. Officer Wells directed the driver to pull over to the curb. The Officer approached the driver and requested his driver's license and car registration. While inspecting the license, Officer Wells noticed that the license had been revoked. Officer Wells took the license, issued a receipt, and placed the driver under arrest. Officer Cortese legally parked the car under a tree.
In this situation, the actions taken by Officers Wells and Cortese were

    A. *proper,* primarily because the driver had a revoked license
    B. *improper,* primarily because he should have taken the license and registration
    C. *proper,* primarily because the driver almost caused an accident
    D. *improper,* primarily because the vehicle should have been removed by a licensed driver

12. Under certain circumstances, Police Officers may be required to use their handguns. In which one of the following situations would it be MOST appropriate for an Officer to remove his gun from his holster?
A

    A. man enters a subway station without paying a fare, and as he runs towards a train, he knocks a woman to the ground
    B. person grabs a woman's handbag and runs down a crowded street
    C. woman hits a young boy with her car and begins to drive away without stopping
    D. person is swinging an ax in a crowded area and threatens to kill anyone who comes near him

13. Police Officer Spencer received the following information from a Grand Larceny victims
    Time of Occurrence: 3:45 P.M.
    Place of Occurrence: Uptown #4 train, 14th Street station
    Victim: Louis Smith
    Witness: Cindy Lewis (Smith's girlfriend)
    Description of Suspect: Unknown
    Crime: Grand Larceny, chain snatch
    Officer Spencer is completing a report on the Grand Larceny.
    Which one of the following expresses the above information MOST clearly and accurately?

    A. Cindy Lewis stated that at 3:45 P.M., while aboard the uptown #4 train, an unknown man reached into the train while it was stopped at the 14th Street station and snatched the chain of her boyfriend, Louis Smith.
    B. A male, unidentified by Louis Smith, reached in and stole his chain from an uptown #4 train at the 14th Street station. Cindy Lewis said she was his girlfriend and unable to identify the suspect, who did the snatch at 3:45 P.M.
    C. On the #4 train going uptown, Louis Smith had his chain snatched at the 14th Street station when a man reached in the train. He was travelling with his girlfriend, Cindy Lewis, and they were both unable to identify him when it occurred at 3:45 P.M.
    D. At 3:45 P.M., Cindy Lewis was unable to identify the man who snatched her boyfriend's chain at the 14th Street station. They were travelling uptown on the #4 train when someone reached in and took Smith's chain.

14. While on patrol, Officer Casio responds to a Grand Larceny. The following details were obtained at the scene:

Time of Crime:	Between 9:30 P.M. and Midnight
Place of Crime:	In front of 119-30 Long Street
Crime:	Car theft
Vehicle Stolen:	1983 Renault
Victim:	San Andrews
Suspect:	Unidentified

Officer Casio is completing a report on the incident.
Which one of the following expresses the above information MOST clearly and accurately?

    A. Between 9:30 P.M. and Midnight, Sam Andrews was in front of 119-30 Long Street. A 1983 Renault was stolen by an unidentified person.
    B. An unidentified person stole Sam Andrews' 1983 Renault from in front of 119-30 Long Street between 9;30 P.M. and Midnight.
    C. An unidentified person in front of 119-30 Long Street stole a car between 9:30 P.M. and Midnight. Sam Andrews has a 1983 Renault.
    D. A 1983 Renault was stolen in front of Sam Andrews at 119-30 Long Street between 9:30 P.M. and Midnight by an unidentified person.

Questions 15-17.

DIRECTIONS: Questions 15 through 17 are to be answered SOLELY on the basis of the following map. The flow of traffic is indicated by the arrows. If there is only one arrow shown, then traffic flows only in the direction indicated by the arrow. If there are two arrows shown, then traffic flows in both directions. You must follow the flow of traffic.

7 (#1)

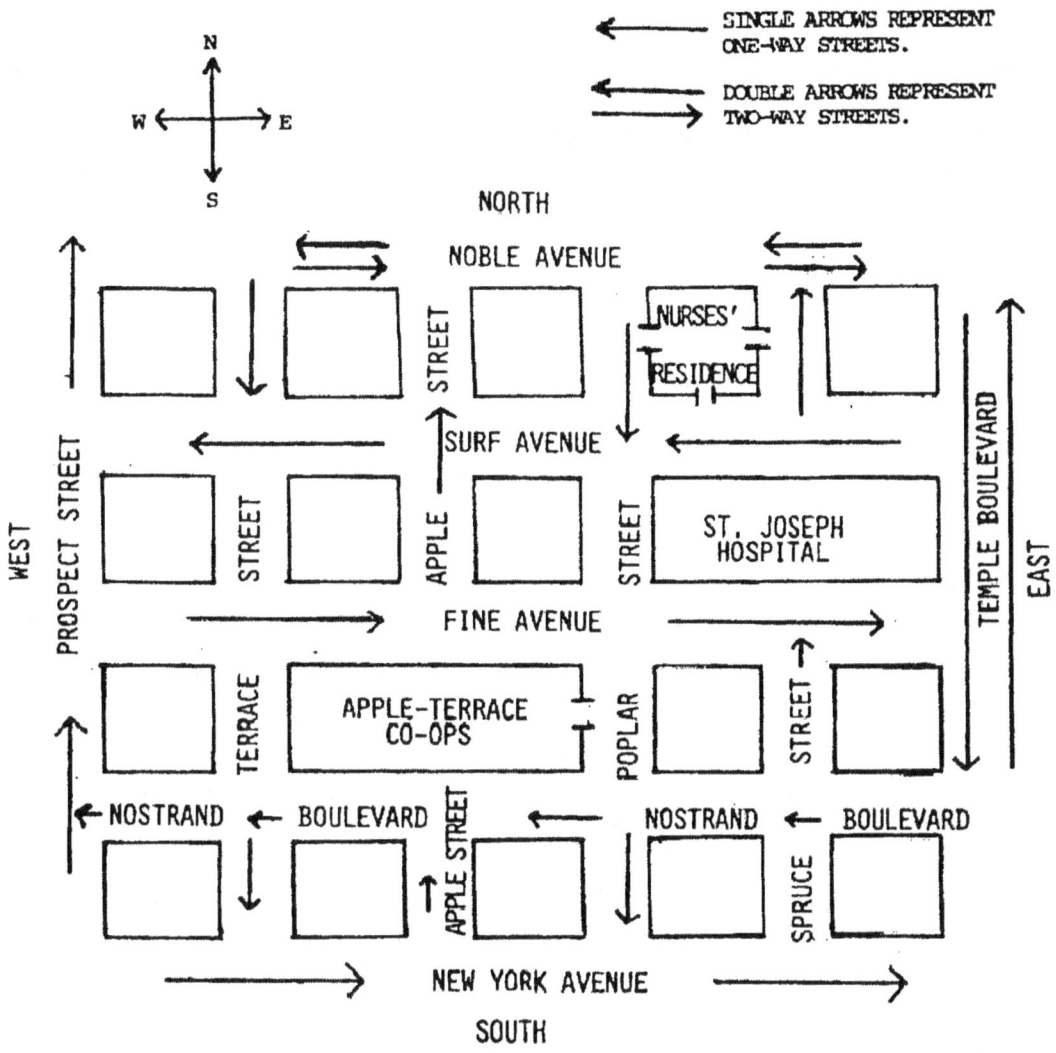

15. Police Officers Gannon and Vine are located at the intersection of Terrace Street and Surf Avenue when they receive a call from the radio dispatcher stating that they need to respond to an attempted murder at Spruce Street and Fine Avenue.
Which one of the following is the SHORTEST route for them to take in their patrol car, making sure to obey all traffic regulations? Travel _____ to Spruce Street.

   A. west on Surf Avenue, then north on Prospect Street, then east on Noble Avenue, then south on Poplar Street, then east on Fine Avenue
   B. east on Surf Avenue, then south on Poplar Street, then east on Fine Avenue
   C. west on Surf Avenue, then south on Prospect Street, then east on Fine Avenue
   D. south on Terrace Street, then east on Fine Avenue

15.____

16. Police Officers Sears and Ronald are at Nostrand Boulevard and Prospect Street. They receive a call assigning them to investigate a disruptive group of youths at Temple Boulevard and Surf Avenue.
Which one of the following is the SHORTEST route for them to take in their patrol car, making sure to obey all traffic regulations? Travel

   A. north on Prospect Street, then east on Surf Avenue to Temple Boulevard

16.____

43

B. north on Prospect Street, then east on Noble Avenue, then south on Temple Boulevard to Surf Avenue
C. north on Prospect Street, then east on Fine Avenue, then north on Temple Boulevard to Surf Avenue
D. south on Prospect Street, then east on New York Avenue, then north on Temple Boulevard to Surf Avenue

17. While on patrol at Prospect Street and New York Avenue, Police Officers Ross and Rock are called to a burglary in progress near the entrance to the Apple-Terrace Co-ops on Poplar Street midway between Fine Avenue and Nostrand Boulevard.
Which one of the following is the SHORTEST route for them to take in their patrol car, making sure to obey all traffic regulations?
Travel _____ on Poplar Street.

   A. east on New York Avenue, then north
   B. north on Prospect Avenue, then east on Fine Avenue, then south
   C. north on Prospect Street, then east on Surf Avenue, then south
   D. east on New York Avenue, then north on Temple Boulevard, then west on Surf Avenue, then south

18. While on patrol, Officer Smith responded to the scene of a robbery. Upon his arrival, Mrs. Mary Taylor told Officer Smith that the following items were taken from her at gunpoint:

Cash	$ 150.00
3 bracelets, each valued at	$ 95.00
2 rings, each valued at	$ 70.00
1 leather handbag, valued at	$ 100.00

Later that day, Mary Taylor telephoned Officer Smith and informed him that she found a receipt for the leather bag that was taken, and it is actually valued at $159.00. Officer Smith is preparing a Complaint Report on the robbery.
Which one of the following is the TOTAL value of the property and cash taken from Mrs. Taylor?
   A. $415.00   B. $474.00   C. $675.00   D. $734.00

19. Three rapes occurred in the 141st Precinct during the month of April. The reported description of each of the suspects is as follows:

Rape No. 1 - Male, White, about 25 years old, short brown hair, gray pants, white tank top shirt, black shoes, scar above right eye and across right cheek, earring in left ear.
Rape No. 2 - Male, White, early 40's, black hair, gray pants, white shirt, black shoes, black suit jacket, wearing sunglasses.
Rape No. 3 - Male, White, 21 years old, black hair, blue dungarees, white sneakers, black leather vest, white T-shirt, tattoo on left arm, earring in right ear.

On April 21, Police Officer Johnson arrested a suspect during an attempted rape. The description of the suspect is as follows:

Rape No. 4 - Male, White, 20 years old, short black hair, blue jeans, white sneakers, white T-shirt, tattoo of a ghost on left arm, earring in left ear.

Based on the descriptions of the suspects in the first three rapes, Officer Johnson should consider the suspect in the fourth rape as a suspect in Rape No.

   A. 1 only   B. 3 only   C. 1 and 3   D. 1 and 2

20. While on patrol, Police Officer Rucco witnesses a robbery and apprehends the suspect. The following information relates to this incident:

Place of Robbery: In front of 311 Sutter Avenue
Victim: Veronica Stables, not injured
Suspect: Male, White, wearing blue jeans, white sneakers, leather jacket
Action Taken: Suspect apprehended and arrested on the corner of Canal and Vestry Streets

Officer Rucco is completing a report on the incident.

Which one of the following expresses the above information MOST clearly and accurately?

- A. Wearing blue jeans, white sneakers, and a leather jacket in front of 311 Sutter Avenue, Veronica Stables was robbed by the suspect and not injured. The White male was apprehended and arrested on the corner of Canal and Vestry Streets.
- B. On the corner of Canal and Vestry Streets was apprehended and arrested a White male. Veronica Stables was robbed and not injured by the suspect wearing blue jeans, white sneakers, and a leather jacket in front of 311 Sutter Avenue.
- C. A White male wearing blue jeans, white sneakers, and a leather jacket in front of 311 Sutter Avenue was apprehended and arrested on the corner of Canal and Vestry Streets. Veronica Stables was not injured and robbed by the suspect.
- D. A White male wearing blue jeans, white sneakers, and a leather jacket robbed Veronica Stables in front of 311 Sutter Avenue. The suspect was apprehended and arrested on the corner of Canal and Vestry Streets.

Question 21.

DIRECTIONS: Question 21 is to be answered SOLELY on the basis of the following information.

Police Officers may arrest a person for driving while under the influence of alcohol and then test the person for alcohol use at a police facility. Upon making such an arrest, a Police Officer should do the following in the order given:

  I. Remove the prisoner to the precinct station house.
  II. Inform the Desk Officer of the arrest.
  III. Request the Communications Division to dispatch Highway Police Officers to the testing location where the alcohol test will be conducted.
  IV. Remove the prisoner to the testing location in order to have the Highway Police Officers conduct a chemical test of the prisoner.
  V. Record the results of the test on an Intoxicated Driver Examination Report.
  VI. Return the prisoner to the precinct station house.

21. While on patrol, Police Officers Riglioni and Cardaci observe the driver of a red Chevrolet driving erratically. The Officers stop the vehicle and ask the driver to get out. The driver gets out of the vehicle and is obviously drunk. The Officers arrest the driver for operating a vehicle while under the influence of alcohol. The Officers take the prisoner to the precinct station house and report the arrest to the Desk Officer.
The NEXT step the Officers should take is to

   A. request the Communications Division to send the Highway Police
   B. bring the prisoner to the testing location
   C. conduct a test to determine if the prisoner is drunk
   D. complete the Intoxicated Driver Examination Report

22. Police Officers must sometimes rely on eyewitness accounts of incidents, even though eyewitnesses may make mistakes with regard to some details.
Mrs. Levy was the victim of a hit-and-run accident. When Police Officer Murphy arrived at the scene, he interviewed four witnesses who saw a black car strike the victim and leave the scene. The following are license plate numbers provided by the four witnesses. Which one of these numbers should Officer Murphy consider MOST likely to be correct?

   A. P-82324   B. P-82342   C. F-83424   D. F-62323

Question 23.

DIRECTIONS: Question 23 is to be answered SOLELY on the basis of the following information.

When Police Officers respond to investigate a complaint of unnecessary loud noise, they should do the following in the order given:

   I. Respond to the location of the unnecessary noise.
   II. Interview the complainant, if possible.
   III. Interview the violator.
   IV. Correct the condition by advising and warning the violator.
   V. Give the violator a summons if the warning is ignored.
   VI. Make a Memo Book entry concerning the incident.
   VII. Report all actions taken to the Desk Officer.

23. While on patrol, Police Officer Ryan receives a call at 3 A.M. to respond to 225 Kent Street, Apt. 4J, concerning a complaint of loud music. Upon his arrival, the Officer is met by Mr. Templer, who states that his neighbor has been continuously playing his stereo very loudly. As the Officer is speaking to Mr. Templer, he hears a loud stereo playing from the next door apartment. Officer Ryan goes to the apartment and informs the violator, Mr. Nelson, that Mr. Templer has complained about the noise. Mr. Nelson immediately apologizes for playing his stereo loudly and then lowers the stereo saying he will be more thoughtful in the future.
Police Officer Ryan should NEXT

   A. interview Mr. Templer
   B. give Mr. Nelson a summons
   C. make a Memo Book entry
   D. give Mr. Templer a summons

24. When a motorist commits a traffic violation, a Police Officer may give the motorist either a warning or a traffic ticket.
In which one of the following situations should a Police Officer issue a traffic ticket instead of a warning?
A
   A. woman is adjusting her child's seat belt while driving
   B. man who is driving on a busy street turns his head away from the road to watch a young woman pass by
   C. woman who is applying lipstick while driving goes through a stop sign
   D. man who is talking to his friend comes to a sudden halt at a red traffic light

Question 25.

DIRECTIONS: Question 25 is to be answered SOLELY on the basis of the following information.

Grand Larceny 2nd Degree - occurs when a person steals property and when the value of the property is greater than $1500.

Unauthorized Use of a Vehicle - occurs when a person knowingly takes, operates, rides in, or otherwise uses a vehicle without the consent of the owner.

25. Will Walker, a car mechanic at a gas station, repairs Mr. Smith's car. Knowing that Mr. Smith is away, Walker decides to borrow the car for the weekend. He drives the car home, parks it on the street, and accidentally leaves the keys in the ignition. Several hours-later, Ben Barnes walks past the car and notices the keys in the ignition. Knowing that the car is worth at least $7,000, Barnes breaks into the car and drives it away. Barnes later sells the car to a used car salesman for $8,000.
In this situation,

   A. both Barnes and Walker should be charged only with Grand Larceny 2nd Degree
   B. Barnes should be charged with Grand Larceny 2nd Degree and Unauthorized Use of a Vehicle, and Walker should be charged with Unauthorized Use of a Vehicle
   C. both Barnes and Walker should be charged only with Unauthorized Use of a Vehicle
   D. Barnes should be charged with Unauthorized Use of a Vehicle, and Walker should be charged with Grand Larceny 2nd Degree and Unauthorized Use of a Vehicle

KEY (CORRECT ANSWERS)

1. A
2. B
3. D
4. A
5. B

6. A
7. D
8. D
9. C
10. B

11. A
12. D
13. A
14. B
15. D

16. C
17. B
18. D
19. B
20. D

21. A
22. A
23. C
24. C
25. B

TEST 2

DIRECTIONS: Each question or incomplete statement is followed by several suggested answers or completions. Select the one that BEST answers the question or completes the statement. *PRINT THE LETTER OF THE CORRECT ANSWER IN THE SPACE AT THE RIGHT.*

1. Police Officer Clay obtained the following information at the scene of burglary: 1.____
   Time of Occurrence: 3:00 P.M. Place of Occurrence:
   350 Lenox Avenue Suspect: Male
   Crime: Burglary; TV and VCR stolen
   Witness: Ed Simms
   Victim: Mrs. Lester
   Police Officer Clay is preparing a report on the burglary. Which one of the following expresses the above information MOST clearly and accurately?

   A. At 3:00 P.M., Mrs. Lester's house at 350 Lenox Avenue was burglarized. Ed Simms reported seeing a man leaving Mrs. Lester's house with a TV and VCR.
   B. Mrs. Lester's house was burglarized at 3:00 P.M. A man took a TV and a VCR. Mr. Ed Simms saw a man. She lives at 350 Lenox Avenue.
   C. At 350 Lenox Avenue, Mrs. Lester's house was burglarized. Mr. Ed Simms saw a man leaving her house at 3:00 P.M. He was carrying a TV and a VCR.
   D. Ed Simms stated that he witnessed a burglary. It happened at 350 Lenox Avenue, at 3:00 P.M. A man took a TV set and a VCR from Mrs. Lester's house.

Question 2.

DIRECTIONS: Question 2 is to be answered SOLELY on the basis of the following information.

While on patrol in September 2002, Police Officer Harris received several reports from people who were robbed as they exited the Georgia Street subway station. The description of each suspect is as follows:

Robbery No. 1 - Male, Black, early 20's, 5'10", 180 lbs., dark hair, moustache, blue jeans, black jacket, running shoes. Robbery No. 2 - Male, Black, 25 to 30 years old, 5'9", 165 lbs., dark hair, dark moustache, glasses, black jeans, green sweat shirt, running shoes.
Robbery No. 3 - Male, Black, 40 to 45 years old, 5'8", 150 lbs., 'dark hair, clean-shaven, blue jeans, black jacket, running shoes.

On October 6, 2002, a woman was robbed by a male who was loitering near the Georgia Street subway station. Police Officer Harris witnessed the, robbery and apprehended the suspect four blocks away. The description of the suspect is as follows:
Robbery No. 4 - Male, Black, 20-25 years old, 5'10", 175 lbs., dark hair, moustache, blue jeans, black jacket, black cap, sneakers.

2. Based on the above description of the suspects in the first three robberies, Officer Brown 2.____
   should consider the suspect in the fourth robbery as a suspect in Robbery No.

   A. 1 *only*   B. 1 and 2
   C. 2 and 3   D. 1, 2, and 3

49

3. Officer Stanley obtained the following information regarding a call for help:
   Time of Occurrence: 6:40 A.M.
   Place of Occurrence: 452 Hull Street, Apt. 4A
   Crime: Rape
   Victim: Jane Allen
   Suspect: Male, White
   Officer Stanley is completing a report on the incident.
   Which one of the following expresses the above information MOST clearly and accurately?

   A. Raped at 452 Hull Street, at 6:40 A.M., was Jane Allen in Apt. 4A by a White male.
   B. At 6:40 A.M., Jane Allen was raped by a White male living at 452 Hull Street, Apt. 4A.
   C. A White male at 452 Hull Street, Apt. 4A, raped Jane Allen at 6:40 A.M.
   D. At 6:40 A.M., Jane Allen was raped at 452 Hull Street, Apt. 4A, by a White male.

Question 4.

DIRECTIONS: Question 4 is to be answered SOLELY on the basis of the following information.

Complaint - is a report of an unlawful or improper act, or any condition which requires investigation by the Police to determine if an unlawful act has occurred.

Complaints should be recorded in a particular precinct when:

   I. There is an arrest for an unlawful act in that precinct; or
   II. A resident of that precinct is reported missing; or
   III. A dead human body is found on the piers or in the waters bordering that precinct; or
   IV. Property is lost and the loss is first discovered in that precinct.

4. Police Officer Menke, of the 126th Precinct, is assigned to prepare the Precinct's Complaint Reports.
   Which one of the following situations should be recorded as a Complaint by Officer Menke?

   A. While having lunch in the 44th Precinct, Ray Shaw, a businessman, who lives in the 126th Precinct, discovers that his briefcase has been stolen.
   B. David Spooner, who lives in the 126th Precinct, is arrested for possession of cocaine in the 56th Precinct.
   C. A dead human body is found floating in the West River approximately fifteen feet from the riverbank bordering the 126th Precinct.
   D. Richard Warman, of the 126th Precinct, reports that his 23-year-old daughter, who lives in the 130th Precinct, has been missing for 48 hours.

Question 5.

DIRECTIONS: Question 5 is to be answered SOLELY on the basis of the following information.

Police Officers Smith and Jones are on patrol when, at approximately 10:00 A.M., James Banks runs up to the patrol car and informs the Officers that he has just been robbed. Mr. Banks is told to get into the patrol car, and the Officers proceed to drive around the immediate area in search of the suspect. Mr. Banks gives the following description of the suspect:

Male, Black, about 18 years old, 6'1", 190 lbs., wearing
blue dungarees, red button-down shirt, red and white sneakers,
blue cap, long sideburns, and has a gold front tooth.

Officer Smith is aware that this is the fourth robbery in this area during the past month. The reported descriptions of the suspects involved in the previous three robberies are as follows:

Robbery No. 1 - Male, Black, 21 years old, 6'0", 180 lbs.,
wearing blue pants, red shirt, red sneakers, blue ski cap,
wearing a slight beard.
Robbery No. 2 - Male, Black, 19 years old, 6'0", 185 lbs.,
wearing blue jeans, red shirt, white sneakers, blue baseball
cap, wearing long sideburns.
Robbery No. 3 - Male, Black, 18 years old, 5'7", 150 lbs.,
wearing blue dungarees, red sweat shirt, red and white
sneakers, blue hat, wearing long sideburns.

5. Based on the descriptions that were given of the suspects for the first three robberies, Officer Smith should consider the suspect in the Banks robbery as a suspect in Robbery No.

   A. 2 *only*   B. 1 and 2
   C. 2 and 3   D. 1, 2, and 3

6. Police Officer Roland responded to 233 Main Street to investigate a past burglary. Officer Roland arrived at the scene and interviewed Mrs. Joan Bates. Mrs. Bates stated that her apartment was broken into, and the following items were missing:

1 ring valued at	$415.00
Cash	$220.00
Coin collection, valued at	$410.00
3 cameras, each valued at	$175.00

Officer Roland is preparing a report on the burglary. Which one of the following is the TOTAL value of the missing property and cash?
   A. $1,220.00   B. $1,395.00
   C. $1,570.00   D. $1,615.00

Questions 7-9.

DIRECTIONS: Questions 7 through 9 are to be answered SOLELY on the basis of the following passage.

Police Officers Ryder and Brown respond to a call concerning a past burglary in a private house located at 1296 Brentwood Road. When the Officers arrive, they are met by William Parker, who owns the house. Mr. Parker tells the Officers that he had been out of town for the entire weekend and, upon his return twenty minutes ago, discovered that the lock on his back door was broken. He also discovered that several items were missing from around his house. At this point, Officer Ryder asks Mr. Parker to show her where the burglars entered. Meanwhile, Officer Brown makes a search of the immediate area. Officer Ryder's investigation reveals that the burglars had cut a wire located by the front basement window in order to disable the alarm system. The burglars then forced open the lock with a metal bar of some kind. Officer Brown's search of the area uncovers no evidence. Officer Ryder then asks Mr. Parker to describe the items which are missing. Mr. Parker says that his 19" color television and clock radio are gone, along with several items which were borrowed from various friends. Among the missing items are a compact disc player owned by David Mills, a videotape recorder owned by Samantha Burns, and a portable tape player with headphones owned by Roger Denning. Officer Ryder lists the missing items and the owners' names in her report and tells Mr. Parker to call the station house in the morning to obtain a report number which he can use if he files an insurance claim.

7. The thieves broke the lock of which entrance?

   A. Side   B. Front   C. Basement   D. Back

8. Which of the missing items were owned by William Parker?

   A. Color television and clock radio
   B. Compact disc player and tape player
   C. Videotape recorder and compact disc player
   D. Portable tape player and headphones

9. With what crime is this passage PRIMARILY concerned?

   A. Arson   B. Assault   C. Burglary   D. Fraud

Question 10.

DIRECTIONS: Question 10 is to be answered SOLELY on the basis of the following information.

When a person commits an offense for which a summons may be served, a Police Officer should:

   I. Inform the violator of each offense committed.
   II. Request that the violator show proof of identity and residence.
   III. Take the violator to the station house for investigation if doubt exists concerning his identity.
   IV. Enter only one offense on a summons.
   V. Use a separate summons for any additional offense.

10. Police Officer Hayes stops a motorist for driving through a red light and asks him for his driver's license, registration, and insurance card. The motorist apologizes to Officer Hayes and explains that he left his house in a hurry and forgot his wallet, which contained all of his identification. Officer Hayes asks the driver to state his name and address and advises him that, in addition to receiving a summons for going through the red light, he will receive three summonses for driving without his license, registration, and insurance card.
The actions taken by Officer Hayes in this situation were

A. *proper,* primarily because the driver may have been lying when he said that he forgot his wallet
B. *improper,* primarily because he did not take the driver to the station house
C. *proper,* primarily because there was no need to investigate further since the driver willingly gave his name and address
D. *improper,* primarily because he should have followed the driver home to check his identification

11. Police Officer Greg responds to the apartment of a complainant who just reported a child missing. He obtains the following information:

    Complainant: Francis Fallen
    Missing Child: Johnny Red
    Age of Child: 5 years old
    Description of Child: Male, White, wearing a red T-shirt and blue jeans
    Time and Place Last Seen: Thomas Park, 4:20 P.M.

    Officer Greg is about to radio this information to the dispatcher.
    Which one of the following expresses the above information MOST clearly and accurately?

    A. Francis Fallen reported that Johnny Red, a 5-year-old White male, was last seen at 4:20 P.M. in Thomas Park. He was wearing a red T-shirt and blue jeans.
    B. Wearing a red T-shirt and blue jeans, Francis Fallen reported that Johnny Red was last seen at 4:20 P.M. in Thomas Park. He is a White 5-year-old male.
    C. In Thomas Park, Francis Fallen reported that 5-year-old Johnny Red, a White male, was last seen wearing a red T-shirt and blue jeans at 4:20 P.M.
    D. At 4:20 P.M., Francis Fallen reported in Thomas Park that 5-year-old Johnny Red, a White male, was last seen wearing a red T-shirt and blue jeans.

12. Police Officer Zacks responds to 57th Avenue and Broadway and obtains the following information regarding a vandalism complaint:

    Time of Occurrence: 12:00 P.M.
    Place of Occurrence: In front of 5716 Broadway
    Damage: Shattered front windshield of car
    Complainant: Daniel Molley, Owner of car
    Suspect: Unidentified teenager

    Officer Zacks is completing a report on the incident. Which one of the following expresses the above information MOST clearly and accurately?

    A. At 12:00 P.M., an unidentified teenager shattered his car's front windshield in front of 5716 Broadway reported Daniel Molley.
    B. At 12:00 P.M., in front of 5716 Broadway, an unidentified teenager shattered the front windshield of Daniel Molley's car.
    C. At 12:00 P.M., Daniel Molley reported an unidentified teenager in front of 5716 Broadway. His front car windshield was shattered.
    D. A teenager, unidentified, was in front of 5716 Broadway. At 12:00 P.M., Daniel Molley's front windshield was shattered on his car.

Question 13.

DIRECTIONS: Question 13 is to be answered SOLELY on the basis of the following information.

When a juvenile, less than 16 years old, is arrested and charged as a juvenile offender, the arresting Police Officer should do the following in the order given:

    I. Bring the juvenile to the station house.
    II. Notify parents that the juvenile is in custody and of the location of the juvenile.
    III. If parents are unavailable to come to the station house, then:
        a. advise juvenile of constitutional rights; and
        b. begin questioning the juvenile
    III. If parents are coming to the station house, then:
        a. advise juvenile of constitutional rights in the parents'" presence;
        b. begin questioning the juvenile in the parents' presence
    V. Prepare an Arrest Report.

13. While patrolling, Police Officer Martin observes a male juvenile carrying a gun and robbing an elderly woman. Officer Martin confiscates the gun and arrests 15-year-old Tom Hill. The Officer takes Hill to the station house. The Desk Officer advises Officer Martin to take Hill to the room selected for the questioning of juveniles. Officer Martin then contacts Hill's parents. They inform her that they will be there as soon as possible.
Officer Martin should NEXT

    A. begin questioning the juvenile about the offense
    B. prepare an Arrest Report detailing the events of the crime
    C. inform the juvenile of his constitutional rights once his parents arrive and are in the room
    D. request the parents to wait in another room during questioning

14. While on patrol, Officer Woods responds to a robbery that occurred earlier. Officer Woods obtains the following information at the scene:

Crime:	Robbery
Time of Crime:	7:30 P.M.
Place of Crime:	1177 103rd Avenue
Victim:	Erica Russell
Suspect:	Floyd Benett
Witness:	Ben Jamin

Officer Woods is completing a report on the incident.
Which one of the following expresses the above information MOST clearly and accurately?

    A. At 1177 103rd Avenue, Ben Jamin stated that Floyd Benett was seen robbing Erica Russell at 7:30 P.M.
    B. At 7:30 P.M., Ben Jamin witnessed Floyd Benett rob Erica Russell at 1177 103rd Avenue.
    C. At 7:30 P.M., Ben Jamin stated that he saw Floyd Benett rob Erica Russell at 1177 103rd Avenue.
    D. Ben Jamin witnessed Floyd Benett at 1177 103rd Avenue. At 7:30 P.M., Erica Russell was robbed.

15. Police Officer Joplin has finished investigating a report of Grand Larceny and has obtained the following information:
    Place of Occurrence: Orchard Street Furs, 121 Orchard St.
    Time of Occurrence: 4:00 P.M.
    Victim: Sam Houston, owner of store
    Crime: $3,000 stolen
    Suspect: Unknown Black male
    Officer Joplin is preparing a report on the incident.
    Which one of the following expresses the above information MOST clearly and accurately?

    A. Sam Houston, owner of Orchard Street Furs, located at 121 Orchard Street, reported that at 4:00 P.M. an unknown Black male stole $3,000 from his store.
    B. Orchard Street Furs is located at 121 Orchard Street. Sam Houston reported at 4:00 P.M. an unknown Black male stole $3,000 from his store.
    C. At 4:00 P.M., $3,000 was stolen from the owner of Orchard Street Furs. Sam Houston was robbed by a Black male at 121 Orchard Street.
    D. At 4:00 P.M., an unknown Black male stole $3,000. Sam Houston's store, Orchard Street Furs, is located at 121 Orchard Street.

16. Officers Reed and Shaw respond to the scene of a robbery and obtain the following information from a witness:

Crime:	Bank Robbery, $20,000 stolen
Bank:	Federal Conserve Bank
Time of Crime:	2:30 P.M.
Suspect:	Female, White, armed with a shotgun
Witness:	Frank Count, bank teller

    Officer Reed is recording the details of the crime in her Memo Book.
    Which one of the following expresses the above information MOST clearly and accurately?

    A. At 2:30 P.M., Frank Count, a bank teller at Federal Conserve Bank, reported a robbery. The bank was robbed of $20,000 by a shotgun and a White female.
    B. Frank Count, a bank teller, reported that the Federal" Conserve Bank was robbed of $20,000 at 2:30 P.M. by a White female armed with a shotgun.
    C. A bank teller, reported Frank Count, robbed the Federal Conserve Bank of $20,000. She was White and armed with a shotgun.
    D. At 2:30 P.M., the Federal Conserve Bank was robbed of $20,000. Frank Count, a bank teller, reported a White female armed with a shotgun.

Question 17.

DIRECTIONS: Question 17 is to be answered SOLELY on the basis of the following information.

When a Police Officer receives property found by someone other than a Police Officer, he should:

   I. Issue a receipt, including a description of the property, to the person delivering the property. Enter the facts in the Activity Log.
   II. Prepare a Property Clerk's Invoice.

III. Deliver the property and invoice to the Desk Officer.
IV. Resume patrol

17. Arlene Harris found a brown leather wallet containing twenty dollars and two credit cards. She approached Police Officer Taylor, who was patrolling on the corner of Concorde and Broadway. Officer Taylor took the wallet and handed Ms. Harris a signed note which stated: *Received property from Ms. Arlene Harris.* He thanked Ms. Harris for her honesty and then entered the events, including Ms. Harris1 address and telephone number, in his Activity Log. He then went directly to the precinct where he prepared a Property Clerk's Invoice, which he gave, along with the wallet, to Sgt. Mead, the Desk Officer. Officer Taylor then returned to patrol. In this situation, Officer Taylor's actions were.... 17.____

A. *proper,* primarily because he thanked Ms. Harris for her honesty
B. *improper,* primarily because he should have asked Ms. Harris to take the wallet to the precinct
C. *proper,* primarily because he did not leave his post to return the wallet
D. *improper,* primarily because he did not give Ms. Harris a proper receipt for the wallet

18. Police Officer Hoff responds to the scene of a hit-and-run accident and obtains the following information: 18.____

Occurrence:	Woman hit by a speeding car
Time of Occurrence:	1:30 P.M.
Location of Occurrence:	35th Avenue between 4th and 5th Streets
Description of Car:	Green Ford
Victim:	Lois Nettle
Injuries:	Broken right leg

Officer Hoff is radioing for an ambulance. Which one of the following expresses the above information MOST clearly and accurately?

A. Lois Nettle broke her right leg between 4th and 5th Streets on 35th Avenue. At 1:30 P.M., a woman was hit by a speeding green Ford.
B. A car hit Lois Nettle and broke her right leg at 1:30 P.M. A green Ford was speeding on 35th Avenue between 4th and 5th Streets.
C. Lois Nettle broke her right leg when a speeding green Ford hit her at 1:30 P.M. on 35th Avenue between 4th and 5th Streets.
D. At 1:30 P.M., a green Ford was speeding. On 35th Avenue, between 4th and 5th Streets, Lois Nettle broke her right leg when she was hit.

Questions 19-21.

DIRECTIONS: Questions 19 through 21 are to be answered SOLELY on the basis of the following passage.

Police Officers Wilson and Mills receive a radio call to investigate an auto accident involving injuries. Upon their arrival, Officer Mills approaches a Mustang convertible which had been driven into the side of an Oldsmobile sedan. There is also a small Dodge truck several feet away which had crashed into a fire hydrant. Officer Mills immediately determines that no one is injured and radios the dispatcher to cancel the ambulance. Meanwhile, Officer Wilson interviews Sam Thomas, who is the owner and driver of the Mustang. Mr. Thomas states that he was driving south on Bedford Avenue when a large Oldsmobile pulled out of a parking lot in front of him. Mr. Thomas goes on to say that he immediately hit his brakes but slid into the side of the Oldsmobile. Officer Mills interviews Thomas Parker, who is the driver of the Oldsmobile. Mr. Parker admits that he drove out of the parking lot without looking for oncoming traffic. He tells Officer Mills that he is not used to driving and borrowed the Oldsmobile from his brother, Harold Parker, who is the owner of the car. Finally, Officer Wilson interviews Rutger Schmidt, who is the driver of the Dodge truck. Mr. Schmidt indicates that, in an attempt to avoid the accident, he swerved out of the way, lost control of the truck, and ran into a fire hydrant. Mr. Schmidt tells Officer Wilson that he works for the Acme Exterminating Company, which owns the truck. Following the interviews, the two Officers write their accident report and indicate the damage to each vehicle. The Mustang had a damaged front bumper and grill, and broken headlights; the Oldsmobile had a dented driver's side quarter panel; the Dodge truck had a crumpled bumper and blown right front tire.

19. Who was the owner of the Oldsmobile sedan?

    A. Sam Thomas   B. Thomas Parker
    C. Harold Parker   D. Rutger Schmidt

20. What was damaged on the Dodge truck?

    A. Driver's side quarter panel
    B. Bumper and right front tire
    C. Tailgate and tail lights
    D. Front bumper, grill, and headlights

21. The driver of which vehicle was the PRIMARY cause of the accident?
The

    A. Mustang convertible   B. patrol car
    C. Dodge truck   D. Oldsmobile sedan

Question 22.

DIRECTIONS: Question 22 is to be answered SOLELY on the basis of the following information.

Upon observing a vehicle.accident, a Police Officer should do the following in the order given:

    I. Park the patrol car so that it will not block traffic.
    II. Determine if there are any injuries and request an ambulance, if needed.
    III. Divert traffic if necessary.
    IV. Obtain drivers' licenses, vehicle registrations, and insurance identification cards of the drivers involved.
    V. Have vehicles removed from the roadway.
    VI. Determine the cause of the accident.

22. Officer Jackson responds to the scene of an accident. Upon arrival, Officer Jackson parks his patrol car in a spot where it is not blocking traffic. As he approaches the intersection on foot, he sees that a taxicab and a white Toyota have been involved in a head-on collision. He also notices that a large crowd has gathered around the damaged vehicles. Traffic is backed up in all directions leading into the intersection, and a man who is bleeding from the head is lying on the roadway.
The NEXT step Officer Jackson should take is to

    A. request an ambulance
    B. direct traffic away from the accident
    C. have the vehicles removed from the roadway
    D. determine the cause of the accident

22.____

23. Police Officer Boyle was driving his patrol car in the snow when he was involved in a car accident. The following information was obtained at the scene of the accident:

    Place of Occurrence: Intersection of Canal and Church Streets
    Time of Occurrence: 10:15 A.M.
    Vehicle Number: 5729
    Damage to Vehicle: Hood, right fender, and windshield
    Injuries Sustained by Officer: Two broken arms

    Police Officer Nevins is completing a report on the accident. Which one of the following expresses the above information MOST clearly and accurately?

    A. Police Officer Boyle had two broken arms at 10:15 A.M. Vehicle 5729 was in a car accident at the intersection of Canal and Church Streets. It has a damaged hood, right fender, and windshield.
    B. At 10:15 A.M., Vehicle 5729 and Police Officer Boyle were in a car accident. At the intersection of Canal and Church Streets, they suffered two broken arms, a damaged hood, right fender, and windshield.
    C. Vehicle 5729 had a damaged hood, right fender, and windshield at 10:15 A.M. At the intersection of Canal and Church Streets, Police Officer Boyle had two broken arms in a car accident.
    D. At 10:15 A.M., Police Officer Boyle was in a car accident at the intersection of Canal and Church Streets. Officer Boyle suffered two broken arms, and Vehicle 5729 sustained damage to the hood, right fender, and windshield.

23.____

Question 24.

DIRECTIONS: Question 24 is to be answered SOLELY on the basis of the following information.

Juvenile - a child who is at least seven years of age but less than sixteen years of age.

A juvenile report should be prepared for the following:

    I. All violations and offenses except felonies, unlawful assembly, and photographable offenses.
    II. Petty violations
    III. A juvenile in need of supervision.

IV. An intoxicated juvenile.
V. A stranded juvenile.
VI. A runaway juvenile (city resident).

24. Police Officer Fillmore apprehends Walter Gardiner, who is fifteen years old. Walter was participating in a political demonstration in front of his 5th Avenue apartment in Manhattan. The protesters did not have a valid permit allowing them to demonstrate at that location. A witness states that she saw Walter drinking alcohol, but Police Officer Fillmore sees no indication that the youth is intoxicated. The Officer believes that the youth's parents were also participants in the demonstration. Walter has no previous arrest record. Officer Fillmore decides to prepare a Juvenile Report for unlawful assembly for Walter.
The action taken by Police Officer Fillmore is

   A. *improper,* primarily because a Juvenile Report should not be prepared for unlawful assembly
   B. *proper,* primarily because Walter is a city resident who has not reached his sixteenth birthday
   C. *improper,* primarily because Walter has the right to express his political beliefs
   D. *proper,* primarily because a Juvenile Report should be prepared for a juvenile who has been drinking

25. Police Officer Frankle responds to the scene of an abused child. Officer Frankle obtains the following information:
   Complainant: Gladys Jones
   Date of Complaint: October 12
   Time of Complaint: 2:00 P.M.
   Name of Child: Henry Worth
   Child's Injuries: Bruises to face and arms
   Police Officer Frankle is notifying the Bureau of Child Welfare about this incident.
   Which one of the following expresses the above information MOST clearly and accurately?

   A. On October 12, Henry Worth had bruises on his face and arms, reported Gladys Jones at 2:00 P.M.
   B. With bruises to the face and arms, Gladys Jones reported Henry Worth on October 12 at 2:00 P.M.
   C. On October 12, at 2:00 P.M., Gladys Jones reported that Henry Worth had bruises on his face and arms.
   D. Henry Worth, with bruises to his face and arms, reported Gladys Jones on October 12 at 2:00 P.M.

KEY (CORRECT ANSWERS)

1. A
2. B
3. D
4. C
5. B

6. C
7. D
8. A
9. C
10. B

11. A
12. B
13. C
14. B
15. A

16. B
17. D
18. C
19. C
20. B

21. D
22. A
23. D
24. A
25. C

TEST 3

DIRECTIONS: Each question or incomplete statement is followed by several suggested answers or completions. Select the one that BEST answers the question or completes the statement. *PRINT THE LETTER OF THE CORRECT ANSWER IN THE SPACE AT THE RIGHT.*

1. <u>Burglary 1st Degree</u> - occurs when a person knowingly enters or remains unlawfully in a dwelling with intent to commit a crime therein, and when, in entering or while in the dwelling or in immediate flight from it, he or another participant in the crime: 1.____
    I. Is armed with explosives or a deadly weapon; or
    II. Causes physical injury to any person who is not a participant in the crime; or
    III. Displays what appears to be a pistol, revolver, rifle, shotgun, machine gun, or other firearm

    <u>Dwelling</u> - a building which is usually occupied by a person living there at night.
    Which one of the following situations is the BEST example of Burglary in the First Degree?

    A. Carrying only a flashlight, Thomas Jackson climbs through the dining room window of the Bentley estate and steals $20,000 worth of jewelry.
    B. Bill Watson breaks into a house to steal a VCR. While in the house, he sees Mrs. Campbell. Watson then pulls out a gun and tells her to give him her VCR or he will kill her.
    C. Joe Smith and Mark Star, each carrying revolvers, unlawfully break into an office building to commit a robbery. While inside the building, they hear a noise and try to run out. On their way out, Star pushes Smith to the ground, causing him physical injury.
    D. Tommy Taylor breaks into a department store at 2:00 A.M. to steal a television set. When a security guard confronts him, Taylor pulls out a gun and pushes the guard to the ground, causing him physical injury.

2. To ensure fair and proper proceedings when investigations are conducted, a Police Officer must do the following in the order given: 2.____
    I. Inform the suspect that he must appear in a lineup for identification in connection with the crime.
    II. Arrest the suspect if he does not agree to voluntarily appear in the lineup.
    III. Notify the detective supervisor who will personally supervise the lineup.
    IV. Give the suspect Miranda Warnings if he is to be questioned before or after the lineup.

    Police Officers Shore and Thompson are looking for a male who was involved in a robbery and stabbing. A witness to the crime gives the Officers a description that matches the description of a person named Rodney Pitts. The Officers find Mr. Pitts at his home and tell him that he must appear in a lineup because he fits the description of a man who committed a robbery and stabbing. Mr. Pitts angrily denies his involvement with the crimes but agrees to take part in the lineup. The NEXT step the Officers should take is to
    A. tell Mr. Pitts that he must appear in a lineup
    B. contact the detective supervisor
    C. place the suspect under arrest
    D. advise Mr. Pitts of Miranda Warnings

61

3. Police Officer Pepper responds to a shooting and obtains the following information:

Victim:	John Rice
Suspect:	Rudy Johnson
Witness:	Mary Rice, wife of victim
Location:	Rudy's Bar, 1492 York Avenue
Weapon:	.38 caliber revolver
Injury:	Wound to left leg

Officer Pepper is preparing a report on the incident.
Which one of the following expresses the above information MOST clearly and accurately?

- A. Rudy Johnson, witnessed by his wife Mary Rice, shot John Rice with a .38 caliber revolver in Rudy's Bar, 1492 York Avenue. Mr. Rice had a wound to his left leg.
- B. With a wound to the left leg, Mary Rice witnessed Rudy Johnson shoot John Rice in Rudy's Bar at 1492 York Avenue. Mr. Johnson had a .38 caliber revolver.
- C. Mary Rice witnessed Rudy Johnson shoot her husband, John Rice, with a .38 caliber revolver in Rudy's Bar at 1492 York Avenue. Mr. Rice was wounded in the left leg.
- D. Rudy Johnson was in Rudy's Bar at 1492 York Avenue. Mary Rice witnessed her husband shot by a .38 caliber revolver in the left leg.

4. Police Officers Simon and Peters receive a call to respond to a possible child abuse case. The following information was obtained by the Officers:

Occurrence:	Child found alone in apartment
Time of Occurrence:	11:00 P.M.
Place of Occurrence:	463 Lott Street, Apt. 3A
Child Found By:	Deborah Fields, neighbor
Child:	Angela Bolds, three years old
Parent of Child:	Mary Bolds, mother

Officers Simon and Peters are completing a report for the Bureau of Child Welfare.
Which one of the following expresses the above information MOST clearly and accurately?

- A. Angela Bolds, three years old, was found in Apt. 3A of 463 Lott Street, by herself without her mother, Mary Bolds, by a neighbor who is named Deborah Fields at 11:00 P.M.
- B. At 463 Lott Street, Apt. 3A, Deborah Fields, a neighbor, found Angela Bolds, who is three years old, by herself in her apartment. Her mother, Mary Bolds, was not home at 11:00 P.M.
- C. Deborah Fields, a neighbor, found Angela Bolds, three years old, by herself in Apt. 3A at 11:00 P.M. The child's mother, Mary Bolds, who resides at 463 Lott Street, was not home.
- D. At 11:00 P.M., Deborah Fields, a neighbor, found three-year-old Angela Bolds alone in Apt. 3A of 463 Lott Street. Mrs. Fields stated that the child's mother, Mary Bolds, was not at home.

5. Police Officer Johnson responds to the scene of an assault and obtains the following information:

Time of Occurrence:	8:30 P.M.
Place of Occurrence:	120-18 119th Avenue, Apt. 2A
Suspects:	John Andrews, victim's ex-husband and unknown White male
Victim:	Susan Andrews
Injury:	Broken right arm

Officer Johnson is preparing a complaint report on the incident.
Which one of the following expresses the above information MOST clearly and accurately?

A. Susan Andrews was assaulted at 120-18 119th Avenue, Apt. 2A. At 8:30 P.M., her ex-husband, John Andrews, and an unknown White male broke her arm.
B. At 8:30 P.M., Susan Andrews was assaulted at 120-18 119th Avenue, Apt. 2A, by her ex-husband, John Andrews, and an unknown White male. Her right arm was broken.
C. John Andrews, an unknown -White male, and Susan Andrews' ex-husband, assaulted and broke her right arm at 8:30 P.M., at 120-18 119th Avenue, Apt. 2A.
D. John Andrews, ex-husband of Susan Andrews, broke her right arm with an unknown White male at 120-18 119th Avenue, at 8:30 P.M. in Apt. 2A.

Questions 6-8.

DIRECTIONS: Questions 6 through 8 are to be answered SOLELY on the basis of the following passage.

Police Officer Lombardo was dispatched to the scene of an apparently dead human body. His supervisor and another Officer were at the scene, as were two paramedics. The paramedics, Pete Lizzo and Erick Clark, had just pronounced the body dead at 6:55 P.M. There were no relatives present, and a neighbor, Eddie Torres, told Officer Lombardo that the dead person lived alone and had no family. Mr. Torres agreed to be a witness to the search of the premises. Officer Lombardo knew that the police were required to voucher or hold all valuables and important papers for safekeeping if a close relative did not live with the dead person. The apartment was filled with a large number of possessions, including two gold rings, a gold watch, $200 in cash, and kitchen and living room furniture. They also found an old black and white television set, old clothing, and numerous kitchen utensils. In a tin box, the Officer found a birth certificate, social security card, and the dead person's diary. After the search was completed, the jewelry, cash, birth certificate, and social security card were vouchered. Eddie Torres signed Officer Lombardo's Memo Book.

6. Of the following, which items were vouchered by Officer Lombardo?

A. Two gold rings, a gold watch, a social security card, birth certificate, and $200 in cash
B. A gold watch, two gold rings, $200 cash, a diary, and a social security card
C. A birth certificate, social security card, diary, jewelry, and $200 in cash
D. A social security card, two gold watches, a gold ring, a birth certificate, and $200 cash

7. The search was witnessed by a   7.____

   A. neighbor   B. relative
   C. Police Officer   D. paramedic

8. Officer Lombardo vouchered the dead person's property because   8.____

   A. the paramedics were present
   B. a supervisor was not available
   C. there was only one witness
   D. there, was no relative living with the dead person

9. When Police Officers arrive at the scene of a fire, they should do the following in the   9.____
   order given:
   I. Send an alarm or make sure one has been sent.
   II. Direct a responsible person to remain at the alarm box in order to direct fire vehicles.
   III. Park the patrol car in a location that will not interfere with fire-fighting operations.
   IV. Warn and assist occupants in evacuation of building.
   V. Upon arrival of fire vehicles, establish police lines beyond the fire apparatus and hydrants in use.

   While on patrol, Police Officers Gannett and James see flames and smoke coming from the top floor of an apartment building and notice that the Fire Department is not on the scene. Officer Gannett double-parks his vehicle in front of the building. Officer James immediately walks to the alarm box on the corner, pulls the alarm, and awaits the arrival of the Fire Department.
   The NEXT step Officer Gannett should take is to

   A. ask the building landlord to find an alarm box and direct Fire Department vehicles
   B. enter the building in order to warn and evacuate occupants
   C. establish police lines so that fire vehicles will be able to get to the building
   D. park his patrol car in a spot where it will not block fire vehicles

10. While on patrol, Officers Banks and Thompson see a man lying on the ground bleeding.   10.____
    Officer Banks records the following details about the incident:
    Time of Incident: 3:15 P.M.
    Place of Incident: Sidewalk in front of 517 Rock Avenue
    Incident: Tripped and fell
    Name of Injured: John Blake
    Injury: Head wound
    Action Taken: Transported to Merry Hospital
    Officer Banks is completing a report on the incident.
    Which one of the following expresses the above information MOST clearly and accurately?

    A. At 3:15 P.M., Mr. John Blake was transported to Merry Hospital. He tripped and fell, injuring his head on the sidewalk in front of 517 Rock Avenue.
    B. Mr. John Blake tripped and fell on the sidewalk at 3:15 P.M. in front of 517 Rock Avenue. He was transported to Merry Hospital while he sustained a head wound.
    C. Mr. John Blake injured his head when he tripped and fell on the sidewalk in front of 517 Rock Avenue at 3:15 P.M. He was transported to Merry Hospital.

D. A head was wounded on the sidewalk in front of 517 Rock Avenue at 3:15 P.M. Mr. John Blake tripped and fell and was transported to Merry Hospital.

11. When assigned to investigate a complaint, a Police Officer should
    I. Interview witnesses and obtain facts.
    II. Conduct a thorough investigation of circumstances concerning the complaint.
    III. Prepare a Complaint Report.
    IV. Determine if the Complaint Report should be closed or referred for further investigation.
    V. Enter Complaint Report on the Complaint Report Index and obtain a Complaint Report Number at the station house.

    While on patrol, Police Officer John is instructed by his supervisor to investigate a complaint by Mr. Stanley Burns, who was assaulted by his brother-in-law, Henry Traub. After interviewing Mr. Burns, Officer John learns that Mr. Traub has been living with Mr. Burns for the past two years. Officer John accompanies Mr. Burns to his apartment but Mr. Traub is not there. Officer John fills out the Complaint Report and takes the report back to the station house where it is entered on the Complaint Report Index and assigned a Complaint. Report Number. Officer John's actions were

    A. *improper*, primarily because he should have stayed at Mr. Burns' apartment and waited for Mr. Traub to return in order to arrest him
    B. *proper*, primarily because after obtaining all the facts, he took the report back to the station house and was assigned a Complaint Report Number
    C. *improper*, primarily because he should have decided whether to close the report or refer it for further investigation
    D. *proper*, primarily because he was instructed by his supervisor to take the report from Mr. Burns even though it involved his brother-in-law

12. Police Officers are sometimes required to respond to family disputes and, when appropriate, refer a person to Family Court for counseling or other appropriate services.
    In which one of the following situations would it be MOST appropriate for an Officer to refer the person involved to Family Court?

    A. A husband who is threatening to harm his wife because she spends too much money
    B. Two sisters arguing over the use of the telephone
    C. Three roommates arguing about their recent rent increase
    D. A mother yelling at her 16-year-old son for failing his history test

Questions 13-20.

DIRECTIONS: Questions 13 through 20 are to be answered SOLELY on the basis of the following sketches. The first face on top is a sketch of an alleged criminal based on witnesses' descriptions at the crime scene. One of the four sketches below that face is the way the suspect looked after changing appearance. ASSUME THAT NO SURGERY HAS BEEN DONE ON THE SUSPECT. Select the face which is MOST likely that of the suspect

6 (#3)

13. 13.____

A.   B.   C.   D.

14. 14.____

   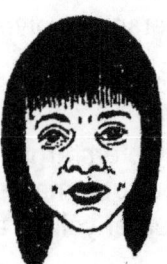

A.   B.   C.   D.

15.  15.____

A.   B.   C.   D.

16. 16.____

A.   B.   C.   D.

8 (#3)

17.   17.____

A.   B.   C.   D.

18.   18.____

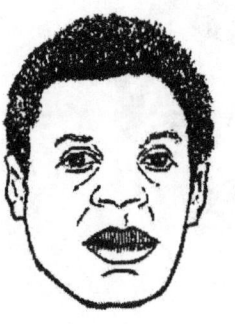

A.   B.   C.   D.

19.

20.

KEY (CORRECT ANSWERS)

1. B
2. B
3. C
4. D
5. B

6. A
7. A
8. D
9. D
10. C

11. C
12. A
13. B
14. C
15. D

16. A
17. A
18. D
19. B
20. C

EXAMINATION SECTION
TEST 1

DIRECTIONS: Each question or incomplete statement is followed by several suggested answers or completions. Select the one that BEST answers the question or completes the statement. *PRINT THE LETTER OF THE CORRECT ANSWER IN THE SPACE AT THE RIGHT.*

<u>MEMORY PAGES</u>

Memory Scene 1 is on Pages 2 and 3. Memory Scene 2 is on Pages 4 and 5. You are to study Scene 1 carefully and try to remember as many details in the scene as you can. You should pay equal attention both to objects and to people shown in the scene. Then turn to Questions 1 through 6 which follow and answer these questions based upon what you remember from Scene 1. Do not turn back to Scene 1 while answering. After you complete Questions 1 through 6, study Memory Scene 2. Then turn to Questions 7 through 12 and answer them based on Scene 2.

SCENE 1

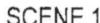

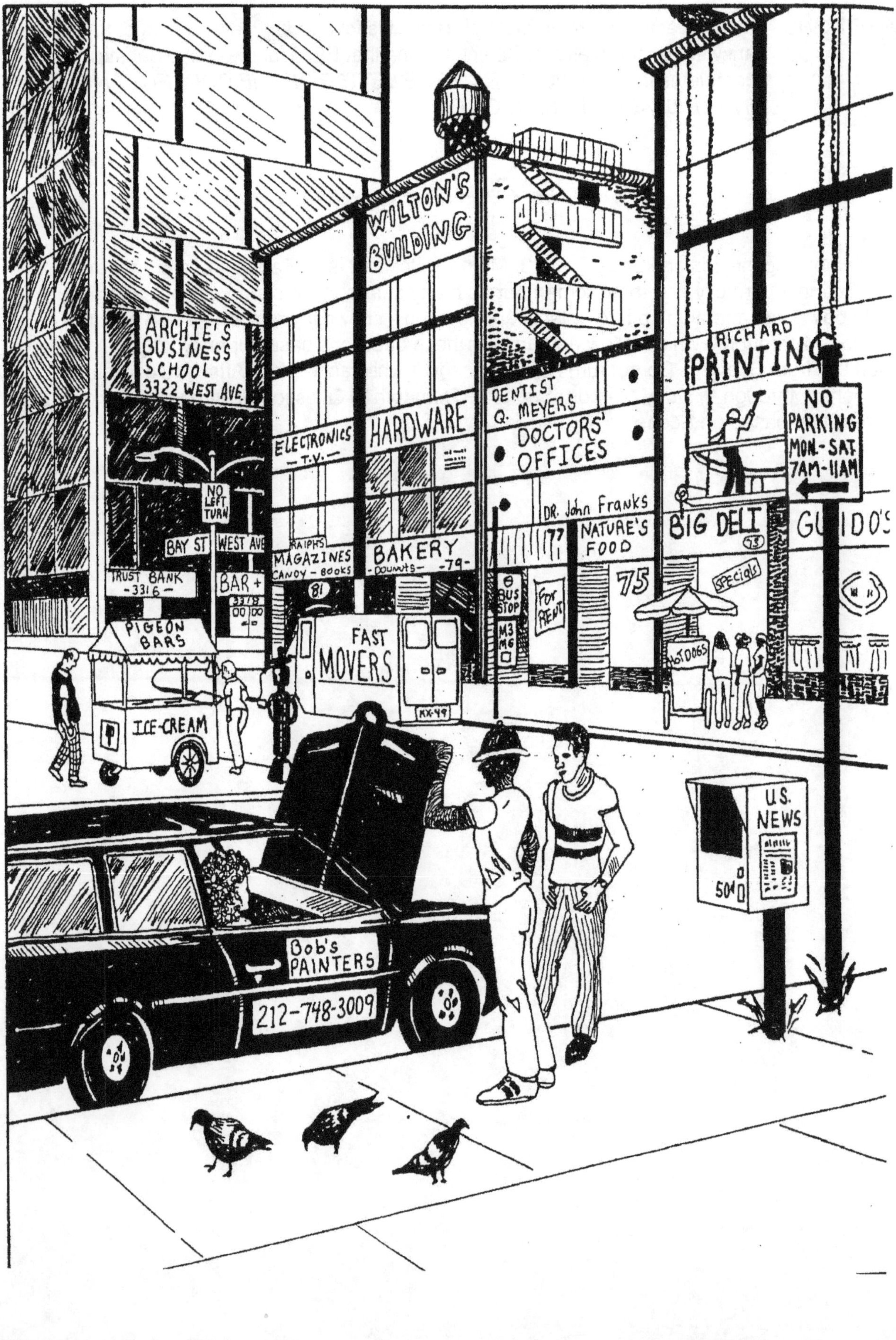
ARCHIE'S BUSINESS SCHOOL 3322 WEST AVE.
WILTON'S BUILDING
ELECTRONICS
T.V.
HARDWARE
DENTIST Q. MEYERS
DOCTORS' OFFICES
RICHARD PRINTING
NO PARKING MON.-SAT. 7AM-11AM
NO LEFT TURN
BAY ST
WEST AVE
TRUST BANK -3316-
BAR
PIGEON BARS
ICE-CREAM
RALPH'S MAGAZINES CANDY - BOOKS
81
BAKERY DONUTS -79-
FAST MOVERS
KX-49
BUS STOP
M3 M6
FOR RENT
DR. John Franks
77
NATURE'S FOOD
75
BIG DELI
73
SPECIALS
HOT DOGS
GUIDO'S
U.S. NEWS
50¢
Bob's PAINTERS
212-748-3009

SCENE 2

5 (#1)

SCENE 2

Questions 1-6.

DIRECTIONS: Questions 1 through 6 are to be answered SOLELY on the basis of Sketch Number 1.

1. Which one of the following is printed on the side of the black vehicle with the open hood?

    A. Richard Printing
    B. Archie's Business School
    C. Bob's Painters
    D. Nature's Food

2. When is parking prohibited on East Avenue?

    A. Monday-Friday, 7:00 A.M. to 11:00 P.M.
    B. Friday-Saturday, 7:00 P.M. to 11:00 A.M.
    C. Monday-Saturday, 7:00 A.M. to 11:00 A.M.
    D. Friday-Saturday, 7:00 P.M. to 11:00 P.M.

3. Which one of the following is printed on the side of the white vehicle on Bay Street?

    A. Bob's Painters
    B. Uptown Express
    C. Guido's
    D. Fast Movers

4. The man standing on the sidewalk with the woman is wearing

    A. black pants and is holding a white jacket
    B. a white jacket and black pants
    C. white pants and is holding a black jacket
    D. a black jacket and white pants

5. Which one of the following is shown as a one-way street?

    A. East Avenue
    B. Bay Street
    C. Jewel Street
    D. West Avenue

6. How many men are standing next to the station wagon with the hood up?

    A. One   B. Two   C. Three   D. Four

Questions 7-12.

DIRECTIONS: Questions 7 through 12 are to be answered SOLELY on the basis of Sketch Number 2.

7. What words are written on the shirt of the man carrying a knife?

    A. Beach Bum
    B. Grateful Dead
    C. He-Man
    D. Big Blue

8. Which one of the following BEST describes the victim of the crime?

    A. White female, striped pants, and blonde hair
    B. White female, dark hair, and black and white blazer
    C. Asian female, black pants, wearing glasses
    D. Black female, striped pants, and white blazer

9. A man is shown taking something from a woman's purse. The man is using his _____ hand, and the purse is on the woman's _____ shoulder.

   A. right; right
   B. left; right
   C. right; left
   D. left; left

10. The youth who is holding a knife is wearing

    A. jeans and a jacket
    B. shorts and a short-sleeve shirt
    C. jeans and a short-sleeve shirt
    D. shorts and a T-shirt

11. Which store has a *CLOSED* sign in its window?

    A. Ave. R Discount
    B. Gourmet Supermarket
    C. Book Store
    D. Rubber Stamps

12. The Electronics store is located

    A. on Ave. R
    B. at the corner of Ave. R and E. 3rd St.
    C. on E. 3rd St.
    D. at the corner of Ave. R and W. 3rd St.

Questions 13-14.

DIRECTIONS: Questions 13 and 14 are to be answered SOLELY on the basis of the following information.

Police Officer Thomas is aware that within his assigned sector all rapes occur on Clark Street, all robberies occur on Gaston Street, and all assaults occur on Pine Grove Avenue. Most robberies occur on Wednesdays and Fridays, most rapes occur on Tuesdays and Thursdays, and most assaults occur on Mondays and Tuesdays. Most rapes occur between 7:00 M. and 11:30 A.M., most assaults occur between 2:30 P.M. and 5:00 P.M., and most robberies occur between 3:30 P.M. and 9:30 P.M.

13. Officer Thomas would MOST likely be able to reduce the number of robberies if he patrolled

    A. Pine Grove Avenue on Wednesdays from 8:00 A.M. to 4:00 P.M.
    B. Gaston Street on Wednesdays from Midnight to 8:00 A.M.
    C. Gaston Street on Fridays from 4:00 P.M. to Midnight
    D. Clark Street on Mondays from 2:00 P.M. to 10:00 P.M.

14. To reduce the number of rapes, Officer Thomas is assigned to work a steady tour. For this purpose, it would be MOST appropriate for Officer Thomas to work

    A. Saturday through Wednesday, 8:00 A.M. to 4:00 P.M.
    B. Thursday through Monday, 2:00 P.M. to 10:00 P.M.
    C. Monday through Friday, 5:00 P.M. to 1:00 A.M.
    D. Sunday through Thursday, 6:00 A.M. to 2:00 P.M.

15. Police Officer Salley has been selected to serve on a special task force designed to identify possible locations of drug sales in the precinct. He is assigned a post at the intersection of Rochester Avenue and Bergen Street between the hours of 9:00 A.M. and 5:00 P.M., Mondays through Fridays.
Which one of the following observations made by Officer Salley MOST likely indicates possible drug activity?

    A. A continuous flow of people frequent Benny's Grocery Store and leave without packages.
    B. A hot dog vendor arrives at the Bergen Street construction site each day at 11:30 A.M. and leaves at 2:00 P.M.
    C. Many of the students from Rochester Avenue Elementary School go into Harry's Candy Store after school.
    D. Many students from Bergen Street High School gather in the video arcade on Rochester Avenue during lunch periods and after school

15.____

16. Police Officer Gattuso responded to a report of a robbery and obtained the following information regarding the incident:

    Place of Occurrence: Princess Grocery, 6 Sutton Place
    Time of Occurrence: 6:00 P.M.
    Crime: Robbery of $200
    Victim: Sara Davidson, owner of Princess
    Grocery Description of Suspect: White, female, red hair, blue jeans, and white
    T-shirt Weapon: Knife

    Officer Gattuso is preparing a report on the incident. Which one of the following expresses the above information MOST clearly and accurately

    A. Sara Davidson reported at 6:00 P.M. her store Princess Grocery was robbed at knifepoint at 6 Sutton Place. A white woman with red hair took $200 from her wearing blue jeans and a white T-shirt.
    B. At 6:00 P.M. a red-haired woman took $200 from 6 Sutton Place at Princess Grocery owned by Sara Davidson, who was robbed by the white woman. She was wearing blue jeans and a white T-shirt and used a knife.
    C. In a robbery that occurred at knifepoint, a red-haired white woman robbed the owner of Princess Grocery. Sara Davidson, the owner of the 6 Sutton Place store which was robbed of $200, said she was wearing blue jeans and a white T-shirt at 6:00 P.M.
    D. At 6:00 P.M. Sara Davidson, owner of Princess Grocery, located at 6 Sutton Place, was robbed of $200 at knifepoint. The suspect is a white female with red hair wearing blue jeans and a white T-shirt.

16.____

17. Murder 1st Degree - occurs when a person intentionally causes the death of another person.
Which one of the following situations is the BEST example of Murder in the First Degree?

    A. Sam is riding the train with Brenda who suddenly passes out, stops breathing, and dies *even* though Sam attempts to *revive* her.
    B. Jennifer shoots and kills her husband after a friend tells her that her husband is seeing another woman.

17.____

C. A taxi driver goes through a red light because he is in a hurry and runs over Albert, breaking his arm and leg.
D. Joe is standing on a very crowded subway platform when he accidentally pushes an elderly woman who falls onto the tracks and is killed by an oncoming train.

18. Police Officer Martinez responds to a report of an assault and obtains the following information regarding the incident:

Place of Occurrence:	Corner of Frank and Lincoln Avenues
Time of Occurrence:	9:40 A.M.
Crime:	Assault
Victim:	Mr. John Adams of 31-20th Street
Suspect:	Male, White, 5'11", 170 lbs., dressed in gray
Injury:	Victim suffered a split lip
Action Taken:	ictim transported to St. Mary's Hospital

Officer Martinez is completing a report on the incident. Which one of the following expresses the above information MOST clearly and accurately?

A. At 9:40 A.M., John Adams was assaulted on the corner of Frank and Lincoln Avenues by a White male, 5'11", 170 lbs., dressed in gray, suffering a split lip. Mr. Adams lives at 31-20th Street and was transported to St. Mary's Hospital.
B. At 9:40 A.M., John Adams was assaulted on the corner of Frank and Lincoln Avenues by a White male, 5'11", 170 lbs., dressed in gray, and lives at 31-20th Street. Mr. Adams suffered a split lip and was transported to St. Mary's Hospital.
C. John Adams, who lives at 31-20th Street, was assaulted at 9:40 A.M. on the corner of Frank and Lincoln Avenues by a White male, 5'11", 170 lbs., dressed in gray. Mr. Adams suffered a split lip and was transported to St. Mary's Hospital.
D. Living at 31-20th Street, Mr. Adams suffered a split lip and was transported to St. Mary's Hospital. At 9:40 A.M., Mr. Adams was assaulted by a White male, 5'11", 170 lbs., dressed in gray.

19. Police Officer Hooks has been instructed by his Precinct Commander to identify the locations in his patrol area where particular patterns of complaints have been reported. In reviewing recent complaint reports, Officer Hooks finds that most noise complaints occur on Beeker Street between Bay Boulevard and 79th Avenue. Larceny complaints are reported along Sutton Place between Church Street and Jerome Avenue. The majority of complaints concerning double-parked cars occur on Main Street between Flushing Street and Ocean Boulevard. Most of the larcenies occur between 7:00 A.M. and 10:00 A.M., the noise complaints between 11:00 P.M. and 2:00 A.M., and the complaints regarding double-parked cars between 1:00 P.M. and 4:00 P.M.
Officer Hooks is working a 1:00 P.M. to 9:00 P.M. shift. From which area should he receive the MOST complaints?

A. Sutton Place between Jerome Avenue and Church Street
B. Beeker Street between Bay Boulevard and 79th Avenue
C. Main Street between Flushing Street and Ocean Boulevard
D. Main Street between Jerome Avenue and Church Street

Questions 20-23.

DIRECTIONS: Questions 20 through 23 are to be answered SOLELY on the basis of the following passage.

Police Officer Richards, performing an 8:00 A.M. to 4:00 P.M. tour of duty, is designated as the station house cell block attendant. During Officer Richards patrol, he hears moaning sounds coming from cell block number six, which is occupied by Sam Galvez. Mr. Galvez is complaining of abdominal pain and requests to go to the hospital. Officer Richards follows the procedure for a prisoner requiring medical attention by requesting that an ambulance respond to the precinct and also notifying the Desk Officer, Lt. Schwinn, who is talking with Captain Small. When the Emergency Medical Service attendants arrive, Officer Richards escorts them toward the cell block. John Ross, a medical attendant, determines after a brief examination of Mr. Galvez that his pain is probably due to his appendix.

John Ross and Jack Ryan, the other medical attendant, recommend that the prisoner be removed to the hospital. Lieutenant Schwinn assigns Police Officer Ellen Gray to rear handcuff Mr. Galvez and escort him to the hospital in the ambulance. At the hospital, Mr. Galvez is seen by Dr. Keegan, the attending physician, who requests that Officer Gray remove the handcuffs so he may conduct a complete physical examination. Officer Gray complies with Dr. Keegan's request. After Dr. Keegan examines the patient, he recommends that Mr. Galvez be admitted for an appendectomy. Police Officer Gray notifies the Hospitalized Prisoner Unit at the Court Division, completes the entries on the Medical Treatment of Prisoners form, and remains with Mr. Galvez until the arrival of a uniformed Police Officer, who relieves her.

20. Who assigned Officer Gray to accompany the prisoner?

    A. Police Officer Richards
    B. Captain Small
    C. Police Officer Ryan
    D. Lieutenant Schwinn

21. The Medical Treatment of Prisoner form was completed by the

    A. escorting Officer
    B. cell block attendant
    C. Desk Officer
    D. medical attendant

22. Prior to examining Mr. Galvez, Dr. Keegan requested that Officer Gray

    A. handcuff Mr. Galvez
    B. leave the examination room
    C. remove the handcuffs from Mr. Galvez
    D. submit a copy of the Medical Treatment form

23. Officer Gray obtained the medical diagnosis from Dr. Keegan and then notified the

    A. Hospitalized Prisoner Unit at the Court Division
    B. Emergency Medical Service attendant, John Ross
    C. Desk Officer, Lieutenant Schwinn
    D. cell block attendant, Police Officer Richards

24. The Commanding Officer of each precinct often assigns Police Officers to special conditions patrols which are designed to handle problems unique to that precinct. Officers Martin and Spector are assigned to a special narcotics vehicle.
    Which one of the following should they give the MOST attention to as a possible drug dealing location?

A. A schoolyard where a group of 15 youths are playing basketball and listening to the radio at 4:30 P.M.
B. A street corner where a group of people are standing next to an out-of-order telephone at 3:30 A.M.
C. Outside a YMCA center where a group of kids are getting on bicycles at 10:30 P.M.
D. Near an outdoor pool where twenty teenagers are waiting for an approaching bus at 4:00 P.M.

25. While reviewing crime statistics for his patrol area, Police Officer Jones, of the 25th Precinct, notices that most of the homicides occur between 1:00 A.M. and 3:00 A.M., chain snatches between 10:00 A.M. and 2:00 P.M., and assaults between 5:00 A.M. and 6:00 A.M. Most of the homicides seem to occur on Thursdays, most of the chain snatches on Fridays, and most of the assaults on Fridays and Saturdays.
Police Officer Jones is instructed to work a steady tour that would allow him to concentrate on homicides and assaults within his patrol area.
In order to do this, it would be MOST appropriate for Officer Jones to work   25._____

A. 1:00 A.M. to 9:00 A.M., Monday through Friday
B. 5:00 A.M. to 1:00 P.M., Tuesday through Saturday
C. Midnight to 8:00 A.M., Wednesday through Sunday
D. 10:00 A.M. to 6:00 P.M., Monday through Friday

KEY (CORRECT ANSWERS).

1. C
2. C
3. D
4. A
5. B

6. B
7. A
8. B
9. D
10. C

11. D
12. A
13. C
14. D
15. A

16. D
17. B
18. C
19. C
20. D

21. A
22. C
23. A
24. B
25. C

TEST 2

DIRECTIONS: Each question or incomplete statement is followed by several suggested answers or completions. Select the one that BEST answers the question or completes the statement. *PRINT THE LETTER OF THE CORRECT ANSWER IN THE SPACE AT THE RIGHT.*

1. <u>Assault 3rd Degree</u> - occurs when a person intentionally causes physical injury to another person.
   Which one of the following situations is the BEST example of Assault in the Third Degree?

   A. Jennifer and Joe were talking on a street corner when Sam approached Jennifer, snatcher her pocketbook, and fled.
   B. Arthur and Jennifer were standing on a street corner arguing over Jennifer's daughter when Arthur punched Jennifer in the face, causing her mouth to bleed.
   C. Sam and Arthur were arguing on a street corner when Sam's head was struck and bruised by a brick falling from a nearby building.
   D. In order to avoid paying a debt, Sam ran away from Joe, who was chasing after him on foot. Joe was then hit by a passing car.

2. The following information was obtained by Police Officer Adams at the scene of an auto accident:
   Date of Occurrence: August 7, 2003
   Place of Occurrence: 541 W. Broadway
   Time of Occurrence: 12:45 P.M.
   Drivers: Mrs. Liz Smith and Mr. John Sharp
   Action Taken: Summons served to Mrs. Liz Smith
   Officer Adams is completing a report on the accident. Which one of the following expresses the above information MOST clearly and accurately?

   A. At 541 W. Broadway Mr. John Sharp and Mrs. Liz Smith had an auto accident at 12:45 P.M. Mrs. Smith received a summons on August 7, 2003.
   B. Mrs. Liz Smith received a summons at 12:45 P.M. on August 7, 2003 for an auto accident with Mr. John Sharp at 541 W. Broadway.
   C. Mr. John Sharp and Mrs. Liz Smith were in an auto accident. At 541 W. Broadway on August 7, 2003 at 12:45 P.M. Mrs. Smith received a summons.
   D. On August 7, 2003 at 12:45 P.M. at 541 W. Broadway, Mrs. Liz Smith and Mr. John Sharp were involved in an auto accident. Mrs. Smith received a summons.

3. Police Officer Gold and his partner were directed by the radio dispatcher to investigate a report of a past burglary. They obtained the following information at the scene:
   Date of Occurrence: April 2, 2003
   Time of Occurrence: Between 7:30 A.M. and 6:15 P.M.
   Place of Occurrence: 124 Haring Street, residence of victim
   Victim: Mr. Gerald Palmer
   Suspect: Unknown
   Crime: Burglary
   Items Stolen: Assorted jewelry, $150 cash, T.V., VCR
   Officer Gold must complete a report on the incident. Which one of the following expresses the above information MOST clearly and accurately?

A. Mr. Gerald Palmer stated that on April 2, 2003, between 7:30 A.M. and 6:15 P.M., while he was at work, someone broke into his house at 124 Haring Street and removed assorted jewelry, a VCR, $150 cash, and a T.V.
B. Mr. Gerald Palmer stated while he was at work that somebody broke into his house on April 2, 2003 and between 7:30 A.M. and 6:15 P.M. took his VCR, T.V., assorted jewelry, and $150 cash. His address is 124 Haring Street.
C. Between 7:30 A.M. and 6:15 P.M. on April 2, 2003 Mr. Gerald Palmer reported an unknown person at 124 Haring Street took his T.V., VCR, $150 cash, and assorted jewelry from his house. Mr. Palmer said he was at work at the time.
D. An unknown person broke into the house at 124 Haring Street and stole a T.V., VCR, assorted jewelry, and $150 cash from Mr. Gerald Palmer. The suspect broke in on April 2, 2003; while he was at work, reported Mr. Palmer between 7:30 A.M. and 6:15 P.M.

4. When a Police Officer observes a person in custody or possession of a rifle or shotgun in public, the Officer should do the following in the order given:
    I. Determine if person possesses a valid permit or certificate of registration.
    II. Inform person not possessing permit or certificate of registration that:
        a. he may accompany the Officer to the precinct and surrender the firearm; or
        b. he may surrender the firearm at the scene, after which a receipt will be given.
    III. Serve a summons returnable to appropriate criminal court.
    IV. Make a prompt arrest if violator refuses to surrender weapon.
    V. Prepare a Property Clerk's Invoice and voucher weapons as evidence.

Police Officers Stromm and Rivers receive a call from the radio dispatcher that a male Black, wearing sunglasses, is creating a disturbance in front of Joe's Grocery Store, located at 592 Pit Avenue. When they arrive, the Officers observe a male fitting the description showing the rifle to a small crowd that has gathered. The man, identified as Jerry Perkins, informs the Officers that he does not have a permit for the rifle and has no intention of accompanying them to the precinct to surrender his gun. The NEXT thing that the Officers should do is

A. promptly place Perkins under arrest at the scene
B. inform Perkins that a receipt will be given to him if he surrenders the weapon on the spot
C. issue Perkins a summons returnable to the appropriate criminal court
D. inform Perkins that he must have a valid permit or certificate of registration

5. Police Officers must sometimes rely on eyewitness accounts of incidents, even though eyewitnesses may make mistakes with regard to some details.
While on patrol, Police Officers Black and Beck receive a call from the radio dispatcher regarding a bank robbery in progress. When they arrive on the scene, they see that one of the bank employees has been wounded. While Officer Beck attends to the wounded employee, Officer Black interviews four witnesses who saw a man carrying a gun get into a blue late-model Cadillac and flee from the scene. The following are license plate numbers that were observed by the witnesses.
Which one of these plates should Officer Black consider MOST likely to be the correct one?

A. N.J. Plate ACE-1780
B. N.Y. Plate ADE-1780
C. N.Y. Plate BDE-1780
D. N.J. Plate ADE-1680

6. While on patrol, Police Officers Morris and Devine receive a call to respond to a reported burglary. The following information relating to the crime was obtained by the Officers:

Time of Occurrence: 2:00 A.M.
Place of Occurrence: 2100 First Avenue
Witness: David Santiago
Victim: John Rivera
Suspect: Joe Ryan
Crime: Burglary, video tape recorder stolen

The Officers are completing a report on the incident.
Which one of the following expresses the above information MOST clearly and accurately?

A. David Santiago, the witness reported at 2:00 A.M. he saw Joe Ryan leave 2100 First Avenue, home of John Rivera, with a video tape recorder.
B. At 2:00 A.M. David Santiago reported that he had seen Joe Ryan go into 2100 First Avenue and steal a video tape recorder. John Rivera lives at 2100 First Avenue.
C. David Santiago stated that Joe Ryan burglarized John Rivera's house at 2100 First Avenue. He saw Joe Ryan leaving his house at 2:00 A.M. with a video tape recorder.
D. David Santiago reported that at 2:00 A.M. he saw Joe Ryan leave John Rivera's house, located at 2100 First Avenue, with Mr. Rivera's video tape recorder.

7. When a Police Officer responds to an incident involving the victim of an animal bite, the Officer should do the following in the order given:
   I. Determine the owner of the animal.
   II. Obtain a description of the animal and attempt to locate it for an examination if the owner is unknown.
   III. If the animal is located and the owner is unknown, comply with the Care and Disposition of Animal procedure.
   IV. Prepare a Department of Health Form 480BAA and deliver it to the Desk Officer with a written report.
   V. Notify the Department of Health by telephone if the person has been bitten by an animal other than a dog or cat.

Police Officer Rosario responds to 1225 South Boulevard where someone has been bitten by a dog. He is met by John Miller who informs Officer Rosario that he was bitten by a large German Shepard. Mr. Miller also states that he believes the dog belongs to someone in the neighborhood but does not know who owns it. Officer Rosario searches the area for the dog but is unable to find it. What should Officer Rosario do NEXT?

A. Locate the owner of the animal.
B. Notify the Department of Health by telephone.
C. Prepare a Department of Health Form 480BAA.
D. Comply with the Care and Disposition of Animal procedure.

8. The following details were obtained by Police Officer Howard at the scene of a hit-and-run accident:

   Place of Occurrence: Intersection of Brown Street and Front Street
   Time of Occurrence: 11:15 A.M.
   Victim: John Lawrence
   Vehicle: Red Chevrolet, License Plate 727PQA
   Crime: Leaving the scene of an accident

   Officer Howard is completing a report on the incident. Which one of the following expresses the above information MOST clearly and accurately?

   A. A red Chevrolet license plate 727PQA hit John Lawrence. It left the scene of the accident at 11:15 A.M. at the intersection of Brown and Front Streets.
   B. At 11:15 A.M. John Lawrence was walking at the intersection of Brown Street and Front Street when he was struck by a red Chevrolet, license plate 727PQA, which left the scene.
   C. It was reported at 11:15 A.M. that John Lawrence was struck at the intersection of Brown Street and Front Street. The red Chevrolet, license plate 727PQA, left the scene.
   D. At the intersection of Brown Street and Front Street, John Lawrence was the victim of a car at 11:15 A.M. which struck him and left the scene. It was a red Chevrolet license plate 727PQA.

9. Police Officer Donnelly has transported an elderly male to Mt. Hope Hospital after finding him lying on the street. At the hospital, Nurse Baker provided Officer Donnelly with the following information:

   Name: Robert Jones
   Address: 1485 E. 97th St.
   Date of Birth: May 13, 1917
   Age: 90 years old
   Type of Ailment: Heart condition

   Officer Donnelly is completing an Aided Report. Which one of the following expresses the above information MOST clearly and accurately?

   A. Mr. Robert Jones, who is 90 years old, born on May 13, 1917, collapsed on the street. Mr. Jones, who resides at 1485 E. 97th Street, suffers from a heart condition.
   B. Mr. Robert Jones had a heart condition and collapsed today on the street, and resides at 1485 E. 97th Street. He was 90 years old and born on May 13, 1917.
   C. Mr. Robert Jones, who resides at 1485 E. 97th Street, was born on May 13, 1917, and is 90 years old, was found lying on the street from a heart condition.
   D. Mr. Robert Jones, born on May 13, 1917, suffers from a heart condition at age 90 and was found lying on the street residing at 14*85 E. 97th Street.

10. Police Officers on patrol are often called to a scene where a response from the Fire Department might be necessary.
    In which one of the following situations would a request to the Fire Department to respond be MOST critical?

    A. A film crew has started a small fire in order to shoot a scene on an October evening.
    B. Two manhole covers blow off on a September afternoon.

C. Homeless persons are gathered around a trash can fire on a February morning.
D. A fire hydrant has been opened by people in the neighborhood on a July afternoon.

11. Upon coming into possession of found property, a Police Officer should do the following in the order given:
    I. Issue a receipt to person delivering property if other than a Police Officer.
        a. If property is turned in at station house, Station House Clerk will prepare a Property Clerk's Invoice and give finder a copy as a receipt.
        b. If property is delivered to a Police Officer on patrol, prepare a receipt including a description of the property and signature of receiving Officer.
    II. Enter facts in Memo Book.
    III. Prepare worksheet of Property Clerk's Invoice.
    IV. Deliver property and worksheet to Station House Officer.
    V. Verify accuracy of Property Clerk's Invoice by signing name in the appropriate box.

    Police Officer Bestwell, while on patrol, finds a black leather purse near a subway entrance. The bag contains a wallet with personal papers and other miscellaneous items. After logging the items that were contained in the bag into his Memo Book, Officer Bestwell asks Mrs. Robinson, a witness, to sign the book to verify that he found the property and that he was going to deliver it to the station house. Officer Bestwell's NEXT step should be to

    A. give Mrs. Robinson a receipt describing the property
    B. have the Station House Clerk prepare a Property Clerk's Invoice and give a copy to Mrs. Robinson
    C. prepare a worksheet of the Property Clerk's Invoice
    D. deliver property and Property Clerk's Invoice to the Station House Officer

12. Police Officer Rogers was dispatched to investigate a report of drugs being sold. The Officer obtained the following information:
    Place of Occurrence: In front of 109-30 Hollis Avenue
    Time of Occurrence: Between 3:00 P.M. and 6:00 P.M.
    Reporter: Mrs. Williams, who resides at 109-30 Hollis Avenue
    Crime: Drug sales
    Suspects: Male students from PS 182

    Officer Rogers is preparing a report on the investigation. Which one of the following expresses the above information MOST clearly and accurately?

    A. Mrs. Williams reports between the hours of 3:00 P.M. and 6:00 P.M. drugs are sold. She lives at 109-30 Hollis Avenue where a group of boys from PS 182 sell drugs outside of her home.
    B. Male students selling drugs from PS 182 are creating a problem for Mrs. Williams. She reports this takes place in front of her home. She resides at 109-30 Hollis Avenue. The sales take place from 3:00 P.M. to 6:00 P.M.
    C. Drugs are being sold in front of 109-30 Hollis Avenue. Mrs. Williams reported a group of boys from PS 182 are responsible in front of her home at 109-30 Hollis Avenue. The drugs sell from 3:00 P.M. to 6:00 P.M.
    D. Mrs. Williams reports that a group of boys from PS 182 are selling drugs in front of her home at 109-30 Hollis Avenue. She further reports that the drug sales occur between 3:00 P.M. and 6:00 P.M.

13. <u>Rape 1st Degree</u> - occurs when a male engages in sexual intercourse with a female: 13.____
    I. by forcible compulsion; or
    II. who is incapable of consent by reason of being physically helpless; or
    III. who is less than eleven years old

    Liz and Marie, while returning home from school, walked by a wooded area near their home. The girls, both 10 years old, were spotted by their neighbor, Mr. Walls, who invited them to his house for ice cream. The girls followed Mr. Walls home where Joe, Mr. Walls' friend, joined them. After finishing their ice cream, the girls decided to go home but were unable to leave because Joe had locked the door. The girls were pushed into a room by Joe and Mr. Walls. The men then tore the girls' clothes off and tied them to a bed. Mr. Walls engaged in sexual intercourse with the girls while Joe watched. Who should be charged with Rape 1st Degree?

    A. Mr. Walls
    B. Joe
    C. Both Joe and Mr. Walls
    D. Neither Joe nor Mr. Walls

Questions 14-15.

DIRECTIONS: Questions 14 and 15 are to be answered SOLELY on the basis of the map which appears on the following page. The flow of traffic is indicated by the arrows. If there is only one arrow shown, then traffic flows only in the direction indicated by the arrow. If there are two arrows shown, then traffic flows in both directions. You must follow the flow of traffic.

7 (#2)

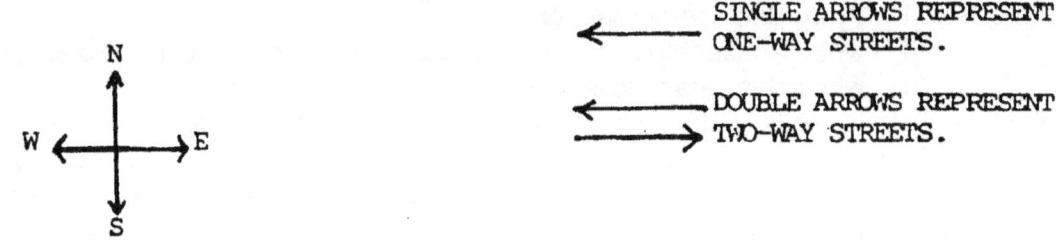

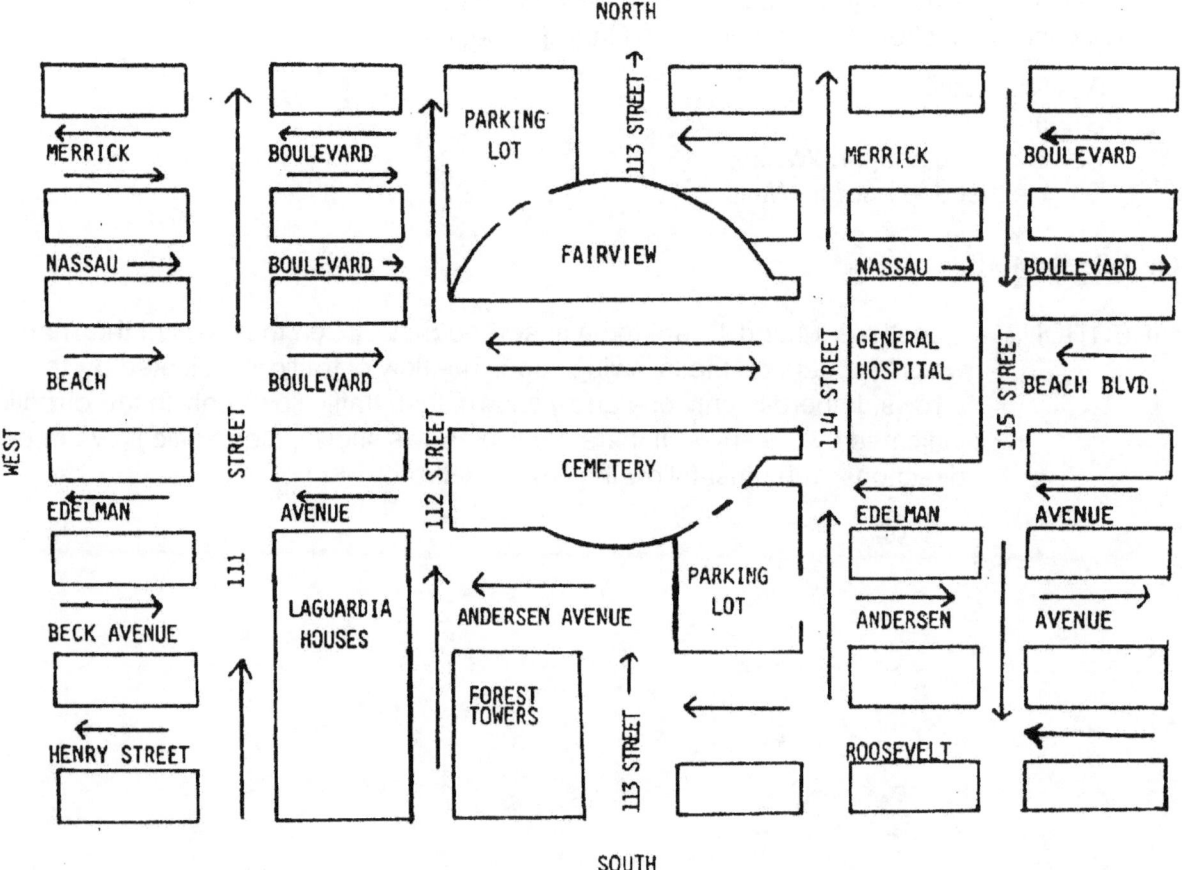

14. Police Officers Glenn and Albertson are on 111th Street at Henry Street when they are dispatched to a past robbery at Beach Boulevard and 115th Street. Which one of the following is the SHORTEST route for the Officers to follow in their patrol car, making sure to obey all traffic regulations?
Travel north on IIIth Street, then east on _____ south on 115th Street.

   A. Edelman Avenue, then north on 112th Street, then east on Beach Boulevard, then north on 114th Street, then east on Nassau Boulevard, then one block
   B. Beach Boulevard, then north on 114th Street, then east on Nassau Boulevard, then one block
   C. Merrick Boulevard, then two blocks
   D. Nassau Boulevard, then south on 112th Street, then east on Beach Boulevard, then north on 114th Street, then east on Nassau Boulevard, then one block

15. Later in their tour, Officers Glenn and Albertson are driving on 114th Street. If they make a left turn to enter the parking lot at Andersen Avenue, and then make a U-turn, in what direction would they now be headed?

   A. North   B. South   C. East   D. West

16. On Monday, October 12, Police Officers Reynolds and Cornan responded to a past burglary at the Electronic Center. The manager of the store stated that the following merchandise was taken:

2 Portable tape players, each valued at	$ 99.00
3 Compact disc players, each valued at	$ 290.00
5 Telephone sets, each valued at	$ 50.00
1 VCR valued at	$ 470.00
1 TV set valued at	$ 600.00
1 Stereo rack system valued at	$ 975.00
1 Walkman stereo valued at	$ 70.00

   In addition to the above items, the manager told the Officers that his calculator, worth $50, was also taken from behind the counter.
   Officer Reynolds is preparing a Complaint Report on the burglary.
   Which one of the following is the TOTAL value of the property stolen?

   A. $2,554   B. $2,604   C. $3,433   D. $3,483

Questions 17-21.

DIRECTIONS: Questions 17 through 21 are to be answered SOLELY on the basis of the following passage.

At 10:30 P.M., while parked in front of a clothing store at 1925 First Avenue, Police Officers Cole and Reese received a radio call to investigate a possible burglary at 1423 Second Avenue. The Officers were to meet the complainant in front of the location given by the dispatcher.

Upon arriving at the scene, the Officers were met by Mr. Rivers, the owner of the Melody Grocery Store, located at 1425 Second Avenue. He explained that he had called the Police because he noticed the bicycle shop next door had been left open. Mr. Rivers further stated that the shop owner, Mr. Rose, usually closes at 9:00 P.M. Mr. Reyes, who lives at 1923 First

Avenue and works with Mr. Rivers, noticed that the store gate had been partially closed and upon checking saw that the lights were off and the door was not locked.

At 10:40 P.M., Police Officer Reese radioed for a Supervisor before entering the premises. Sgt. Parker arrived ten minutes later and supervised a search to find out if the owner was sick, injured, or incapacitated somewhere in the store. The results proved negative. Apparently nothing had been taken or disturbed, and there were no visible signs of a forced entry. The Sergeant instructed Officer Reese to guard the premises while his partner contacted Police Officer Craig, the Precinct Telephone Switchboard Operator, who would check the precinct merchant index file and then notify Mr. Rose of the situation.

17. The Sergeant supervised a search to determine if the

    A. store was being burglarized
    B. owner was sick or injured
    C. store had been ransacked
    D. owner was working late

18. The Police dispatcher received a call regarding a possible burglary at _____ Avenue.

    A. 1423 Second   B. 1923 First
    C. 1425 Second   D. 1925 First

19. What type of business was left unsecured?

    A. Florist Shop   B. Bicycle Shop
    C. Grocery Store   D. Clothes Store

20. At what time did the Sergeant arrive? _____ P.M.

    A. 10:30   B. 10:40   C. 10:45   D. 10:50

21. Which Police Officer would attempt to contact the store owner?

    A. Reese   B. Parker   C. Craig   D. Cole

22. While on patrol, Police Officer Willis responds to a report of unusual odors at an apartment complex. The following information was obtained by the Officer:
    Place of Occurrence: 173 Concord Avenue, Apartment 17
    Time of Occurrence: 1:10 A.M.
    Caller: Mrs. Denise Mathis
    Odors: Gas and ammonia
    Source of Odors: Janitor's supply room
    Action Taken: Fire Department called
    Officer Willis is completing a report on the incident.
    Which one of the following expresses the above information MOST clearly and accurately?

    A. At 173 Concord Avenue, Apartment 17, the smell of gas and ammonia prompted Mrs. Denise Mathis to call 911. The Fire Department responded to the scene of the janitor's supply room. It was 1:10 A.M.
    B. Mrs. Denise Mathis smelled gas and ammonia from her home at 173 Concord Avenue, Apartment 17. She called 911. The source was found in the janitor's supply room after being noticed at 1:10 A.M., and the Fire Department was called.

C. At 1:10 A.M., Mrs. Denise Mathis of 173 Concord Avenue, Apartment 17, smelled gas and ammonia, and called 911. The odors were found to be coming from the janitor's supply room. The Fire Department was called to the scene.
D. Unusual odors of gas and ammonia were noticed by Mrs. Denise Mathis at 173 Concord Avenue, Apartment 17 at 1:10 A.M. The janitor's supply room was responsible. She called 911. The Fire Department was called.

23. Police Officers must sometimes rely on eyewitness accounts of incidents, even though eyewitnesses may make mistakes with regard to some details.
While crossing the street, ten-year-old Nerissa King is struck by a car at the corner of James Street and Paul Avenue. Police Officer Lou responds to the scene and questions four witnesses who saw the vehicle which struck Nerissa. The following are descriptions of the vehicle given by the witnesses.
Which one of these descriptions should Officer Lou consider MOST likely to be correct?

   A. Red Ford Mustang, NY Plate 2198 CAT
   B. Red Ford Mustang, NY Plate 2998 KAT
   C. Burgundy Ford Pinto, NY Plate 2198 CAT
   D. Red Ford Mustang, NY Plate 2198 COT

24. Police Officer Kelly responds to a call from the radio dispatcher regarding a small boy who has fallen down while running in a schoolyard. Officer Kelly has obtained the following information:
Time of Incident: 8:00 A.M.
Place of Incident: PS 27 schoolyard at 1313 Thorn Lane
Victim: Henry Ruiz
Injury: Broken right index finger
Officer Kelly is writing a report on the incident.
Which one of the following expresses the above information MOST clearly and accurately?

   A. While running in the PS 27 schoolyard Henry Ruiz broke his right index finger. At 8:00 A.M. an accident occurred at 1313 Thorn Lane.
   B. At 8:00 A.M. a little boy broke his finger in the schoolyard at 1313 Thorn Lane. Henry Ruiz was running and it was his right index finger he broke at PS 27.
   C. Henry Ruiz fell down while running at 8:00 A.M. at 1313 Thorn Lane. The small boy broke his right index finger in the schoolyard of PS 27.
   D. At 8:00 A.M. in the schoolyard of PS 27, 1313 Thorn Lane, Henry Ruiz fell down while running and broke his right index finger.

25. Police Officer Covatti was on patrol when he received the following information relating to a person in need of assistance:
Place of Occurrence: Canal Street and Ludlow Place
Date of Occurrence: May 25
Person Aided: Unidentified woman, unconscious and bleeding from the head
Reporter: Laura Gallo
Disposition: Victim transported by ambulance to Beth Israel Hospital

11 (#2)

Officer Covatti is about to enter the details regarding this incident in his Memo Book. Which one of the following expresses the above information MOST clearly and accurately?

- A. An unconscious woman was transported to Beth Israel Hospital by ambulance. Laura Gallo reported that she was bleeding from the head at the corner of Canal Street and Ludlow Place on May 25th. She was unidentified.
- B. On May 25th, Laura Gallo reported that there was an unconscious woman bleeding from the head on the corner of Canal Street and Ludlow Place. An ambulance responded and transported the woman, who was unidentified, to Beth Israel Hospital.
- C. Laura Gallo reported that there was an unconscious unidentified woman bleeding from the head on the corner of Canal Street and Ludlow Place. On May 25th, an ambulance transported the woman to Beth Israel Hospital.
- D. An ambulance transported an unconscious woman, bleeding from the head, to Beth Israel Hospital.
  On May 25th, Laura Gallo reported that an unidentified woman was on the corner of Canal Street and Ludlow Place.

KEY (CORRECT ANSWERS)

1. B
2. D
3. A
4. B
5. B

6. D
7. C
8. B
9. A
10. B

11. C
12. D
13. A
14. B
15. C

16. D
17. B
18. A
19. B
20. D

21. C
22. C
23. A
24. D
25. B

TEST 3

DIRECTIONS: Each question or incomplete statement is followed by several suggested answers or completions. Select the one that BEST answers the question or completes the statement. *PRINT THE LETTER OF THE CORRECT ANSWER IN THE SPACE AT THE RIGHT.*

1. When transporting emotionally disturbed people, a Police Officer should: 1.____
    I. Have person removed to the hospital in an ambulance.
        A. Restraining equipment, including handcuffs, may be used if patient is violent or resists.
        B. When possible, a female patient being transported should be accompanied by another female or by an adult member of her immediate family.
    III. Ride in body of ambulance with patient.
        A. Two Police Officers are needed if more than one patient is being transported.
        B. If an ambulance is not available and the situation warrants, transport the patient to the hospital by patrol car, if able to do so with reasonable restraint.

On Monday, while working an 8:00 P.M. to 4:00 A.M. shift, Police Officer Crown is assigned to patrol the Broadway-Lafayette subway station. At 2:15 A.M., he observes a middle-aged man wearing only red shorts pacing up and down the platform yelling, *Aliens are coming, Aliens are coming.* Officer Crown approaches the man, later identified as Robert Grover, and asks, *What's the matter?* Mr. Grover begins swinging his arms at the Officer and shouts, *Don't touch me. When the next train comes, I'm jumping in front of it.* Officer Crown immediately handcuffs him and calls for an ambulance. When it arrives, Officer Crown places Mr. Grover into the back of the ambulance. Just as the ambulance is about to leave for the hospital, Police Officer Cook arrives with two emotionally disturbed females, both in handcuffs. The women are placed into the ambulance, along with Mr. Grover. Officer Cook stays behind to console Mrs. Susan Helms, the mother of one of the two females. Officer Crown accompanies Mr. Grover and the females to the hospital, telling Officer Cook, *I'll see you later at the hospital.* In this situation, the actions taken by the Officer were

   A. *proper,* primarily because Officer Cook attempted to console Mrs. Helms, the mother of one of the women
   B. *improper,* primarily because Officer Crown handcuffed Mr. Grover without good cause
   C. *proper,* primarily because Officer Cook accompanied the females to the hospital in an ambulance
   D. *improper,* primarily because Officer Crown accompanied more than one patient to the hospital

Questions 2-3.

DIRECTIONS: Questions 2 and 3 are to be answered SOLELY on the basis of the following information.

Police Officer Malone is instructed by his supervisor to analyze the crime statistics in his patrol sector in order to reduce the number of burglaries, auto thefts, and robberies. Through his analysis, Officer Malone finds that a large percentage of the burglaries take place on East 99th Street, the majority of auto thefts along East 100th Street, and most of the robberies on Park Avenue. The burglaries occur after most people go to bed, the auto thefts during the afternoon rush hours, and the robberies during the evening hours. For the most part, burglaries take place on Thursdays and Fridays, auto thefts on Mondays and Wednesdays, and robberies on Fridays and Saturdays..

2. Officer Malone would be MOST effective in reducing the number of burglaries and robberies if he patrolled from

 A. 9:00 P.M. to 5:00 A.M., Wednesday through Sunday, on E. 99th Street and Park Avenue
 B. 8:00 A.M. to 4:00 P.M., Monday through Friday, on E. 99th and E. 100th Streets
 C. Noon to 8:00 P.M., Wednesday through Sunday, on E. 99th Street and Park Avenue
 D. 1:00 A.M. to 9:00 A.M., Friday through Tuesday, on Park Avenue and E. 100th Street

3. In order to most effectively reduce the number of auto thefts in his sector, Officer Malone's Supervisor asked him to work a steady tour that would allow him to concentrate on that crime.
For this purpose, it would be MOST appropriate for Officer Malone to work

 A. Tuesday through Saturday, 3:00 A.M. to 11:00 A.M.
 B. Saturday through Wednesday, 8:00 A.M. to 4:00 P.M.
 C. Monday through Friday, 4:00 P.M. to Midnight
 D. Monday through Friday, Midnight to 8:00 A.M.

4. It is sometimes necessary for a Police Officer to call for back-up assistance in certain situations.
In which one of the following situations would it be MOST appropriate for Police Officers to call for back-up?

 A. A group of people playing a radio loudly in the park
 B. Two children fighting in front of a school
 C. A shop owner who wants a drunk removed from his doorway
 D. Two men shaking sticks at each other while arguing in front of a bar

5. Police Officers coming into possession of a recovered weapon are required to voucher it by taking the following steps in the order given:
  I. Unload ammunition from the chamber or magazine.
  II. Scratch an identifying mark on the side of each cartridge case removed from the weapon.
  III. Place the ammunition in an envelope.
  IV. Write *Ammunition Removed from Firearm* and the weapon's serial number (if available) across the face of the envelope.
  V. Place additional ammunition, other than that removed from firearm, in a separate envelope.
  VI. Deliver the firearm and ammunition to the Desk Officer of the precinct of occurrence.

Police Officer Black is acting as vouchering officer for recovered weapons at the Midtown South Precinct. He is given a loaded .357 magnum revolver and 20 additional rounds of ammunition to be vouchered. Officer Black removes the bullets from the revolver's chamber and, with a nail, engraves *P.O.B.* on the side of each cartridge case. He then places the bullets into a large brown envelope and writes *Ammunition Removed from Firearm* and the revolver's serial number across the envelope's face. The NEXT step Officer Black should take is to

- A. scratch an identifying mark on each of the additional 20 rounds of ammunition
- B. put the additional 20 rounds of ammunition in another envelope
- C. give the revolver and bullets to the Desk Officer of the precinct where the revolver was recovered
- D. scratch an identifying mark on the barrel of the revolver

6. Police Officers Davis and Lewis are assigned to cover Sector A. They have been working this area for six months now and have noticed that a lot of the rapes take place on Saturdays, most of the drug sales take place on Fridays and Saturdays, and the majority of the robberies occur on Mondays and Fridays. The primary hours when the rapes occur are between 3:00 P.M. and 10:00 P.M., the drug sales take place between 9:00 'M. and 6:00 P.M., and the robberies happen between 1:00 P.M. and Midnight.
The Officers are instructed to work a steady tour that would allow them to concentrate on robberies and rapes within their patrol area.
For this purpose, it would be MOST appropriate for the Officers to work

- A. 3:00 P.M. to 11:00 P.M., Thursday through Monday
- B. 10:00 A.M. to 6:00 P.M., Tuesday through Saturday
- C. 8:00 A.M. to 4:00 P.M., Monday through Friday
- D. 4:00 P.M. to Midnight, Wednesday through Sunday

Questions 7-9.

DIRECTIONS: Questions 7 through 9 are to be answered SOLELY on the basis of the following passage.

Police Officers Wilson and Jost are assigned to a patrol car and receive a call from the dispatcher to respond to a shooting at 236 Bever Street between Hoyt and Clinton Avenues. The two Officers arrive at the scene at 5:20 P.M. and see a man, later identified as David Smith of 242 Bever Street, lying on the sidewalk and bleeding from the chest. An ambulance arrives at 5:35 P.M., and the attendant, Peter Johnson, pronounces Mr. Smith dead from a gunshot wound on the left side of the chest. Officer Jost begins to walk along Bever Street looking for witnesses. Suddenly, William Jones comes out of his store, located at 239 Beyer Street, and tells Officer Jost that he heard a gunshot at 5:15 P.M. and saw two White males going through the victim's pockets. Meanwhile, Walter Garvey, of 247 Bever Street, approaches Officer Wilson and tells him that he saw the victim fall to the ground and then observed two White males search the victim before they ran west on Bever Street toward Clinton Avenue. Mr. Garvey describes one suspect as having blonde hair and wearing a blue jacket with black jeans, and the other suspect as having brown hair and wearing a white jacket and blue jeans.

After interviewing Mr. Jones, Officer Jost is approached by Doris Finkle, owner of the Sweet Shop located at 238 Bever Street. She tells him that the victim was walking along

Bever Street when two White males came from behind and pushed Mr. Smith against the wall. She also says that a man with blonde hair started talking to the victim when suddenly a man wearing a white jacket fired a gun and Mr. Smith fell to the ground. Mrs. Finkle tells the Officer that the two suspects searched the victim and then ran away.

7. Who pronounced David Smith dead?

    A. William Jones
    B. Doris Finkle
    C. Peter Johnson
    D. Walter Garvey

8. Which of the following persons was the FIRST to report hearing a gunshot?

    A. Police Officer Jost
    B. Walter Garvey
    C. Peter Johnson
    D. William Jones

9. Who was the FIRST witness to give a description of the suspects' clothing?

    A. Mrs. Finkle
    B. Mr. Garvey
    C. Mr. Jones
    D. Mr. Johnson

10. Police Officers Carrano and Lee have responded to the scene of a burglary and obtained the following information:

    Place of Occurrence: 289 Orchard Street
    Time of Occurrence: 1:35 A.M.
    Witness: Ms. Perez
    Suspect: A female Hispanic, 5'10", 140 lbs., wearing a black jacket and blue jeans
    Crime: Burglary of a clothing store, three coats taken

    Officers Lee and Carrano are filing the initial report on the incident.
    Which one of the following expresses the above information MOST clearly and accurately?

    A. At 1:35 A.M., Ms. Perez reported a woman stole three coats while wearing a black jacket and blue jeans in the store at 289 Orchard Street. The Hispanic is 5'10" and 140 lbs.
    B. A female Hispanic witnessed by Ms. Perez was wearing blue jeans and a black jacket. A store at 289 Orchard Street was robbed of three coats by a suspect weighing 140 lbs. at 5'10" at 1:35 A.M.
    C. Ms. Perez witnessed a burglary when she saw a woman steal three coats. She was wearing blue jeans and a black jacket. At 1:35 A.M. she burglarized a store at 289 Orchard Street. The Hispanic suspect was 5'10" and 140 lbs.
    D. At 1:35 A.M., Ms. Perez reportedly saw a female Hispanic steal three coats from a store at 289 Orchard Street. The suspect was described as being 5'10", 140 lbs., wearing blue jeans and a black jacket.

11. Police Officer Sanchez has just finished investigating a report of a rape and has obtained the following information:

    Time of Occurrence: 9:10 A.M.
    Place of Occurrence: Tony's Bodega, 109 Victory Boulevard
    Victim: Joyce Rivera, employee
    Crime: Rape
    Suspect: Male, White, carrying a gun

    Officer Sanchez is completing a report on the incident.

Which one of the following expresses the above information MOST clearly and accurately?
- A. Joyce Rivera is an employee at Tony's Bodega located at 109 Victory Boulevard. She reported that at 9:10 A.M. a White male went into the Bodega and raped her at gunpoint.
- B. While working in Tony's Bodega, located at 100 Victory Boulevard, Joyce Rivera reported at 9:10 A.M. she was raped at gunpoint by a male White.
- C. The time was 9:10 A.M., when a White male went into Tony's Bodega and pointed a gun at an employee. He then raped Joyce Rivera. The Bodega is located at 109 Victory Boulevard.
- D. At 9:10 A.M. Joyce Rivera reported that she was in Tony's Bodega, located at 109 Victory Boulevard. A White male went in and raped her while she was working at gunpoint.

12. When evidence is required for presentation in court, a Police Officer must do the following:
    - I. Request evidence from Officer assigned to Property Clerk facility where it is stored.
    - II. Give the Officer the Property Clerk's Invoice Number.
    - III. Present shield and identification card.
    - IV. If the evidence is held by the court, obtain a receipt and notify the Property Clerk's Office.
    - V. If the evidence is not held, return all evidence to the Property Clerk's Office.

    Police Officer Johnson of the 105th Precinct was notified to appear in Queens Supreme Court to testify in a case involving an arrest he made the previous month. Officer Johnson needed the evidence, which consisted of two 9mm pistols and one hunting knife, before he could testify. Officer Johnson went to the 112th Precinct, where the Property Clerk's Office is located, gave the invoice number for the evidence, and presented his shield and D. card. Officer Johnson obtained the evidence and proceeded to the courthouse. After four hours of testimony by various witnesses, the trial was adjourned for the day and the weapons were taken into custody by the court officer. After obtaining a receipt, Officer Johnson returned to the 105th Precinct where he completed his tour.
    In this situation, the actions taken by Officer Johnson were

    - A. *proper,* primarily because he obtained a receipt for the evidence before going to court
    - B. *improper,* primarily because he did not notify the Property Clerk's Office
    - C. *proper,* primarily because he presented his shield and D. card to obtain the evidence from the court officer
    - D. *improper,* primarily because he did not return the evidence before ending his tour

13. Captain Rutherford assigns Police Officer Haskel to a post in the Washington Avenue subway station. Officer Haskel is informed that there has been an increase in chain snatching at the location, and he is instructed to observe anyone who looks suspicious. Which one of the following situations should Officer Haskel monitor more closely?

    - A. A teenage boy who is standing on the platform and constantly checking the time on his watch
    - B. A man wearing a white robe selling incense and jewelry on the platform

C. A woman who has been standing against a post for the past hour watching passengers as they exit trains
D. Two teenagers walking down the stairs and onto an awaiting train

14. Police Officer Mercardo has been assigned to inspect Patrol Car #785 for its equipment and general condition. The following information has been obtained by the Officer:
    I. Total mileage of car: 76,561
    II. Exterior of car: poor
        A. Broken right headlight
        B. Dents on right fender and right door
        C. Front tires flat
    III. Interior of car: poor
        A. Seats ripped
        B. Dashboard lights broken
        C. Glove compartment door missing

    Officer Mercado is completing a report on his inspection of the car.
    Which one of the following expresses the above information MOST clearly and accurately?

    A. Patrol Car #785 has a total mileage of 76,561 miles and is in poor condition in that the exterior of the car has a broken right headlight. It also has flats on both front tires and dents are on right fender and door. The interior of the car shows ripped seats and no glove compartment door with the dashboard lights broken.
    B. Patrol Car #785, which is in poor condition, has a total mileage of 76,561 miles. The exterior of the car has a broken right headlight and dents on the right fender and right door. Both front tires are flat. The interior of the car reveals that the seats are ripped, the dashboard lights don't work, and the door to the glove compartment is missing.
    C. Patrol Car #785 has on the exterior a broken right headlight, dents to the fender and door which can be found on the right side, and two flat tires in the front. For the interior, the seats are ripped, the dashboard lights are broken, and the glove compartment needs to be fixed. The general condition of the car is poor, which has a total mileage of 76,561.
    D. Patrol Car #785 has in the interior ripped seats and a missing glove compartment door. Also the dashboard lights don't come on. The condition of the car is poor, it has a total mileage of 76,561 miles on it. The exterior of the car has two front tires that are flat, a broken right headlight and dents to the right fender. The door is also dented.

15. Police Officers may become involved in cases regarding children who are lost. When a lost child is brought to a Police Officer, the Officer should do the following in the order given:
    I. Notify Desk Officer and radio dispatcher.
    II. Conduct a brief investigation in vicinity of place where child was found.
    III. Bring child to the Precinct station house if parents or relatives are not found.
    IV. Prepare an Aided Report.
    V. Telephone Missing Persons Squad and give a description.
    VI. Complete captions on Aided Report and process in normal manner.

Police Officer Davis, while assigned to patrol on White Street, was approached by Mr. Franklin, the custodian at 274 Lafayette Street, and a small child. Mr. Franklin explained that he found the child walking alone on the fifth floor of his building. Officer Davis radioed the dispatcher, telephoned his Desk Officer, and then escorted the child to the station house.

When Officer Davis arrived at the Precinct, the Desk Officer reminded him that, prior to bringing the child in, Officer Davis should have

- A. prepared an Aided Report
- B. called the radio dispatcher
- C. notified the Missing Persons Squad
- D. made inquiries in the building about the child

16. Police Officer Cohen is on patrol and receives a call to respond to a disturbance at a local grocery store. The following information is given to the Officer at the scene:

    Place of Occurrence: Joe's Mini-Mart
    Complainant: Tom Callas
    Crime: Loitering and using abusive language
    Suspect: Male, Hispanic
    Action Taken: The suspect was removed from premises

    Officer Cohen is completing a report on the incident. Which one of the following expresses the above information MOST clearly and accurately?

    - A. Tom Callas called the Police because a male Hispanic was loitering and using abusive language in Joe's Mini-Mart. The male Hispanic was removed from the premises by Police.
    - B. A male Hispanic was removed from Joe's Mini-Mart. Tom Callas called the Police. He was loitering and using abusive language when he was removed from the premises.
    - C. At Joe's Mini-Mart, a male Hispanic was loitering and using abusive language. Tom Callas called the Police. They removed him from the premises.
    - D. The Police removed a male Hispanic from Joe's Mini-Mart. Tom Callas called them because he was loitering and using abusive language.

Questions 17-18.

DIRECTIONS: Questions 17 and 18 are to be answered SOLELY on the basis of the following information.

Upon notification or observation of a vehicle accident, a Police Officer should do the following in the order given:

       I. Park radio motor patrol car behind vehicles involved so that traffic will not be blocked.
     II. Determine if there are any injuries and request an ambulance if needed.
    III. Divert traffic if necessary.
   IV. Obtain the driver's license, vehicle registration, and insurance identification card of driver(s) so that required information can be recorded.
    V. Determine the cause of the accident by inquiry and observation.
   VI. Prepare one copy of Police Accident Report.

17. While on Highway Patrol, Police Officer Quinn witnesses a serious three vehicle accident and immediately stops to assist. While exiting his patrol car, he notices that one of the drivers involved in the accident is bleeding heavily from the mouth and that a serious traffic condition is developing on both sides of the intersection. The NEXT step Officer Quinn should take is to

    A. reduce congestion by diverting the traffic
    B. request driver's licenses, vehicle registration, and insurance cards from the drivers
    C. obtain medical assistance for the injured
    D. radio for a tow truck to remove accident vehicles

17.____

18. Police Officers Velazquez and Degas are on vehicle patrol and passing through an intersection when a pedestrian flags them down to report a traffic accident. Officer Velazquez stops behind the vehicles involved in the accident, gets out of the car, and asks the two drivers if anyone is injured. They both say that they are all right. Officer Velazquez then asks them for their licenses, registrations, and insurance cards. Officer Degas notices that traffic is beginning to back up at the intersection, so she starts to direct traffic around the accident.
    The NEXT step that Officers Velazquez and Degas should take is to

    A. request that an ambulance respond to the scene
    B. divert traffic if necessary
    C. prepare one copy of a Police Accident Report
    D. determine the cause of the accident

18.____

19. During his last tour of duty, Police Officer Meehan observed a robbery in progress and arrested the suspect. The following details are related to the robbery:
    Place of Occurrence: Corner of Ludlow and Rivington Streets
    Date of Occurrence: June 10
    Weapon: .357 Magnum
    Crime: Robbery
    Officer Meehan is completing a request for departmental recognition for this arrest. Which one of the following expresses the above information MOST clearly and accurately?

    A. On June 10th, I apprehended a perpetrator without assistance on the corner of Ludlow and Rivington Streets. I observed a robbery in progress and recovered a .357 Magnum.
    B. On June 10th, I observed a robbery in progress on the corner of Ludlow and Rivington Streets. I apprehended the perpetrator without assistance and recovered a .357 Magnum.
    C. I observed a robbery in progress and without assistance I apprehended the perpetrator with a .357 Magnum. This took place on the corner of Ludlow and Rivington Streets. The incident occurred on June 10.
    D. On June 10th, I recovered a .357 Magnum when I observed a robbery in progress. I apprehended the perpetrator on Ludlow and Rivington Streets without assistance.

19.____

20. After a suspicious person has been stopped, questioned, and frisked, the Police Officer should do the following in the order given:

20.____

I. Request the person's name and address.
II. Prepare a Stop and Frisk Report.
III. Enter the details in the Activity Log.
IV. Inform the Supervisor of the facts.
V. Submit a Stop and Frisk Report to the Desk Officer.
VI. Get the Precinct Log number.

Police Officer O'Boyle is dispatched to investigate a suspicious male with a knife in Van Cortland Park. When the Officer arrives on the scene, he notices a male fitting the description he has been given. Officer O'Boyle stops, questions, and frisks the male but finds nothing on him. What should the Officer do NEXT?

A. Inform his Supervisor of the facts.
B. Prepare a Stop and Frisk Report.
C. Request the person's name and address.
D. Enter the details in the Activity Log.

21. During the winter, when the temperature drops below 32 and the Department of Health declares a Cold Weather Emergency, Police Officers are required to:
    I. Require all homeless people to go to a shelter
    II. Give transportation to homeless people looking for shelter
    III. If a homeless person refuses to go to a shelter and has no home, use force if necessary to get the person to a hospital for psychiatric evaluation.

It is 3:00 A.M. on a Tuesday, and the temperature has dropped from 34 to 28. A Cold Weather Emergency has just been declared. During his patrol, Police Officer Georgia notices a middle-aged woman lying near a metal grate on the sidewalk near the corner of Main Street and Craig Avenue. The woman is surrounded by shopping bags and appears to be disoriented. The Officer asks her where she lives, and she says *many places*. He asks if she has any friends or relatives, and she says that she does not know anyone. The Officer then asks her if she would like to go to a shelter and she refuses. When asked for identification, she hands the Officer a wallet containing a few meaningless scraps of paper. The Officer then calls for a Supervisor and an ambulance to transport her to a hospital for psychiatric evaluation.
In this situation, the actions taken by Officer Georgia were

A. *improper,* primarily because the woman had not committed a crime or bothered anyone
B. *proper,* primarily because she was obviously in need of psychiatric evaluation
C. *improper,* primarily because the woman was more in need of shelter than of a psychiatric evaluation
D. *proper,* primarily because the woman had refused shelter despite the Cold Weather Emergency

22. Criminal Sale of a Controlled Substance 5th Degree -occurs when a person knowingly and unlawfully sells a controlled substance, such as cocaine, marijuana, heroin.
Sell means to sell, give, or dispose of to another, or to offer or agree to do the same.
Which one of the following situations is the BEST example of Criminal Sale of a Controlled Substance in the Fifth Degree?

A. James and Cathy dispose of six vials of cocaine by burying them in their backyard.
B. Harry and Jack sit in a stairwell and pass a lit pipe filled with marijuana between them.

C. Thomas opens his dresser drawer and exchanges a bag full of cocaine for a bag of marijuana.
D. John laces his neighbor's dogfood with heroin.

23. After arresting a suspect, Police Officers are required to take fingerprints in order to establish positive identification. When taking fingerprints, Police Officers must do the following in the order given:
    I. Police Officers should be extremely careful when fingerprinting to have no weapons on their person.
    II. Inform person to relax hands and fingers and let the Officer do the rolling.
    III. Prepare fingerprint charts as follows:
        A. Two copies of Criminal Fingerprint Record
        B. One copy of FBI Fingerprint Chart
        C. One copy of State Fingerprint Chart
    IV. In the case of a juvenile, prepare one copy of State Juvenile Fingerprint Chart.
    V. Whenever arrested persons are fingerprinted, palm prints and photographs may also be taken.

Police Officer Lane has arrested a juvenile and is about to process his arrest. Before taking the fingerprints, Officer Lane hands his revolver to Lt. Cronin, who secures it in the weapons locker. The youth is told to relax his hand and fingers and to let Officer Lane do the rolling. The Officer begins to prepare two Criminal Fingerprint Records, an FBI Fingerprint Chart, and a State Fingerprint Chart.
After completing this, the NEXT step Officer Lane should take is to

A. take palm prints and photographs of the juvenile
B. prepare an additional Criminal Fingerprint Record
C. deliver the fingerprint reports to the appropriate agency
D. prepare a State Juvenile Fingerprint Chart

24. Police Officer Roach responded to the home of Audrey Seager regarding a past burglary. Ms. Seager reported that, while she was at work, someone broke into her home and stole the property listed below. She further stated that a piece of her luggage worth approximately $150.00 was also taken and was probably used by the robber to carry the following property out of her apartment:

2 35mm cameras, each valued at	$289.00
2 video cassette recorders, each valued at	$329.00
Miscellaneous jewelry valued at	$455.00
Cash	$350.00
Stock certificates valued at	$1500.00

Officer Roach is completing a Complaint Report. Which one of the following is the TOTAL value of the property and cash stolen from Ms. Seager?

A. $2,923   B. $3,073   C. $3,691   D. $3,991

Question 25.

DIRECTIONS: Question 25 is to be answered SOLELY on the basis of the following information.

Serious Physical Injury - injury which creates a substantial risk of death, or serious and prolonged disfigurement, prolonged impairment of health, or loss or impairment of function of any bodily organ.

Assault 2nd Degree - occurs when, with intent to cause physical injury to another, a person causes such injury to such person or to a third person by means of a deadly weapon or dangerous instrument.

Manslaughter 1st Degree - occurs when, with intent to cause serious physical injury to another, a person causes death to that person or to a third person.

Murder 2nd Degree - occurs when, with intent to cause the death of another, a person causes the death of such person or a third person.

25. Police Officers Harris and Linden were dispatched to Clare's Bar. Upon their arrival, they observed two dead bodies lying on the floor. After interviewing witnesses at the bar, they learned that an elderly man known as *Whiskey Bill* had given the victims homemade liquor. Whiskey Bill was placed under arrest. During the interrogation, Bill admitted that he knew that the liquor would be fatal if someone drank it, but he wanted to get even with Joe, who was one of the victims.
It would be MOST appropriate for the Officers to charge Bill with

   A. Murder 2nd Degree
   B. Serious Physical Injury
   C. Assault 2nd Degree
   D. Manslaughter 1st Degree

KEY (CORRECT ANSWERS)

1. D
2. A
3. C
4. D
5. B

6. A
7. C
8. D
9. B
10. D

11. A
12. B
13. C
14. B
15. D

16. A
17. C
18. D
19. B
20. C

21. D
22. B
23. D
24. C
25. A

EXAMINATION SECTION
TEST 1

DIRECTIONS: Each question or incomplete statement is followed by several suggested answers or completions. Select the one that BEST answers the question or completes the statement. *PRINT THE LETTER OF THE CORRECT ANSWER IN THE SPACE AT THE RIGHT.*

Questions 1-3.

DIRECTIONS: Questions 1 through 3 are to be answered SOLELY on the basis of the map which appears on the next page. The flow of traffic is indicated by the arrow. If there is only one arrow shown, then traffic flows only in the direction indicated by the arrow. If there are two arrows shown, then traffic flows in both directions. You must follow the flow of traffic.

2 (#1)

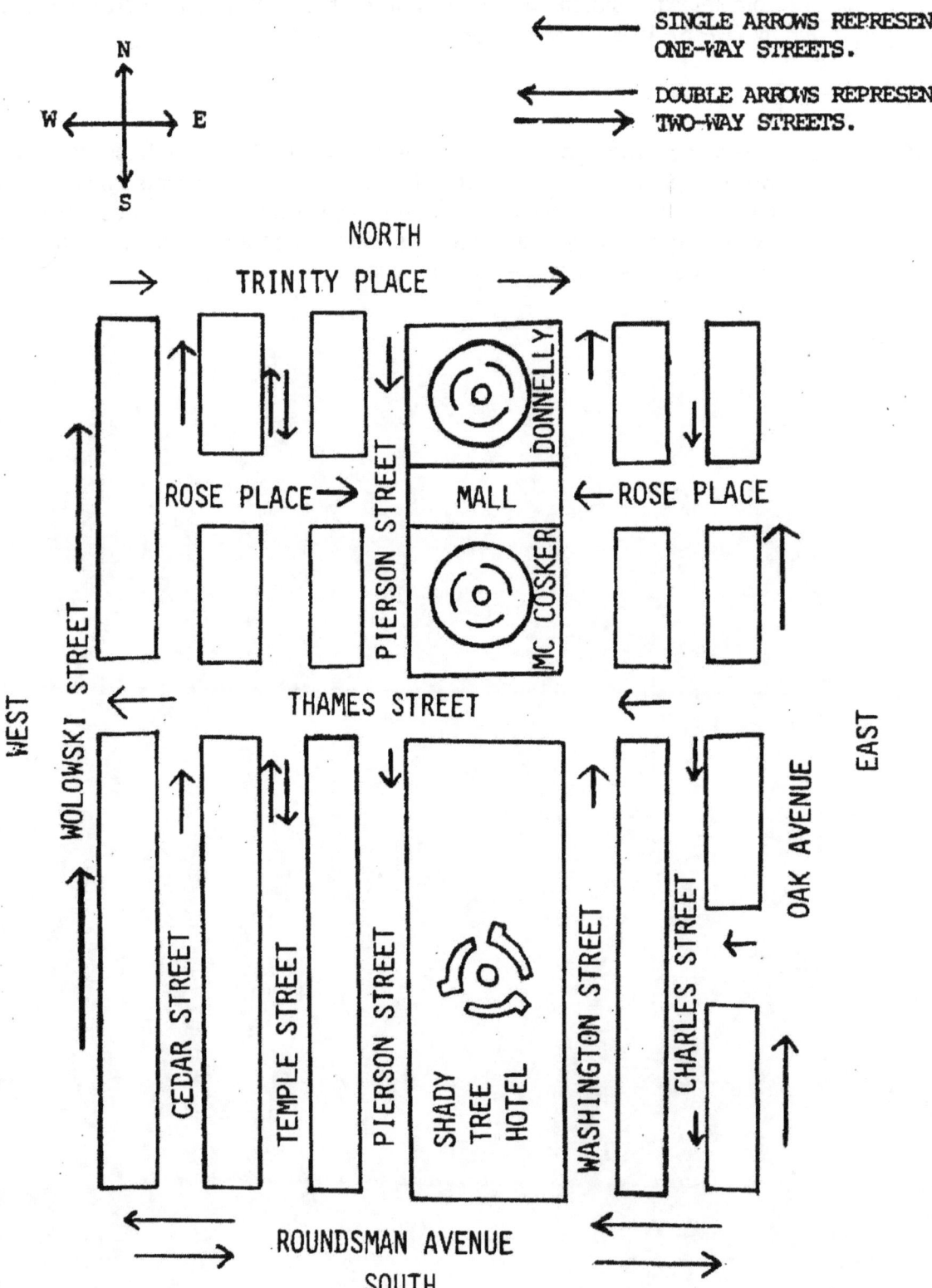

1. Police Officers Simms and O'Brien are located at Roundsman Avenue and Washington Street. The radio dispatcher has assigned them to investigate a motor vehicle accident at the corner of Pierson Street and Rose Place.
   Which one of the following is the SHORTEST route for them to take in their patrol car, making sure to obey all traffic regulations? Travel

   A. west on Roundsman Avenue, then north on Temple Street, then east on Thames Street, then north on Pierson Street to Rose Place
   B. east on Roundsman Avenue, then north on Oak Avenue, then west on Rose Place to Pierson Street
   C. west on Roundsman Avenue, then north on Temple Street, then east on Rose Place to Pierson Street
   D. east on Roundsman Avenue, then north on Oak Avenue, then west on Thames Street, then north on Temple Street, then east on Rose Place to Pierson Street

2. Police Officers Sears and Castro are located at Cedar Street and Roundsman Avenue. They are called to respond to the scene of a burglary at Rose Place and Charles Street. Which one of the following is the SHORTEST route for them to take in their patrol car, making sure to obey all traffic regulations? Travel

   A. east on Roundsman Avenue, then north on Oak Avenue, then west on Rose Place to Charles Street
   B. east on Roundsman Avenue, then north on Washington Street, then east on Rose Place to Charles Street
   C. west on Roundsman Avenue, then north on Wolowski Street, then east on Trinity Place, then south on Charles Street to Rose Place
   D. east on Roundsman Avenue, then north on Charles Street to Rose Place

3. Police Officer Glasser is in an unmarked car at the intersection of Rose Place and Temple Street when he begins to follow two robbery suspects. The suspects go south for two blocks, then turn left for two blocks, then make another left turn for one more block. The suspects realize they are being followed and make a left turn and travel two more blocks and then make a right turn.
   In what direction are the suspects now headed?

   A. North B. South C. East D. West

4. Police Officer Miller is assigned to the 72nd Precinct and observes that most of the rapes in his sector are committed on Bay Street between President Street and Alabama Street. All the assaults are committed on Nelson Street between Carroll Street and Lewis Street, and all the homicides are committed on Third Avenue between Tinton Street and Union Street. Most of the rapes happen on Thursdays and Fridays between 10:00 P.M. and 2:00 A.M.; the assaults on Saturdays between 10:00 A.M. and 1:00 P.M.; and most of the homicides on Saturdays and Sundays between 1:00 A.M. and 4:00 A.M. Officer Miller would MOST likely be able to reduce the number of homicides by patrolling

   A. Bay Street on Thursdays and Fridays between 10:00 P.M. and 2:00 A.M.
   B. Alabama Street on Saturdays between 10:00 A.M. and 1:00 P.M.
   C. Carroll Street on Wednesdays between 11:00 A.M. and 3:00 P.M.
   D. Third Avenue on Saturdays and Sundays between 1:00 A.M. and 4:00 A.M.

5. Police Officer Ross has been assigned to investigate a recent increase in the number of token booth hold-ups committed by pairs of youths in the Chamber Street Station. He has been instructed to pay special attention to any activity that appears to be suspicious. Which one of the following situations should Officer Ross monitor more closely?

   A. A male youth talking to the token clerk while the clerk is counting money
   B. A youth looking at a subway map near the booth while holding a black canvas bag
   C. One youth standing by the token booth while his friend waits on the stairs
   D. Two female youths engaged in a fistfight near the turnstile

6. When a prisoner in custody is admitted to a hospital, the arresting Police Officer should do the following in the order given:
   I. Notify Desk Officer in the precinct of arrest.
   II. Search male prisoner at hospital in presence of witnesses if prisoner was removed from scene of arrest directly to hospital.
   III. Have hospital personnel search female prisoners.
   IV. Search prisoner's personal clothing, after removal by hospital personnel, for weapons, evidence, or contraband.
   V. Give hospital authorities receipt for property received.
   VI. Enter in Activity Log list of property removed and any information necessary to process arrest.
   VII. Report to precinct of arrest to continue arrest processing when relieved by guarding Officer

   While Police Officer Smith was arresting Michelle Hart for the robbery of a jewelry store, Ms. Hart suffered an asthma attack and had to be hospitalized immediately. Officer Smith requested that an ambulance respond to the scene and informed Lt. Brandon, the Desk Officer in the precinct, of details regarding the arrest. He then rode to the hospital in the ambulance with his prisoner. After informing hospital personnel of the circumstances concerning the arrest, the NEXT thing Officer Smith should do is

   A. report to the precinct of arrest and continue arrest processing
   B. search the prisoner in presence of hospital personnel
   C. enter in his Activity Log the time of arrest and identity of prisoner
   D. direct hospital personnel to search the prisoner

7. When a person is arrested for possession of a firearm, the arresting Officer should:
   I. Seize the weapon
   II. Base the charge on the violation of Penal Law or Administrative Code
   III. Prepare the Request for Laboratory Examination form
   IV. Bring weapon and Request form to the Ballistics Unit
   V. After examination by Ballistics Unit, deliver weapon to Property Clerk with Property Clerk's Invoice.

   Police Officer Livingston has received a call from the dispatcher regarding shots fired. Upon arriving at the scene, Officer Livingston finds a loaded 9mm automatic pistol in the possession of John Blake. Officer Livingston secures the firearm and arrests John Blake, charging him with Criminal Use of a Firearm in the 1st Degree, a violation of the Penal Law. Once at the station house, Officer Livingston is instructed to prepare a form requesting a Laboratory Examination of the firearm.

   After this has been completed, Officer Livingston leaves the form with his Supervisor and takes the firearm to the Ballistics Unit, where it is examined. It is learned that the gun was used in a number of crimes, including the shooting of a Police Officer. Officer Livingston delivers the gun to the Property Clerk's Office with a Property Clerk's Invoice. Officer Livingston's actions were

A. *improper,* primarily because the laboratory request was not brought to the Ballistics Unit
B. *proper,* primarily because the gun was brought to the Ballistics Unit where it was learned that the gun was used in other crimes
C. *improper,* primarily because the Property Clerk's Invoice should have been given to his Supervisor after it was completed
D. *proper,* primarily because Mr. Blake was charged with Criminal Use of a Firearm in the 1st Degree, a violation of the Penal Law

8. Police Officers are sometimes required to request emergency transportation for seriously injured people. For which one of the following people would it be MOST appropriate for a Police Officer to request emergency transportation?
A(n)

   A. pregnant woman who complains of feeling faint
   B. elderly man who has been drinking complains about his vision
   C. young boy who is rollerskating falls down and is knocked unconscious
   D. teenage girl slips while iceskating and limps off the ice

Questions 9-12.

DIRECTIONS: Questions 9 through 12 are to be answered SOLELY on the basis of the following passage.

On May 10, at 5:30 P.M., Police Officers Swift and Monroe were on routine patrol when they were dispatched to 1180 Albany Avenue, Apartment 3C, on an assault in progress. They arrived at the apartment at 5:40 P.M. and were met by Mr. Raymond Ambrose. Mr. Ambrose said he called the Police because he heard yelling and screaming coming from Apartment 3A, but it had since stopped. Mr. Ambrose told the Officers that the tenant in 3A, Helen Gray, lived alone ever since her divorce.

Officer Monroe knocked on the door of Apartment 3A and noticed that the door was partially opened. The Officers cautiously entered the apartment, which appeared to have been ransacked. Officer Swift checked the fire escape while his partner searched the bedroom, where he found Mrs. Gray, unconscious, lying on the floor and bleeding heavily from the head. A blood-covered baseball bat was found next to her. The Officer called for an ambulance to respond while Officer Swift tried to gather information from neighbors.

Mary Grable, age 68, of Apartment 3B, Ben Grim, age 16 of Apartment 1A, and Angela Arnold, age 27, of 1162 Albany Avenue were standing in the hallway. Ms. Arnold stated that she and Mrs. Gray are close friends, and she became concerned when she saw Stuart Gray in the neighborhood around 5:10 P.M. Ms. Arnold told Officer Swift, *Since they've been divorced, Stuart visits Helen to get money to support a "crack" habit, and it always leads to an argument.* Grable said she heard a commotion, but didn't know who was involved. Grim told Officer Swift that he saw Stuart Gray running from the building at about 5:35 P.M. with blood on his hands and shirt.

Paramedics arrived at 5:50 P.M. and transported Mrs. Gray to the hospital, where she died at 6:30 P.M. without regaining consciousness. Stuart Gray was arrested at 7:15 the next morning at the home of his mother, Valerie Gray, and was charged with the homicide.

9. From the information given, it is MOST likely that the crime was committed between

    A. 5:10 A.M. - 5:35 A.M.
    B. 5:10 P.M. - 5:35 P.M.
    C. 5:30 P.M. - 5:35 P.M.
    D. 5:30 P.M. - 5:50 P.M.

10. Who was the FIRST person to find Mrs. Gray?

    A. Officer Monroe
    B. Mr. Ambrose
    C. Officer Swift
    D. Ms. Arnold

11. Whose information tied Stuart to the crime?

    A. Ms. Arnold and Ben Grim
    B. Mr. Ambrose and Ms. Arnold
    C. Ben Grim and Valerie Gray
    D. Ms. Arnold and Ms. Grable

12. Stuart Gray was arrested on

    A. May 10 at 6:30 P.M.
    B. May 11 at 7:15 P.M.
    C. May 10 at 7:15 A.M.
    D. May 11 at 7:15 A.M.

13. The following details were obtained by Police Officer Dwight at the scene of a family dispute:

    Place of Occurrence: 77 Baruch Drive
    Victim: Andrea Valdez, wife of Walker
    Violator: Edward Walker
    Witness: George Valdez, victim's brother
    Crime: Violation of Order of Protection
    Action Taken: Violator arrested

    Police Officer Dwight is preparing a report on the incident.
    Which one of the following expresses the above information MOST clearly and accurately?

    A. George Valdez saw Edward Walker violate his sister's Order of Protection at 77 Baruch Drive. Andrea Valdez's husband was arrested for this violation.
    B. Andrea Valdez's Order of Protection was violated at 77 Baruch Drive. George Valdez saw his brother-in-law violate his sister's Order. Edward Walker was arrested.
    C. Edward Walker was arrested for violating an Order of Protection held by his wife, Andrea Valdez. Andrea's brother, George Valdez, witnessed the violation at 77 Baruch Drive.
    D. An arrest was made at 77 Baruch Drive when an Order of Protection held by Andrea Valdez was violated by her husband. George Valdez, her brother, witnessed Edward Walker.

14. Endangering the Welfare of a Child - occurs when a person knowingly acts in a manner likely to be injurious to the physical, mental, or moral welfare of a male child less than 16 years old or a female child less than 17 years old.
    Which one of the following situations is the BEST example of Endangering the Welfare of a Child?

A. John spanks his seven-year-old son because he has been misbehaving in school.
B. Linda slaps her sixteen-year-old brother for punishing her child.
C. Beverly leaves her four-year-old son unattended to go to a party in the next building.
D. Gary sends his twelve-year-old daughter to her room with no dinner for bringing home a bad report card.

15. Police Officer Clay responds to the scene of a found child where he obtains the following information:

Child's Name:	Craig Gildae
Age:	4 years
Location Found:	Wandering around in front of 501 E. 204th Street
Description:	Male, White, blond hair, blue eyes, wearing red overalls, white T-shirt, and blue high-top sneakers

Officer Clay is about to transmit this information to the radio dispatcher.
Which one of the following expresses the above information MOST clearly and accurately?

A. In front of 501 E. 204th Street a male White, Craig Gildae, was found wandering around with blond hair, blue eyes, wearing a white T-shirt, red overalls, and blue high-top sneakers. The child is four years old.
B. Four-year-old Craig Gildae was found wandering around in front of 501 E. 204th Street. He is a male, White, blond hair, blue eyes, wearing red overalls, a white T-shirt, and blue high-top sneakers.
C. A blond hair, blue-eyed male was found wandering around wearing red overalls, white T-shirt, and blue high-top sneakers. Four-year-old Craig Gildae was found in front of 501 E. 204th Street.
D. Found wandering around in front of 501 E. 204th Street male, White, with blond hair, blue eyes, wearing red overalls, white T-shirt, and blue high-top sneakers identified as four-year-old Craig Gildae.

16. The following details were obtained by Police Officer Jackson at the scene of a robbery:

Place of Occurrence:	Chambers Street, northbound A platform
Victim:	Mr. John Wells
Suspect:	Joseph Miller
Crime:	Robbery, armed with knife, wallet taken
Action Taken:	Suspect arrested

Officer Jackson is completing a report on the incident.
Which one of the following expresses the above information MOST clearly and accurately?

A. At Chambers Street northbound A platform Joseph Miller used a knife to remove the wallet of John Wells while waiting for the train. Police arrested him.
B. Mr. John Wells, while waiting for the northbound A train at Chambers Street, had his wallet forcibly removed at knifepoint by Joseph Miller. Joseph Miller was later arrested.
C. Joseph Miller was arrested for robbery. At Chambers Street John Wells stated that his wallet was taken. The incident occurred at knifepoint while waiting on a northbound A platform.
D. At the northbound Chambers Street platform, John Wells was waiting for the A train. Joseph Miller produced a knife and removed his wallet. He was arrested.

17. When a Police Officer stops a vehicle and discovers that the operator is driving with a suspended or revoked driver's license, the Officer should do the following in the order given:
    I. Confiscate the driver's license.
    II. Prepare a Seized Driver's License Report.
    III. Give operator of vehicle a receipt for license:
        A. If operator has two or more unrelated suspensions, or his license has been revoked for any reason, remove the motorist to the precinct of arrest and process a Desk Appearance Ticket.
        B. If operator has one or more suspensions regarding the same violation, a Universal Summons should be issued.
    III. Do not mark or mutilate license in any manner.
    IV. Have the violator's vehicle parked in a legal parking area until the registered owner can arrange to have the vehicle removed from the scene by a licensed operator.

    Police Officers Harris and Lowe are on patrol in their radio car when they stop a vehicle driven by Dennis Clarke. Clarke, whose license had been suspended once before for speeding, was driving over the speed limit. Officer Harris confiscates Clarke's license, prepares the required report, and issues him a receipt for his license.
    The NEXT thing Officer Harris should do is

    A. have Clarke park his vehicle in a legal parking area until he can arrange to have a licensed operator remove it
    B. issue Clarke a Universal Summons and have him drive his vehicle to his home
    C. remove Clarke to the precinct and process him for a Desk Appearance Ticket
    D. issue Clarke a Universal Summons and have his car parked in a legal parking area

18. Police Officer Hayes is informed by Sergeant Holt that drugs are being sold from autos on Officer Hayes post. He is directed to observe stopped vehicles if he believes the occupants' actions are suspicious.
    Which one of the following should Officer Hayes consider MOST suspicious?

    A. Two men sit in a parked auto in front of a schoolyard during recess and after school
    B. An auto drops off a man and then quickly speeds away
    C. A car service driver reads a newspaper and is parked in the same spot for 45 minutes
    D. Four teenagers sit in a parked convertible by a busy recreation area while listening to a radio

19. Upon uncovering illegal drugs during an investigation, Police Officers should do the following in the order given:
    I. Bring the drugs to the station house of the precinct where the discovery was made.
    II. Notify the Station House Officer.
    III. Prepare a Property Clerk's Invoice.
    IV. Request a laboratory analysis of the drugs.
    V. Mark the drugs for future identification.
    VI. Request specially secured envelopes from the Station House Officer.
    VII. Deliver the drugs to the laboratory.

In the course of a drug investigation in the 2nd Precinct, Police Officer Wells has come into possession of 100 vials of refined cocaine. He brought his find to the Station House Officer in the 2nd Precinct, filled out a Property Clerk's Invoice, and called for a laboratory analysis of the narcotics. He then labelled each individual vial so that the vials could be identified by other Officers if necessary. The NEXT step Officer Wells should take is to

- A. deliver the drugs to the laboratory
- B. consecutively number all the vials of cocaine with the Officer's initials
- C. ask the Station House Officer for specially secured envelopes
- D. prepare a request for a laboratory examination of the drugs

20. Theft of Services - occurs when a person intentionally fails to pay or avoids the payment of lawful charges for any public transportation service.
Which one of the following is the BEST example of Theft of Services?

- A. A shabbily dressed elderly man crawls under a turnstile in a subway station to retrieve a quarter he accidentally dropped. When a train pulls into the station, he retrieves the quarter and quickly gets on.
- B. In the middle of dinner at a restaurant, Tom and Janet complain about the quality of service. They refuse to pay their bill and immediately leave the restaurant and hail a taxi.
- C. Harry is driving home and pulls up to a toll booth to pay a quarter toll. Harry misses the coin box with the quarter and drives away.
- D. John hails a cab to take him to his office. When he arrives, he realizes that he has no cash with him and asks the cabdriver to wait while he gets some from his office safe.

21. Police Officer Bellows responds to a report of drugs being sold in the lobby of an apartment building. He obtains the following information at the scene:

Time of Occurrence:	11:30 P.M.
Place of Occurrence:	1010 Bath Avenue
Witnesses:	Mary Markham, John Silver
Suspect:	Harry Stoner
Crime:	Drug sales
Action Taken:	Suspect was gone when Police arrived

Officer Bellows is completing a report of the incident. Which one of the following expresses the above information MOST clearly and accurately?
- A. Mary Markham and John Silver witnessed drugs being sold and the suspect flee at 1010 Bath Avenue. Harry Stoner was conducting his business at 11:30 P.M. before Police arrival in the lobby.
- B. In the lobby, Mary Markham reported at 11:30 P.M. she saw Harry Stoner, along with John Silver, selling drugs. He ran from the lobby at 1010 Bath Avenue before Police arrived.
- C. John Silver and Mary Markham reported that they observed Harry Stoner selling drugs in the lobby of 1010 Bath Avenue at 11:30 P.M. The witnesses stated that Stoner fled before Police arrived.
- D. Before Police arrived, witnesses stated that Harry Stoner was selling drugs. At 1010 Bath Avenue, in the lobby, John Silver and Mary Markham said they observed his actions at 11:30 P.M.

22. While on patrol, Police Officer Fox receives a call to respond to a robbery. Upon arriving at the scene, he obtains the following information:

    Time of Occurrence: 6:00 P.M.
    Place of Occurrence: Sal's Liquor Store at 30 Fordham Road
    Victim: Sal Jones
    Suspect: White male wearing a beige parka
    Description of Crime: Victim was robbed in his store at gunpoint

    Officer Fox is completing a report on the incident.
    Which one of the following expresses the above information MOST clearly and accurately?

    A. I was informed at 6:00 P.M. by Sal Jones that an unidentified White male robbed him at gunpoint at 30 Fordham Road while wearing a beige parka at Sal's Liquor Store.
    B. At 6:00 P.M., Sal Jones was robbed at gunpoint in his store. An unidentified White male wearing a beige parka came into Sal's Liquor Store at 30 Fordham Road, he told me.
    C. I was informed at 6:00 P.M. while wearing a beige parka an unidentified White male robbed Sal Jones at gunpoint at Sal's Liquor Store at 30 Fordham Road.
    D. Sal Jones informed me that at 6:00 P.M. he was robbed at gunpoint in his store, Sal's Liquor Store, located at 30 Fordham Road, by an unidentified White male wearing a beige parka.

23. Police Officer Daily has been informed by Sergeant Newman that there have been three purse snatches on his post during the past two weeks. The description of each of the suspects is as follows:

    Incident No. 1 - Male, Black, 24 years old, 5'9", 185 lbs., scar on left side of face, blue dungarees, white sneakers, long brown hair, earring in right ear.
    Incident No. 2 - Male, Black, about 25 years old, 170 lbs., 5'9", long black hair, black dungarees, white sneakers, white tank top, scar on right side of face.
    Incident No. 3 - Male, Black, 27 to 30 years old, 5'8", 190 lbs., long curly hair, blue T-shirt, earring in left ear, black sneakers, black dungarees, tattoo on right arm.

    On April 20, Police Officer Daily arrested a suspect during an attempted purse snatch. The description of the suspect is as follows:

    Incident No. 4 - Male, Black, 5'9", 180 lbs., 23 years old, white tank top, white sneakers, long, straight brown hair, black dungarees, gold earring in right ear, scar on left side of face.

    Based on the above descriptions of the suspects in the first three incidents, Officer Daily could consider the suspect in the fourth purse snatching as a suspect in

    A. Incident No. 1 *only*
    B. Incident No. 3 *only*
    C. Incidents No. 1 and 2
    D. Incidents No. 2 and 3

24. Robbery - occurs when a person steals property by using or threatening the immediate use of physical force upon another person.
    Which one of the following is the BEST example of Robbery?

    A. Bill casually bumps into Raymond, removes Raymond's wallet from his back pocket, and runs away.
    B. Carol and John are approached by Marty, who takes their money after saying he would slash Carol's face with a knife.

C. Karen approaches Grace, who is sleeping on the train, slices her purse strap with a razor, grabs the purse, and walks away.
D. Fred threatens to find Peter's daughter and hurt her if Peter does not hand over his gold watch.

25. The following details were obtained by Police Officer Connors at the scene of a bank robbery:

    Time of Occurrence: 10:21 A.M.
    Place of Occurrence: Westbury Savings and Loan
    Crime: Bank Robbery
    Suspect: Male, dressed in black, wearing a black woolen ace mask
    Witness: Mary Henderson of 217 Westbury Avenue
    Amount Stolen: $6141 U.S. currency

    Officer Connors is completing a report on the incident. Which one of the following expresses the above information MOST clearly and accurately?

    A. At 10:21 A.M. the Westbury Savings and Loan was witnessed being robbed by Mary Henderson of 217 Westbury Avenue. The suspect fled dressed in black with a black woolen face mask. He left the bank with $6141 in U.S. currency.
    B. Dressed in black wearing a black woolen face mask, Mary Henderson of 217 Westbury Avenue saw a suspect flee with $6141 in U.S. currency after robbing the Westbury Savings and Loan. The robber was seen at 10:21 A.M.
    C. At 10:21 A.M., Mary Henderson, of 217 Westbury Avenue, witness to the robbery of the Westbury Savings and Loan, reports that a male, dressed in black, wearing a black face mask, did rob said bank and fled with $6141 in U.S. currency.
    D. Mary Henderson, of 217 Westbury Avenue, witnessed the robbery of the Westbury Savings and Loan at 10:21 A.M. The suspect, a male, was dressed in black and was wearing a black woolen face mask. He fled with $6141 in U.S. currency.

KEY (CORRECT ANSWERS)

1. C
2. A
3. A
4. D
5. C

6. D
7. A
8. C
9. B/C
10. A

11. A
12. D
13. C
14. C
15. B

16. B
17. D
18. A
19. C
20. A

21. C
22. D
23. A
24. B
25. D

TEST 2

DIRECTIONS: Each question or incomplete statement is followed by several suggested answers or completions. Select the one that BEST answers the question or completes the statement. *PRINT THE LETTER OF THE CORRECT ANSWER IN THE SPACE AT THE RIGHT.*

1. Police Officers sometimes have to make notifications to the Bureau of Child Welfare when they determine that a child may have been abused, maltreated, or neglected. In which one of the following cases would it be MOST appropriate for a Police Officer to notify the Bureau of Child Welfare?
   A

   A. woman is pulling a screaming child across the street while the traffic light is about to turn red against them
   B. man is spanking his son with his bare hands because his son refused to get out of the swimming pool when he was told to
   C. mother is cooking with hot oil while her children are running around in the kitchen. One bangs into the stove and burns his hand slightly.
   D. father is playing softball in the park while his infant takes a nap alone in their apartment

   1.____

2. At the scene of a dispute, Police Officer Johnson made an arrest after obtaining the following information:
   Place of Occurrence: 940 Baxter Avenue
   Time of Occurrence: 3:40 P.M.
   Victim: John Mitchell
   Suspect: Robert Holden, arrested at scene
   Crime: Menacing
   Weapon: Knife
   Time of Arrest: 4:00 P.M.
   Officer Johnson is completing a report of the incident.
   Which one of the following expresses the above information MOST clearly and accurately?

   A. John Mitchell was menaced by a knife at 940 Baxter Avenue. Robert Holden, owner of the weapon, was arrested at 4:00 P.M., twenty minutes later, at the scene.
   B. John Mitchell reports at 3:40 P.M. he was menaced at 940 Baxter Avenue by Robert Holden. He threatened him with his knife and was arrested at 4:00 P.M. at the scene.
   C. John Mitchell stated that at 3:40 P.M. at 940 Baxter Avenue he was menaced by Robert Holden, who was carrying a knife. Mr. Holden was arrested at the scene at 4:00 P.M.
   D. With a knife Robert Holden menaced John Mitchell at 3:40 P.M. The knife belonged to him and he was arrested at the scene of 940 Baxter Avenue at 4:00 P.M.

   2.____

117

3. Officer Nieves obtained the following information after he was called to the scene of a large gathering:

Time of Occurrence: 2:45 A.M.
Place of Occurrence: Mulberry Park
Complaint: Loud music
Complainant: Mrs. Simpkins, 42 Mulberry Street, Apartment 25
Action Taken: Police Officer dispersed the crowd

Officer Nieves is completing a report on the incident. Which one of the following expresses the above information MOST clearly and accurately?

A. Mrs. Simpkins, who lives at 42 Mulberry Street, Apartment 25, called the Police to make a complaint. A large crowd of people were playing loud music in Mulberry Park at 2:45 A.M. Officer Nieves responded and dispersed the crowd.
B. Officer Nieves responded to Mulberry Park because Mrs. Simpkins, the complainant, lives at 42 Mulberry Street, Apartment 25. Due to a large crowd of people who were playing loud music at 2:45 A.M., he immediately dispersed the crowd.
C. Due to a large crowd of people who were playing loud music in Mulberry Park at 2:45 A.M., Officer Nieves responded and dispersed the crowd. Mrs. Simpkins called the Police and complained. She lives at 42 Mulberry Street, Apartment 25.
D. Responding to a complaint by Mrs. Simpkins, who resides at 42 Mulberry Street, Apartment 25, Officer Nieves dispersed a large crowd in Mulberry Park. They were playing loud music. It was 2:45 A.M.

4. While patrolling the subway, Police Officer Clark responds to the scene of a past robbery where he obtains the following information:

Place of Occurrence: Northbound E train
Time of Occurrence: 6:30 P.M.
Victim: Robert Brey
Crime: Wallet and jewelry taken
Suspects: 2 male Whites armed with knives

Officer Clark is completing a report on the incident.
Which one of the following expresses the above information MOST clearly and accurately?

A. At 6:30 P.M. Robert Brey reported he was robbed of his wallet and jewelry. On the northbound E train, two White males approached Mr. Brey. They threatened him before taking his property with knives.
B. While riding the E train northbound, two White men approached Robert Brey at 6:30 P.M. They threatened him with knives and took his wallet and jewelry.
C. Robert Brey was riding the E train at 6:30 P.M. when he was threatened by two Whites. The men took his wallet and jewelry as he was traveling northbound.
D. Robert Brey reports at 6:30 P.M. he lost his wallet to two White men as well as his jewelry. They were carrying knives and threatened him aboard the northbound E train.

5. Whenever a Police Officer responds to the scene of a family offense, the Officer should do the following in the order given:
   I. Obtain medical assistance if requested or need is apparent.
   II. Determine if:
      A. A crime has been committed; or
      B. An Order of Protection has been obtained by complainant.

III. Arrest offender if a crime has been committed.

Police Officers Harley and Morris are dispatched to the scene of a family dispute at 734 E. 180th Street, Apartment 2E. As the Officers enter the apartment, they see a man and a woman struggling on the floor while cursing at each other. The Officers immediately separate the two, who are identified as Herbert and Mary Jones. Officer Harley attempts to question the two individuals to determine what happened, while Officer Morris keeps them separated. Both parties blame each other for starting the fight. Although neither spouse seems to be physically hurt, Mrs. Jones insists she be examined by a doctor. What should the Officers do NEXT?

    A. Call for medical assistance.
    B. Arrest Mr. Jones for committing the offense.
    C. Find out if Mrs. Jones has obtained an Order of Protection.
    D. Determine whether a family offense has been committed by either spouse.

Questions 6-9.

DIRECTIONS: Questions 6 through 9 are to be answered SOLELY on the basis of the following passage.

While returning to the 15th Precinct from court, Police Officer Moody encountered an armed robbery in progress outside of 238 Madison Street. When the perpetrator saw the Officer, he fled into the building and attempted to enter the second floor apartment of Maria Vasquez. Ms. Vasquez had previously opened the door when she heard the noise downstairs. When Ms. Vasquez saw the perpetrator approaching her with a gun in his hand, she immediately closed and locked the door. Since the perpetrator was not able to gain entrance to the apartment, he jumped out of the hallway window and hid in the courtyard. When Officer Moody arrived at the bottom of the second floor stairway, he heard Ms. Vasquez crying hysterically from inside the apartment. He banged on the door and called to her to see if she was all right. Ms. Vasquez did not speak English and, thinking it was the perpetrator, she refused to open the door. As a result, Officer Moody assumed that the woman was being held hostage by the perpetrator. Officer Moody immediately stepped away from the door, advised the radio dispatcher of the circumstances, and requested back-up assistance.

Every sector car in the precinct responded to assist Officer Moody; and each, with the exception of sectors Adam and Charlie, took up a strategic location outside of the building. Officers O'Connor and Torres, of sector Adam, went up to the second floor to guard the apartment door with Officer Moody. Officer Perez, of sector Charlie, went up to the roof. Officer Donadio, also of sector Charlie, started to enter the courtyard when he observed the perpetrator hiding in the bushes. Officer Donadio quickly took cover behind the cement wall entrance of the courtyard and ordered the perpetrator at gunpoint to surrender. The perpetrator surrendered his weapon and allowed himself to be easily apprehended. Officer Donadio then advised the other Officers by radio that the perpetrator was in custody and that Ms. Vasquez was not being held hostage.

6. Which Officer went up to the roof?

    A. O'Connor   B. Perez   C. Donadio   D. Moody

7. Officer Moody chased the perpetrator because he

   A. was trying to get into the apartment of Maria Vasquez
   B. was holding Maria Vasquez hostage
   C. was attempting to commit an armed robbery
   D. jumped out the second floor hallway window

8. Which Officer was NOT on the second floor?

   A. Moody   B. Torres   C. O'Connor   D. Donadio

9. While Officer Moody was standing at the bottom of the stairs, the suspect was

   A. in Ms. Vasquez's apartment
   B. in the courtyard
   C. on the roof
   D. on the second floor fire escape

10. *Police Officers must sometimes rely on eyewitness accounts of incidents, even though eyewitnesses may make mistakes with regard to some details.*
    While coming from the bank, Sal Shure was mugged and killed at the corner of W. 238th Street and Oxford Avenue. Police Officer Farris responds to the scene and questions four witnesses who saw the person that killed Shure. The following are descriptions of the suspect given by the witnesses.
    Which one of these descriptions should Officer Farris consider MOST likely to be correct?
    Male,

    A. White, 5'9", 185 lbs., brown hair, black eyes
    B. Hispanic, 5'11", 175 lbs., brown hair, brown eyes
    C. White, 5'10", 190 lbs., black hair, hazel eyes
    D. White, 5'11", 190 lbs., brown hair, brown eyes

11. Police Officer Johnson has just finished investigating a report of a burglary and has obtained the following information:
    Place of Occurrence: Victim's residence
    Time of Occurrence: Between 8:13 P.M. and 4:15 A.M.
    Victim: Paul Mason of 1264 Twentieth Street, Apartment 3D
    Crime: Burglary
    Damage: Filed front door lock
    Officer Johnson is preparing a report of the incident. Which one of the following expresses the above information MOST clearly and accurately?

    A. Paul Mason's residence was burglarized at 1264 Twentieth Street, Apartment 3D, between 8:13 P.M. and 4:15 A.M. by filing the front door lock.
    B. Paul Mason was burglarized by filing the front door lock and he lives at 1264 Twentieth Street, Apartment 3D, between 8:13 P.M. and 4:15 A.M.
    C. Between 8:13 P.M. and 4:15 A.M. the residence of Paul Mason, located at 1264 Twentieth Street, Apartment 3D, was burglarized after the front door lock was filed.
    D. Between 8:13 P.M. and 4:15 A.M., at 1264 Twentieth Street, Apartment 3D, after the front door lock was filed, the residence of Paul Mason was burglari

12. Grand Larceny 4th Degree - occurs when a person steals property and when the
    I. value of the property is greater than one thousand dollars; or
    II. property consists of secret scientific material; or
    III. property consists of a credit card; or
    IV. property, regardless of its nature and value, is taken from the body or clothing of another person; or
    V. property, regardless of its nature and value, is obtained through fear.

    Which one of the following is the BEST example of Grand Larceny in the Fourth Degree?

    A. Jim finds a briefcase on the downtown E train. Inside the briefcase, he notices an envelope which contains $900.00. He removes the money from the envelope and exits the train, leaving the briefcase behind.
    B. Jane finds a wallet on the street which contains several papers and an American Express card, which she sends back to the company.
    C. Bruce, a gang member, goes into an all-night produce market and orders the owner, Mr. Wong, to pay him $50.00 for protection or his store will be destroyed. Mr. Wong refuses and dials 911 as Bruce flees from the store.
    D. Without Elaine's knowledge, Grace removes a costume jewelry bracelet valued at about $15.00 from Elaine's wrist.

13. Police Officer Lowell has just finished investigating a burglary and has received the following information:

    Place of Occurrence: 117-12 Sutphin Boulevard
    Time of Occurrence: Between 9:00 A.M. and 5:00 P.M.
    Victim: Mandee Cotton
    Suspects: Unknown

    Officer Lowell is completing a report on this incident.
    Which one of the following expresses the above information MOST clearly and accurately?

    A. Mandee Cotton reported that her home was burglarized between 9:00 A.M. and 5:00 P.M. Ms. Cotton resides at 117-12 Sutphin Boulevard. Suspects are unknown.
    B. A burglary was committed at 117-12 Sutphin Boulevard reported Mandee Cotton between 9:00 A.M. and 5:00 P.M. Ms. Cotton said unknown suspects burglarized her home.
    C. Unknown suspects burglarized a home at 117-12 Sutphin Boulevard between 9:00 M. and 5:00 P.M. Mandee Cotton, homeowner, reported.
    D. Between the hours of 9:00 A.M. and 5:00 P.M. it was reported that 117-12 Sutphin Boulevard was burglarized. Mandee Cotton reported that unknown suspects are responsible.

14. When a prisoner in custody requires medical or psychiatric treatment, a Police Officer should do the following in the order given:
    I. Request an ambulance and remove prisoner to hospital directly from place of arrest, if necessary.
        A. Accompany prisoner to hospital.
        B. Notify Desk Officer.
    II. Handcuff prisoner, hands in rear, before transporting.
    III. Remain with prisoner at all times in hospital.

IV. Request room change if security is inadequate.
V. Do not remove handcuffs, unless requested by attending physician.
VI. Remain immediately outside room and attempt to maintain visual contact, even if requested to leave examination room after informing physican of circumstances of arrest.

Police Officer Schultz calls for an ambulance to remove a prisoner from the precinct to Grant Hospital's Emergency Room due to chest pains which the prisoner is experiencing. The Desk Officer, Lt. Collins, orders Officer Schultz to ride in the ambulance with the prisoner and reminds him to rearcuff the prisoner before removing him from the holding cell. Officer Schultz does so and escorts the prisoner into the ambulance. When they arrive at the hospital, Officer Schultz questions Dr. Carson about the security status of the Emergency Room. Dr. Carson informs Officer Schultz that they haven't had any problems since the hospital opened ten years ago. Officer Schultz's NEXT step should be to

A. remove the prisoner's handcuffs to allow Dr. Carson to examine him
B. describe the details of the prisoner's arrest to Dr. Carson
C. keep an eye on the prisoner if requested to leave the examining room by Dr. Carson
D. ask Dr. Carson to examine prisoner in a more secure location in the hospital

15. Under certain circumstances, Police Officers are authorized to search a person suspected of having committed a crime.
Which one of the following people would a Police Officer MOST likely search?
A

A. person who is suspected by a store owner of selling watches on the street without a license
B. motorist who is stopped by a Traffic Enforcement Agent for going through a red light
C. poorly dressed man who is obviously intoxicated staggering down the street
D. man who is recognized by a woman as being recently involved in an armed robbery

16. Larceny - occurs when a person, without the use or threat of force, wrongfully takes, obtains, or withholds property from the owner.
Robbery - occurs when a person uses, or threatens the immediate use of, force on the victim or on another person in the course of stealing property.
Burglary - occurs when a person knowingly and unlawfully enters or remains in a building with intent to commit a crime therein.
Kevin Watts follows Jane Robinson, his ex-girlfriend, to her home one night after work and decides that he wants to make her pay for breaking off their engagement. While Jane is in the kitchen preparing her dinner, Kevin climbs up the fire escape and enters her bedroom through the window. He then threatens to beat Jane *to a pulp* if she tries to stop him from taking her cash, jewelry, and television set. Kevin takes her property and leaves. In this situation, Watts should be charged with

A. Burglary and Larceny
B. Burglary and Robbery
C. Robbery and Larceny
D. Robbery, Burglary, and Larceny

17. Police Officer Dale has just finished investigating a report of attempted theft and has obtained the following information:

    Place of Occurrence: In front of 103 W. 105th Street
    Time of Occurrence: 11:30 A.M.
    Victim: Mary Davis
    Crime: Attempted theft
    Suspect: Male, Black, scar on right side of face
    Action Taken: Drove victim around area to locate suspect

    Officer Dale is preparing a report on the incident.
    Which one of the following expresses the above information MOST clearly and accurately?

    A. Mary Davis was standing in front of 103 W. 105th Street when Officer Dale arrived after an attempt to steal her pocketbook failed at 11:30 A.M. Officer Dale canvassed the area looking for a Black male with a scar on the right side of his face with Ms. Davis in the patrol car.
    B. Mary Davis stated that, at 11:30 A.M., she was standing in front of 103 W. 105th Street when a Black male with a scar on the right side of his face attempted to steal her pocketbook. Officer Dale canvassed the area with Ms. Davis in the patrol car.
    C. Officer Dale canvassed the area by putting Mary Davis in a patrol car looking for a Black male with a scar on the right side of his face. At 11:30 A.M. in front of 103 W. 105th Street she said he attempted to steal her pocketbook.
    D. At 11:30 A.M., in front of 103 W. 105th Street, Officer Dale canvassed the area with Mary Davis in a patrol car who said that a Black male with a scar on the right side of his face attempted to steal her pocketbook.

18. While on patrol, Police Officer Santoro received a call to respond to the scene of a shooting. The following details were obtained at the scene:

    Time of Occurrence: 4:00 A.M.
    Place of Occurrence: 232 Senator Street
    Victim: Mike Nisman
    Suspect: Howard Conran
    Crime: Shooting
    Witness: Sheila Morris

    Officer Santoro is completing a report on the incident. Which one of the following expresses the above information MOST clearly and accurately?

    A. Sheila Norris stated at 4:00 A.M. she witnessed a shooting of her neighbor in front of her building. Howard Conran shot Mike Nisman and ran from 232 Senator Street.
    B. Mike Nisman was the victim of a shooting incident seen by his neighbor. At 4:00 M. Sheila Norris saw Howard Conran shoot him and run in front of their building. Norris and Nisman reside at 232 Senator Street.
    C. Sheila Norris states that at 4:00 A.M. she witnessed Howard Conran shoot Mike Nisman, her neighbor, in front of their building at 232 Senator Street. She further states she saw the suspect running from the scene.
    D. Mike Nisman was shot by Howard Conran at 4:00 A.M. His neighbor, Sheila Norris, witnessed him run from the scene in front of their building at 232 Senator Street.

19. When a Police Officer arrives at a scene where there is a dead human body, the Officer should do the following in the order given:
    I. Request an ambulance and a patrol supervisor.
    II. Exclude unauthorized persons from the scene.
    III. Obtain the names of witnesses and keep them at the scene if the death is suspicious.
    IV. Screen the area from public view, if possible.
    V. Cover the body with waterproof covering, if publicly exposed.

    Police Officer Wong is dispatched to 365 E. 52nd Street. Upon arriving, he sees a man who is apparently dead and lying face down in an alley behind the building. Officer Wong immediately calls for an ambulance and his patrol supervisor. While waiting, the Officer notices that a large crowd is beginning to gather around the uncovered body. The NEXT step Officer Wong should take is to

    A. cover the body with a waterproof covering
    B. keep unauthorized people away from the scene
    C. screen the area from public view
    D. obtain the names of witnesses

20. Police Officer Taylor responds to the scene of a serious traffic accident in which a car struck a telephone pole, and obtains the following information:

    Place of Occurrence: Intersection of Rock Street and Amboy Place
    Time of Occurrence: 3:27 A.M.
    Name of Injured: Carlos Black
    Driver of Car: Carlos Black
    Action Taken: Injured taken to Beth-El Hospital

    Officer Taylor is preparing a report on the accident. Which one of the following expresses the above information MOST clearly and accurately?

    A. At approximately 3:27 A.M. Carlos Black drove his car into a telephone pole located at the intersection of Rock Street and Amboy Place. Mr. Black, who was the only person injured, was taken to Beth-El Hospital.
    B. Carlos Black, injured at the intersection of Rock Street and Amboy Place, hit a telephone pole. He was taken to Beth-El Hospital after the car accident which occurred at 3:27 A.M.
    C. At the intersection of Rock Street and Amboy Place, Carlos Black injured himself and was taken to Beth-El Hospital. His car hit a telephone pole at 3:27 A.M.
    D. At the intersection of Rock Street and Amboy Place at 3:27 A.M., Carlos Black was taken to Beth-El Hospital after injuring himself by driving into a telephone pole.

21. While on patrol in the Jefferson Housing Projects, Police Officer Johnson responds to the scene of a Grand Larceny. The following information was obtained by Officer Johnson:

    Time of Occurrence: 6:00 P.M.
    Place of Occurrence: Rear of Building 12A
    Victim: Maria Lopez
    Crime: Purse snatched
    Suspect: Unknown

    Officer Johnson is preparing a report on the incident.
    Which one of the following expresses the above information MOST clearly and accurately?

A. At the rear of Building 12A, at 6:00 P.M., by an unknown suspect, Maria Lopez reported her purse snatched in the Jefferson Housing Projects.
B. Maria Lopez reported that at 6:00 P.M. her purse was snatched by an unknown suspect at the rear of Building 12A in the Jefferson Housing Projects.
C. At the rear of Building 12A, Maria Lopez reported at 6:00 P.M. that her purse had been snatched by an unknown suspect in the Jefferson Housing Projects.
D. In the Jefferson Housing Projects, Maria Lopez reported at the rear of Building 12A that her purse had been snatched by an unknown suspect at 6:00 P.M.

22. Criminal Possession of Stolen Property 2nd Degree - occurs when a person knowingly possesses stolen property with intent to benefit himself or a person other than the owner, or to prevent its recovery by the owner, and when the
    I. value of the property exceeds two hundred fifty dollars; or
    II. property consists of a credit card; or
    III. person is a pawnbroker or is in the business of buying, selling, or otherwise dealing in property; or
    IV. property consists of one or more firearms, rifles, or shotguns.

    Which one of the following is the BEST example of Criminal Possession of Stolen Property in the Second Degree?

    A. Mary knowingly buys a stolen camera valued at $225.00 for her mother's birthday.
    B. John finds a wallet containing $100.00 and various credit cards. John keeps the money and turns the credit cards in at his local precinct.
    C. Mr. Varrone, a pawnbroker, refuses to buy Mr. Cutter's stolen VCR valued at $230.00.
    D. Mr. Aquista, the owner of a toy store, knowingly buys a crate of stolen water pistols valued at $260.00.

23. Police Officer Dale has just finished investigating a report of menacing and obtained the following information:
    Time of Occurrence: 10:30 P.M.
    Place of Occurrence: (Hallway) 77 Hill Street
    Victim: Grace Jackson
    Suspect: Susan, White female, 30 years of age
    Crime: Menacing with a knife

    Officer Dale is preparing a report on the incident.
    Which one of the following expresses the above information MOST clearly and accurately?

    A. At 10:30 P.M., Grace Jackson was stopped in the hallway of 77 Hill Street by a 30-year-old White female known to Grace as Susan. Susan put a knife to Grace's throat and demanded that Grace stay out of the building or Susan would hurt her.
    B. Grace Jackson was stopped in the hallway at knifepoint and threatened to stay away from the building located at 77 Hill Street. The female who is 30 years of age known as Susan by Jackson stopped her at 10:30 P.M.
    C. At 10:30 P.M. in the hallway of 77 Hill Street Grace Jackson reported a White female 30 years of age put a knife to her throat. She knew her as Susan and demanded she stay away from the building or she would get hurt.
    D. A White female 30 years of age known to Grace Jackson as Susan stopped her in the hallway of 77 Hill Street. She put a knife to her throat and at 10:30 P.M. demanded she stay away from the building or she would get hurt.

24. Police Officer Bennett responds to the scene of a car accident and obtains the following information from the witness:

    Time of Occurrence: 3:00 A.M.
    Victim: Joe Morris, removed to Methodist
    Hospital Crime: Struck pedestrian and left the scene of accident
    Description of Auto: Blue 1988 Thunderbird, license plate BOT-3745

    Officer Bennett is preparing an Accident Report. Which one of the following expresses the above information MOST clearly and accurately?

    A. Joe Morris, a pedestrian, was hit at 3:00 A.M. and removed to Methodist Hospital. Also a blue Thunder-bird, 1988 model left the scene, license plate BOT-3745.
    B. A pedestrian was taken to Methodist Hospital after being struck at 3:00 A.M. A blue automobile was seen leaving the scene with license plate BOT-3745. Joe Morris was knocked down by a 1988 Thunderbird.
    C. At 3:00 A.M. Joe Morris, a pedestrian, was struck by a blue 1988 Thunderbird. The automobile, license plate BOT-3745, left the scene. Mr. Morris was taken to Methodist Hospital.
    D. Joe Morris, a pedestrian at 3:00 A.M. was struck by a Thunderbird. A 1988 model, license plate BOT-3745, blue in color, left the scene and the victim was taken to Methodist Hospital.

25. <u>Burglary</u> - occurs when a person knowingly enters or remains unlawfully in a building with the intent to commit a crime therein.
    Which one of the following situations is the BEST example of Burglary?

    A. John Moss, an employee at the Forever Toys Warehouse, enters the locked warehouse at 10:30 P.M. through an open window in order to get his wallet, which he had forgotten in his desk when he left work at 5:30 P.M.
    B. Mary Hargrove, not wanting to walk around the block to get to the train station, decides to take a shortcut by slipping through a hole in the fence and walking across a field. There are signs posted which state that the field is a restricted area and unauthorized persons would be prosecuted. Although Hargrove is not authorized to be on the property, she continues anyway.
    C. Wayne Moore, after being locked out of his home by his wife, goes to a neighbor's house in the hope that he would be able to spend the night. Although the neighbors are not home, Moore notices that a window leading to the basement is unlocked. He climbs through the window and falls asleep on a basement sofa.
    D. Harold Weeks decides to steal from an antique store valuable items which he will later sell. Weeks enters the premises by picking the lock on the back door and is confronted by the owner before he is able to take anything.

KEY (CORRECT ANSWERS)

1. D
2. C
3. A
4. B
5. A

6. B
7. C
8. D
9. B
10. D

11. C
12. D
13. A
14. B
15. D

16. B
17. B
18. C
19. B
20. A

21. B
22. D
23. A
24. C
25. D

TEST 3

DIRECTIONS: Each question or incomplete statement is followed by several suggested answers or completions. Select the one that BEST answers the question or completes the statement. *PRINT THE LETTER OF THE CORRECT ANSWER IN THE SPACE AT THE RIGHT.*

Questions 1-3.

DIRECTIONS: Questions 1 through 3 are to be answered SOLELY on the basis of the following passage.

Police Officer Berman has been assigned to a steady post from Hartman Boulevard to Bement Street on Forest Avenue for the past two years. Officer Berman's duties involve walking along Forest Avenue and in and out of stores talking with the people on his post to ensure that everything is all right. While on duty at 11:30 on Saturday morning, Officer Berman walks into Pete Arturo's Boutique, which is normally filled with female customers because of the type of merchandise sold there. Today, the Officer sees only three young men in the store. Officer Berman looks around and notices that Pete is not in sight. Officer Berman notices a thin man whom he has never seen behind the register. Officer Berman decides to ask for Mrs. Arturo, knowing that Pete is not married, because he suspects that something is wrong. The thin man replies with a smile, *She will be in a little later.* Officer Berman then walks out of the boutique and calls for back-up assistance on a possible robbery in progress. At 11:40, Police Officers Fernandez and Heck arrive at the side of Arturo's Boutique. Five minutes later, Police Officer Jones arrives in his scooter. The Officers are now waiting for a Supervisor to arrive so they can proceed with the plan of action, which they have already discussed. Two minutes after Officer Jones arrives, Sgt. Demond pulls up with his driver, Police Officer Ricco, and gathers all of the information. Sgt. Demond then calls the boutique by phone, identifies himself, and advises the man who answers to give himself up so that nobody will get hurt. Sgt. Demond also tells the man on the phone that he has the store surrounded and will give them five minutes to surrender. The three men walk out of the boutique with Mr. Arturo, who is unharmed. Officer Berman recovers three loaded .38 caliber revolvers from the suspects.

1. How many Police personnel responded to Officer Berman's call for assistance?   1._____
    A. Four   B. Five   C. Six   D. Seven

2. At what time did Sergeant Demond arrive at the boutique? _____ A.M.   2._____
    A. 11:40   B. 11:42   C. 11:45   D. 11:47

3. Which of the following Officers arrived in the scooter?   3._____
    A. Berman   B. Fernandez   C. Jones   D. Heck

Questions 4-6.

DIRECTIONS: Questions 4 through 6 are to be answered SOLELY on the basis of the following information.

Police Officer Keenan has been ordered to improve the traffic flow on his post by issuing summonses on West 231st Street from Maple Lane to Kingsway Avenue. Officer Keenan has noticed that, between 8:00 A.M. and 10:00 A.M. at W. 231st Street and Maple Lane, cars park in the bus stop on the north side of the street. This has forced the buses to stop in the middle of the street, blocking traffic for several minutes at a time. In addition, from 10:00 A.M. to 3:00 P.M., cars doublepark on both sides of W. 231st Street from Maple Lane to Kingsway Avenue, which slows the traffic throughout the day. Officer Keenan has also noticed that from 4:00 P.M. to 6:00 P.M., cars park in the bus stop on the south side of W. 231st Street and Kingsway Avenue, again forcing the buses to stop in the middle of the street.

4. Officer Keenan would be MOST effective at improving the traffic condition between 8:00 M. and 9:00 A.M. by issuing summonses 4._____

   A. between Kingsway Avenue and Maple Lane
   B. on the north side of W. 231st Street and Maple Lane
   C. on the south side of W. 231st Street and Maple Lane
   D. between Kingsway Avenue and W. 231st Street

5. In order to keep traffic flowing between Noon and 1:00 P.M., Officer Keenan should issue summonses on 5._____

   A. the north side of Kingsway Avenue
   B. both sides of Maple Lane
   C. both sides of W. 231st Street
   D. the south side of Kingsway Avenue

6. To keep traffic flowing between 5:00 P.M. and 6:00 P.M., Officer Keenan should issue summonses on the _____ side of W. 231st Street and _____ . 6._____

   A. south; Kingsway Avenue   B. south; Maple Lane
   C. north; Kingsway Avenue   D. north; Maple Lane

Questions 7-9.

DIRECTIONS: Questions 7 through 9 are to be answered SOLELY on the basis of the following passage.

Police Officer Smith was reassigned to the Parkhill Housing Complex, which consists of nine 8-story buildings. He was told that nine rapes had occurred in the last eight days in the complex and all had taken place between 9:00 A.M. and 6:00 P.M. On May 2, Officer Smith was working the 10:00 A.M. to 6:00 P.M. shift. At the beginning of Officer Smith's shift, his Supervisor, Sergeant Larry, gave him the suspected rapist's description, which had been obtained on April 27 from Nancy Lewis, one of the rape victims. The suspect was described as a male, Black, 6'2", approximately 210 lbs., having a light complexion and the word *Budda* tattooed on his left forearm.

While on patrol several blocks from the Parkhill Complex at Noon of the same day, Officer Smith was called by the dispatcher and told to respond to a complaint at 110 Park Avenue, Apartment 3C, located in the complex. Upon his arrival at the apartment, he was met by Mary Wilson, who told him that her 16-year-old daughter Tammy had just been raped in the building elevator. Tammy stated that when she entered her building, a Black male, approximately 26 years old, about 6'1", wearing a suit, had been waiting for the elevator. She also told Officer Smith that when she entered the elevator with this man, he forced her to the floor, raped her, and pushed her out of the elevator on the 7th floor.

On May 3, at 8:00 A.M., an individual fitting the descriptio given by Ms. Lewis was apprehended in front of 55 Hill Street, another building in the Parkhill Complex. The suspect's name was John Jones. At 12:30 P.M. of the same day, Ms. Wilson and Ms. Le went to the Precinct station house and identified John Jones as the person who raped them.

7. Who was the FIRST person to give Officer Smith a description of the rapist?

    A. Sergeant Larry
    B. Tammy Wilson
    C. Mary Wilson
    D. Nancy Lewis

8. Where was Tammy Wilson raped?

    A. In the elevator at 55 Hill Street
    B. On the 5th floor at 110 Park Avenue
    C. In the elevator at 110 Park Avenue
    D. On the 7th floor at 55 Hill Street

9. John Jones was apprehended the

    A. same day as the rape of Nancy Lewis
    B. day after the rape of Nancy Lewis
    C. same day as the rape of Tammy Wilson
    D. day after the rape of Tammy Wilson

10. At 11:30 A.M., Police Officers Newman and Johnson receive a radio call to respond to a reported robbery. The Officers obtained the following information:
    Time of Occurrence: 11:20 A.M.
    Place of Occurrence: Twenty-four hour newsstand at 2024 86th Street
    Victim: Sam Norris, owner
    Amount Stolen: $450.00
    Suspects: Two male Whites
    Officer Newman is completing a complaint report on the incident.
    Which one of the following expresses the above information MOST clearly and accurately?

    A. At 11:20 A.M. it was reported by the newsstand owner that two male Whites robbed $450.00 from Sam Norris. The Twenty-four hour newsstand is located at 2024 86th Street.
    B. At 11:20 A.M., Sam Norris, the newsstand owner, reported that the Twenty-four hour newsstand located at 2024 86th Street was robbed by two male Whites who took $450.00.
    C. Sam Norris, the owner of the Twenty-four hour newsstand located at 2024 86th Street, reported that at 11:20 A.M. two White males robbed his newsstand of $450.00.
    D. Sam Norris reported at 11:20 A.M. that $450.00 had been taken from the owner of the Twenty-four hour newsstand located at 2024 86th Street by two male Whites.

11. Police Officers are often required to handle cases where the occupant of a residence has died. Upon arrival at the scene of a dead human body, Police Officers should do the following in the order given:
    I. Request an ambulance and patrol supervisor to respond.
    II. Determine if the death is suspicious or of natural causes.

III. Determine facts and notify the Desk Officer as soon as possible.
IV. Notify station house and get aided and complaint report numbers.
V. Notify medical examiner and get log number.
VI. Notify precinct Detective Unit.
VII. If apparent homicide or suicide, notify Crime Scene Unit.

Police Officer Casin and his Supervisor, Sergeant Velez, are in Apartment 1-H at 3333 Hudson Parkway. The occupant of the apartment, Tom Acheson, age 65, is lying face up on the kitchen floor, dead. The ambulance attendant is present and informs the Sergeant that the occupant died of natural causes and has probably been dead for about four days. Officer Berberich arrives on the scene, and Sgt. Velez gives Officer Berberich the above information, instructing him to make the proper notifications. Which one of the following should Officer Berberich notify FIRST? The

A. Desk Officer
B. precinct Detective Unit
C. occupant's immediate family
D. medical examiner

12. While on patrol, Police Officer Adams is dispatched to investigate a reported burglary. When he arrives, Officer Adams is informed by Ms. Bond, an artist, that when she returned home from an appointment, she found that her front door had been forced open and the following pieces of her artwork were missing:

3 Sculptures, each valued at	$2000.00
2 Oil paintings, each valued at	$ 500.00
1 Ceramic vase, valued at	$ 375.00
1 Portrait, valued at	$2500.00
2 Small watercolors, each valued at	$ 75.00

In addition to the artwork, Ms. Bond told Officer Adams that a brooch and bracelet, each valued at $250.00, and $50.00 in cash were also missing.
Officer Adams is preparing a Complaint Report on the burglary.
Which one of the following is the TOTAL value of the property and cash stolen?

A. $5,450   B. $5,750   C. $10,325   D. $10,575

13. Police Officers are often required to respond to the scene of a serious crime, such as robbery, rape, or burglary. When a Police Officer responds to a crime scene, he should do the following in the order given:
    I. Interview the complainant and witnesses, obtain the facts, and gather evidence.
    II. Conduct a thorough field investigation.
    III. Prepare a Complaint Report.
    IV. Determine if the complaint should be closed or referred for further investigation.

Police Officers Pastorino and Longo are driving down Longwood Avenue near Snyder Street while on patrol. They notice that a woman, later identified as Grace Thomas, is lying on the sidewalk in front of 1237 Snyder Street. Officer Pastorino approaches her, notices that she has sustained a minor stab wound on her left arm, and radios for an ambulance. Officer Longo then asks the victim to explain what happened. She tells him that she has just been robbed and assaulted and gives a description of the suspect. Meanwhile, Officer Pastorino searches the area thoroughly and finds a knife but no witnesses. The NEXT step that the Officers should take is to

A. prepare a Complaint Report
B. determine if the complaint should be closed or referred for further investigation
C. conduct a thorough field investigation
D. interview the complainant and witnesses

14. <u>Dwelling</u> - a building which is usually occupied by a person lodging there at night.
<u>Burglary 1st Degree</u> - occurs when a person knowingly enters or remains unlawfully in a dwelling at night with the intent to commit a crime therein, and when, while entering or while in the dwelling, or in immediate flight therefrom, he or another participant in the crime:
   I. Is armed with explosives or a deadly weapon; or
   II. Causes physical injury to any person who is not a participant in the crime; or
   III. Uses or threatens the immediate use of a dangerous instrument; or
   IV. Displays what appears to be a pistol, revolver, rifle, shotgun, machine gun, or other firearm.

Which one of the following situations is the BEST example of Burglary in the First Degree?

A. Sam enters Joanne's apartment by breaking the lock on her door in order to get warm during the cold weather.
B. Ernest remains in Doreen's Department Store after store hours and removes five diamond rings from the showcase. On his way out, he injures a security guard who tries to apprehend him.
C. Roger enters the courtyard of a large apartment building and breaks a bedroom window with the butt of his pistol in order to gain entry. The tenant awakens moments later and sees Roger leaving through the window with her VCR.
D. At 2:00 A.M. on a Sunday, Kevin enters Tom's 24-Hour Deli, removes two cases of beer without paying for them, and runs to an awaiting vehicle.

15. While on patrol, Police Officers Carter and Popps receive a call to respond to an assault in progress. Upon arrival, they receive the following information:

Place of Occurrence:	27 Park Avenue
Victim:	John Dee
Suspect:	Michael Jones
Crime:	Stabbing during a fight
Action Taken:	Suspect arrested

The Officers are completing a report on the incident.
Which one of the following expresses the above information MOST clearly and accurately?

A. In front of 27 Park Avenue, Michael Jones was arrested for stabbing John Dee during a fight.
B. Michael Jones was arrested for stabbing John Dee during a fight in front of 27 Park Avenue.
C. During a fight, Michael Jones was arrested for stabbing John Dee in front of 27 Park Avenue.
D. John Dee was stabbed by Michael Jones, who was arrested for fighting in front of 27 Park Avenue.

16. When a child under ten years of age is reported to be missing, a Police Officer should:
    I. Respond to the scene and interview the complainant in order to obtain details, including an accurate description of the child and the location where last seen.
    II. Notify Desk Officer of details.
    III. Start an immediate search for the child.
    IV. Request Patrol Supervisor to respond.

Police Officers Cippillone and Carey are dispatched to 2501 Richmond Road to investigate a report of a missing child. When the Officers arrive at the location, they are told by Mr. and Mrs. Williams that their eight-year-old daughter Jill was due back from her friend's house three hours ago and she has still not returned. The Williams describe Jill as 4'3" tall, having brown hair, green eyes, and weighing 60 lbs. She was wearing a yellow dress and a white sweater when she left home. The Officers ask the Williams for the name and address of Jill's friends, particularly the last one she had visited. After obtaining this information, the Officers notify their Desk Officer and begin a thorough search for Jill. After a half hour, Officer Carey finds Jill inside a nearby candy store and returns her to her parents' home. Officer Cippillone informs the Desk Officer of the situation, and both Officers go back out on patrol. In this situation, the actions taken by the Officers were

A. *proper,* primarily because they conducted a thorough search and located Jill
B. *improper,* primarily because they should have broadcasted Jill's description to other Officers over the radio
C. *proper,* primarily because they were able to locate the child without the help of their Supervisor
D. *improper,* primarily because the Patrol Supervisor should have been requested

Questions 17-25.

DIRECTIONS: Questions 17 through 25 are to be answered SOLELY on the basis of the following sketches. The first face on top is a sketch of an alleged criminal based on witnesses' descriptions at the crime scene. One of the four sketches below that face is the way the suspect looked after changing appearance. Assume that NO surgery has been done on the suspect. Select the face which is MOST likely that of the suspect.

7 (#3)

17. 17.____

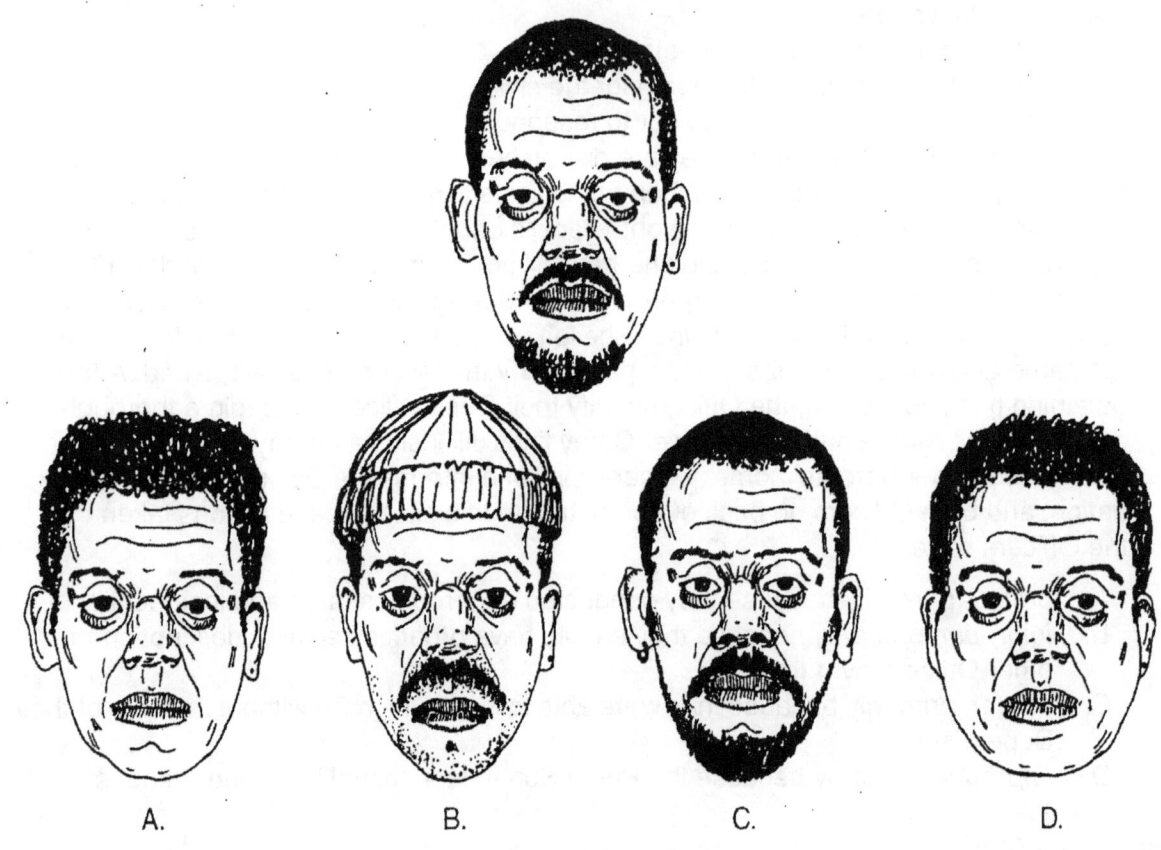

A. B. C. D.

18. 18.____

   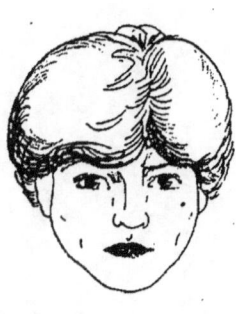

A. B. C. D.

19.  19.____

A.   B.   C.   D.

20.  20.____

A.   B.   C.   D.

9 (#3)

21.    21. ____

A.   B.   C.   D.

22.      22. ____

A.   B.   C.   D.

23.   23.____

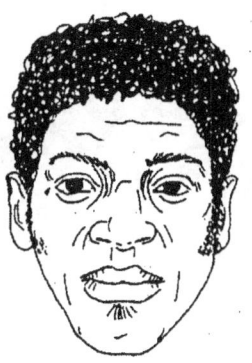

A.   B.   C.   D.

24.   24.____

A.   B.   C.   D.

25.

 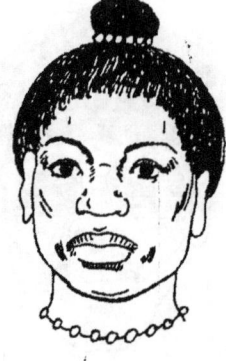  

A.   B.   C.   D.

KEY (CORRECT ANSWERS)

1.	B	11.	A
2.	D	12.	D
3.	C	13.	A
4.	B	14.	C
5.	C	15.	B
6.	A	16.	D
7.	A	17.	A
8.	C	18.	C
9.	D	19.	B
10.	C	20.	D

21. A
22. B
23. D
24. B
25. C

EXAMINATION SECTION
TEST 1

DIRECTIONS: Each question or incomplete statement is followed by several suggested answers or completions. Select the one that BEST answers the question or completes the statement. *PRINT THE LETTER OF THE CORRECT ANSWER IN THE SPACE AT THE RIGHT.*

MEMORY PAGES

Memory Scene 1 is on Pages 2 and 3. Memory Scene 2 is on Pages 4 and 5. You are to study Scene 1 carefully and try to remember as many details in the scene as you can. You should pay equal attention both to objects and to people shown in the scene. Then turn to Questions 1 through 6 which follow and answer these questions based upon what you remember from Scene 1. Do not turn back to Scene 1 while answering. After you complete Questions 1 through 6, study Memory Scene 2. Then turn to Questions 7 through 12 and answer then based on Scene 2.

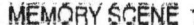

MEMORY SCENE 1

4 (#1)

MEMORY SCENE 2

142

Questions 1-6.

DIRECTIONS: Questions 1 through 6 are to be answered SOLELY on the basis of Memory Scene 1.

1. What does the sign at the subway entrance say?

   A. Uptown 3
   B. Downtown 1
   C. Uptown A
   D. Downtown B

2. At which one of the following times can a legal left turn be made from Avenue C onto Park?

   A. 8:30 A.M. Mondays
   B. 9:30 A.M. Tuesdays
   C. 12:00 P.M. Wednesdays
   D. 1:00 P.M. Thursdays

3. Which one of the following persons is wearing glasses? The

   A. postal employee
   B. woman pushing the stroller
   C. newspaper vendor
   D. man wearing baseball cap and sneakers

4. What is the plate number on the bus?

   A. 313   B. 530   C. 731   D. 848

5. What is the last pick-up time shown on the mailbox? ____ P.M.

   A. 4:30   B. 5:00   C. 5:30   D. 6:00

6. What is the address of the bank?

   A. 33 Park
   B. 25 Avenue C
   C. 33 Avenue C
   D. 25 Park

Questions 7-12.

DIRECTIONS: Questions 7 through 12 are to be answered SOLELY on the basis of Memory Scene 2.

7. On what day is the Variety Store closed?

   A. Friday   B. Saturday   C. Sunday   D. Monday

8. In front of which building is a crime taking place?

   A. 483   B. 487   C. 489   D. 498

9. Which one of the following BEST describes the perpetrator? ____ male, ____ jacket, ____ pants.

   A. White; plaid; black
   B. Black; white; white
   C. White; black; white
   D. Black; plaid; black

10. Of the following, it appears that the victim of the crime is

    A. standing by the telephone booth
    B. buying a hot dog
    C. reading a newspaper
    D. lighting a cigarette

11. Which one of the following BEST describes the victim? Male _____, _____ pants, _____ jacket, _____ shoes.

    A. white; striped; white; black
    B. black; white; striped; white
    C. white; white; black; black
    D. black; black; white; white

12. The woman who is CLOSEST to the crime is wearing

    A. a dress and carrying a pocketbook
    B. striped pants and eating a hotdog
    C. shorts and standing by the phone booth
    D. a skirt and holding a cigarette

13. Police Officer Daniels has just finished investigating a report of criminal mischief and has obtained the following information:
    Place of Occurrence: In front of victim's residence
    Time of Occurrence: Between 5:15 A.M. and 5:30 A.M.
    Victim: Carl Burns, of 1856 Lenox Street, owner of vehicle
    Crime: Criminal Mischief
    Damage: Paint poured onto his vehicle
    Officer Daniels is preparing a report on the incident.
    Which one of the following expresses the above information MOST clearly and accurately?

    A. While parked in front of his residence, Carl Burns stated between 5:15 A.M. and 5:30 A.M., that paint was poured onto his vehicle at 1856 Lenox Street.
    B. Carl Burns, of 1856 Lenox Street, stated that between 5:15 A.M. and 5:30 A.M., paint was poured onto his vehicle while it was parked in front of his residence.
    C. Between 5:15 A.M. and 5:30 A.M., Carl Burns of 1856 Lenox Street stated, while parked in front of his residence, that paint was poured on his vehicle.
    D. Carl Burns between 5:15 A.M. and 5:30 A.M. while parked at 1856 Lenox Street, his residence, stated that paint was poured onto his vehicle.

14. Police Officer Johnson arrives at the National Savings Bank five minutes after it has been robbed at gunpoint. The following are details provided by eyewitnesses:
    Suspect
    Sex: Male
    Ethnicity: White
    Height: 5'10" to 6'2"
    Weight: 180 lbs. to 190 lbs.
    Hair Color: Blonde
    Clothing: Black jacket, blue dungarees
    Weapon: .45 caliber revolver

Officer Johnson is completing a report on the incident. Which one of the following expresses the above information MOST clearly and accurately?
A white male

- A. weighing 180-190 lbs. robbed the National Savings Bank. He was White with a black jacket with blonde hair, is 5'10" to 6"2", and blue dungarees. The robber was armed with a .45 caliber revolver.
- B. weighing around 180 or 190 lbs. was wearing a black jacket and blue dungarees. He had blonde hair and had a .45 caliber revolver, and was 5'10" to 6'2". He robbed the National Savings Bank.
- C. who was 5'10" to 6'2" and was weighing 180 to 190 lbs., and has blonde hair and wearing blue dungarees and a black jacket with a revolver, robbed the National Savings Bank.
- D. armed with a .45 caliber revolver robbed the National Savings Bank. The robber was described as being between 180-190 lbs., 5'10" to 6'2", with blonde hair. He was wearing a black jacket and blue dungarees.

15. Police Officers may have to close an area to traffic in certain situations, such as an accident, fire, or explosion.
In which one of the following situations would it be MOST appropriate for an Officer to close off traffic?
A(n)

- A. airplane skids off the runway onto the air field, causing minor injuries to passengers
- B. car hits a tree late at night on a dead-end street, resulting in a broken headlight
- C. manhole cover explodes on a street in the afternoon, causing damage to nearby buildings
- D. fire breaks out on a boat while it is anchored in the middle of the harbor

16. Police Officer Engle is completing a Complaint Report of a burglary which occurred at Monty's Bar. The following five sentences will be included in the Complaint Report:
    I. The owner said that approximately $600 was taken along with eight bottles of expensive brandy.
    II. The burglar apparently gained entry to the barthrough the window and exited through the front door.
    III. When Mr. Barrett returned to reopen the bar at 1:00 P.M., he found the front door open and items thrown all over the bar.
    IV. Mr. Barrett, the owner of Monty's Bar, said he closed the bar at 4:00 A.M. and locked all the doors.
    V. After interviewing the owner, I conducted a search of the bar and found that a window in the back of the bar was broken.

    The MOST logical order for the above sentences to appear in the report is

    A. II, IV, III, V, I   B. IV, III, I, V, II
    C. IV, II, III, I, V   D. II, V, TV, III, I

17. <u>Reckless endangerment</u> - the crime of reckless endangerment occurs when one engages in conduct which creates a substantial risk of serious physical injury to another person, in that one is aware of the risk of such conduct but continues anyway.
Which one of the following is the BEST example of reckless endangerment?

A. Bill, a construction worker on a skyscraper, walks on a narrow beam hundreds of feet above the ground, even though if he falls he will probably die.
B. Jason, a security guard in a warehouse, fires his revolver at an armed robber who is shooting at him, but misses and nearly hits a woman who has just walked in.
C. George, who used to be an acrobat, walks on the ledge of a roof on his hands and does cartwheels in order to win a bet.
D. John, while working on a scaffold, removes broken bricks from a building and throws them to the ground, even though people on the street below are shouting that he could hurt someone.

Questions 18-20.

DIRECTIONS: Questions 18 through 20 are to be answered SOLELY on the basis of the following passage.

Police Officers Gillespie and Henderson, working an 8:00 A.M. to 4:00 P.M. shift in the 87th Precinct, receive a radio call to investigate a theft from an automobile at 870 Bayard Street. Officer Gillespie explains to his partner, who is new to the Precinct, that the Precinct receives a lot of calls around 9:30 A.M. regarding thefts from automobiles. This occurs because people come out at that time to move their cars due to the 10:30 A.M. - 1:30 P.M. alternate side parking regulation.

Turning onto Bayard Street, the Officers notice that there are six automobiles parked on the south side of the street. Officer Gillespie pulls into a spot behind the last car, in front of 871 Bayard Street, and is greeted by Mrs. Blount. She tells the Officers that at 9:15 A.M. she discovered that the right front vent window of her green 1982 Pontiac had been smashed and her car radio worth $500 had been stolen. She mentions that the cars of two of her neighbors, Mr. Abernathy and Pete Shaw, were also broken into.

Mr. Abernathy, who lives at 870 Bayard Street, comes out of his home and walks across the street to speak to the Officers. As Officer Henderson takes Mrs. Blount's report, Officer Gillespie walks with Mr. Abernathy to his car to fill out a report. Mr. Abernathy saw a white male trying to break into his silver gray Le Sabre at 11:05 on the previous night. Mr. Abernathy called the police, but the Officers who responded were unable to complete the report because they received a radio call to respond to an assault in progress. Officer Gillespie takes Mr. Abernathy's report and then rejoins his partner, who is already completing a report on Pete Shaw's automobile. Having been on the scene for an hour and ten minutes, they notice it is now 10:50 A.M., and all of the vehicles have been removed, except those whose owners have just given reports.

18. Officer Henderson completed reports on 18._____

    A. Mrs. Blount and Mr. Abernathy
    B. Mr. Abernathy and Pete Shaw
    C. Mrs. Blount and Pete Shaw
    D. Mr. Abernathy, Pete Shaw, and Mrs. Blount

19. Which side of Bayard Street did Mr. Abernathy live on? 19._____

    A. North   B. South   C. East   D. West

20. When Officers Gillespie and Henderson file the reports, for which person will the date of the crime be different from the others?

  A. Mrs. Blount   B. Mr. Abernathy
  C. Mr. Shaw   D. Mr. Blount

Question 21.

DIRECTIONS: Question 21 is to be answered SOLELY on the basis of the following information.

Police Officers are required to handle calls regarding abused children. Officers handling cases of abused children should do the following in the order given:

  I. Remove the child from the home with consent of the parents if continued presence may cause an immediate danger to the child's life or health.
  II. Remove the child from home without the parents' consent if continued presence may cause an immediate danger to the child's life or health and there is insufficient time to apply for a court order as directed by the Patrol Supervisor.
  III. Bring child to precinct unless immediate hospitalization is necessary.
  IV. Prepare necessary reports.
  V. Telephone facts to the Bureau of Child Welfare.
  VI. Obtain serial number and enter it on pertinent reports.
  VII. Telephone facts to the Society for the Prevention of Cruelty to Children.
  VIII. Inform parents or guardian to contact the Department of Social Services caseworker.

21. Police Officers Gray and Turner are assigned to a radio patrol car. At approximately 3:30 P.M., they are dispatched to 305 Maplewood Terrace to handle an abused child case. Upon their arrival, the Officers are informed by Mrs. Smith that her husband continually beats her son for no apparent reason. She further states that her husband is extremely violent and is a heavy drinker. The Officers complete all steps up to and including the preparation of the necessary reports.
Officers Gray and Turner should NEXT

  A. inform the parents to contact the Department of Social Services caseworker
  B. apply for a court order after conferring with the Patrol Supervisor
  C. telephone the facts to the Society for the Prevention of Cruelty to Children
  D. telephone the facts to the Bureau of Child Welfare

22. *Police Officers often have to handle emotionally disturbed persons who may be a danger to others.*
At 10:30 P.M., while patrolling the Times Square area, Police Officer Larsen observes four emotionally disturbed persons within a three-block radius.
Which one of the following would MOST likely present the GREATEST problem for Officer Larsen?
A(n)

  A. elderly woman is chanting loudly to people waiting in line for a movie
  B. youth is quickly pacing back and forth while cursing at people waiting for a bus
  C. woman is standing on a corner arguing loudly with herself about her son
  D. man is preaching to a crowd about the world coming to an end

23. While on patrol, Police Officer Rogers is approached by Terry Conyers, a young woman whose pocketbook has been stolen. Ms. Conyers tells Officer Rogers that the following items were in her pocketbook at the time it was taken:
    4 Traveler's checks, each valued at $20.00
    3 Traveler's checks, each valued at $25.00
    Cash of $212.00
    1 wedding band valued at $450.00
    Officer Rogers is preparing a Complaint Report on the robbery.
    Which one of the following is the TOTAL value of the property and cash taken from Ms. Conyers?

    A. $707.00 B. $807.00 C. $817.00 D. $837.00

24. While on patrol, Police Officer Scott is dispatched to respond to a reported burglary. Two burglars entered the home of Mr. and Mrs. Walker and stole the following items:
    3 watches valued at $65.00 each
    1 VCR valued at $340.00
    1 television set valued at $420.00
    Officer Scott is preparing a Complaint Report on the burglary.
    Which one of the following is the TOTAL value of the property stolen?

    A. $707.00 B. $825.00 C. $920.00 D. $955.00

25. While on patrol, Police Officer Smith is dispatched to investigate a grand larceny. Deborah Paisley, a businesswoman, reports that her 1998 Porsche was broken into. The following items were taken:
    1 car stereo system valued at $2,950.00
    1 car phone valued at $1,060.00
    Ms. Paisley's attache case valued at $200.00 was also taken from the car in the incident. The attache case contained two new solid gold pens valued at $970.00 each. Officer Smith is completing a Complaint Report. Which one of the following is the TOTAL dollar value of the property stolen from Ms. Paisley's car?

    A. $5,180.00   B. $5,980.00
    C. $6,040.00   D. $6,150.00

KEY (CORRECT ANSWERS)

1. D
2. A
3. C
4. D
5. C

6. A
7. B
8. B
9. A
10. D

11. C
12. D
13. B
14. D
15. C

16. B
17. D
18. C
19. A
20. B

21. D
22. B
23. C
24. D
25. D

TEST 2

DIRECTIONS: Each question or incomplete statement is followed by several suggested answers or completions. Select the one that BEST answers the question or completes the statement. *PRINT THE LETTER OF THE CORRECT ANSWER IN THE SPACE AT THE RIGHT.*

Questions 1-2.

DIRECTIONS: Questions 1 and 2 are to be answered SOLELY on the basis of the map which appears on the following page. The flow of traffic is indicated by the arrows. If there is only one arrow shown, then traffic flows only in the direction indicated by the arrow. If there are two arrows shown, then traffic flows in both directions. You must follow the flow of traffic.

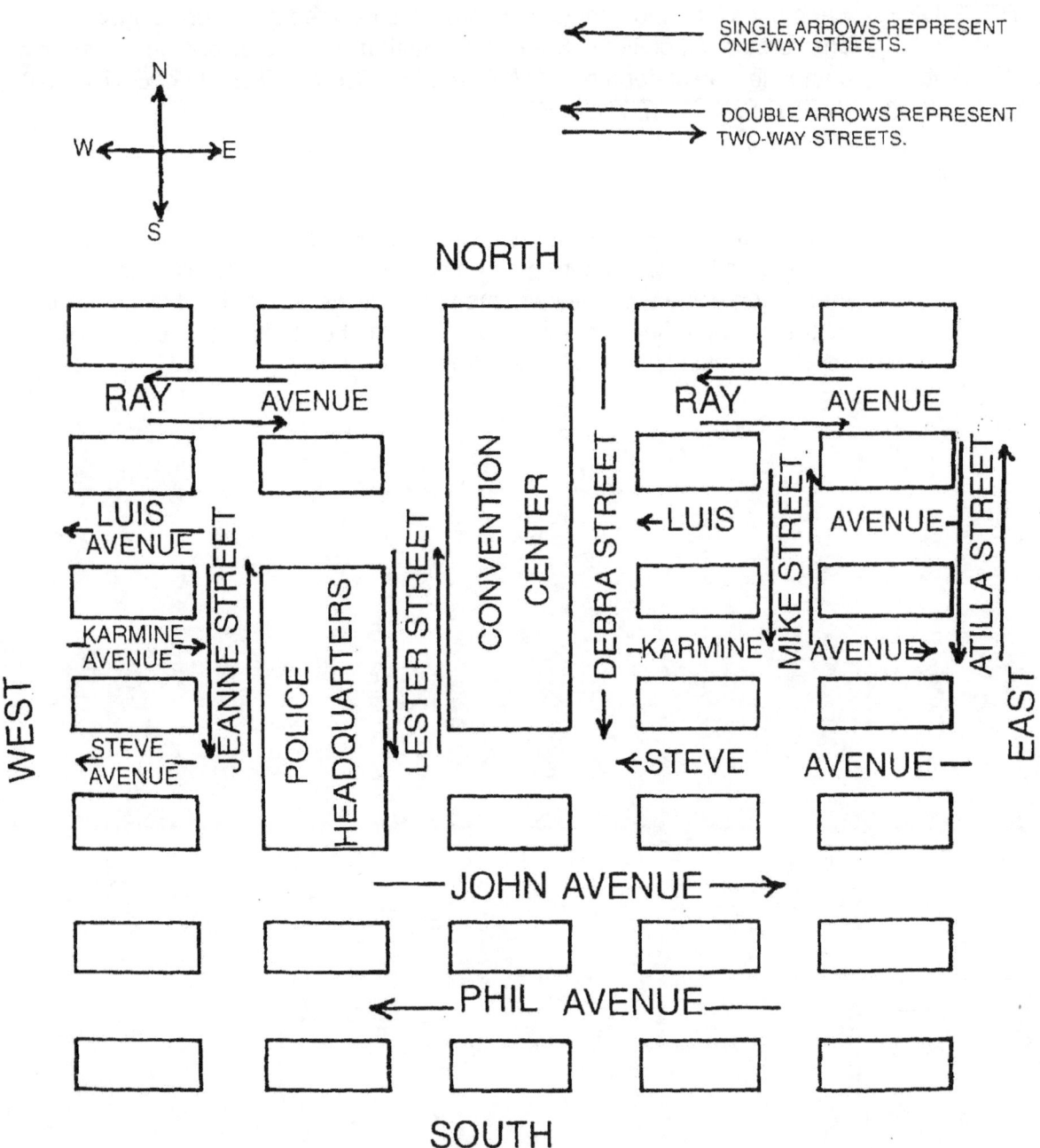

1. While in a patrol car located at Ray Avenue and Atilia Street, Police Officer Ashley receives a call from the dispatcher to respond to an assault at Jeanne Street and Karmine Avenue.
   Which one of the following is the SHORTEST route for Officer Ashley to follow in his patrol car, making sure to obey all traffic regulations?
   Travel

   A. south on Atilla Street, west on Luis Avenue, south on Debra Street, west on Steve Avenue, north on Lester Street, west on Luis Avenue, then one block south on Jeanne Street
   B. south on Atilla Street, then four blocks west on Phil Avenue, then north on Jeanne Street to Karmine Avenue

1.____

152

C. west on Ray Avenue to Debra Street, then five blocks south to Phil Avenue, then west to Jeanne Street, then three blocks north to Karmine Avenue
D. south on Atilla Street, then four blocks west on John Avenue, then north on Jeanne Street to Karmine Avenue

2. After taking a complaint report from the assault victim, Officer Ashley receives a call from the dispatcher to respond to an auto larceny in progress at the corner of Debra Street and Luis Avenue.
Which one of the following is the SHORTEST route for Officer Ashley to follow in his patrol car, making sure to obey all traffic regulations?
Travel

   A. south on Jeanne Street to John Avenue, then east three blocks on John Avenue, then north on Mike Street to Luis Avenue, then west to Debra Street
   B. south on Jeanne Street to John Avenue, then east two blocks on John Avenue, then north on Debra Street to Luis Avenue
   C. north on Jeanne Street two blocks, then east on Ray Avenue for one block, then south on Lester Street to Steve Avenue, then one block east on Steve Avenue, then north on Debra Street to Luis Avenue
   D. south on Jeanne Street to John Avenue, then east on John Avenue to Atilla Street, then north three blocks to Luis Avenue, then west to Debra Street

3. Police Officer Revson is writing a report concerning a vehicle pursuit. His report will include the following five sentences:
   I. I followed the vehicle for several blocks and then motioned to the driver to pull the car over to the curb and stop.
   II. I informed the radio dispatcher that I was in a high-speed pursuit.
   III. When the driver ignored me, I turned on my siren and the driver increased his speed.
   IV. The vehicle hit a tree, and I was able to arrest the driver.
   V. While on patrol in car #4135, I observed a motorist driving suspiciously.
   The MOST logical order for the above sentences to appear in the report is

   A. V, I, III, II, IV   B. II, V, III, I, IV   C. V, I, II, IV, III   D. II, I, V, IV, III

4. Police Officer Grundig is writing a Complaint Report regarding a burglary and assault case. Officer Grundig has obtained the following facts:
Place of Occurrence: 2244 Clark Street
Victim: Mrs. Willis
Suspect: Mr. Willis, victim's ex-husband
Complaint: Unlawful entry; head injury inflicted with a bat
Officer Grundig is completing a report on the incident. Which one of the following expresses the above information MOST clearly and accurately?

   A. He had no permission or authority to do so and it caused her head injuries, when Mr. Willis entered his ex-wife's premises. Mrs. Willis lives at 2244 Clark Street. He hit her with a bat.
   B. Mr. Willis entered 2244 Clark Street, the premises of his ex-wife. He hit her with a bat, without permission and authority to do so. It caused Mrs. Willis to have head injuries.
   C. After Mr. Willis hit his ex-wife, Mrs. Willis, at 2244 Clark Street, the bat caused her to have head injuries. He had no permission nor authority to do so.
   D. Mr. Willis entered his ex-wife's premises at 2244 Clark Street without her permission or authority. He then struck Mrs. Willis with a bat, causing injuries to her head.

5. While on patrol, Police Officer York responds to a case of a missing child. The following information relating to this case was obtained by the Officer:

Name of Missing Child: Susan Spencer
Age: 7 years old
School: Mountainside School
Information Provided By: Mary Templeton, Principal
Disposition of Case: Child is all right; she arrived at school five minutes before Officer York arrived

Officer York is completing a report on the incident. Which one of the following expresses the above information MOST clearly and accurately?

A. Only five minutes before my arrival she was at the school and was all right. Mary Templeton, the Principal of Mountainside School said that the missing child, Susan Spencer was seven years old.
B. I arrived at Mountainside School and spoke with Mary Templeton, the Principal. She informed me that the missing child, Susan Spencer, age seven, had arrived five minutes before I did and is fine.
C. She arrived five minutes before I did. The Principal of Mountainside School, Mary Templeton, informed me that the missing child was seven years old, Susan Spencer, and was fine.
D. Seven year old Susan Spencer was missing. Mary Templeton, Principal, Mountainside School said that only five minutes before my arrival she was at the school and was fine.

5.____

Question 6.

DIRECTIONS: Question 6 is to be answered SOLELY on the basis of the following information.

Police Officers may be confronted with a situation involving a mentally ill or emotionally disturbed person who does not voluntarily seek medical assistance. When a Police Officer has reason to believe that an individual is mentally ill or emotionally disturbed, the Officer should do the following in the order given:

I. Request an ambulance if one has not already been dispatched and determine whether the Patrol Supervisor is responding; if not, request response.
II. Attempt to comfort the mentally ill or emotionally disturbed person.
III. Attempt to isolate and contain the mentally ill or emotionally disturbed person until the arrival of the Patrol Supervisor and the Emergency Service Unit.
IV. Establish police lines.
V. After the person has been restrained, remove property that is dangerous to life or might help the person to escape.
VI. Have person removed to hospital in ambulance.
VII. Ride in the body of the ambulance with the person.
VIII. Safeguard the person at the hospital until examined by the psychiatrist.

6. Police Officer Emilio, while on foot patrol, is informed by Mr. Green, the superintendent of the building at 285 Jay Street, that there is a male tenant with a known history of mental illness in Apartment 3A yelling loudly that space aliens are controlling his thoughts and actions. The tenant is reported to have a violent temper and can be heard throwing things around the apartment. The building superintendent has already called an ambulance, and Officer Emilio has requested that the Patrol Supervisor respond.
The NEXT step that Officer Emilio should take is to

   A. have the tenant taken to the hospital in the ambulance
   B. try to calm the tenant and comfort him
   C. establish police lines
   D. attempt to isolate and contain the tenant for his safety

7. *Menacing* - *A person is guilty of menacing when, by physical means, he intentionally places or attempts to place another person in immediate fear of serious physical injury.*
Which one of the following situations is the BEST example of menacing?

   A. Debbie walks up to Brian, says *I'm going to punch you,* then punches Brian in the face, causing his jaw to ache for several hours.
   B. A terrorist secretly places a time bomb which could cause serious injury to many people in a busy shopping mall.
   C. During a heated argument, Tom picks up a knife, holds it to Mike's throat, and tells Mike that he will cut his throat.
   D. Roy, who strongly dislikes his neighbor John, tells John that if he does not move out of his apartment within the next month, Roy will set it on fire when John is not around to stop him.

8. On occasion, Police Officers may require back-up assistance from other Officers. While on patrol, Police Officer Casey observes a number of situations.
For which one of the following would it be MOST appropriate for Officer Casey to request back-up assistance?

   A. A woman looking under the hood of the car while parked on the highway shoulder
   B. A fight between two groups of teenage boys in a park concerning the use of a baseball field
   C. A man who changes lanes as he drives without signaling
   D. An argument between two women concerning who will park in a vacant space

9. Police Officer Webster is preparing an Arrest Report which will include the following five sentences:
   I. I noticed that the robber had a knife placed at the victim's neck.
   II. I told the robber to drop the knife.
   III. While on patrol, I observed a robbery which was in progress.
   IV. I grabbed the robber, placed him in handcuffs, and took him to the precinct.
   V. The robber dropped the knife and tried to flee.

   The MOST logical order for the above sentences to appear in the report is

   A. I, II, V, IV, III
   B. III, I, II, V, IV
   C. III, II, IV, I, V
   D. I, III, IV, V, II

10. When a patrol car must be repaired, Police Officers should do the following in the order given:
    I. Notify the Desk Officer.
    II. Call for an appointment as follows:
       A. Make an appointment with the Borough Service Station for all repairs during normal business hours.
       B. Make an appointment with the Central Repair Shop for all repairs during other than normal business hours.
    III. Prepare an Emergency Repair Requisition and drive the vehicle in for repairs at the appointed time.

    Police Officer Visconti, while performing a night tour, checks her patrol car and notices a problem with the transmission. She calls the Desk Officer at 1:00 A.M. to report the problem. The NEXT step the Police Officer should take is to

    A. call and make an appointment with the Borough Service Station
    B. prepare an Emergency Repair Requisition on her way to the repair shop
    C. arrange for an appointment with the Central Repair Shop
    D. drive the vehicle back to the precinct station house

11. Police Officers are sometimes required to provide emergency transportation for seriously injured persons. Police Officer Phelan arrives at the 103rd Street subway station to provide assistance to a critically injured elderly man who fell from the stairs onto the platform. Which one of the following would be the MOST serious situation for the Officer to deal with?

    A. A crowd of onlookers has gathered ten feet away from the injured man.
    B. The ambulance dispatcher informs the Officer that an ambulance would not be available for twenty minutes.
    C. The injured man is unable to provide the Officer with the name of a relative to be contacted.
    D. Several onlookers start to complain about a delay in train service.

Questions 12-14.

DIRECTIONS: Questions 12 through 14 are to be answered SOLELY on the basis of the following passage.

At 2:00 P.M., while sitting in front of 215 Rover Street, Police Officers Casey and Rogers receive a radio call to investigate a suspected case of child abuse at 415 Dover Street, Apartment 12B. The radio dispatcher informs the Officers that the call came from Apartment 12A. The Officers arrive at the location and decide to go to the apartment the complaint came from to investigate. When the Officers knock, both Mr. and Mrs. Fine come to the door. Mrs. Fine states that she has heard a child crying since noon and asked her husband to call the police. The Officers thank Mr. and Mrs. Fine, go on to Apartment 12B, and knock on the door.

A male named John Brice opens the door and asks what seems to be the problem. After Officer Casey explains why they are at the apartment, Mr. Brice states that he works nights and often falls into a deep sleep. The crying of his child did not awaken him. Officer Casey asks to see the child, and Mr. Brice complies. Officer Casey looks at the child and notices bruises and burn marks on the child's feet. The Officers then request a Patrol Supervisor and an ambulance. Sergeant Ramos arrives at the apartment at 2:30 P.M. and orders the child removed to a hospital. Fifteen minutes later, Mr. Brice is arrested. At 3:00 P.M., another patrol car is sent to notify Mrs. Brice at 725 Clover Street.

12. The police dispatcher received the call from _____ Street, Apartment _____.   12._____
    A. 725 Clover; 12C
    B. 415 Dover; 12A
    C. 215 Rover; 12B
    D. 415 Dover; 12B

13. Who called the police?   13._____
    A. Mrs. Fine
    B. Mr. Brice
    C. Mr. Fine
    D. Mrs. Brice

14. From which of the following persons did the Officers receive initial information regarding this complaint?   14._____
    A. Mrs. Brice
    B. Mrs. Fine
    C. Mr. Brice
    D. Mr. Fine

Question 15.

DIRECTIONS: Question 15 is to be answered SOLELY on the basis of the following information.

Definitions:

Aided case: Any occurrence coming to the attention of a uniformed member of the service which requires that a person, other than a prisoner, receive medical aid or assistance because such person is
   A. sick or injured (except vehicle accident)
   B. dead (except vehicle accident)
   C. a lost person
   D. mentally ill
   E. an abandoned, destitute, abused, or neglected child

Vehicle accident: One which occurs on a public highway or on a street between building lines and involves a vehicle, including a parked vehicle, attended or unattended, or vehicles on private property to which the public has access.

Procedures:

Upon arrival at the scene of a vehicle accident, a Police Officer shall prepare a Police Accident Report.

Upon arrival at the scene of an aided incident, a Police Officer shall render appropriate aid to the sick or injured person, request an ambulance or doctor if necessary, and prepare an aided report.

15. At about 6:00 P.M. on February 5, 2000, Police Officer Malone receives a radio call to respond to the scene of an accident. Witnesses inform him that a newspaper truck was struck in the rear by a garbage truck at the intersection of Mica and Gold Streets. The driver of the newspaper truck sustained a broken leg and a very bad facial cut. The driver of the garbage truck suffered a cut on his left arm. A female passerby, about 70 years old, observed the accident and had a heart attack. She was lying on the sidewalk, having trouble breathing.
    In addition to making the necessary notifications, Police Officer Malone should prepare a(n)   15._____

A. Police Accident Report and an Aided Report for the victims of the vehicle accident
B. Aided Report and a Police Accident Report for the passerby
C. Police Accident Report for the vehicle accident only
D. Police Accident Report for the vehicle accident and an Aided Report for the passerby

16. Police Officer Lee is preparing a report regarding someone who apparently attempted to commit suicide with a gun. The report will include the following five sentences:
    I. At the location, the woman pointed to the open door of Apartment 7L.
    II. I called for an ambulance to respond.
    III. The male had a gun in his hand and a large head wound.
    IV. A call was received from the radio dispatcher regarding a woman who heard a gunshot at 936 45th Avenue.
    V. Upon entering Apartment 7L, I saw the body of a male on the kitchen floor.

    The MOST logical order for the above sentences to appear in the report is

    A. IV, I, V, III, II
    B. I, III, V, IV, II
    C. I, V, III, II, IV
    D. IV, V, III, II, I

Question 17.

DIRECTIONS: Question 17 is to be answered SOLELY on the basis of the following information.

Police Officers are sometimes required to arrest a person for whom a warrant has been issued. When making such an arrest, Officers should do the following in the order given:

   I. Inform defendant of the warrant and the reason it was issued, unless physical resistance, escape, or other factors make this impractical.
   II. Show warrant, if requested.
   III. Announce authority and purpose, if premises are involved and there is reasonable cause to believe that the defendant is inside, UNLESS giving such notice may
      A. endanger the life or safety of the Officer or another person
      B. result in defendant attempting to escape
      C. result in material evidence being destroyed, damaged, or hidden
   IV. Break into premises, if necessary.
   V. Make arrest.
   VI. Take the prisoner to the station house.

17. Police Officers Haggerty and Adams are enroute to 2112 Jefferson Street, Apartment 2B, with a warrant to arrest Mark Johnson. The arrest warrant was issued when Mr. Johnson failed to appear in court on charges of bank robbery and rape. Upon arrival at Mr. Johnson's residence, Officer Haggerty knocks on the door and announces herself. Without hearing any acknowledgment from anyone, the Officers suddenly hear glass breaking inside the apartment. Officer Adams then forces the apartment door open, rushes inside, and stops a man who fits Mark Johnson's description from escaping through a bedroom window.
    The NEXT step the Officers should take is to

    A. take Mr. Johnson to the station house for booking
    B. present the warrant to Mr. Johnson
    C. inform Mr. Johnson of the reason why a warrant was issued for his arrest
    D. arrest Mr. Johnson

Questions 18-20.

DIRECTIONS: Questions 18 through 20 are to be answered SOLELY on the basis of the following passage.

Police Officers Wilson and Mylers had just begun their 4:00 P.M. to Midnight tour of duty when they received a radio call to investigate a case of possible child abuse. Mrs. Margaret Volkman had called 911 and said she was going to hurt her two daughters. Mary Watson, Mrs. Volkman's mother, had urged her daughter to call the police after speaking with her over the phone. Mrs. Volkman had been drinking, and her mother knew from past occasions that her daughter could become very aggressive after one or two beers. In fact, last year Mrs. Volkman's neighbor, Joyce Hill, had called the police to complain about Margaret's *drunken behavior*. When the Officers arrived at 51 Broadway, Apartment 4C, they spoke briefly to Mrs. Volkman, who appeared to be very agitated. She stated that being a single parent of two young girls is very difficult and there are times when she feels she is at her wit's end. Officer Wilson asked if he could speak to the two children alone, and she agreed to wait in the living room. She stated to Officer Mylers that she loved her girls and would never do anything to hurt them. Officer Wilson spoke to Gayle, the 13-year-old daughter, who told him that her mother *gets very worked up when she drinks and begins to scream at me and Mattie and cry at the same time, but has never tried to hurt us. After awhile, she just falls asleep.* After hearing this, Officer Wilson decided the children were not in any immediate danger. Before leaving, the Officers told Mrs. Volkman to call the precinct if she felt she might try to hurt her children again.

18. The call which prompted the Officers to respond to 51 Broadway was placed by   18.____

   A. Mary Watson   B. Margaret Volkman
   C. Joyce Hill   D. Gayle Mylers

19. Officer Wilson decided that the children were not in any danger after speaking with   19.____

   A. Mattie Volkman   B. Joyce Hill
   C. Gayle Volkman   D. Mary Watson

20. Which one of the following persons had made a complaint in the past concerning Margaret's drinking?   20.____
    Her

   A. mother   B. daughter   C. grandmother   D. neighbor

21. At 10:20 A.M., Police Officer Medina responds to a report of a robbery. The Officer obtains the following information regarding the incident:
Time of Occurrence: 10:15 A.M.
Place of Occurrence: Mike's Deli 1700 E. 9th Street
Victim: Chuck Baker, owner of Mike's Deli
Amount Stolen: $500.00
Suspects: 3 male Whites
Officer Medina is completing a report on the incident. Which one of the following expresses the above information MOST clearly and accurately?

- A. Chuck Baker, the owner of Mike's Deli, located at 1700 E. 9th Street, reported that at 10:15 A.M. three White males robbed his deli of $500.00.
- B. At 10:15 A.M., Chuck Baker, deli owner, reported that Mike's Deli, located at 1700 E. 9th Street, was robbed of $500.00 by three White males.
- C. Chuck Baker reported that $500.00 had been taken from the owner of Mike's Deli, located at 1700 E. 9th Street at 10:15 A.M. by three White males.
- D. At 10:15 A.M. it was reported by the deli owner that three White males robbed $500.00 from Chuck Baker. Mike's Deli is located at 1700 E. 9th Street.

22. While on patrol, Police Officers Rydell and Francis receive a call to respond to a reported robbery. The following information related to the crime is obtained by the Officers:
Time of Occurrence: 10:00 A.M.
Place of Occurrence: 8012 Liberty Street
Victim: Leslie Reese, friend of witness
Witness: Lorraine Mitchell
Suspect: Bill Clark
Crime: Money and jewelry stolen
Officer Francis is completing a report on the incident.
Which one of the following expresses the above information MOST clearly and accurately?

- A. Lorraine Mitchell stated that while responding to a robbery, at 10:00 A.M., she was a witness at 8012 Liberty Street. Her friend, Leslie Reese, had her jewelry and money taken from her by Bill Clark.
- B. Lorraine Mitchell stated that at 10:00 A.M. she saw Bill Clark approach her friend, Leslie Reese, and take money and jewelry from her. The crime took place at 8012 Liberty Street.
- C. At 8012 Liberty Street, stolen money and jewelry were reported. This was witnessed by Lorraine Mitchell and her friend, Leslie Reese, who was also robbed of her money and jewelry. The incident occurred at 10:00 A.M. The suspect is Bill Clark.
- D. At 10:00 A.M. Lorraine Mitchell saw Bill Clark enter 8012 Liberty Street. At that point, Leslie Reese owned jewelry and money which were stolen.

23. When assigned to safeguard a crime scene, a Police Officer should:
    I. Request that a Patrol Supervisor respond to the scene.
    II. Notify the Precinct Detective Unit.
    III. Make sure that evidence found at scene is not disturbed.
    IV. Record in Memo Book any important observations, such as identity of suspects and witnesses.
    V. Advise the Patrol Supervisor and Detectives of any witnesses detained and any other information regarding the crime.

    Police Officer Best is assigned to a foot post on Rock Avenue between East Street and Pitt Street. While working an 8:00 A.M. to 4:00 P.M. shift, Officer Best hears what appears to be three gunshots coming from an apartment building located at 1400 Rock Avenue. After noting the time (10:00 A.M.) and address, Officer Best investigates and notices that the door of a first-floor apartment is open. She walks into the apartment and discovers a male, Black, approximately 35 years old, with three bullet holes in his chest lying on the floor. Officer Best checks for a pulse, but the man is dead. Next to the body there is a .38 caliber revolver. Officer Best checks the rest of the apartment. When satisfied that everything is secure, she, without touching anything, uses her radio to request that a Supervisor and the Detective Unit respond to the scene. Officer Best leaves the apartment and questions the people who have gathered outside the victim's apartment. She asks if anyone there knew the victim. Two people state that they did, and Officer Best records their names in her Memo Book. The actions of Officer Best were

    A. *improper*, primarily because she should have picked up the revolver to see if there were three bullets missing from it
    B. *proper*, primarily because she was able to respond to the scene quickly
    C. *improper*, primarily because she should not have felt the man's pulse to determine if he was alive
    D. *proper*, primarily because she did not disturb any possible evidence at the scene

24. Police Officers are sometimes required to request transportation for seriously injured persons.
    In which one of the following cases would it be MOST appropriate for a Police Officer to request emergency transportation?
    A(n)

    A. man using an electric hedge trimmer accidentally scratches his finger
    B. nine-year-old girl falls off her bicycle, twists her ankle, and suffers abrasions on her knees
    C. elderly man falls down a flight of stairs and is knocked unconscious
    D. young mother complains of feeling faint

25. Upon arrival at the scene of a hit-and-run accident involving property damage, a Police Officer should do the following in the order given:
   I. Prepare a Complaint Report.
   II. If a New York license number is obtained for vehicle leaving the scene:
      A. Determine from the Stolen Property Inquiry Section if vehicle is reported stolen
      B. Obtain the name and address of registered owner
      C. Give the information to complainant
   III. If the vehicle leaving the scene is registered in If the vehicle leaving the scene is registered in another state:
      A. Request identity of registered owner from Inter-City Correspondence Unit
      B. Inform complainant of identity of owner if obtained

Police Officer Murphy responds to the scene of a hit-and-run accident involving damage to a black Chevrolet, with New York license plate number 315 ALV, owned by Mr. Mangione. He tells Officer Murphy that his car was hit by a blue Ford, bearing New Jersey license plate number 461 ESP. Mr. Mangione states that immediately after the collision, the unknown driver left the scene in his blue Ford.

After preparing a Complaint Report, Officer Murphy's NEXT step should be to

A. determine from Stolen Property Inquiry Section if the hit-and-run vehicle is stolen
B. provide operator of vehicle with name and address of hit-and-run driver
C. try to learn identity of registered owner of hit-and-run vehicle from Inter-City Correspondence Unit
D. request a computer check from the radio dispatcher to determine the identity of the hit-and-run driver

KEY (CORRECT ANSWERS)

1.	A		11.	B
2.	A		12.	B
3.	A		13.	C
4.	D		14.	B
5.	B		15.	D
6.	B		16.	A
7.	C		17.	D
8.	B		18.	B
9.	B		19.	C
10.	C		20.	D

21. A
22. B
23. D
24. C
25. C

TEST 3

DIRECTIONS: Each question or incomplete statement is followed by several suggested answers or completions. Select the one that BEST answers the question or completes the statement. *PRINT THE LETTER OF THE CORRECT ANSWER IN THE SPACE AT THE RIGHT.*

1. Police Officer Modrak is completing a Memo Book entry which will include the following five sentences:

    I. The victim, a male in his thirties, told me that the robbery occurred a few minutes ago.
    II. My partner and I jumped out of the patrol car and arrested the suspect.
    III. We responded to an armed robbery in progress at Billings Avenue and 59th Street.
    IV. On Chester Avenue and 68th Street, the victim spotted and identified the suspect.
    V. I told the victim to get into the patrol car and that we would drive him around the area.

    The MOST logical order for the above sentences to appear in the Memo Book is

    A. III, I, V, IV, II
    B. I, III, V, II, IV
    C. I, IV, III, V, II
    D. III, V, I, II, IV

1.____

Question 2.

DIRECTIONS: Question 2 is to be answered SOLELY on the basis of the following information.

Hazardous Material - any chemical, biological, or radiological substance which a Police Officer believes to be dangerous to health. In a hazardous material incident, a Police Officer shall establish minimum *frozen areas* (where the public cannot enter) as follows:
    A. <u>Outdoors</u> - At least 150 feet from hazardous material source or spillage.
    B. <u>Indoors</u> - Evacuate room in which material is located.
    C. <u>Tanker Truck or Military Shipment</u> - Extend frozen area to at least 300 feet in radius.
    D. <u>Explosion or Fire</u> -
        (1) <u>Outdoors</u> - at least 1000 feet in radius from explosive; at least 300 feet in radius from fire.
        (2) <u>Indoors</u> - extend frozen area to include all areas or rooms where a person might be exposed to material; include floors above and below the materials.
        (3) <u>Tanker Truck or Military Shipment</u> - extend frozen areato at least 1000 feet in radius.

2. While on patrol, Police Officers Hunt and Richardson were driving eastbound on the Soundview Highway, which was wet after heavy rains. At approximately 3:00 P.M., a tanker truck containing nuclear waste spun around and turned on its side approximately 300 feet in front of the patrol car. Officer Hunt immediately notified the radio dispatcher because there was liquid leaking from the tank which spread approximately 150 feet west of the truck. After about ten minutes, an explosion occurred which caused a fire. Officers Hunt and Richardson decided to block off the roadway and evacuate pedestrians in the area.
In this situation, which of the following would be the MOST appropriate action for the Officers to take? Establish a frozen area

2.____

163

A. 1000 feet west of the tanker truck
B. 300 feet in radius around the tanker truck
C. 1200 feet in radius from the tanker truck
D. 100 feet from the source of the leak

3. Recently, there has been a significant increase in the number of drug sales at the Havenbrook High School. Police Officer Mair has been assigned to a special team to investigate this situation. He has been instructed to monitor closely any activities that appear to be suspicious.
Which one of the following should Officer Mair monitor?

   A. The school principal arriving one hour before the beginning of class every day
   B. Teachers who double park in front of the school every morning
   C. A hot dog vendor who arrives five minutes before the end of the lunch period every day
   D. Two students who are picked up at the school gate immediately after classes every Friday

Questions 4-6.

DIRECTIONS: Questions 4 through 6 are to be answered SOLELY on the basis of the following passage.

Five minutes after the end of his Noon to 1:00 P.M. lunch hour, Police Officer Miller is approached by two obviously frightened teenaged boys. The boys report being robbed by three men while they were listening to music under the boardwalk about twenty minutes earlier.

Danny Brown, the older teenager, informs the Officer that the robbers took his large radio, silver watch, and twenty dollars. His friend, Larry Jones, reports that they took a gold watch and ten dollars from him. The victims report that the perpetrators fled underneath the boardwalk towards the amusement area.

The victims are able to describe the robbers. All three are White males in their late twenties. The first is about 5'6", 160 lbs., wearing white jeans and a blue shirt. The second is about 5'10", 145 lbs., and of dark complexion. The third is known to the younger victim as Redeye and is believed to be a resident of that neighborhood. During the robbery, Redeye was armed with a knife. He is described as being about the same height as the second perpetrator but at least ten pounds heavier than the first. Officer Miller gave the descriptions to the dispatcher.

Officer McMillan, working in the amusement park area, observes three men fitting the description of the robbers. One of the three is carrying a large radio, while the other two are carrying baseball bats and wearing walkman stereos. Officer McMillan quickly requests a police back-up unit to assist in the arrest.

Officers Smith and Campbell respond to provide back-up. Immediately after the three men are apprehended by Officer McMillan and the back-up officers, Officer Miller arrives on the scene accompanied by the victims. The victims identify the three men as the robbers, and the Officers arrest them.

4. What weapon was used in the robbery?

   A. Baseball bat
   B. Knife
   C. Handgun
   D. Sword

5. Which one of the following BEST describes Redeye?

   A. Hispanic, 5'6", dark complexion
   B. White, 5'10", 170 lbs.
   C. Hispanic, 5'6", 160 lbs.
   D. White, 5'10", 155 lbs.

6. Which one of the following Officers was NOT present at the time the suspects were apprehended?

   A. McMillan   B. Campbell   C. Smith   D. Miller

7. When a Police Officer receives a complaint concerning a crime that occurred in another precinct, the Officer should do the following in the order given:
   I. Interview the complainant and obtain facts.
   II. Prepare a Complaint Report.
   III. Telephone complaint to the precinct of occurrence.
   IV. Record the name of the member of the department receiving the complaint at the precinct of occurrence under the *Details* section of the report.
   V. Make Memo Book entries and forward all copies of the Complaint Report to the precinct of occurrence.

   While walking his assigned foot post in the 99th Precinct, Police Officer Jones is approached by an elderly woman who states that her pocketbook had been snatched from her shoulder just four blocks away, in the 98th Precinct. Police Officer Jones speaks to the woman and records all the facts related to the incident. He then prepares a Complaint Report.
   At the Precinct, the NEXT step Police Officer Jones should take is to

   A. make appropriate Memo Book entries and forward all copies of the Complaint Report
   B. telephone the complaint to the precinct of occurrence
   C. prepare a Complaint Report
   D. record the name of the member of the department receiving the complaint at the precinct of occurrence under the *Details* section of the report

8. Police Officer Rodriguez is preparing a report concerning an incident in which she used her revolver. Her report will include the following five sentences:
   I. Upon seeing my revolver, the robber dropped his gun to the ground.
   II. At about 10:55 P.M., I was informed by a passerby that several people were being robbed at gunpoint on 174th Street and Walton Avenue.
   III. I was assigned to patrol on 174th Street and Ghent Avenue during the evening shift.
   IV. I saw a man holding a gun on three people, took out my revolver, and shouted, *Police, don't move!*
   V. After calling for assistance, I went to 174th Street and Walton Avenue and took cover behind a car.

   The MOST logical order for the above sentences to appear in the report is

   A. II, III, IV, V, I
   B. III, II, V, IV, I
   C. IV, V, I, III, II
   D. II, IV, I, V, III

9. Procedure for Safeguarding a Hospitalized Patient Permit only the following persons on official business to interview the prisoner:
   I. Ranking Officer of the Police Department
   II. Detective
   III. District Attorney or representative
   IV. Chief Medical Examiner or representative
   V. Clergyman (if requested by prisoner)

   Police Officer Roger Ziegler is guarding a prisoner at County Hospital. He is approached by Reverend Falter, a minister who wishes to speak with the prisoner, who is a member of his congregation. Reverend Falter feels that he might be able to persuade the prisoner to discuss his case. Also present at the hospital is Captain Lattimore of the Police Academy. The Captain, who is visiting a friend in the hospital while off duty, knows the minister from a previous assignment. The Captain tells Officer Ziegler that he can see no reason to keep Reverend Falter from talking with the prisoner. Officer Ziegler then permits Reverend Falter to see the prisoner. This action by Officer Ziegler was

   A. proper, primarily because Captain Lattimore gave his approval
   B. improper, primarily because the prisoner did not ask to speak with Reverend Falter
   C. proper, primarily because Reverend Falter might be helpful in solving the case
   D. improper, primarily because Captain Lattimore was off duty at the time

10. While on patrol, Police Officers routinely observe motorists and evaluate their capability to operate a motor vehicle. At times, it is necessary to pull someone over to the side of the road when the driver's capability is questionable.
    In which one of the following cases would a Police Officer be LEAST likely to pull the motorist over?
    A

    A. man who weaves his car back and forth over the white dividing line
    B. woman in the car who suddenly swerves to avoid a dog
    C. man who changes lanes without looking behind him, cutting other motorists off
    D. woman who turns her head to reach for something in the back seat and goes through a stop sign

Questions 11-13.

DIRECTIONS: Questions 11 through 13 are to be answered SOLELY on the basis of the following passage.

On July 19, while walking home from the subway, Paul Carro was assaulted by three males on the corner of Evergreen Street and Appleseed Avenue. Mr. Carro suffered a slight concussion, a broken nose, and cuts on his face.

When Police Officers James and Blake arrived on the scene, Mr. Carro was lying on the ground in a semi-conscious state in front of the subway station. Just as the Officers arrived, a Mrs. Frankel of 1785 Appleseed Avenue, Mr. Jones of 1783 Appleseed Avenue, Ms. Brown of 851 Evergreen Street, and Mr. Peters of 1787 Appleseed Avenue came out of their apartments to see what had happened.

Officer James immediately radioed for an ambulance and then attempted to question Mr. Carro about the incident. Mr. Carro stated that *there were three young male Whites wearing dungarees, sneakers, and T-shirts.* Mr. Carro also said that he hit one of the males in the face and kicked another before he was knocked to the ground.

In the meantime, Officer Blake interviewed the neighbors who were present. Mr. Jones gave the Officer Mr. Carro's address and stated that he was Mr. Carro's roommate. He also stated that he heard a lot of noise on the street; but by the time he came outside, Mr. Carro was lying on the ground. Both Ms. Brown and Mr. Peters stated that they saw the three youths who attacked Mr. Carro because of a remark he made to them. Mr. Peters further stated that Mr. Carro did not fight back, and at one point said, *Please leave me alone.* Mrs. Frankel stated that she rushed out of her apartment just in time to see the young men running off. She said that Mr. Carro pursued them for a half a block and then collapsed on the sidewalk. Mrs. Frankel further stated that this was not the first time that Mr. Carro had started trouble in the neighborhood.

11. Where did Mr. Carro live?

    A. 1783 Appleseed Avenue
    B. 1785 Appleseed Avenue
    C. 851 Evergreen Street
    D. 1787 Appleseed Avenue

12. Whose statement to the police directly contradicted Mr. Carro's statement?

    A. Mr. Peters
    B. Mr. Jones
    C. Ms. Brown
    D. Mrs. Frankel

13. Which one of the following witnesses was the FIRST to be interviewed by Officer Blake?

    A. Mr. Peters
    B. Mr. Jones
    C. Ms. Brown
    D. Mrs. Frankel

14. The following details were obtained by Police Officer Talbert at the scene of a shooting:
    Place of Occurrence: 77 Greene Street, inside the Video
    Arcade Victim: Mr. Gerald Jackson, Video Arcade
    customer Suspect: Mr. Michael Benton, Video Arcade owner
    Crime: Shooting
    Action Taken: Suspect arrested
    Officer Talbert is completing a report on the incident. Which one of the following expresses the above information MOST clearly and accurately?

    A. Gerald Jackson was present in the Video Arcade when Michael Benton, the Arcade owner, was involved in a shooting. The shooting occurred at 77 Greene Street. An arrest was made.
    B. Michael Benton and Gerald Jackson were in a shooting at the Video Arcade located at 77 Greene Street. The person shot by the owner was a customer. An arrest was made.

C. Gerald Jackson, a customer at the Video Arcade, located at 77 Greene Street, was shot by Michael Benton, the Arcade owner. Mr. Benton was arrested.
D. Michael Benton, owner of the Video Arcade, located at 77 Greene Street, and Gerald Jackson, an Arcade customer were involved in a shooting. An arrest was made.

15. While on patrol, Police Officers Cando and Poppy receive a call to respond to a reported burglary. The following information relating to the crime is obtained by the Police Officers:

Time of Occurrence: 4:00 A.M.
Place of Occurrence: 81-31 Mitts Street
Witness: Jennifer Wink
Victim: Bette Miller, neighbor
Suspect: John Haysport, neighbor
Crime: House burglarized; TV set stolen

The Officers are completing a report on the incident. Which one of the following expresses the above information MOST clearly and accurately?

A. Jennifer Wink, while on patrol, stated to me that the house next to her house at 81-31 Mitts Street was burglarized. The crime was committed by John Haysport. The crime was the TV set was no longer there. Bette Miller, a neighbor could not find her T
B. At 4:00 A.M. Jennifer Wink, the witness, reported to me that before she had seen John Haysport, a neighbor, go into 81-31 Mitts Street and steal a TV set. The TV belonged to Bette Miller who also lives nearby.
C. Jennifer Wink, the witness, states that John Haysport, burglarized her neighbor's house at 81-31 Mitts Street. She saw her neighbor leaving her neighbor's house at 4:00 A.M. with a TV set. The house was Bette Miller's house.
D. Jennifer Wink, the witness, states that her neighbor's house located at 81-31 Mitts Street was burglarized. Mrs. Wink further states that at 4:00 A.M. she saw a neighbor, John Haysport, leave Mrs. Miller's house with a TV set.

Questions 16-18.

DIRECTIONS: Questions 16 through 18 are to be answered SOLELY on the basis of the map which appears on the following page. The flow of traffic is indicated by the arrows. If there is only one arrow shown, then traffic flows only in the direction indicated by the arrow. If there are two arrows, then traffic flows in both directions. You must follow the flow of traffic.

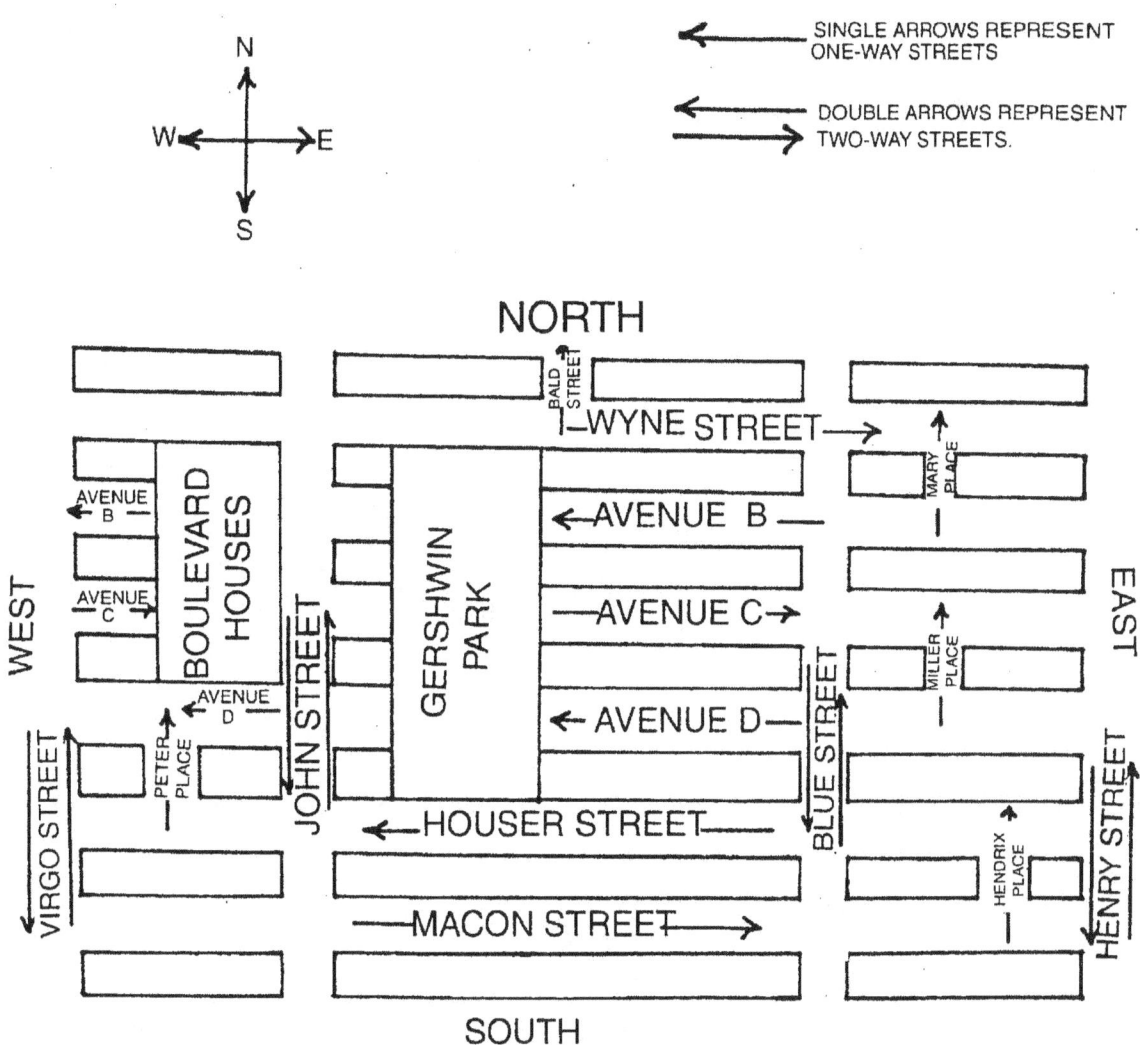

16. Police Officers Ranking and Fish are located at Wyne Street and John Street. The radio dispatcher has assigned them to investigate a motor vehicle accident at the corner of Henry Street and Houser Street.
Which one of the following is the SHORTEST route for them to take in their patrol car, making sure to obey all traffic regulations?
Travel

   A. four blocks south on John Street, then three blocks east on Houser Street to Henry Street
   B. two blocks east on Wyne Street, then two blocks south on Blue Street, then two blocks east on Avenue C, then two blocks south on Henry Street
   C. two blocks east on Wyne Street, then five blocks south on Blue Street, then two blocks east on Macon Street, then one block north on Henry Street
   D. five blocks south on John Street, then three blocks east on Macon Street, then one block north to Houser Street

16.____

17. Police Officers Rizzo and Latimer are located at Avenue B and Virgo Street. They respond to the scene of a robbery at Miller Place and Avenue D.
Which one of the following is the SHORTEST route for them to take in their patrol car, making sure to obey all traffic regulations?
Travel _____ to Miller Place.

   A. one block north on Virgo Street, then four blocks east on Wyne Street, then three blocks south on Henry Street, then one block west on Avenue D
   B. four blocks south on Virgo Street, then two blocks east on Macon Street, then two blocks north on Blue Street, then one block east on Avenue D
   C. three blocks south on Virgo Street, then east on Houser Street to Henry Street, then one block north on Henry Street, then one block west on Avenue D
   D. four blocks south on Virgo Street, then four blocks east to Henry Street, then north to Avenue D, then one block west

18. Police Officer Bendix is in an unmarked patrol car at the intersection of John Street and Macon Street when he begins to follow a robbery suspect. The suspect goes one block east, turns left, travels for three blocks, and then turns right. He drives for two blocks and then makes a right turn. In the middle of the block, the suspect realizes he is being followed and makes a U-turn. In what direction is the suspect now headed?

   A. North   B. South   C. East   D. West

Questions 19-20.

DIRECTIONS: Questions 19 and 20 are to be answered SOLELY on the basis of the following table.

CRIMES IN SECTOR C FOR JANUARY

Report #	Date	Day	Offense	Time	Location
1465	1/3	Friday	Robbery	2:00 AM	2300 Creston Avenue
1470	1/6	Monday	Burglary	3:20 PM	2650 Morris Avenue
1474	1/6	Monday	Assault	8:00 AM	2020 Davidson Avenue
1477	1/8	Wednesday	Assault	11:00 AM	2350 Creston Avenue
1478	1/10	Friday	Burglary	3:00 AM	2500 Creston Avenue
1480	1/10	Friday	Robbery	5:00 PM	2025 Morris Avenue
1484	1/10	Friday	Burglary	2:45 AM	2420 Cummings Street
1486	1/11	Saturday	Robbery	4:00 PM	2650 Morris Avenue
1488	1/15	Wednesday	Robbery	7:00 PM	2400 Morris Avenue
1490	1/17	Friday	Burglary	1:15 AM	2620 Creston Avenue
1494	1/20	Monday	Assault	7:00 AM	2515 Davidson Avenue
1498	1/21	Tuesday	Assault	11:45 AM	2614 Creston Avenue
1503	1/21	Tuesday	Burglary	5:00 AM	2230 Morris Avenue
1510	1/24	Friday	Burglary	7:00 AM	2719 Creston Avenue
1512	1/25	Saturday	Robbery	11:00 PM	2485 Davidson Avenue
1518	1/31	Friday	Robbery	4:00 PM	2355 Davidson Avenue

19. A Police Officer would MOST likely be able to reduce the number of burglaries by patrolling

   A. Creston Avenue between 7:00 A.M. and 3:00 P.M. on Mondays
   B. Morris Avenue between Noon and 8:00 P.M. on Sundays
   C. Creston Avenue between Midnight and 8:00 A.M. on Fridays
   D. Morris Avenue between Midnight and 8:00 A.M. on Mondays

9 (#3)

20. A Police Officer would MOST likely be able to reduce the number of robberies by patrolling

    A. Davidson Avenue between 3:00 P.M. and 11:00 P.M., Tuesday through Saturday
    B. Morris Avenue between 2:00 P.M. and 10:00 P.M., Monday through Friday
    C. Morris Avenue between 3:00 P.M. and 11:00 P.M., Tuesday through Saturday
    D. Davidson Avenue between Noon and 8:00 P.M., Monday through Friday

21. Police Officer Stacy has been directed to observe stopped vehicles if he believes the occupants' actions are suspicious.
    Which one of the following should Officer Stacy consider MOST suspicious?

    A. A man and woman kissing in a parked van in front of a hospital
    B. Three men sitting in a parked car outside a closed liquor store
    C. Two women strolling down the street glancing in shop windows
    D. A man quickly running from a double-parked car into a pharmacy which is about to close

22. When assigned to investigate a rape, Police Officers should do the following in the order given:
    I. Interview the victim and any witnesses, obtain the facts, and protect evidence.
    II. Transmit a description of the suspect if it is known
    III. over the Police radio.
    IV. Detain witnesses if there are any.
    V. Prepare a Complaint Report Worksheet.
    VI. Determine if the case should be closed or referred for further investigation.
    VII. Notify Precinct Detectives and Sex Crime Squad if further investigation is required.

    Police Officer Johnson responds to a rape. She completes all appropriate actions through notifying the Precinct Detectives.
    The NEXT step Officer Johnson should take is to

    A. interview the witnesses further
    B. prepare a Complaint Report Worksheet
    C. inform the Sex Crime Squad
    D. transmit a description of the suspect

23. Police Officer Roberts, a rookie, has been informed by some of the veteran Police Officers in his precinct that certain streets in his sector have unusually high rates of violent crime. All of the homicides take place on Locust Street between Ash Boulevard and Spruce Avenue. Most of the rapes take place on Ash Boulevard between Locust Street and Ennis Place. All of the assaults take place on Spruce Avenue between Ennis Place and Kama Drive. The rapes occur between 9:00 P.M. and 12:00 P.M.; the assaults occur between 4:00 P.M. and 12:00 P.M.; and most of the homicides occur between 7:00 P.M. and 11:00 P.M. The assaults usually occur on Wednesdays and Thursdays; the homicides occur on Mondays and Tuesdays; and the rapes occur on Fridays and Saturdays. Officer Roberts would MOST likely be able to reduce the number of homicides by patrolling

    A. Ash Boulevard between Spruce Avenue and Ennis Place on Mondays and Tuesdays between 8:00 P.M. and 4:00 A.M.

B. Locust Street between Ash Boulevard and Spruce Avenue on Fridays and Saturdays between 7:00 P.M. and 11:00 P.M.
C. Spruce Avenue between Kama Drive and Ennis Place on Wednesdays and Thursdays between 4:00 P.M. and Midnight
D. Locust Street between Ash Boulevard and Spruce Avenue on Mondays and Tuesdays between 8:00 P.M. and Midnight

24. The procedure that a Police Officer should follow when making an arrest is:
    I. Inform the person in custody of the reason for his arrest.
    II. Handcuff the person with hands behind his back.
    III. Immediately search the person for weapons or evidence.
    IV. Advise the person of his legal rights.

Police Officer Jelko, while doing his regular 4:00 P.M. to Midnight foot patrol, was approached by Sister Maria, who told him that she had just had her pocketbook stolen at gunpoint. Sister Maria further stated that the man who robbed her was standing across the street. Officer Jelko, after being assured by Sister Maria that the man did commit the crime, walked up to him and stated, *You are under arrest for robbery.* Officer Jelko then proceeded to handcuff the man's hands behind his back, advise him of his legal rights, and take him to the precinct. The actions taken by Officer Jelko were

A. *proper,* primarily because the prisoner was handcuffed from behind
B. *improper,* primarily because Sister Maria also should have gone to the precinct since she was the victim
C. *proper,* primarily because the prisoner was positively identified by Sister Maria
D. *improper,* primarily because the prisoner was not searched for any weapons or evidence

25. Police Officer Davis is completing an Activity Log entry which will include the following five sentences:
    I. A radio car was dispatched and the male was taken to Greenville Hospital.
    II. Several people saw him and called the police.
    III. A naked man was running down the street waving his arms above his head and screaming, *Insects are all over me!*
    IV. I arrived on the scene and requested an ambulance.
    V. The dispatcher informed me that no ambulances were available.

The MOST logical order for the above sentences to appear in the Activity Log is:

A. III, IV, V, I, II
B. II, III, V, I, IV
C. III, II, IV, V, I
D. II, IV, III, V, I

KEY (CORRECT ANSWERS)

1. A
2. C
3. C
4. B
5. B

6. D
7. B
8. C
9. B
10. B

11. A
12. A
13. B
14. C
15. D

16. B
17. A
18. C
19. C
20. C

21. B
22. C
23. D
24. D
25. C

EXAMINATION SECTION
TEST 1

DIRECTIONS: Each question or incomplete statement is followed by several suggested answers or completions. Select the one that BEST answers the question or completes the statement. *PRINT THE LETTER OF THE CORRECT ANSWER IN THE SPACE AT THE RIGHT.*

Questions 1-3.

DIRECTIONS: Questions 1 through 3 are to be answered SOLELY on the basis of the following passage.

    Housing Police Officer Lewis is patrolling Woodrow Houses, a housing project consisting of ten 14-story apartment buildings. Officer Lewis is working a Midnight to 8 A.M. tour of duty. Before going to his assigned post, Officer Lewis was told by Sergeant Smith that there has been an increase in the number of apartment burglaries on his post. Sergeant Smith also stated that the burglaries are occurring between 10 P.M. and 6 A.M. A male Hispanic, 5'5" tall, dark complexion, tattoo of a cross on right forearm, large black mustache, and wearing dark sunglasses has been seen in the area just prior to a number of the burglaries. At 3:00 M., Officer Lewis is patrolling his post and notices a male Hispanic, 5"5", dark complexion, no mustache, no sunglasses, a tattoo of a cross on his right forearm, exiting an apartment building carrying a portable TV and a Sony radio. Officer Lewis stops the man and asks him where he was coming from. The man says that he was just coming from his friend's 6th floor apartment and that he was going to have the TV and radio repaired in the morning. Officer Lewis asks the man to return to the apartment with him. The man then drops the TV and radio and starts to run. Officer Lewis pursues and apprehends the man and places him under arrest.

    A short time later, Officer Lewis learns that a burglary had occurred in a 6th floor apartment in the same building that the male Hispanic was seen leaving. Among the items stolen were a TV and radio.

1. What did the male Hispanic have in his possession when he was stopped by Officer Lewis?
A

    A. portable radio and a Sony TV
    B. portable TV and a Sony radio
    C. Sony TV and a Zenith radio
    D. Zenith TV and a Sony radio

1.____

2. Sergeant Smith informed Officer Lewis of burglaries occurring on his post in the

    A. late evening and early morning
    B. early morning and early afternoon
    C. early afternoon and late afternoon
    D. late morning and early evening

2.____

3. The man Officer Lewis stopped to question

    A. was about 5'5" tall and wore dark sunglasses
    B. had a dark complexion and a large black mustache
    C. had a large black mustache and a tattoo on his forearm
    D. had a tattoo on his forearm and was about 5'5" tall

3.____

4. Police Officers must sometimes rely on eyewitness accounts of incidents, even though eyewitnesses may make mistakes with regard to some details.
Police Officer Ballard responds to the report of a mugging. When she arrives at the scene, she interviews four witnesses who saw a man flee the scene in a white car. The following are license plate numbers provided by the four witnesses.
Which one of these numbers should Officer Ballard consider MOST likely to be correct?

   A. L-41688 B. L-41638 C. L-41238 D. L-31638

5. Upon arriving at the scene of a fire, a Police Officer should do the following in the order given:
   I. Send an alarm to the Fire Department or make sure
   II. one has been sent.
   III. Direct a responsible person to remain at the alarm box to direct fire apparatus (if the fire is not in view).
   IV. Park patrol car to prevent interference with fire-fighting operation.
   V. Warn occupants of building and assist them in leaving.
   VI. Take other action required by the situation.
   VII. Establish police lines beyond the fire apparatus and hydrants in use.

While on patrol, Police Officers Kittle and Chiu are flagged down by a man running from an apartment building. The man tells the Officers that there is a fire on most of the fifth floor of the building located at 330 State Street. The man also tells the Officers that he has already notified the Fire Department by using the fire alarm box, located at the corner of State Street and Bushwick Avenue. Officer Kittle tells the man to wait by the fire alarm box and to direct Fire Department personnel to the exact location of the fire when they arrive. The NEXT step Officers Kittle and Chiu should take is to

   A. set up police lines beyond the fire apparatus and hydrants in use
   B. position their patrol car so it will prevent interference with firefighting operations
   C. warn occupants of the building and help them leave
   D. direct someone to remain at the alarm box to direct the fire apparatus

6. According to the Criminal Procedure Law, a Police Officer may temporarily stop a person in a public place for questioning when the Officer reasonably suspects a person is committing, has committed, or is about to commit a crime. The grounds for reasonable suspicion may include any overheard conversations of the suspect, any information received from third parties, the time of day or night, the particular streets or area involved, or the actions of a suspect.
In which one of the following situations would it be LEAST appropriate for the Officer to stop and question the other person?

   A. Officer Hicks sees Randy Jones, whom he arrested a year ago for shoplifting, walk into Lacy's Department Store.
   B. Officer Lance notices a person checking cars to see if the doors have been left open.
   C. Officer Blake is given a description of a man offering rides to little girls as they are leaving school.
   D. Officer Hines, while working in plain clothes, hears a man on a public phone discussing plans for a bank robbery.

7. Police Officer Jenner responds to the scene of a burglary at 2106 La Vista Boulevard. He is approached by an elderly man named Richard Jenkins, whose account of the incident includes the following five sentences:
   I. I saw that the lock on my apartment door had been smashed and the door was open.
   II. My apartment was a shambles; my belongings were everywhere and my television set was missing.
   III. As I walked down the hallway toward the bedroom, I heard someone opening a window.
   IV. I left work at 5:30 P.M. and took the bus home.
   V. At that time, I called the police.

   The MOST logical order for the above sentences to appear in the report is

   A. I, V, IV, II, III
   B. IV, I, II, III, V
   C. I, V, II, III, IV
   D. IV, III, II, V, I

Questions 8-9.

DIRECTIONS: Questions 8 and 9 are to be answered SOLELY on the basis of the following information.

Police Officer Meadows is aware that in his sector all of the robberies take place on Edgewater Street; all of the homicides happen on Bay Street; and all of the assaults take place on Went-worth Avenue. Most of the homicides occur between Midnight and 4:00 A.M.; most of the robberies take place between 8:00 P.M. and 11:00 P.M.; and most of the assaults happen from 7:00 P.M. to Midnight. Most of the robberies occur on Saturdays, most of the assaults on Fridays, and most of the homicides on Wednesdays and Fridays.

8. Officer Meadows would be MOST able to reduce the number of assaults if he patrolled

   A. Edgewater Street on Wednesdays from 7:00 P.M. to Midnight
   B. Bay Street on Thursdays from 8:00 P.M. to 11:00 P.M.
   C. Wentworth Avenue on Fridays from Midnight to 4:00 A.M.
   D. Wentworth Avenue on Fridays from 7:00 P.M. to Midnight

9. In order to reduce the number of homicides in his sector, Officer Meadows' superiors ask him to work a steady tour that would allow him to concentrate on that crime.
   For this purpose, it would be MOST appropriate for Officer Meadows to work

   A. Tuesday through Saturday, 4:00 P.M. to Midnight
   B. Saturday through Wednesday, 8:00 P.M. to 4:00 A.M.
   C. Tuesday through Saturday, Midnight to 8:00 A.M.
   D. Monday through Friday, 4:00 P.M. to Midnight

10. While on patrol, Police Officer Richardson receives a call to respond to a Grand Larceny. The following information relating to the crime is obtained by the Officer:
    Time of Occurrence: Between 3:00 A.M. and 4:00 A.M.
    Place of Occurrence: In front of 1122 Dumont Avenue
    Victim: Bart Edwards
    Crime: Car Theft
    Type of Car: 2003 Monte Carlo

    Officer Richardson is completing a report on the incident. Which one of the following expresses the above information MOST clearly and accurately?

A. Reported stolen at 3:00 A.M. and 4:00 A.M. in front of 1122 Dumont Avenue was Bart Edwards' 2003 Monte Carlo.
B. Bart Edwards reported that at some time between 3:00 A.M. and 4:00 A.M. his 2003 Monte Carlo was stolen from in front of 1122 Dumont Avenue.
C. Between 3:00 A.M. and 4:00 A.M. Bart Edwards reported that his 2003 Monte Carlo was stolen in front of 1122 Dumont Avenue.
D. In front of 1122 Dumont Avenue between 3:00 A.M. and 4:00 A.M., Bart Edwards reported that his 2003 Monte Carlo was stolen.

11. While on patrol, Police Officers Coates and Hall respond to a complaint about a stolen vehicle. The following information relating to the incident is obtained by the Officers:

Time of Occurrence:	3:00 A.M.
Stolen Vehicle:	2004 Corvette
Witness:	Mark Wondon
Place:	In front of 12-14 Diamond Street
Victim:	John Silber
Suspect:	James Frank

Officer Hall is completing a report on the incident.
Which one of the following expresses the above information MOST clearly and accurately?

11.____

A. Mark Wondon reports that at 3:00 A.M. he witnessed James Frank steal a 2004 Corvette from in front of 12-14 Diamond Street. Mr. Wondon states that the car belongs to John Silber.
B. Mark Wondon reports that the 2004 Corvette taken was for John Silber. In front of 12-14 Diamond Street it was taken. The car was robbed by James Frank at 3:00 M.
C. At 3:00 A.M. a 2004 Corvette stolen by James Frank was reported. Mark Wondon saw it in front of 12-14 Diamond Street. It was owned by John Silber.
D. At 12-14 Diamond Street, a 2004 Corvette was reported by Mark Wondon at 3:00 A.M. John Silber, the car owner, was the victim. It was done by James Frank.

Questions 12-15.

DIRECTIONS: Questions 12 through 15 are to be answered SOLELY on the basis of the following passage.

At 3:55 A.M. on August 3, Police Officer Snow observed four male Hispanics standing by the emergency exit at the 14th Street and Union Square subway station. After one of the males spotted Officer Snow, they all ran down the subway platform. Three of the males ran out the exit gate and up into the street, while the fourth male loitered on the platform, stuffing what appeared to be candy into a paper bag. At 3:57 A.M., Officer Snow stopped and questioned the male. While Officer Snow was questioning the male, a call came over her portable radio requesting her to search the station for unidentified vandals. Officer Snow decided to detain the male because of the radio call and proceeded to interview the railroad clerk who had called the police.

At 4:00 A.M., the railroad clerk, Mr. Wallace, stated that four male Hispanics had broken into the concession stand and removed several bars of candy, cigarettes, and some cash. Officer Snow arrested the male she had detained after the railroad clerk identified him as one of the thieves. Officer Snow read the suspect his constitutional rights at 4:02 A.M., and Sergeant Burns transported Officer Snow and the suspect to the District 4 office.

The suspect was identified as Louie Rodriguez, of 2948 W. 38th Street, New York, New York, age seventeen, 5'10", 145 lbs., with brown eyes and black hair. Officer Snow described one of the other three suspects as a male Hispanic, approximately 17 to 20 years old, 5'10", slim build, mustache, wearing a black leather jacket, blue jeans, and white Puma sneakers.

The prisoner was searched by Officer Snow and drugs were found on his person. Lieutenant Nicholson classified the crime as Burglary and Unlawful Possession of a Controlled Substance. Officer Snow entered the crime classification on her arrest forms at 4:54 A.M. and fingerprinted and photographed the prisoner at 5:04 A.M. Officer Snow then called the Warrant Division by telephone to make sure the perpetrator did not have any outstanding warrants. In accordance with procedures, Officer Snow secured the drugs in a sealed envelope containing a serial number.

12. Who transported Officer Snow and the prisoner to the District 4 office?

    A. Lieutenant Nicholson B. Lieutenant Wallace
    C. Sergeant Burns   D. Sergeant Rodriguez

13. What time did Police Officer Snow fingerprint the prisoner?
    _____ A.M.

    A. 3:57   B. 4:02   C. 4:54   D. 5:04

14. When Officer Snow first observed the four males, they were standing by the

    A. exit gate   B. emergency exit
    C. concession stand   D. token booth

15. How did Officer Snow safeguard the drugs?

    A. Stored them in a locked safe   B. Gave them to the supervisor
    C. Placed them in a sealed envelope   D. Sent them to the lab for analysis

16. When Police Officers arrive at the scene of a serious crime, they should protect any evidence and detain witnesses for further investigation. The following steps should be taken in the order given:
    I. Call for the Patrol Supervisor, Detectives, and any other person that may be required.
    II. Remove unauthorized persons from the area and secure the crime scene. Do not disturb any evidence found at the scene.
    III. Detain witnesses and persons with information concerning the crime.
    IV. Record in Memo Book all observations, as well as the names, addresses, and telephone numbers of witnesses, and relevant statements made by anyone, whether casually or as a formal statement.
    V. Advise the Patrol Supervisor and Detectives of the identity of witnesses detained and any other information regarding the crime.

Police Officer Hayward responds to a secluded area in Greenville Park after receiving an anonymous report that a dead body is at the location. When the Officer arrives, there is no one around, but the Officer sees what appears to be a body wrapped in plastic. Officer Hayward notifies the Patrol Supervisor and Detectives and calls for an ambulance.
After roping off the area, the Officer should NEXT

- A. detain witnesses to the crime
- B. cut open the bag to determine if it actually contains a dead body
- C. write the appropriate entries in his Memo Book
- D. advise the Patrol Supervisor of all relevant details when the Supervisor arrives

17. Police Officer LaJolla is writing an Incident Report in which back-up assistance was required. The report will contain the following five sentences:
    I. The radio dispatcher asked what my location was and he then dispatched patrol cars for back-up assistance.
    II. At approximately 9:30 P.M., while I was walking my assigned footpost, a gunman fired three shots at me.
    III. I quickly turned around and saw a White male, approximately 5'10", with black hair, wearing blue jeans, a yellow T-shirt, and white sneakers, running across the avenue carrying a handgun.
    IV. When the back-up Officers arrived, we searched the area but could not find the suspect.
    V. I advised the radio dispatcher that a gunman had just fired a gun at me, and then I gave the dispatcher a description of the man.

    The MOST logical order for the above sentences to appear in the report is

    A. III, V, II, IV, I
    B. II, III, V, I, IV
    C. III, II, IV, I, V
    D. II, V, I, III, IV

Question 18.

DIRECTIONS: Question 18 is to be answered SOLELY on the basis of the following information.

Serious Physical Injury - injury which creates a substantial risk of death, or serious and protracted disfigurement, protracted impairment of health, or loss or impairment of function of any bodily organ.

Assault 2nd Degree - occurs when, with intent to cause physical injury to another, a person causes such injury to such person or to a third person by means of a deadly weapon or dangerous instrument.

Assault 1st Degree - occurs when a person intends to cause serious physical injury to another and causes such injury to that person or to a third person by means of a deadly weapon or dangerous instrument.

Manslaughter 1st Degree - occurs when, with intent to cause serious physical injury to another, a person causes death to that person or to a third person.

Murder 2nd Degree - occurs when, with intent to cause the death of another, a person causes the death of such person or third person.

18. Police Officers Hudson and Ellis are dispatched to the scene of a vehicle accident at 7th Avenue and Valentine Street. Upon their arrival, they observe a man standing over a body lying in the gutter. The man, Ralph Vanderbilt, tells the Officers that he was stopped at a red light in his 1999 Lincoln Continental when he was struck from behind by a car driven by Richard Verde. Intending to break Verde's ribs, Vanderbilt took a baseball bat from his car and swung it at Mr. Verde. In trying to avoid the blow, Verde slipped and was struck in the head by the bat. Soon after, the Patrol Supervisor and an ambulance arrive at the scene. Officers Hudson and Ellis place Mr. Vanderbilt under arrest. The Supervisor then informs the Officers that Mr. Verde is dead. In this situation, it would be MOST appropriate for the Officers to charge Mr. Vanderbilt with _____ Degree.   18.____

    A. Assault 1st
    B. Murder 2nd
    C. Manslaughter 1st
    D. Assault 2nd

19. Police Officers are required to observe locations where criminal activities may be taking place.   19.____
    Which one of the following locations would MOST likely require further observation?

    A. Neighborhood residents complain that young people enter and quickly leave an abandoned building all day long
    B. A diner which is open twenty-four hours a day and frequented by travelers from a nearby motel
    C. A fast food outlet which has become a hang-out for a young crowd
    D. Numerous middle-aged and elderly women are observed entering office buildings in the late afternoon and leaving around midnight

Questions 20-23.

DIRECTIONS: Questions 20 through 23 are to be answered SOLELY on the basis of the following passage.

Police Officers Ruden and Elliot were on routine patrol on the night of August 21 at 11 P.M. when they were dispatched to the scene of a shooting. They were told to respond to 228 West 64th Street. When they arrived at 11:03 P.M., they saw a man lying in the street in front of 226 West 64th Street. He was bleeding from a gunshot wound to the head. The injured man was identified as Raymond Lopez, a resident of 229 West 64th Street, Apartment 5C. A small crowd gathered along the sidewalk.

An ambulance arrived at 11:06 P.M. Police Officer Keyes helped to put Mr. Lopez into the ambulance, and then accompanied him in the ambulance to try to get more information on the shooting. Two paramedics, John Hayes and Robert Shelton, tried their best to save Mr. Lopez' life but failed. He died at 11:12 P.M. on the way to the hospital. Officer Ruden remained at the scene to get a description of the man who shot Lopez, but witnesses were afraid to talk. Three persons were questioned: Ralph Ricardo, male Hispanic, businessman, age 39, lives at 230 West 64th Street, Apartment 4C; John Fitzpatrick, male White, age 25, cabdriver; and Jimmy Warren, male Black, age 13, who stated that he saw Arthur Gonzalez, the superintendent at 229 West 64th Street, shoot Lopez. Jimmy's mother agreed to let him testify against Gonzalez, who was arrested at 11:29 P.M. on November 25, when he returned to his apartment to get some clothes.

20. Which of the following persons claimed to have seen the shooting? 20.____

    A. Ricardo   B. Warren   C. Lopez   D. Fitzpatrick

21. When was Gonzalez arrested? 21.____

    A. 11:03 P.M., November 24   B. 11:06 P.M., November 25
    C. 11:12 P.M., November 24   D. 11:29 P.M., November 25

22. The person who was arrested was 22.____

    A. a superintendent   B. a cabdriver
    C. a businessman   D. unemployed

23. Where did the Police find Raymond Lopez? 23.____

    A. In Apartment 5C, 228 West 64th Street
    B. Opposite 229 West 64th Street
    C. In Apartment 4C, 230 West 64th Street
    D. In front of 226 West 64th Street

Questions 24-25.

DIRECTIONS: Questions 24 and 25 are to be answered SOLELY on the basis of the following information.

Police Officer Quincy observes that all the cocaine sales in her sector take place on Bucket Avenue; all the heroin sales occur on Jones Road between Bucket Avenue and Wright Street; and all the *crack* sales happen on Albany Road between Hamilton Street and Jervis Avenue. Most of the heroin sales take place between 7:00 P.M. and Midnight. Most of the *crack* sales occur between 6:00 P.M. and 10:00 P.M. and between 10:00 A.M. and 2:00 P.M. Most of the cocaine sales take place between 4:00 P.M. and 10:00 P.M. Most of the *crack* sales happen on Tuesdays; most of the heroin sales take place on Wednesdays and Fridays; and most of the cocaine sales take place on Fridays and Saturdays.

24. Officer Quincy would MOST likely be able to reduce the number of heroin sales by patrolling 24.____

    A. Bucket Avenue on Wednesday and Friday from 4:00 P.M. to 10:00 P.M.
    B. Jones Road on Wednesday and Thursday from 8:00 P.M. to Midnight
    C. Jones Road on Wednesday and Friday from 7:00 P.M. to 11:00 P.M.
    D. Albany Road on Tuesday from 6:00 P.M. to 10:00 P.M.

25. Based on her knowledge of the drug sale patterns in her sector, Officer Quincy's supervisor wants her to work a steady tour each week that would allow her to concentrate on cocaine, heroin, and *crack* sales within her sector. 25.____
    For this purpose, it would be MOST appropriate for Officer Quincy to work

    A. Tuesday through Saturday, 4:00 P.M. to Midnight
    B. Tuesday through Saturday, 2:00 P.M. to 10:00 P.M.
    C. Monday through Friday, 4:00 P.M. to Midnight
    D. Wednesday through Sunday, 2:00 P.M. to 10:00 P.M.

KEY (CORRECT ANSWERS)

1. B
2. A
3. D
4. B
5. B

6. A
7. B
8. D
9. C
10. B

11. A
12. C
13. D
14. B
15. C

16. C
17. B
18. C
19. A
20. B

21. D
22. A
23. D
24. C
25. A

TEST 2

DIRECTIONS: Each question or incomplete statement is followed by several suggested answers or completions. Select the one that BEST answers the question or completes the statement. *PRINT THE LETTER OF THE CORRECT ANSWER IN THE SPACE AT THE RIGHT.*

1. Police Officer Davis is preparing a written report concerning child abuse. The report will include the following five sentences:
    I. I responded to the scene and was met by an adult and a child who was approximately four years old.
    II. I was notified by an unidentified pedestrian of a possible case of child abuse at 325 Belair Terrace.
    III. The adult told me that the child fell and that the police were not needed.
    IV. I felt that this might be a case of child abuse, and I requested that a Sergeant respond to the scene.
    V. The child was bleeding from the head and had several bruises on the face.

    The MOST logical order for the above sentences to appear in the report is

    A. II, I, V, III, IV
    B. I, II, IV, III, V
    C. I, III, IV, II, V
    D. II, IV, I, V, III

    1.___

2. While on patrol in the subway, Police Officer Conway is notified, via radio, to respond to the northbound platform to investigate a crime. The following information relating to the crime was obtained by the Officer:
    Time of Occurrence: 5:30 P.M.
    Place: Northbound A train
    Witness: Gertrude Stern
    Victim: Matilda Jones
    Crime: Chain Snatch

    Officer Conway is completing a report on the incident.
    Which one of the following Memo Book entries expresses the above information MOST clearly and accurately?

    A. There was a chain snatching incident on the Northbound A train at 5:30 P.M. involving Matilda Jones and Gertrude Stern. There was a witness.
    B. Gertrude Stern, while traveling on the Northbound A train, witnessed a chain snatching with Matilda Jones at 5:30 P.M.
    C. Matilda Jones and Gertrude Stern were on the Northbound A train at 5:30 P.M. when Gertrude witnessed a chain snatching.
    D. Matilda Jones informed me that her chain was snatched aboard a Northbound A train at 5:30 P.M. Gertrude Stern witnessed the chain snatching.

    2.___

3. Police Officers Quinn and Dunn receive a call to respond to a reported robbery. The following information relating to the crime is obtained by the Officers:
    Time of Occurrence: 10:00 P.M.
    Place of Occurrence: 31-42 Maplewood Avenue, Liquor Store
    Victim: Donna Miller, store owner
    Witness: Thomas White, customer
    Suspect: Michael Wall
    Crime: Money stolen from cash register

    3.___

Officers Quinn and Dunn are completing a report on the incident.
Which one of the following expresses the above information MOST clearly and accurately?

- A. The witness said that he got to the liquor store at 10:00 P.M.; and when he got there, the place was being held up. His name was Michael Wall. He took the money from Donna Miller, the owner of the liquor store on 31-42 Maplewood Avenue out of the store cash register. Thomas White reported these facts to us.
- B. At 10:00 P.M., Thomas White, the witness, states that after entering the liquor store at 31-42 Maplewood Avenue, he saw the suspect take money from the cash register which belongs to Donna Miller, the owner. Michael Wall is suspected.
- C. Thomas White reports that at 10:00 P.M. he went to the liquor store at 31-42 Maplewood Avenue and saw Michael Wall take money from the cash register. The store is owned by Donna Miller.
- D. Donna Miller, the owner, was robbed at 10:00 P.M. when the money from her cash register was taken at 31-42 Maplewood Avenue. Thomas White was in the liquor store at the time and saw Michael Wall do it.

Question 4.

DIRECTIONS: Question 4 is to be answered SOLELY on the basis of the following information.

Police Officers may sometimes release persons charged with juvenile delinquency into the custody of a parent or guardian. In such cases, the Officer should:

- I. Determine if the person who would take custody is a parent, guardian, lawful custodian or responsible adult relative by checking the evidence of identity and relationship to the juvenile.
- II. Call the Youth Records Unit to obtain information on the juvenile's prior police contacts.
- III. Call the Central Warrants Unit to determine if juvenile is wanted by the Police on a warrant.

NOTE: Juvenile will NOT be released if:
- I. Person who would take custody is not capable of providing adequate supervision.
- II. Juvenile is wanted on a warrant by the Police.
- III. Juvenile is not likely to appear in court on return date.
- IV. Juvenile's release would be dangerous to the community.

4. Police Officer Gardner arrested Roger Carter, a 15-year-old, for Grand Larceny. Carter gave Officer Gardner the phone number of his sister Ruth, who was then notified to come down to the station house. Officer Gardner checked the Central Warrants Unit and the Youth Records Unit and determined that Carter had no previous contacts with the Police and could be released into a relative's custody.

A half hour later, a young woman who appeared to be intoxicated entered the station house. There was a strong smell of alcohol on her breath. She had identification that proved she was Roger Carter's 21-year-old sister Ruth. Officer Gardner then released Roger Carter into Ruth's custody.
In this situation, Officer Gardner's actions were

A. *proper*, primarily because Ruth Carter could show that she was a relative who was old enough to take custody
B. *improper*, primarily because Ruth Carter did not appear to be capable of providing adequate supervision
C. *proper*, primarily because Roger Carter had no prior Police contacts and was not wanted on any other charges
D. *improper*, primarily because Roger Carter was unlikely to appear in court and would pose a threat to the community

Questions 5-6.

DIRECTIONS: Questions 5 and 6 are to be answered SOLELY on the basis of the following information.

Police Officer Cruz is told by his Supervisor that the sector he is assigned to has a high incidence of car accidents, assaults, burglaries, and robberies. Officer Cruz studies the crime statistics for his sector and notices that all of the assaults occur Tuesdays through Thursdays, car accidents on Fridays and Saturdays, burglaries on Fridays and Saturdays, and robberies on Fridays through Mondays. Most of the assaults occur on Maple Street, robberies on McDonald Street, car accidents on Merrick Street, and burglaries on Mason Street. Officer Cruz also noticed that all robberies occur between 7:00 P.M. and 11:00 P.M., burglaries between 1:00 P.M. and 5:00 P.M., car accidents between 10:00 P.M. and 3:00 A.M., and assaults between 7:00 P.M. and 11:00 P.M.

5. Officer Cruz would MOST likely be able to reduce the incidence of car accidents by patrolling

    A. Mason Street on Friday and Saturday between 10:00 P.M. and 4:00 A.M.
    B. Maple Street on Monday through Wednesday between 7:00 P.M. and 11:30 P.M.
    C. Merrick Street on Friday and Saturday between 10:00 P.M. and 4:00 A.M.
    D. McDonald Street on Tuesday and Thursday between 8:00 P.M. and 1:00 A.M.

6. Officer Cruz's superiors want him to work a steady tour each week that would allow him to concentrate on robberies within his sector.
What would be the MOST appropriate tour for Officer Cruz to work?

    A. Monday through Friday, 4:00 P.M. to Midnight
    B. Thursday through Monday, 1:00 P.M. to 9:00 P.M.
    C. Thursday through Monday, 4:00 P.M. to Midnight
    D. Monday through Friday, 8:00 A.M. to 4:00 P.M.

7. The following five sentences will be part of a Memo Book entry concerning found property:

    I. Mr. Gustav said that while cleaning the lobby he found six credit cards and a passport.
    II. The credit cards and passport were issued to Manuel Gomez.
    III. I went to the precinct to give the property to the Desk Officer.
    IV. I prepared a receipt listing the property, gave the receipt to Mr. Gustav, and had him sign my Memo Book.
    V. While on foot patrol, I was approached by Mr. Gustav, the superintendent of 50-12 Maiden Parkway.
    VI. The MOST logical order for the above sentences to appear in the Memo Book is

A. V, I, II, IV, III
B. I, II, IV, III, V
C. V, I, III, IV, II
D. I, IV, III, II, V

8. When a juvenile is arrested and charged as a juvenile offender, a Police Officer should do the following in the order given:
   I. Bring the juvenile to the area in the station house designated for interrogation of juveniles.
   II. Notify parents or guardian that the juvenile is in custody and where the juvenile is located.
   III. Do not question the juvenile until arrival of parents or guardian.
   IV. Advise juvenile and parents or guardian of constitutional rights prior to interrogation.
   V. Prepare Arrest Report.

   Police Officer Fernandez has made an arrest charging a juvenile as a juvenile offender. After the parents and juvenile have been read their rights before questioning, Officer Fernandez should NEXT

   A. notify the Detectives
   B. fill out an Arrest Report
   C. bring the juvenile to the area in the station house designated for questioning
   D. advise the juvenile and parents of their constitutional rights

9. Police Officers Mains and Jacobs respond to a report of an assault and obtain the following information:
   Time of Occurrence: 8:00 P.M.
   Place of Occurrence: Lobby of 165 E. 210th Street Victim: Charles Rayes, stabbed in chest
   Witness: John McNam
   Suspect: Lydon Syms
   Weapon: Large kitchen knife
   The Officers are completing a report on the incident. Which one of the following expresses the above information MOST clearly and accurately?

   A. Mr. John McNam states that at 8:00 P.M. he observed Lydon Syms stab Charles Rayes in the chest while entering the lobby of 165 E. 210th Street with a large kitchen knife.
   B. At 8:00 P.M. John McNam stated he saw Lydon "Syms use a large kitchen knife on Charles Rayes in the chest in the lobby of 165 E. 210th Street.
   C. At 8:00 P.M. John McNam stated he observed Lydon Syms stab him in the chest with a kitchen knife while in the lobby of 165 E. 210th Street with Charles Rayes.
   D. Mr. John McNam stated that at 8:00 P.M. he observed Lydon Syms stab Charles Rayes in the chest with a large kitchen knife in the lobby of 165 E. 210 Street.

10. Upon arriving at a location where a person is threatening to jump from a structure, a Police Officer should do the following in the order given:
    I. Notify Communications Unit and request an Emergency Service Unit to respond.
    II. Attempt to persuade or prevent the person from jumping.
    III. Seek assistance from the person's relatives, friends, or clergyman if available.
    IV. Confine the person to the side of the building facing the street.
    V. Rope off area below and prevent persons from entering the area.
    VI. Prepare a Complaint Report and make appropriate Memo Book entries.

    Police Officer Samuels is on a footpost when a woman runs up to him and states that her husband is on the roof of their twelve-story apartment building and has threatened to jump. Officer Samuels and the woman go to the roof of the building. The man sees them and shouts, *You come any closer and I'll jump!* Officer Samuels radios the Communications Unit and requests an Emergency Service Unit to respond. While waiting for back-up assistance, Officer Samuels attempts to persuade the man not to jump.
    The NEXT step Officer Samuels should take is to

    A. prepare a Complaint Report and make appropriate Memo Book entries
    B. rope off area below and prevent persons from entering the area
    C. ask the man's wife and any friends who may be present for assistance
    D. keep the man on the side of the building facing the street

11. A Police Officer may on occasion arrest a juvenile who is less than 16 years of age, take him into custody, and charge him with a serious felony. When a juvenile is arrested and charged as a juvenile offender, the Officer should
    I. put the juvenile in the forward compartment of the patrol wagon and adult prisoners in the rear compartment, if they are being transported at the same time
    II. bring the juvenile to an appropriate area designated for questioning at the precinct of arrest
    III. keep the juvenile separated from adult prisoners while in custody

    While on patrol, Police Officer Morgan sees 15-year-old Mary Jarvis robbing a neighborhood candy store. Officer Morgan arrests Mary and calls for the patrol wagon to bring her to the local precinct. When the wagon arrives, a forty-year-old burglar named Harry Ryan is seated in the front compartment. Officer Morgan orders Ryan into the rear compartment and puts Mary in the front. The actions taken by Officer Morgan were

    A. *proper,* primarily because male and female prisoners should not be transported together
    B. *improper,* primarily because Ryan should have been left in the front compartment
    C. *proper,* primarily because Mary belonged in the front compartment
    D. *improper,* primarily because Mary should not be sent to the local precinct

12. Police Officer Thomas is making a Memo Book entry that will include the following five sentences:

    I. My partner obtained a brief description of the suspects and the direction they were heading when they left the store.
    II. Edward Lemkin was asked to come with us to search the immediate area.
    III. I transmitted this information over the radio.
    IV. At the corner of 72nd Street and Broadway, our patrol car was stopped by Edward Lemkin, the owner of PJ Records
    V. He told us that a group of teenagers stole some merchandise from his record store.

    The MOST logical order for the above sentences to appear in the report is

    A. V, IV, I, III, II
    B. IV, V, I, III, II
    C. V, I, III, II, IV
    D. IV, I, III, II, V

13. Police Officer Black has been informed by Police Officer Hunt that there have been three robberies of clothing shops on his assigned patrol post during the month of June. All of the robberies occurred soon after the shops opened, and the suspect escaped on foot. Officer Hunt is in charge of investigating this series of crimes. The description of each of the subjects is as follows:

    Robbery No. 1 - Male, White, about 18 years old, 5'6", 120 lbs. Short hair with a tail on back. Blue dungarees, white sport sleeve shirt, white sneakers, scar from his right wrist to elbow.

    Robbery No. 2 - Male, White, 20 to 23 years old, 5'5", 140 lbs. Short curly black hair, blue dungarees, blue T-shirt, blue sneakers, tattoo on right arm, earring in right ear.

    Robbery No. 3 - Male, White, about 19 years old, 5'6", 135 lbs. Short black hair. Wears an earring in left ear, black jogging pants, black jacket, white sneakers, scar on left hand.
    On July 1, Police Officer Black arrested a suspect during an attempted robbery of another store. The description of this suspect is as follows:

    Robbery No. 4 - Male, White, 20 years old, 5'6", 130 lbs., short straight black hair, white short sleeve shirt, blue dungarees, white sneakers, gold earring in left ear, tattoo on right arm, 4" scar going from left hand to wrist.

    Based on the above descriptions of the suspects in the first three robberies, Officer Black should tell Officer Hunt that the suspect in the fourth robbery should also be considered a suspect in Robbery No.

    A. 1 *only*
    B. 3 *only*
    C. 2 and Robbery No. 3
    D. 1 and Robbery No. 2

14. While on patrol, Police Officers Murray and Crown receive a radio call to respond to a reported assault. The following information is given to them at the scene:

    Time of Occurrence: 6:00 P.M.
    Victim: Sarah Schwartz, wife
    Witness: Cathy Morris, Sarah's sister
    Suspect: Raymond Schwartz, husband
    Crime: Assault with a knife

    The Officers are completing a report on the incident.
    Which one of the following expresses the above information MOST clearly and accurately?

    A. Cathy Morris stated that she was visiting her sister, Sarah Schwartz. They were cooking dinner when Raymond Schwartz, Sarah's husband, came home at 6:00 P.M.
    Raymond was drunk and started an argument with Sarah. During the argument, Raymond picked up a knife and cut Sarah.
    B. Sarah Schwartz stated that she was making dinner with her sister, Cathy Morris. Her husband Raymond came home real angry and was drunk at 6:00 P.M.
    They had an argument and Raymond cut her with a knife.
    C. According to Cathy Morris, her sister Sarah Schwartz was cooking dinner with her. Sarah's husband Raymond came home. They got into an argument. He was drunk and had a knife in his hand and cut her. This happened when he arrived at 6:00 P.M.
    D. Sarah Schwartz' sister reported to me that at 6:00 P.M. her husband Raymond came home drunk. Cathy Morris was with her making dinner. Raymond got mad at her, picked up a knife, and cut her.

15. Police Officer Halloway responds to a call for help inside the Municipal Parking Lot. The following information relating to an assault is obtained by the Officer:

    Place of Occurrence: Municipal Parking Lot
    Victim: Diane Gallagher
    Suspect: Dominick DeLuca, victim's ex-boyfriend
    Crime: Assault

    Officer Halloway is completing a report on the incident. Which one of the following expresses the above information MOST clearly and accurately?

    A. The victim, Diane Gallagher, states that she was in the Municipal Parking Lot with her ex-boyfriend, Dominick DeLuca, when she was assaulted.
    B. Diane Gallagher states that she and her ex-boyfriend were in the Municipal Parking Lot when she was assaulted by Dominick DeLuca.
    C. Diane Gallagher, the victim, in the Municipal Parking Lot with Dominick DeLuca, states that she was assaulted by her ex-boyfriend.
    D. The victim, Diane Gallagher, states that she was assaulted by her ex-boyfriend, Dominick DeLuca, in the Municipal Parking Lot.

16. Police Officer Fox, of the 62nd Precinct, notices that most of the assaults happen between 2:00 A.M. and 6:00 A.M.; most of the burglaries occur between 10:00 A.M. and 3:00 P.M.; and most of the purse snatches take place between 4:00 P.M. and 7:00 A.M. Most of the burglaries occur on Wednesday; most of the assaults take place on Friday; and most of the purse snatches happen on Friday and Saturday. Police Officer Fox's superiors instruct him to work a steady tour each week that would allow him to concentrate on purse snatches and burglaries within his patrol area.
For this purpose, it would be MOST appropriate for Officer Fox to work

   A. 4:00 A.M. to Noon, Tuesday through Saturday
   B. Noon to 8:00 P.M., Wednesday through Sunday
   C. Midnight to 8:00 A.M., Tuesday through Saturday
   D. 4:00 A.M. to Noon, Monday through Friday

17. A Police Officer may issue a Desk Appearance Ticket (DAT) instead of detaining a prisoner if the prisoner qualifies for one. When processing a prisoner charged with a misdemeanor or violation, in addition to following the normal arrest procedure, the arresting officer should do the following in the order given:
   I. Inform the prisoner that he may be issued a DAT instead of detention if he qualifies.
   II. Check the prisoner's name with the Central Warrant Unit to determine if the prisoner is wanted for another crime.
   III. Issue the DAT after you determine that the prisoner is eligible.
   IV. Conduct an interview with the prisoner, using a Desk Appearance Ticket Investigation form.

Police Officer Perez has made an arrest involving a Petit Larceny.
In addition to following the normal arrest procedure, Officer Perez has informed the prisoner that he may be eligible for a Desk Appearance Ticket. Officer Perez should NEXT

   A. find out if the prisoner is wanted for committing another crime
   B. interview the prisoner
   C. inform the prisoner that he may be issued a Desk Appearance Ticket if he qualifies
   D. issue a Desk Appearance Ticket to the prisoner

18. Police Officer Caldwell is completing a Complaint Report. The report will include the following five sentences:
   I. When I yelled, *Don't move, Police,* the taller man dropped the bat and ran.
   II. I asked the girl for a description of the two men.
   III. I called for an ambulance.
   IV. A young girl approached me and stated that a man with a baseball bat was beating another man in front of 1700 Grande Street.
   V. Upon approaching the location, I observed the taller man hitting the other man with the bat.

The MOST logical order for the above sentences to appear in the report is

   A. IV, V, I, II, III
   B. V, IV, II, III, I
   C. V, I, III, IV, II
   D. IV, II, V, I, III

19. When a Police Officer is assigned to guard a hospitalized prisoner, only the following persons are allowed to visit the prisoner:
   I. Lawyer, if requested by the prisoner
   II. Member of the family, after written permission has been granted by the district Desk Officer of the district concerned or on official City Police Department letterhead of the precinct of arrest by the Station House Supervisor.

Agnes Smith, who has recently committed a bank robbery, is a prisoner at Bayview Hospital. In attempting to escape from the scene, Smith injured herself in an auto accident and has not been able to communicate since. Police Officer Cleon, who is guarding Ms. Smith, is approached by Betty Phillips, who requests permission to visit Ms. Smith. Officer Cleon explains to Ms. Phillips the rules for visiting a hospitalized prisoner. Ms. Phillips, who has documentation that shows she is a lawyer, also states that she is Ms. Smith's cousin. A nurse at the hospital, who knows them both, confirms this. In this situation, for Officer Cleon to allow Ms. Phillips to visit Ms. Smith would be

- A. *proper,* primarily because Ms. Phillips is a lawyer
- B. *improper,* primarily because only a doctor can determine who is allowed to see a patient who is seriously ill
- C. *proper,* primarily because Ms. Phillips is a member of Ms. Smith's family
- D. *improper,* primarily because Ms. Phillips lacks written permission to visit the patient

20. When a Police Officer stops a vehicle and discovers that the operator is driving with a suspended or revoked driver's license, the following should be done in the order given:
    - I. Confiscate driver's license.
    - II. Prepare Seized Driver's License Receipt/Report.
    - III. Give operator of the vehicle a receipt for the license.
    - IV. If the driver has two or more unrelated suspensions or his license has been revoked for any reason, arrest him and take him to the precinct.
    - V. Do not mark or mutilate license in any manner.
    - VI. Have violator's vehicle parked in a legal parking area until a registered owner can arrange to have the vehicle removed from the scene by a licensed operator.

    Police Officer Winterman is directing traffic during rush hour at a very busy and dangerous intersection. After observing the driver of a green Volvo make an illegal U-turn at the intersection, Officer Winterman directs the driver to pull his car over to the curb. While inspecting the driver's license, Officer Winterman discovers that the license has been revoked. Officer Winterman should NEXT

    - A. arrest the driver
    - B. take the driver's license,
    - C. give the operator of the vehicle a receipt for taking his license
    - D. have the violator park his car in a legal parking area

21. Police Officers Ortiz and Rinaldi patrol the harbor terminal area. Officer Ortiz works from 8:00 A.M. to 4:00 P.M., Monday through Friday. She takes her meal from Noon to 1:00 P.M. each day. Officer Rinaldi works from 4:00 P.M. to Midnight, Tuesday through Saturday. He takes his meal from 8:00 P.M. to 9:00 P.M. each day. Crime statistics for the terminal area show that most crimes in the daytime occur from 11:45 A.M. to 1:20 P.M. on Mondays, Tuesdays, and Thursdays, and from 12:05 P.M. to 1:20 P.M. on Wednesdays and Fridays. Most crimes at night are committed from 7:30 P.M. to 8:45 P.M. on Tuesdays and Thursdays, and from 8:30 P.M. to 9:15 P.M. on Wednesdays, Fridays, and Saturdays. In order to have an Officer on patrol during the periods when most crimes are committed, which of the following would be the MOST appropriate times for Officers Ortiz and Rinaldi to take their meals?

    Officer Ortiz - _____ ; Officer Rinaldi - _____ .

A. 1:30 P.M. - 2:30 P.M.; 9:00 P.M. - 10:00 P.M.
B. 12:30 P.M. - 1:30 P.M.; 9:30 P.M. - 10:30 P.M.
C. 1:30 P.M. - 2:30 P.M.; 9:30 P.M. - 10:30 P.M.
D. 1:00 P.M. - 2:00 P.M.; 7:00 P.M. - 8:00 P.M.

22. Whenever a Police Officer responds to the scene of a family offense, the Officer should
    I. obtain medical assistance for anyone who appears to need it
    II. determine if an Order of Protection has been obtained by the complainant, which would mean that a violator would be subject to arrest
    III. arrest the offender if a felony has been committed
    IV. not attempt to bring the parties together or mediate the dispute in felony cases - an arrest should be made
    V. arrest the offender in a non-felony case when efforts to mediate are unsuccessful and the complainant wants the offender arrested

    Police Officer Berger responds to a family dispute. After investigating, he determines that a violent argument has occurred between Max Jansen and his wife, Maria. Max apparently slapped Maria in the face more than once. Although she does not need medical attention and does not have an Order of Protection, Mrs. Jansen wants her husband arrested. Officer Berger, who knows that this is a non-felony case, tells Mrs. Jansen that there are problems in many marriages, but she and her husband should be able to work things out. When Mrs. Jansen insists that she wants her husband arrested, Officer Berger tells her to think the matter over for a day or two and then call him at the precinct. In this situation, Officer Berger's actions were

    A. *improper,* primarily because Mrs. Jansen had been struck in the face and should have been taken to the hospital as a precaution
    B. *proper,* primarily because it was not a felony case and Mrs. Jansen did not need medical attention
    C. *improper,* primarily because Mrs. Jansen insisted her husband be arrested
    D. *proper,* primarily because Mrs. Jansen had not obtained an Order of Protection

23. In August, the number of robberies near Montgomery Avenue and Cedar Street sharply increased. Captain Jones decided to assign Police Officer Roberts to a post at that corner. He ordered the Officer to remain visible and observe anyone who looked suspicious. Which one of the following situations should Officer Roberts observe MOST closely?

    A. A man standing near a bank cash machine watching people withdraw money
    B. A cabdriver parked in the same spot for thirty minutes drinking a cup of coffee and smoking a cigar
    C. Two young men running down the block toward the park
    D. A young man walking with an elderly lady into a grocery store

24. Police Officers must sometimes rely on eyewitness accounts of incidents, even though eyewitnesses may make mistakes with regard to some details.
    While walking his dog, Walter Twining is struck by a car at the corner of Bacon Avenue and Jersey Street. Police Officer Bond responds to the scene and questions four witnesses who saw the vehicle that struck Mr. Twining. The following are descriptions of the vehicle given by the witnesses.

Which one of these descriptions should Officer Bond consider MOST likely to be correct?
A

- A. blue Chevrolet, NY Plate 1736BOT
- B. black Chevrolet, NY Plate 1436BAT
- C. blue Oldsmobile, NY Plate 1736 BAI
- D. blue Chevrolet, NY Plate 1736 BAT

25. <u>Robbery 2nd Degree</u> - occurs when a person forcibly steals property and when:
    I. He is aided by another person actually present; or
    II. While committing the crime or immediately fleeing from it, he or another participant in the crime:
        (A) Causes physical injury to any person who is not a participant in the crime; or
        (B) Displays what appears to be a pistol, revolver, rifle, shotgun, machine gun, or other firearm.

    Which one of the following situations is the BEST example of Robbery in the Second Degree?

    - A. Jim Jackson and Martin Hayes decide to rob a grocery store. Unknown to Jackson, Hayes decides to bring along his pistol. They walk into the store, push the owner against the counter, and tell him to hand over the money or they will hurt him. The owner gives them two hundred dollars, and they flee the scene. Hayes never takes out his gun during the entire episode.
    - B. Ben Tyler walks into a grocery store, tells the clerk that he has a gun, and demands money. Tyler has his finger extended in his pocket pretending he has a gun. The clerk becomes frightened and gives Tyler all the money in the cash register.
    - C. Bill Jefferson and Warren Pierce plan to rob a liquor store. While entering the store, Pierce trips over a display and knocks over several bottles. This angers Jefferson, who punches Pierce in the face, causing a bloody nose. They then grab several bottles of liquor and run out of the store.
    - D. John Harrison decides to rob a gas station. He drives up, gets out of his car, takes out a 12" bowie knife, and threatens the attendant with it. The attendant gives $500 to Harrison, who then drives away.

KEY (CORRECT ANSWERS)

1. A
2. D
3. C
4. B
5. C

6. C
7. A
8. B
9. D
10. C

11. C
12. B
13. B/C
14. A
15. D

16. A
17. A
18. D
19. D
20. B

21. C
22. C
23. A
24. D
25. A

TEST 3

DIRECTIONS: Each question or incomplete statement is followed by several suggested answers or completions. Select the one that BEST answers the question or completes the statement. *PRINT THE LETTER OF THE CORRECT ANSWER IN THE SPACE AT THE RIGHT.*

1. When a crime has been committed and a Police Officer makes an arrest, he should do the following in the order given:
    I. Inform the person in custody of the reason for the arrest unless the person arrested physically resists or attempts to flee, or if it would be impractical to do so.
    II. Handcuff the person with hands behind the back.
    III. Immediately search the person for weapons and evidence.
    IV. Advise the person of his legal rights before questioning.

    Police Officers Darcy and Hayward were on patrol when they were approached by a woman on the corner of 236th Street and Katonah Avenue. The woman was very upset and said that an unidentified White male wearing a blue jacket was attempting to remove the stereo from her car, a green Oldsmobile, which was parked one block away on 237th Street. The Officers drove to 237th Street and saw a man fitting the description in the green Oldsmobile. When the Officers approached the auto, the man fled on foot, dropping the stereo as he left the vehicle. Officer Darcy caught the man about a block away, and *after* a brief struggle, placed the man under arrest. Officer Darcy should NEXT

    A. search the man for possible weapons
    B. inform the man of the reason for the arrest
    C. advise the man of his rights before questioning
    D. handcuff the man with his hands behind his back

2. Police Officer Moore is writing a Memo Book entry concerning a summons he issued. The entry will contain the following five sentences:
    I. As I was walking down the platform, I heard music coming from a radio that a man was holding on his shoulder.
    II. I asked the man for some identification.
    III. I was walking in the subway when a passenger complained about a man playing a radio loudly at the opposite end of the station.
    IV. I then gave the man a summons for playing the radio.
    V. As soon as the man saw me approaching, he turned the radio off.
    The MOST logical order for the above sentences to appear in the Memo Book entry is

    A. III, V, II, I, IV
    B. I, II, V, IV, III
    C. III, I, V, II, IV
    D. I, V, II, IV, III

3. Police Officers Janson and Lorenz are assigned to cover Sector C in a patrol car. They have been working together for over a year and know the sector well. They have noticed that all of the auto thefts occur on Diamond Avenue; all of the drug sales take place on Stag Street; most of the assaults occur on Beatle Street; and most of the burglaries occur on Bond Avenue. All of the drug sales occur between 2:00 P.M. and 11:00 P.M., and all of the auto thefts take place between Midnight and 6:00 A.M.

The assaults happen between 6:00 P.M. and 10:00 P.M. All of the burglaries take place between 8:00 P.M. and Midnight.
Officers Janson and Lorenz will be working a steady 10:00 P.M. to 6:00 A.M. tour during the fourth week of October.
During this tour, they would MOST likely decrease the incidence of crime by patrolling on

- A. Bond Avenue
- B. Stag Street
- C. Diamond Avenue
- D. Beatle Street

4. A Police Officer may bring a suspect back to the crime scene for a prompt on-the-spot identification only.
   I. within a reasonable time after the crime was committed; and
   II. the suspect was caught in an area reasonably near the scene of the crime; and
   III. the suspect is shown to the witness as fairly as possible under the circumstances.

   Police Officer Burke's patrol car is flagged down by Ed Weis, owner of Kay's Jewelry Store. Mr. Weis tells Officer Burke that just two minutes earlier his store was robbed. Mr. Weis gives the Officer a description of the robber, as well as the direction of his escape. About five minutes later, Officer Burke sees a male who fits the description acting suspiciously. As soon as the male sees the police car, he begins to run. After a brief chase, the male is apprehended by Officer Burke and brought back to the jewelry store, which is four blocks away. Mr. Weis identifies the male as the robber, and the Officer arrests him. In this situation, Officer Burke's actions were

   A. *improper,* primarily because the suspect was apprehended far away from the jewelry store
   B. *proper,* primarily because the Officer caught the suspect in an area near the scene of the crime and within a short period of time
   C. *improper,* primarily because the Officer deliberately brought the suspect back to the jewelry store to persuade the manager to identify him
   D. *proper,* primarily because the male began to run as soon as he saw the police car

5. Police Officer Kashawahara is completing an Incident Report regarding fleeing suspects he had pursued earlier. The report will include the following five sentences:
   I. I saw two males attempting to break into a store through the front window..
   II. On Myrtle Avenue, they ran into an alley between two abandoned buildings.
   III. I yelled to them, *Hey, what are you guys doing by* that window?
   IV. At that time, I lost sight of the suspects and I returned to the station house
   V. They started to run south on Wycoff Avenue heading towards Myrtle Avenue.
   The MOST logical order for the above sentences to appear in the report is

   A. I, V, II, IV, III
   B. III, V, II, IV, I
   C. I, III, V, II, IV
   D. III, I, V, II, IV

6. Police Officers who observe a person carrying a rifle or shotgun in public should do the following in the order given:
    I. Determine if the person has a valid permit.
    II. If there is no permit:
        a. Inform the person that he may surrender his firearm to the Officer at the scene or at the precinct.
        b. Serve a summons for violation or make an arrest.
        c. Prepare a receipt for the firearm and give a copy to the owner.
        d. Send the firearm to the gun lab if it is believed to have been used in a crime, or safeguard it at the precinct.
        e. Tell the owner to apply for a permit.

    After stopping Mr. Jones for carrying a rifle on the street, Police Officer Scott determines that Mr. Jones does not have a valid permit. While holding Mr. Jones' rifle, Officer Scott writes a summons.
    After giving Mr. Jones a summons for not having a valid permit, Officer Scott should NEXT

    A. tell Mr. Jones to apply for a permit
    B. send the rifle to the gun lab
    C. tell Mr. Jones to surrender his rifle
    D. make out a receipt for the firearm and give a copy to Mr. Jones

7. A Police Officer who attempts to arrest a person for whom a warrant has been issued must do the following:
    I. Inform the person of the warrant and the reason it was issued unless he physically resists or attempts to flee.
    II. Show the warrant if requested.
    III. If premises are involved, do not announce authority and purpose if
        A. A) the life and safety of the Officer or another person is endangered; or
        B. B) an attempt to escape may result; or
        C. C) material evidence might be destroyed, damaged, or hidden
    IV. Break into the premises, if necessary.

    Police Officer Ramos has a warrant for the arrest of Bill Jensen for failure to appear in court on a drug charge. As Officer Ramos approaches Mr. Jensen's apartment door, he hears a female in the apartment scream, *Please don't shoot me!* Without announcing his identity or reason for being at the apartment, Officer Ramos kicks the door open, sees Mr. Jensen, and arrests him. In this situation, the action taken by Officer Ramos was

    A. *proper,* primarily because the life of the female in the apartment was in danger
    B. *improper,* primarily because Officer Ramos should have announced his authority before entering the apartment
    C. *proper,* primarily because Jensen had no opportunity to destroy drug-related evidence
    D. *improper,* primarily because Jensen had made no attempt to escape

8. Police Officer Bloom is completing an entry in his Memo Book regarding a confession made by a perpetrator. The entry will include the following five sentences:

   I. I went towards the dresser and took $400 in cash and a jewelry box with rings, watches, and other items in it.
   II. There in the bedroom, lying on the bed, a woman was sleeping.
   III. It was about 1:00 A.M. when I entered the apartment through an opened rear window.
   IV. I spun around, punched her in the face with my free hand, and then jumped out the window into the street.
   V. I walked back to the window carrying the money and the jewelry box and was about to go out when all of a sudden I heard the woman scream.

   The MOST logical order for the above sentences to appear in the Memo Book entry is

   A. I, III, II, V, IV
   B. I, V, IV, III, II
   C. III, II, I, V, IV
   D. III, V, IV, I, II

9. Resisting Arrest - a person is guilty of resisting arrest when he intentionally prevents or attempts to prevent a Police Officer from making an authorized arrest of himself or another person.
   Tom Turbo is returning home from work when he sees Police Officer Bannon in the process of arresting his friend, Dominick Foss, for an assault that Foss has just committed. Turbo walks up to Officer Bannon and asks him what Foss has done. As Officer Bannon turns to answer Turbo's question, Foss begins to run down the street. Officer Bannon gives chase and recaptures Foss a few seconds later. In this situation,

   A. Turbo should be charged with resisting arrest but Foss should not
   B. Foss should be charged with resisting arrest but Turbo should not
   C. both Turbo and Foss should be charged with resisting arrest
   D. neither Turbo nor Foss should be charged with resisting arrest

10. A Police Officer has discretion regarding when to issue a traffic summons. This is the case when the Officer believes a person did not realize that he was committing the violation and did not intend to commit one. However, a Police Officer should never benefit from using such discretion.
    Police Officer Gray is patrolling at the corner of Tull Street and Burke Avenue. The intersection is crowded with pedestrians and automobiles. The light on Tull Street is red but one man proceeds to cross the street against the light in view of Officer Gray. People standing on the corner waiting for the light to change tell Officer Gray to give the man a summons. Officer Gray questions the man and learns that he is a tourist from a foreign country. The man has just arrived in the United States and is unfamiliar with American traffic regulations. Officer Gray explains what a red light means and tells the man that no summons will be issued this time. The man is extremely thankful and tells Officer Gray that if he ever visits the man's country Officer Gray will be treated to the best meal he has ever eaten. In this situation, the actions of Officer Gray were

    A. *proper,* primarily because the violation that was committed was not important
    B. *improper,* primarily because a summons should be issued whenever an Officer witnesses a violation
    C. *proper,* primarily because the violator was unfamiliar with the traffic regulations
    D. *improper,* primarily because the Officer would benefit by overlooking the violation

11. Police Officer Allan responds to the scene of a robbery. The following information relating to the incident is obtained by the Officer:

    Time of Occurrence: 2:00 A.M.
    Victim: Michael Harper
    Perpetrator: Unknown
    Description of Crime: Victim was grabbed around neck from behind while walking home.
    Money and jewelry taken.

    Police Officer Allan is preparing a report on the robbery.
    Which of the following expresses the above information MOST clearly and accurately?

    A. At 2:00 A.M. while walking home, Michael Harper observed someone he could not identify. The victim was grabbed around the neck, and his money and jewelry were stolen.
    B. At 2:00 A.M. while walking home, Michael Harper was grabbed around the neck from behind. His money and jewelry were stolen. Mr. Harper is unable to identify the perpetrator.
    C. Michael Harper is unable to identify the perpetrator because he grabbed him around the neck while walking home. The victim was robbed of money and jewelry at 2:00 A.M.
    D. Michael Harper was robbed of money and jewelry. The unknown perpetrator was not identified, however he grabbed him from behind while walking home.

11. ____

12. While on patrol, Police Officer Silas responds to a report of a robbery. The following information is obtained by the Officer:

    Time of Occurrence: 5:00 P.M.
    Place of Occurrence: 40 Forman Street
    Victim: Floyd Joy
    Witness: Paul Clay
    Suspect: Joe Lister
    Crime: Robbery

    Officer Silas is completing a report on the incident.
    Which one of the following expresses the above information MOST clearly and accurately?

    A. At 5:00 P.M., Paul Clay witnessed a robbery at 40 Forman Street. Floyd Joy was robbed by Joe Lister.
    B. At 5:00 P.M., Joe Lister was observed committing a robbery with Floyd Joy on 40 Forman Street by Paul Clay.
    C. At 40 Forman Street, Paul Clay stated to me that he had seen Floyd Joy getting robbed. The perpetrator, Joe Lister, committed the robbery at 5:00 P.M.
    D. Paul Clay stated that he witnessed a robbery taking place at 40 Forman Street at 5:00 P.M. with Joe Lister. The subject of the robbery was Floyd Joy.

12. ____

Questions 13-14.

DIRECTIONS: Questions 13 and 14 are to be answered SOLELY on the basis of the following information.

Before engaging in a high-speed pursuit of a vehicle, Police Officers should do the following in the order given:

6 (#3)

   I. Determine whether a high-speed pursuit is necessary.
   II. Notify radio dispatcher at start of pursuit and provide the following information:
      a. Your location
      b. Type of vehicle, color, and direction of travel
      c. Nature of offense
      d. State and number of license plate
      e. Description of contents
      f. Any other pertinent information
   III. Utilize patrol car's emergency signalling devices.
   III. Inform radio dispatcher if vehicle changes direction, give last location of vehicle, as well as speed and direction of travel.
   IV. Notify radio dispatcher if pursued vehicle is lost or pursuit is terminated.

13. While on patrol, Police Officers Montalvo and Casadante observe a vehicle with two White males traveling at a very high speed go through a red light. Officer Montalvo decides to begin a high-speed pursuit. Officer Casadante informs the radio dispatcher that they are in a high-speed pursuit of a black Ford, NY license number UXY918, traveling east on the Grand Central Parkway in the vicinity of LaGuardia Airport. Officer Casadante further advises that the vehicle ran a red light at the intersection of Northern Boulevard and 47th Avenue.
Which one of the following should the Officers do NEXT?

   A. Notify the radio dispatcher that back-up assistance is needed.
   B. Turn on the patrol car's emergency signalling lights and siren.
   C. Notify the radio dispatcher that the vehicle has changed direction.
   D. Give the radio dispatcher a description of the occupants in the Ford.

13._____

14. Assume that the Ford leaves the Grand Central Parkway and continues to travel east. After a mile or so, the Officers lose sight of it.
Officers Montalvo and Casadante should NEXT inform the radio dispatcher

   A. that they are still in pursuit of the black Ford
   B. to advise the local precinct of the description of the vehicle
   C. that the Ford has changed its direction
   D. that they have lost the Ford

14._____

15. Police Officer Sherman received the following information from a robbery victim:
Time of Occurrence: 8:00 P.M.
Place of Occurrence: Jack's Check Cashing Place
Victim: Frank Jackson, owner
Witness: Daryl Green
Description of Suspect: Unknown
Crime: Robbery of $1000
Police Officer Sherman is completing a report on the robbery.
Which one of the following expresses the above information MOST clearly and accurately?

   A. Although Daryl Green, who reported the crime while in progress, was also a witness, "the police arrived minutes after the robbery. Neither Mr. Green nor Mr. Jackson could describe the thief, and, he ran away with $1000. Frank Jackson, who owns Jack's Check Cashing Place, was robbed at 8:00 P.M.

15._____

B. Jack's Check Cashing Place was robbed at 8:00 P.M. The owner, Frank Jackson could not give a description of the thief as the police arrived soon after. Daryl Green, a witness, reported the crime while it was in progress. He first entered the store next to the Check Cashing Place, but came out 10 minutes later. Mr. Jackson said the thief got away with $1000. Mr. Green could not describe the thief either.

C. Frank Jackson, the owner of Jack's Check Cashing Place, was robbed there at 8:00 P.M. Daryl Green, a witness, reported the robbery while it was in progress. The police arrived minutes later. Mr. Jackson and Mr. Green could not provide a description of the thief, who escaped with $1000.

D. The thief escaped with $1000, according to Frank Jackson, the owner. Daryl Green, who witnessed the robbery, could not describe the thief. He reported the incident while the thief was still there. Jack's Check Cashing Place was robbed at 8:00 P.M., however the owner could not describe him either.

16. While on patrol, Police Officer Wright receives a call to respond to a robbery. The following information relating to the crime is obtained by the Officer:

Place of Occurrence: Corner of Rockaway and New York Avenue
Victim: Frank Holt
Suspect: Male White
Weapon: .357 Magnum

Officer Wright is completing a report on the incident. Which one of the following expresses the above information MOST clearly and accurately?

A. On the corner of Rockaway and New York Avenues, Frank Holt reported that he was robbed with a .357 Magnum by a White male.
B. Armed with a .357 Magnum on the corner of Rockaway and New York Avenues, Frank Holt reported that he was robbed by a White male.
C. A White male on the corner of Rockaway and New York Avenues who was armed with a .357 Magnum committed a robbery, reported Frank Holt.
D. Frank Holt reported that he was robbed on the corner of Rockaway and New York Avenues by a White male armed with a .357 Magnum.

Questions 17-25.

DIRECTIONS: Questions 17 through 25 are to be answered SOLELY on the basis of the following sketches. The first face on top is a sketch of an alleged criminal based on witnesses' descriptions at the crime scene. One of the four sketches below that face is the way the suspect looked after changing appearance. Assume that NO surgery has been done on the suspect. Select the face which is MOST likely that of the suspect.

8 (#3)

17. 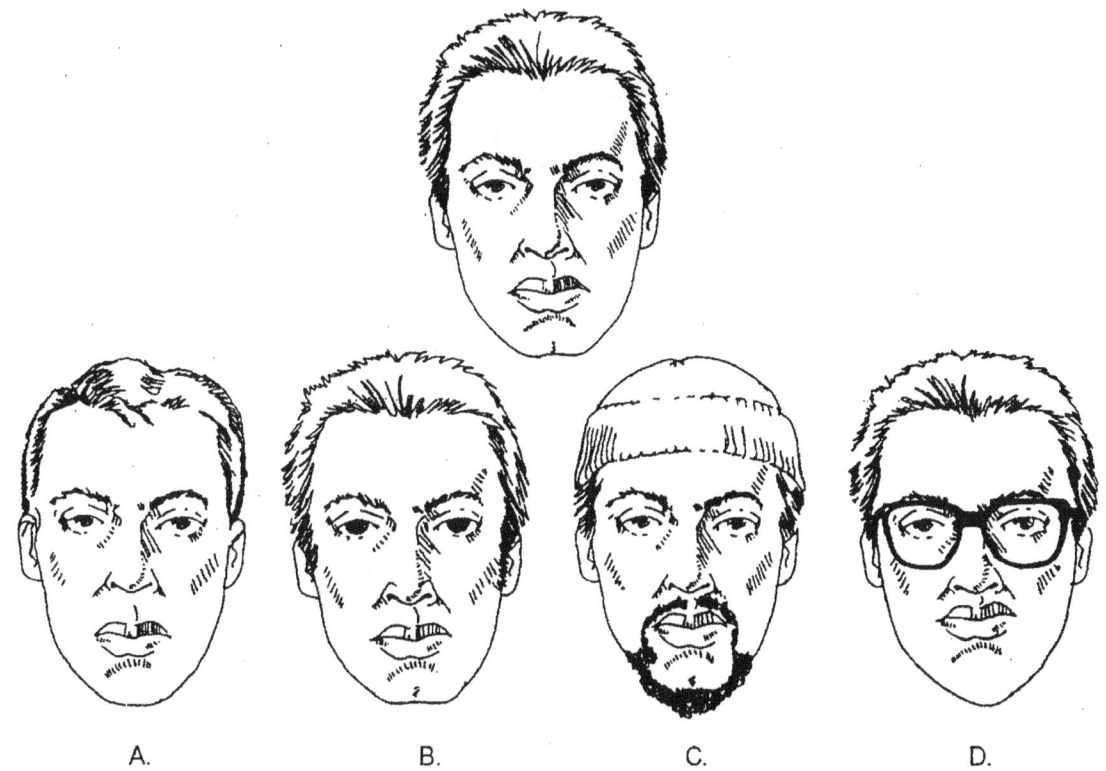 17.____

18. 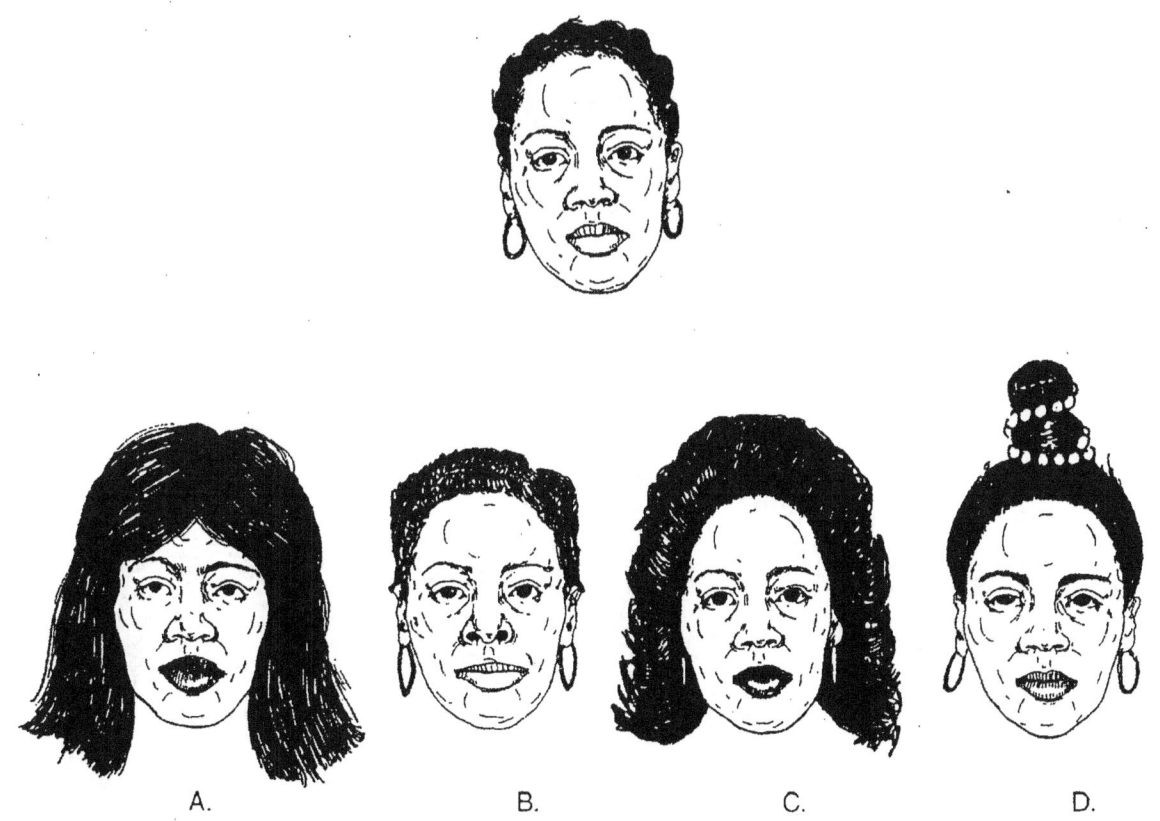 18.____

203

9 (#3)

19.

A.   B.   C.   D.

19._____

20.

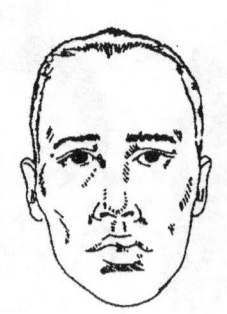  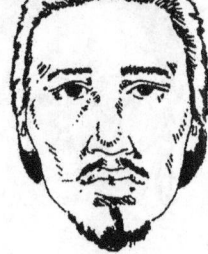 
A.   B.   C.   D.

20._____

10 (#3)

21.  21.____

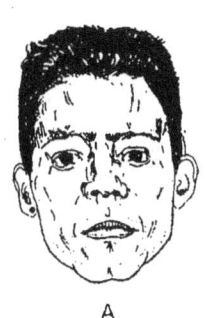   
A. B. C. D.

22.  22.____

 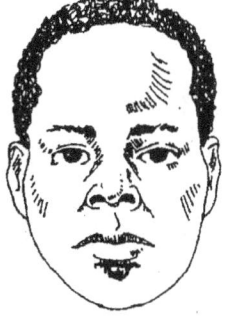  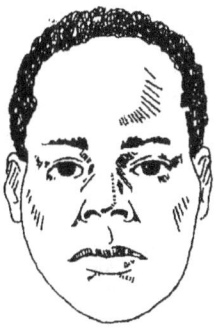
A. B. C. D.

205

11 (#3)

23. 23.____

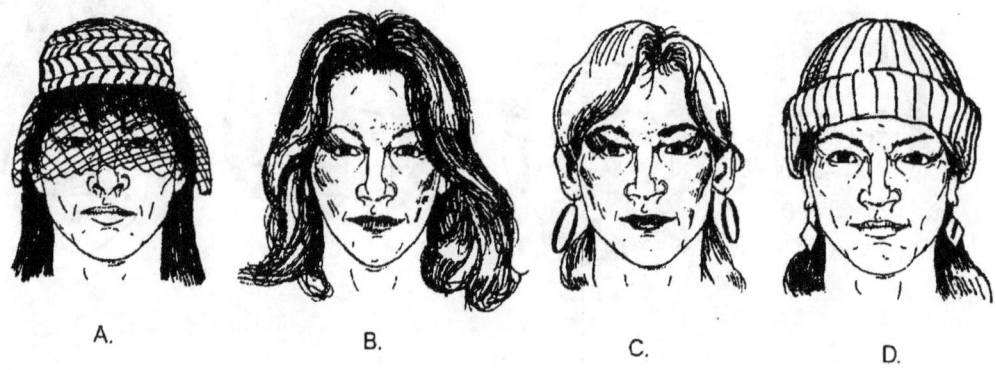

A.　　　　　B.　　　　　C.　　　　　D.

24. 24.____

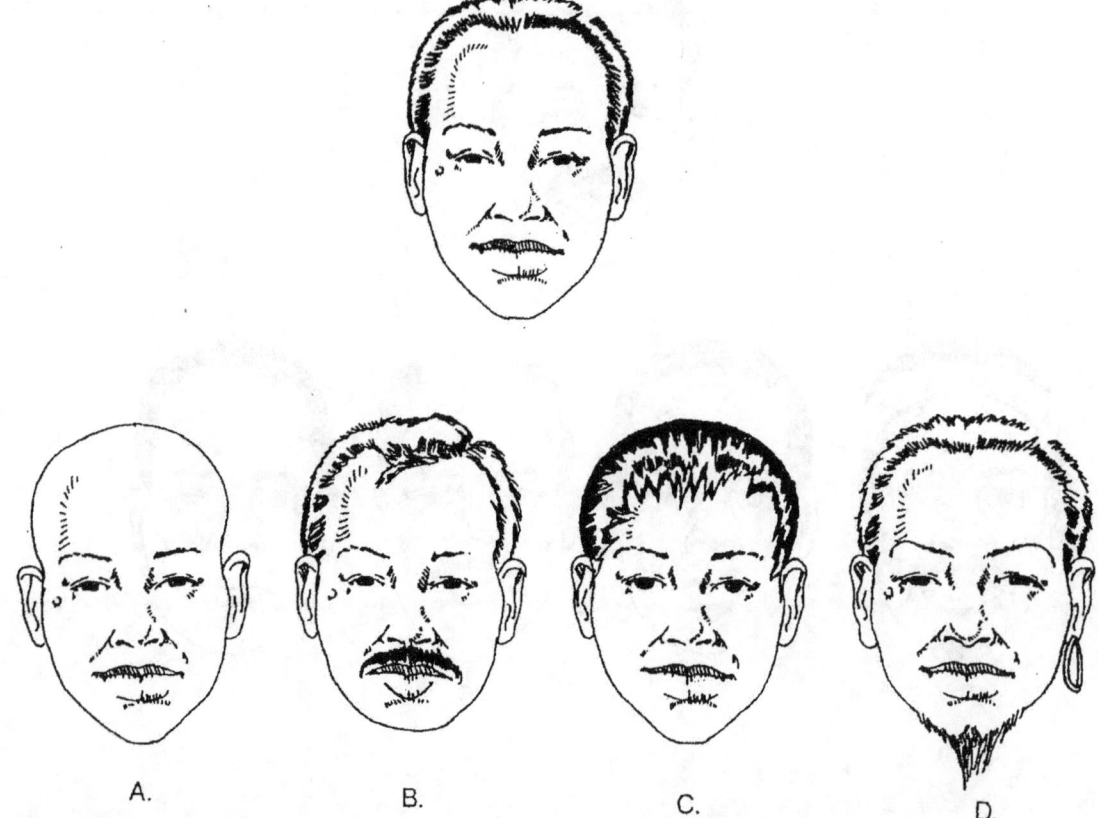

A.　　　　　B.　　　　　C.　　　　　D.

206

12 (#3)

25.   25._____

A.   B.   C.   D.

KEY (CORRECT ANSWERS)

1.	D	11.	B
2.	C	12.	A
3.	C	13.	D
4.	B	14.	D
5.	C	15.	C
6.	D	16.	D
7.	A	17.	C
8.	C	18.	C
9.	B	19.	A
10.	C	20.	A

21. B
22. D
23. C
24. A
25. B

207

EXAMINATION SECTION
TEST 1

DIRECTIONS: Each question or incomplete statement is followed by several suggested answers or completions. Select the one that BEST answers the question or completes the statement. *PRINT THE LETTER OF THE CORRECT ANSWER IN THE SPACE AT THE RIGHT.*

MEMORY PAGES

Memory Scene 1 is on Pages 2 and 3. Memory Scene 2 is on Pages 4 and 5. You are to study Scene 1 carefully and try to remember as many details in the scene as you can. You should pay equal attention both to objects and to people shown in the scene. Then turn to Questions 1 through 7 which follow and answer these questions based upon what you remember from Scene 1. Do not turn back to Scene 1 while answering. After you complete Questions 1 through 7, study Memory Scene 2. Then turn to Questions 8 through 12 and answer them based on Scene 2.

SCENE 2

Questions 1-7.

DIRECTIONS: Questions 1 through 7 are to be answered SOLELY on the basis of Memory Scene 1.

1. What is the license plate number of the truck parked in front of Bloom's Factory Outlet? 1.____

   A. 512-Aut B. MAT-1 C. PAT-1 D. MIDAS-1

2. What is the address of the pet shop outlet? _____ Ann Street. 2.____

   A. 79 B. 89 C. 99 D. 109

3. The person with the sign is walking toward the 3.____

   A. woman with the dog
   B. truck partially parked in the warehouse
   C. woman with the carriage
   D. train

4. There is a picture of a man's face 4.____

   A. on the train
   B. on the nut cart
   C. in the window of the pet store
   D. on the truck in front of Bloom's Factory Outlet

5. The Con Ed man is 5.____

   A. driving the truck
   B. talking to the man crossing the street
   C. carrying boxes
   D. handling a hose near a manhole

6. What kind of school is located above the Barber Shop? 6.____

   A. Dance B. Typing C. Boxing D. Karate

7. How many people are in the scene? 7.____

   A. 6 B. 7 C. 8 D. 9

Questions 8-13.

DIRECTIONS: Questions 8 through 13 are to be answered SOLELY on the basis of Memory Scene 2.

8. The three people standing together are closest to the 8.____

   A. liquor store   B. open manhole
   C. income tax office   D. street light

9. The license plate of the occupied auto is 9.____

   A. ARC 1211 B. BAG 6165 C. GAB 5616 D. ABG 6165

10. What is the TOTAL number of persons in the liquor store?

    A. 1   B. 2   C. 3   D. 4

11. The man dressed in the black outfit is standing in front of the

    A. Chelsea Music Store
    B. 23rd Street Cleaners
    C. liquor store
    D. Fishing-Tackle Store

12. The temperature posted on the sign above the bank is

    A. 15°   B. 25°   C. 50°   D. 51°

13. The Income Tax Office is located between the

    A. liquor store and the bank
    B. 23rd Street Cleaners and the Fishing-Tackle Store
    C. Chelsea Music Store and the bank
    D. Fishing-Tackle Store and the liquor store

14. Police Officer Clay is giving a report to the news media regarding someone who has jumped from the Empire State Building. His report will include the following five sentences:
    I. I responded to the 86th floor, where I found the person at the edge of the roof.
    II. A security guard at the building had reported that a man was on the roof at the 86th floor.
    III. At 5:30 P.M., the person jumped from the building.
    IV. I received a call from the radio dispatcher at 4:50 P.M. to respond to the Empire State Building.
    V. I tried to talk to the person and convince him not to jump.

    The MOST logical order for the above sentences to appear in the report is

    A. I, II, IV, III, v
    B. III, IV, I, II, V
    C. II, IV, I, III, V
    D. IV, II, I, V, III

15. Police Officers are required to notify the proper city agency of a street condition requiring corrective action. When a street condition requires corrective action, a Police Officer should follow these procedures, in the order given:
    I. While on patrol, in the Memo Log, write an entry Bindicating what street condition requires correction.
    II. The Memo Log entry must indicate the location of the street condition.
    III. Inform the telephone switchboard operator of the street condition and location.
    IV. If a traffic signal light is not working properly, take all of the above actions and inform the Department of Traffic.

    Police Officer Flanagan while on patrol observes that a traffic signal light on the corner of Second Avenue and 74th Street in Manhattan doesn't change from red. He takes all appropriate actions through indicating the location of the defective traffic signal light in his Memo Log.
    Police Officer Flanagan should NEXT

A. notify the Department of Traffic
B. inform the telephone switchboard operator of the defective traffic signal light on Second Avenue and 74th Street in Manhattan
C. write an entry in the Memo Log indicating that a street condition exists which requires corrective action
D. write an entry in the Memo Log indicating that the telephone switchboard operator was notified

16. A Police Officer is trained in standard first aid techniques. Listed below are the techniques to stop severe bleeding:
    I. Apply direct pressure by placing the hand directly over the wound, when possible.
    II. Elevate a wound of the hand, neck, arm, or leg unless there is evidence of a broken bone.
    III. Apply pressure on the appropriate artery.
    IV. Use a tourniquet only as a last resort. Its use means sacrificing the injured leg or arm to save the person from bleeding to death.

While on foot patrol in Midtown Manhattan, Police Officer Charles is summoned by a passerby to aid an injured construction worker. The worker fell from a third-floor scaffold and injured his left leg, which is severely bleeding. An" ambulance is on its way; but until its arrival, Police Officer Charles should

A. apply direct pressure to the wound and elevate the leg, even if the leg is broken
B. apply direct pressure to the wound and elevate the leg if it appears there are no broken bones
C. elevate the leg immediately and apply pressure on the appropriate artery
D. elevate the leg, apply pressure on the appropriate artery, and automatically apply a tourniquet to save the leg

17. The following five sentences are part of a report of a burglary written by Police Officer Reed:
    I. When I arrived at 2400 1st Avenue, I noticed that the door was slightly open.
    II. I yelled out, *Police, don't move!*
    III. As I entered the apartment, I saw a man with a T. set passing it through a window to another man standing on a fire escape.
    IV. While on foot patrol, I was informed by the radio dispatcher that a burglary was in progress at 2400 First Avenue.
    V. However, the burglars quickly ran down the fire escape.

The MOST logical order for the above sentences to appear in the report is:

A. I, III, IV, V, II
C. IV, I, III, II, V
B. IV, I, III, V, II
D. I, IV, III, II, V

Questions 18-21.

DIRECTIONS: Questions 18 through 21 are to be answered SOLELY on the basis of the following passage.

At 11:55 A.M., Police Officer Benson was on foot patrol on 44th Street between 6th Avenue and Broadway. This post is known to be a high crime area with a large number of narcotics, robbery, and prostitution arrests. Police Officer Benson approached a young woman he had previously arrested for prostitution. As he was about to question her, he heard a scream coming from the direction of a women's boutique on the opposite side of the street. A young black male was running up 44th Street towards Broadway, followed by a woman yelling *Stop that man!* Police Officer Benson ran after the woman but by the time he caught up with her, she had fallen after tripping on the badly cracked sidewalk. The woman was visibly shaken, and appeared to have broken her arm. Police Officer Benson decided that because the young black male had disappeared from sight, he should stay with the injured woman and call for an ambulance. While awaiting the arrival of the ambulance, the injured woman, Ms. Peever, told Police Officer Benson that she was the owner of the boutique and that the young black male had taken approximately $475 from the cash register while she went to check the price of an item. She also mentioned that the boutique was presently unattended because her two sales people had not come to work that morning.

Police Officer Benson called for back-up assistance at 12:35 P.M. and asked the dispatcher to send a Police Officer directly to the boutique located at 338 West 44th Street. Police Officers Maloney and Hernandez arrived at the boutique at 1:05 P.M. and saw that the store had been ransacked. Racks of clothing had been thrown down, and the floor was littered with garments. The two Police Officers then conducted a search of the premises. When Police Officer Benson arrived at the premises at 1:20 P.M., the Police Officers told him that it would be impossible to determine what items had been taken since they had no listing of the store's merchandise.

A young woman then entered the store and identified herself as Ms. Peake, the part-time assistant whose shift started at 1:30 P.M. On seeing the condition of the store, she asked the Police Officers what had happened. They asked her where the merchandise list for the store was kept, and she informed them that the stock clerks, Ms. Feldman and Mr. Austin, kept that information. Ms. Peake said that she would call Ms. Feldman in order to get a current listing of the store's merchandise.

Ms. Peake advised the Police Officers that several items were missing from the display case, including three fur jackets, seven leather handbags, and four silk blouses, amounting to at least $985 in value.

18. At which one of the following addresses is the boutique located?

    A. 388 East 44th Street
    B. 44th Street and Broadway
    C. 338 West 44th Street
    D. 44th Street and 6th Ave.

19. At what time did Police Officer Benson meet Police Officers Maloney and Hernandez at the boutique? _____ P.M.

    A. 12:35   B. 12:5:5   C. 1:05   D. 1:20

20. Which one of the following people owns the boutique?

    A. Ms. Peever
    B. Mr. Austin
    C. Ms. Feldman
    D. Ms. Peake

21. What is Ms. Peake's starting time at the boutique? _____ P.M.

    A. 12:35   B. 1:05   C. 1:20   D. 1:30

Question 22.

DIRECTIONS: Question 22 is to be answered SOLELY on the basis of the following information.

As a Police Officer in New York City, you may have an occasion to deal with diplomats from other nations. You should be aware of the following definitions and procedure.

Definitions
1. Diplomats: Members of foreign missions, delegations, embassies, and staff (D. cards are signed by United States Secretary of State and Chief of Protocol.)
2. Diplomatic immunity: Diplomats shall NOT be arrested or personally served with a summons. Uniformed members of the service will extend every courtesy and consideration to them. All reasonable assistance will be given to them.

Procedure
1. Take necessary action to protect life and property.
2. Obtain the name and the title of the diplomat and the name of the government he represents.
3. Notify the Operations Unit immediately by telephone that an incident involving a diplomat has occurred.
4. Do not detain a diplomat who has proper I.D.
5. Request a Patrol Supervisor to respond.
6. Telephone details to the Desk Officer.

22. Police Officers Rowan and Nieves are on patrol in the 44th Precinct when they respond to 1278 Sedgwick Avenue for a call of shots fired. They arrive and observe a male with a gun in his hand standing over a body. They order the man to drop the gun. He complies and states he is a member of the Soviet Mission to the U.N. and, therefore, cannot be arrested. He hands the Police Officers a State Department I.D. The Police Officers, after verifying the information, allow the man to leave. The actions of the Police Officers were

A. *proper* because once a diplomat is identified he must be released
B. *improper* because the man should have been arrested for shooting the other person
C. *improper* because they didn't let the Patrol Supervisor make the decision
D. *proper* because they weren't sure that he actually pulled the trigger

Questions 23-24.

DIRECTIONS: Questions 23 and 24 are to be answered SOLELY on the basis of the following information.

A Police Officer may arrest a person for possession of an illegal gun. When the individual is arrested, in addition to following the normal arrest procedure, a Police Officer should follow these procedures in the order given:
  I. Confiscate the illegal gun.
  II. Charge the individual with a violation of the Penal Law or the Administrative Code.
  III. Complete a Request for Laboratory Examination form.
  IV. Take the gun and the completed Request for Laboratory Examination form to the Ballistics Section.
  V. Take the gun and Property Clerk's Invoice to the Property Clerk.

23. Police Officer Ritsik has made an arrest involving possession of an illegal gun. In addition to following the normal arrest procedure, after confiscating the illegal gun involved in the crime, he should

    A. take the illegal gun to the Ballistics Section
    B. complete the Request for Examination form
    C. charge the individual with violation of the Penal Law or the Administrative Code
    D. take the illegal gun and the Property Clerk's Invoice to the Property Clerk

24. Police Officer Ritsik has taken all appropriate actions through completing a Request for Laboratory Examination form.
Police Officer Ritsik should NEXT

    A. take the illegal gun and the Property Clerk's Invoice to the Property Clerk
    B. charge the individual with a violation of the Penal Law or the Administrative Code
    C. take the illegal gun and completed Request for Laboratory Examination form to the Property Clerk
    D. take the illegal gun and the completed Request for Laboratory Examination form to the Ballistics Section

25. When a Police Officer transports a prisoner to the hospital either in the patrol car or an ambulance, the Police Officer will remain with the prisoner at all times, and will not remove the handcuffs from the prisoner unless requested by the attending physician. Upon request, the Police Officer will remove the handcuffs only after informing the physician of the circumstances of the arrest. The handcuffs will be replaced at the completion of the medical exam.
According to the procedure, which one of the following police actions is appropriate?

    A. Handcuff a prisoner when transporting in a patrol car, and remove the handcuffs when riding in an ambulance.
    B. Remove the handcuffs automatically upon arrival of the ambulance at the hospital.
    C. Remove the handcuffs only after explaining the circumstances of the arrest to the requesting physician.
    D. Remove the handcuffs after completing the exam and before transporting to the hospital.

12 (#1)

KEY (CORRECT ANSWERS)

1. B
2. B
3. A
4. D
5. D

6. A
7. C
8. D
9. B
10. B

11. D
12. D
13. B
14. D
15. B

16. B
17. C
18. C
19. D
20. A

21. D
22. A
23. C
24. D
25. C

TEST 2

DIRECTIONS: Each question or incomplete statement is followed by several suggested answers or completions. Select the one that BEST answers the question or completes the statement. *PRINT THE LETTER OF THE CORRECT ANSWER IN THE SPACE AT THE RIGHT.*

1. During an emergency, a Police Officer may be required to go onto subway tracks. In which one of the following cases would it be MOST appropriate for a Police Officer to go onto the tracks?
A

   A. female passenger accidentally drops her handbag containing $2,000 in cash onto the tracks
   B. male passenger while leaning over the platform loses his balance and falls onto the tracks
   C. child is shouting at the top of his voice creating a crowd scene because he dropped a ball which rolled onto the tracks
   D. female passenger drops her last token and it rolls onto the tracks

2. Police Officer Jones is told to notify his Command when he observes dangerous conditions.
For which one of the following should Police Officer Jones notify his Command?

   A. A motorist stalled in a bus stop preventing a bus from discharging passengers
   B. A parking sign that has been painted over
   C. A car's burglar alarm that has gone off late at night
   D. Smoke coming from the first floor window of an apartment building

3. Police Officer Brooks has received three complaints from neighborhood storeowners over a two-week period concerning the theft of merchandise. In each case the perpetrator would run out of the store with an armful of designer jeans as soon as the owner's back was turned. The description of each suspect is as follows:
Incident No. 1 (November 14) - male, White, teenager, 5'11", 180 lbs., curly black hair, long sleeve shirt, blue jeans and black boots, tattoo on right hand.
Incident No. 2 (November 19) - male, White, 20-25, 5'10", 175 lbs., curly black hair, tattoos on upper left arm and hand, tank top, brown pants and sneakers.
Incident No. 3 (November 23) - male, White, 17-21, 5'9 1/2", 183 lbs., short curly blond hair, tattoo on left forearm, sleeveless shirt, blue jeans and sneakers. On November 29th, a fourth incident occurred, but this time the suspect was observed running from the store by a plainclothes Police Officer and was arrested. The description of this suspect is as follows:
Incident No. 4 (November 29) - male, White, 18, 5'10", 180 lbs., short curly black hair, tattoo on chest, left forearm, and right hand, short sleeve shirt, blue jeans and sneakers.
Based on the descriptions given above of the suspects in the first three incidents, the suspect in Incident No. 4 should also be considered a suspect in

   A. Incident Nos. 1 and 2   B. Incident Nos. 1 and 3
   C. Incident No. 2 *only*   D. None of the above

4. Police Officer Jenkins is preparing a report for Lost or Stolen Property. The report will include the following five sentences:
   I. On the stairs, Mr. Harris slipped on a wet leaf and fell on the landing.
   II. It wasn't until he got to the token booth that Mr. Harris realized his wallet was no longer in his back pants pocket.
   III. A boy wearing a football jersey helped him up and brushed off the back of Mr. Harris' pants.
   IV. Mr. Harris states he was walking up the stairs to the elevated subway at Queensborough Plaza.
   V. Before Mr. Harris could thank him, the boy was running down the stairs to the street.

   The MOST logical order for the above sentences to appear in the report is:

   A. IV, III, V, I, II
   B. IV, I, III, V, II
   C. I, IV, II, III, V
   D. I, II, IV, III, V

Question 5.

DIRECTIONS: Question 5 is to be answered SOLELY on the basis of the following information.

Reward for Official Misconduct - As a Police Officer, you are a public servant. There are many laws regarding your conduct. For example,
   1. A public servant may not gain any benefit for violating or overlooking his duty.
   2. A Police Officer may not ask for any such benefit.

However, a Police Officer has discretion regarding when to issue a traffic summons. This is the case when he believes a person did not realize that he was committing the violation, and did not intend to commit one. Nevertheless, the Police Officer must not benefit from using such discretion.

5. Police Officer Whyte on routine foot patrol observes a large group of double-parked cars in front of Joe's Pizzeria. He opens his summons book and is about to issue summonses for the violations when Joe comes out to explain that it is Friday, his busiest night, and that the cars belong to his customers. Joe offers Police Officer Whyte a slice of pizza and a soda. Police Officer Whyte does not issue the summonses, but tells Joe to have the cars moved. He does not accept the pizza and soda.
   Police Officer Whyte's actions were

   A. *proper* because he used his discretion but did not benefit from it
   B. *improper* because he should have contacted his Patrol Supervisor
   C. *proper* because summonses would have hurt Joe's business
   D. *improper* because when a Police Officer witnesses a violation, he must write a summons

6. A Police Officer may have to evacuate people from a dangerous area.
   From which one of the following areas should a Police Officer evacuate people? A(n)

   A. train delay at Grand Central Station
   B. unconscious female on a crowded train
   C. deranged male on a moving subway train
   D. asbestos fire under a train in a tunnel

7. Police Officer Hubbard is completing a report of a missing person. The report will contain the following five sentences:
    I. I visited the store at 7:55 P.M. and asked the employees if they had seen a girl fitting the description I had been given.
    II. She gave me a description and said she had gone into the local grocery store at about 6:15 P.M.
    III. I asked the woman for a description of her daughter.
    IV. The distraught woman called the precinct to report that her daughter, aged 12, had not returned from an errand.
    V. The storekeeper said a girl matching the description had been in the store earlier, but he could not give an exact time.

   The MOST logical order for the above sentences to appear in the report is:

   A. I, III, II, V, IV
   B. IV, III, II, I, V
   C. V, I, II, III, IV
   D. III, I, II, IV, V

7.____

8. The purpose of the Stop and Frisk procedure is to protect a Police Officer from injury while investigating a crime. When a Police Officer suspects a person has committed, is committing, or is about to commit a crime, the Police Officer should:
    I. Stop the person and request identification and an explanation of his conduct.
    II. Frisk if the Police Officer believes he may be physically injured or killed.
    III. Search if the frisk reveals an object which may be a weapon.

   While patrolling along Main Street about 10 P.M., Police Officer Jackson observes a man dressed in dark clothes walking slowly along the quiet street. Police Officer Jackson knows that during the past couple of weeks, a few burglaries have occurred in this area after business hours. Police Officer Jackson sees the man looking into the closed store windows, glancing up and down the street, and shaking the door knobs of various shops. Police Officer Jackson suspects this man is about to burglarize one of the stores on the block.
   According to the Stop and Frisk procedure, the Police Officer should

   A. stop the man and frisk him even though the Police Officer does not feel endangered
   B. not stop the man because he hasn't committed any crime
   C. stop the man and search him because the man has already committed a crime
   D. stop the man and ask him to identify himself and explain his behavior

8.____

9. Police Officers are called upon to deliver a prisoner to court so that charges can be stated against the prisoner. When the Police Officer arrives at the court, the following procedures should be followed in the order given:
    I. Escort the prisoner to the Detention Cell.
    II. Write entries in the Detention Record Book.
    III. Report to the Police Room.
    IV. Complete the Court Attendance Record Form.
    V. Report to the Complaint Room.
    VI. Present one copy of the Arrest Report to the Assistant District Attorney.
    VII. Remove the prisoner from the Detention Cell to the Court Room when the Court Officer instructs you to do so.
    VIII. Do not permit the prisoner to talk to any person or give anything to or accept anything from any person while the prisoner is being escorted to the Court Room.

9.____

IX. If the prisoner is held without bail or cannot post the bail, escort the prisoner back to the Detention Cell.
X. If the prisoner is able to post the bail, escort the prisoner to the Court Clerk.

Police Officer Tanner has escorted a prisoner to court. If all appropriate steps are taken through completing a Court Attendance Record Form, Tanner should NEXT

A. report to the Police Room
B. escort the prisoner to the Detention Cell
C. report to the Complaint Room
D. remove the prisoner from the Detention Cell to the Court Room when instructed to by the Court Officer

10. <u>Criminally Negligent Homicide</u> - The crime of criminally negligent homicide is committed when an individual behaves in such a way that his behavior creates a substantial risk for others, unintentionally causing the death of a person.
<u>Felony Murder</u> - A felony murder is committed when a person, acting alone or together with others, commits or attempts to commit robbery, burglary, kidnapping, arson, or rape; and in the course and furtherance of such crime or of immediate flight there from, he or another participant, if there be any, causes the death of a person other than one of the participants.

What is the difference between Criminally Negligent Homicide and Felony Murder?

A. With Criminally Negligent Homicide, the death that results is unintentional. With Felony Murder, the criminal intends to kill another person.
B. The victim of a Criminally Negligent Homicide is usually an acquaintance of the person committing the crime. The victim of a Felony Murder is usually someone who is trying to prevent the commission of a crime.
C. With Criminally Negligent Homicide, the death that results is unintentional. With a Felony Murder, the criminal intends to commit a crime other than murder but someone dies in the commission of the crime.
D. In Criminally Negligent Homicide, the perpetrator has no control over his behavior and the death resulting from it. With Felony Murder, the criminal is in complete control of his mental faculties and realizes that he may be called on to kill someone in order to successfully commit the crime.

11. When a Police Officer arrests a taxicab driver, he should do the following in the order given:
   I. Prepare a Report of Violation form.
   II. Take the credentials of the taxicab driver only when they have been used as an instrument in, or as evidence of, the crime committed.
   III. Prepare and deliver the form *Receipt for Credentials* to the prisoner if the credentials are taken.
   IV. Prepare a Property Clerk's Invoice form when the credentials are taken.
   V. Note under details on the Arrest Report that a *Report of Violation* has been prepared and, if applicable, the taking of the driver's credentials.

Police Officer Bunker has arrested a taxicab driver for robbery. The taxicab driver had not used his credentials while committing the crime. Police Officer Bunker has followed normal arrest procedures and prepared the *Report of Violation* form.
Which one of the following actions should Police Officer Bunker take NEXT?

A. Take the credentials of the driver.
B. Prepare and deliver the form *Receipt for Credentials* to the driver.
C. Prepare a Property Clerk's Invoice form.
D. Note under details on the Arrest Report preparation of *Report of Violation*.

Questions 12-13.

DIRECTIONS: Questions 12 and 13 are to be answered SOLELY on the basis of the following passage.

On July 10th, 2003, Police Officer William Jenkins, Shield No. 815, of the Housing Authority Police Department, assigned to foot patrol in Sector (C) was dispatched at 4:00 P.M. to respond to 42-48 Colden Street, Apartment 3C, on a past rape. Police Officer Jenkins arrived at the apartment at 4:15 P.M. Mrs. Julia Bookman, a black female, age 42, and her daughter Lucille live at that address.

Mrs. Bookman informs the Police Officer that her daughter Lucille, the rape victim, is in her dedroom. Police Officer Jenkins questions the victim, Lucille Bookman, a black female, age 17, date of birth 3/6/86, who states that she was returning home from school at 3:30 P.M. when an unknown male black entered the elevator with her and pressed the 11th floor button. The elevator door closed, the male pulled a knife from his waist, and informed the victim not to scream. The victim was pulled off the elevator on the llth floor and into the staircase, where she was instructed to remove her skirt and undergarment. The male then raped her on the staircase landing.

Police Officer Jenkins informs the Police Radio Dispatcher at 4:26 P.M. to notify the Housing Sergeant to respond to the crime scene. Miss Bookman describes the suspect as a male black, 6 ft. 2 in., 170 pounds, 20 to 25 years old, dark complexion, missing right front tooth, who was wearing a brown leather jacket, brown pants, dark shoes, and spoke with an accent.

At 5:05 P.M., Police Officer Jenkins and Ambulance Attendant Hall, #1689, removed Miss Bookman to Jamaica Hospital, where she was treated by Dr. Ling and released at 5:45 P.M.

Police Officer Jenkins noted the evidence obtained from Miss Bookman at the hospital. At 8:00 P.M., Police Officer Jenkins completed Police Complaint Report #4073, Aided Report #107, Evidence Report #B129075, and then returned to foot patrol.

12. What is Lucille Bookman's occupation?   12.____

    A. Secretary   B. Student
    C. Housewife   D. Waitress

13. Which one of the following is Miss Bookman's CORRECT home address?   13.____

    A. 42-48 Colden Street, Apartment #3C
    B. 42-48 Colden Street, Apartment #2C
    C. 44-48 Colden Street, Apartment #2C
    D. 44-48 Colden Street, Apartment #3C

14. Police Officers sometimes come upon unsafe street conditions. When such conditions exist, the Police Officers should do the following in the order given:
    I. Make an Activity Log entry of the conditions and the location.
    II. Notify the Telephone Switchboard Operator of the condition so that the Operator can notify the appropriate agency responsible for correcting the condition.
    III. Direct traffic until the appropriate agency corrects the condition.

    Police Officer Wright, while on patrol, noticed that the traffic lights at an intersection were not working. He noticed that the cars were slowing down at the intersection, causing traffic to back up. He also noticed that some cars were going through the intersection without stopping, creating a dangerous condition. Police Officer Wright took out his Activity Log and wrote down the location and conditions.
    Which one of the following should Police Officer Wright do NEXT?

    A. Walk into the middle of the intersection and stop all traffic until the appropriate agency arrives to correct the condition.
    B. Notify the appropriate agency.
    C. Stop traffic from one direction for two minutes and then let traffic from the other direction go for two minutes.
    D. Notify the Telephone Switchboard Operator so that the Operator can notify the agency concerned.

15. A Police Officer is sometimes assigned to control the flow of traffic.
    Police Officer Gaston is assigned to direct traffic at 15th Street and 17th Avenue. While directing traffic, Police Officer Gaston observes a man with dark glasses using a white cane with a red tip step off the curb and continue walking against the red light. What should Police Officer Gaston do?

    A. Allow the man to continue walking, then issue him a summons for jaywalking.
    B. Yell out to a bystander to bring the man back to the curb.
    C. Stop all traffic because the man is blind.
    D. Call for an ambulance because the man is sick.

Questions 16-18.

DIRECTIONS: Questions 16 through 18 are to be answered SOLELY on the basis of the following passage.

On September 17, 2003, at approximately 11:05 A.M. Police Officers Jesse Harris, Shield #115, and William Anderson, Shield #110, assigned to Radio Patrol Car #9770, received a radio call to respond to a past burglary at 1428 Webster Avenue, Apartment 21B. The Police Officers arrived at the apartment at 11:10 A.M. and were greeted by Mr. George Smith, a black male, age 61, date of birth 1/10/42. Mr. Smith informed the Police Officers that his apartment had been burglarized.

Mr. Smith told Police Officer Harris that he left his apartment at 9:30 A.M. that morning, 9/17/03, to shop for groceries. Upon his return at approximately 10:45 A.M., he noticed that the cylinder to his apartment lock was removed. Mr. Smith further stated that he did not enter his apartment but asked a neighbor to call the Police. Police Officers Harris and Anderson entered the apartment and found only the bedroom ransacked. Police Officer Harris asked

Mr. Smith if he noticed any strange or suspicious person on his floor or in the lobby when leaving the building. Mr. Smith reported that he did not notice anyone unusual in the building.

Police Officer Anderson continued the investigation by questioning the tenants who resided on the 21st floor. The tenants questioned were Mrs. Vasques, an Hispanic female, age 40, who lives in Apartment 21E, and Mr. John Fox, a white male, age 32, who lives in Apartment 21F. Police Officer Anderson asked both tenants if they heard or saw anything unusual between the hours of 9:30 A.M. and 10:45 A.M.

At 12:20 P.M., Police Officer Harris notified Police Officer Bell, Shield #169, at the Fingerprint Unit to respond to Mr. Smith's apartment for possible prints. Mr. Smith was informed not to touch anything in the bedroom until the Fingerprint Unit arrived to dust for prints. Police Officer Harris told Mr. Smith to wait until the Fingerprint Unit had completed its work before checking to see what property had been taken. Mr. Smith was told to prepare a list of the missing property and forward it to the precinct.

The Police Officers completed their Police Complaint Report #1010 at 12:40 P.M. and returned to patrol.

16. At what time was the call dispatched to Radio Patrol Car #9770? _____ A.M.

    A. 9:30 B. 10:45 C. 11:05 D. 11:15

17. Which one of the following is Mr. Smith's date of birth?

    A. 10/10/51 B. 10/10/42 C. 1/10/51 D. 1/10/42

18. How was the apartment entered?

    A. Door B. Window C. Roof D. Wall

19. A Police Officer is completing an entry in his Daily Activity Log regarding traffic summonses which he issued. The following five sentences will be included in the entry:
    I. I was on routine patrol parked 16 yards west of 170th Street and Clay Avenue.
    II. The summonses were issued for unlicensed operator and disobeying a steady red light.
    III. At 8 A.M. hours I observed an auto traveling westbound on 170th Street not stop for a steady red light at the intersection of Clay Avenue and 170th Street.
    IV. I stopped the driver of the auto and determined that he did not have a valid driver's license.
    V. After a brief conversation, I informed the motorist that he was receiving two summonses.

    The MOST logical order for the above sentences to appear in the report is:

    A. I, III, IV, V, II
    B. III, IV, II, V, I
    C. V, II, I, III, IV
    D. IV, V, II, I, III

20. The presence of a juvenile under 16 years of age in a bar that is licensed is unlawful. When a Police Officer observes a juvenile under 16 in a bar that is licensed, the Police Officer should do the following in the order given:
    I. Determine the age of the juvenile.
    II. Take the juvenile into protective custody if the presence is unlawful, and arrest the manager or person in charge.
    III. Escort the juvenile home if the home is located within the city.
    IV. Inform the juvenile's parents of the violation and request an explanation of the juvenile's conduct.
    V. Advise the parents of their legal responsibilities.
    VI. Prepare a Juvenile Report to the Desk Officer.
    VII. Submit the Juvenile Report to the Desk Officer at the station house.

    Police Officer Richards is part of an undercover team investigating violations involving a certain bar that is licensed in the Bronx. While on duty, Police Officer Richards and her partner enter a bar and notice a young girl inside who they suspect is underage. Police Officer Richards approaches the girl, identifies herself as a Police Officer, and requests identification. The girl produces a local high school identification card indicating that she is 14 years old. The NEXT step the Police Officers should take is

    A. arrest the bar's manager and take the girl into protective custody
    B. locate the girl's parents and inform them of the violation
    C. arrest the girl and the bar's manager and take them to the station house
    D. escort the girl to her residence

21. The following sentences appeared on an Incident Report:
    I. Three teenagers who had been ejected from the theater were yelling at patrons who were now entering.
    II. Police Officer Dixon told the teenagers to leave the area.
    III. The teenagers said that they were told by the manager to leave the theater because they were talking during the movie.
    IV. The theater manager called the Precinct at 10:20 P.M. to report a disturbance outside the theater.
    V. A patrol car responded to the theater at 10:42 P.M., and two Police Officers went over to the teenagers.

    The MOST logical orderi for the above sentences to appear in the Incident Report is:

    A. I, V, IV, III, III
    B. IV, I, V, III, II
    C. IV, I, III, V, III
    D. IV, III, I, V, II

22. Activity Log entries are completed by Police Officers. Police Officer Samuels has written an entry concerning vandalism and part of it contains the following five sentences:
    I. The man, in his early twenties, ran down the block and around the corner.
    II. A man passing the store threw a brick through a window of the store.
    III. I arrived on the scene and began to question the witnesses about the incident.
    IV. Malcolm Holmes, the owner of the Fast Service Shoe Repair Store, was working in the back of the store at approximately 3 P.M.
    V. After the man fled, Mr. Holmes called the Police.

    The MOST logical order for the above sentences to appear in the Activity Log is:

A. IV, II, I, V, III   B. II, IV, I, III, V
C. II, I, IV, III, V   D. IV, II, V, III, I

23. Police Officer Buckley is preparing a report concerning a dispute in a restaurant. The report will contain the following five sentences:
    I. The manager, Charles Chin, and a customer, Edward Green, were standing near the register arguing over the bill.
    II. The manager refused to press any charges providing Green pay the chesk and leave.
    III. While on foot patrol, I was informed by a passerby of a disturbance in the Dragon Flame Restaurant.
    IV. Green paid the $7.50 check and left the restaurant.
    V. According to witnesses, the customer punched the owner in the face when Chin asked him for the amount due.

    The MOST logical order for the above sentences to appear in the report is:

    A. III, I, V, II, IV   B. I, II, III, IV, V
    C. V, I, III, II, IV   D. III, V, II, IV, I

24. Police Officers in the course of a tour may be confronted with persons who need medical assistance. Police Officers know that in life-threatening situations in which they are the first on the scene, they must administer first aid until medical assistance arrives.
    In which one of the following cases should a Police Officer administer first aid while waiting for medical assistance?
    A

    A. person bleeding profusely from the stomach area
    B. person complaining of back pains
    C. pregnant female in early labor
    D. person complaining of sharp pains in his legs

25. Police Officer Wilkins is preparing a report for leaving the scene of an accident. The report will include the following five sentences:

    I. The Dodge struck the right rear fender of Mrs. Smith's 1994 Ford and continued on its way.
    II. Mrs. Smith stated she was making a left turn from 40th Street onto Third Avenue.
    III. As the car passed, Mrs. Smith noticed the dangling rear license plate #412AEJ.
    IV. Mrs. Smith complained to police of back pains and was removed by ambulance to Bellevue Hospital.
    V. An old green Dodge traveling up Third Avenue went through the red light at 40th Street and Third Avenue.

    The MOST logical order for the above sentences to appear in the report is:

    A. V, III, I, II, IV   B. I, III, II, V, IV
    C. IV, V, I, II, III   D. II, V, I, III, IV

KEY (CORRECT ANSWERS)

1. B
2. D
3. A
4. B
5. A

6. D
7. B
8. D
9. C
10. C

11. D
12. B
13. A
14. D
15. C

16. C
17. D
18. A
19. A
20. A

21. B
22. A
23. A
24. A
25. D

TEST 3

DIRECTIONS: Each question or incomplete statement is followed by several suggested answers or completions. Select the one that BEST answers the question or completes the statement. *PRINT THE LETTER OF THE CORRECT ANSWER IN THE SPACE AT THE RIGHT.*

Questions 1-2.

DIRECTIONS: Questions 1 and 2 are to be answered SOLELY on the basis of the following map. The flow of traffic is indicated by the arrows. If there is only one arrow shown, then traffic flows only in the direction indicated by the arrow. If there are two arrows shown, then traffic flows in both directions. You must follow the flow of traffic.

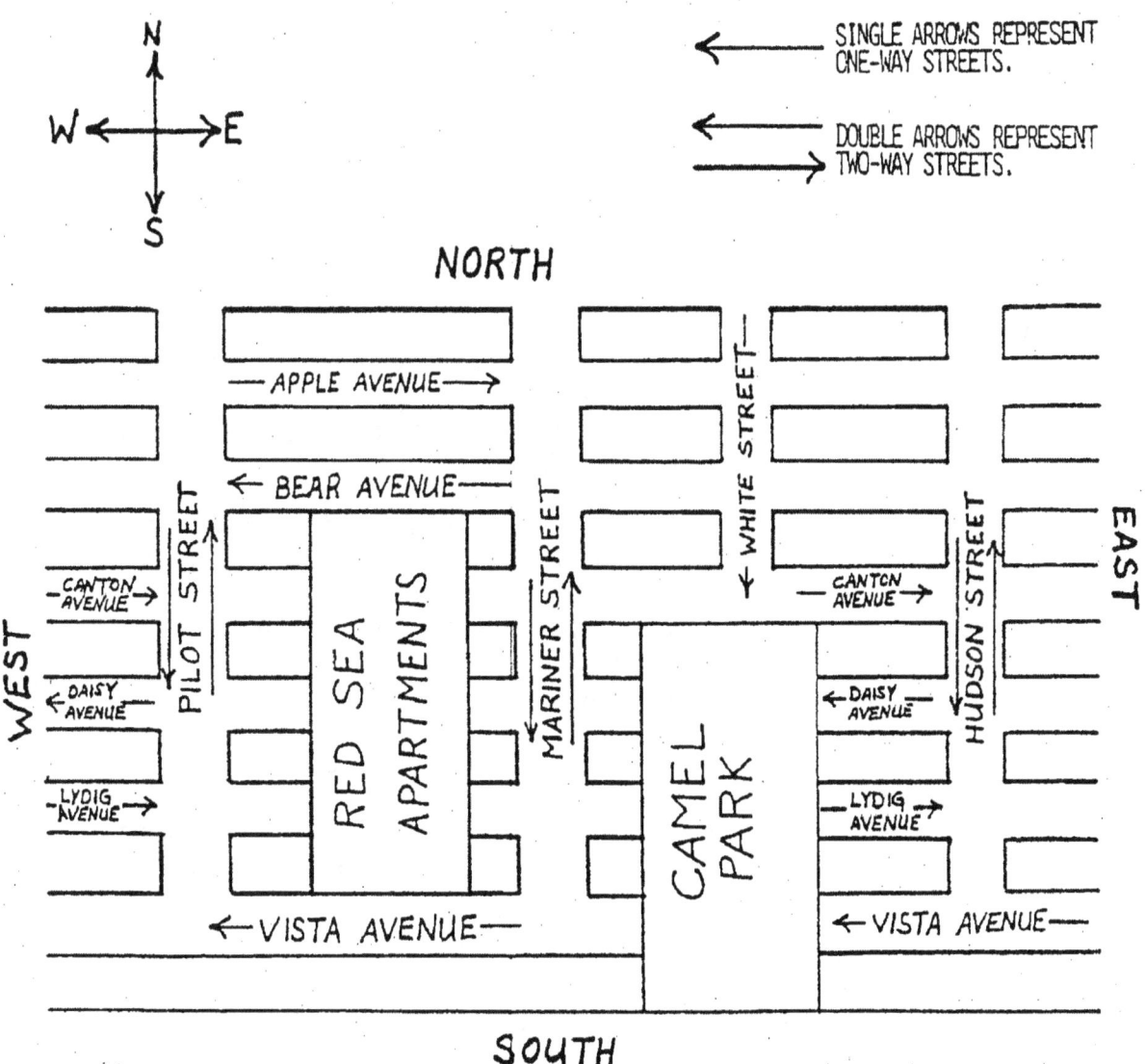

1. You are located at Apple Avenue and White Street. You receive a call to respond to the corner of Lydig Avenue and Pilot Street.
   Which one of the following is the MOST direct route for you to take in your patrol car, making sure to obey all traffic regulations? Travel _____ on Pilot Street.

   A. two blocks south on White Street, then one block east on Canton Avenue, then one block north on Hudson Street, then three blocks west on Bear Avenue, then three blocks south
   B. one block south on White Street, then two blocks west on Bear Avenue, then three blocks south
   C. two blocks west on Apple Avenue, then four blocks south
   D. two blocks south on White Street, then one block west on Canton Avenue, then three blocks south on Mariner Street, then one block west on Vista Avenue, then one block north

2. You are located at Canton Avenue and Pilot Street. You receive a call of a crime in progress at the intersection of Canton Avenue and Hudson Street.
   Which one of the following is the MOST direct route for you to take in your patrol car, making sure to obey all traffic regulations? Travel

   A. two blocks north on Pilot Street, then two blocks east on Apple Avenue, then one block south on White Street, then one block east on Bear Avenue, then one block south on Hudson Street
   B. three blocks south on Pilot Street, then travel one block east on Vista Avenue, then travel three blocks north on Mariner Street, then travel two blocks east on Canton Avenue
   C. one block north on Pilot Street, then travel three blocks east on Bear Avenue, then travel one block south on Hudson Street
   D. two blocks north on Pilot Street, then travel three blocks east on Apple Avenue, then travel two blocks south on Hudson Street

3. Police Officers must follow a set procedure when reporting sick. This is a very important procedure since Police Officers have unlimited sick time. The following steps must be followed in the order given:
   I. Call your Command at least two hours prior to your reporting time.
   II. Contact your District Surgeon within 24 hours.
   III. Follow the directions of your surgeon.
   IV. Remain in your residence while on sick report.
   V. Notify your Command if there is a change in residence.
   VI. Contact Command when you are returned to duty.

   Police Officer Jones becomes ill before going to work one day. He phones his Command three hours before his scheduled time to report. What must he do NEXT?

   A. Notify his Command of a change in his residence.
   B. Follow the directions of the surgeon.
   C. Contact his surgeon within 24 hours.
   D. Remain in his residence while on sick report.

4. When a person commits a traffic infraction, a Police Officer should:
   I. Inform the violatior of the offense committed.

II. Request the violator to show his or her driver's license, vehicle registration, and insurance identification card. Failure to produce this required material may result in additional tickets. (Taxis, buses, and other rented vehicles do not require insurance identification cards.)
III. Enter only one infraction on each ticket.
IV. Use a separate ticket for each additional infraction.

Police Officer Crane is assigned to a traffic post at Broadway and 34th Street to issue tickets for red light violations. Police Officer Crane stops a taxicab for going through a red light at this busy intersection. Police Officer Crane informs the cabdriver of the violation and asks for the required material. The driver hands the Police Officer his license and registration. Police Officer Crane should issue the cabdriver

E. a ticket for the red light violation and a separate ticket for no insurance card
F. one ticket for both the red light violation and no insurance card
G. a ticket only for the red light violation
H. a ticket only for not having an insurance card

5. Police Officer Fitzgrald notices that in his sector all of the burglaries took place on Newton Street. All of the auto thefts occurred on Franklin Street. Most of the rapes took place on Hamburg Avenue. All of the assaults happened on Sparta Place. All of the rapes occurred between 10 P.M and 4 A.M. The auto thefts occurred between Midnight and 6 A.M. All of the burglaries occurred between 10 A.M. and 4 P.M. All of the assaults occurred between 6 P.M. and 10 P.M.

Police Officer Fitzgerald would MOST likely be able to reduce the incidence of rape by patrolling on

A. Sparta Place from 10 A.M. to 4 P.M.
B. Hamburg Avenue from 10 P.M. to 4 A.M.
C. Sparta Place from 10 P.M. to 4 A.M.
D. Hamburg Avenue from 6 P.M. to 10 P.M.

6. Detective Simon is completing a Crime Report. The report contains the following five sentences:
   I. Police Officer Chin, while on foot patrol, heard the yelling and ran in the direction of the man.
   II. The man, carrying a large hunting knife, left the High Sierra Sporting Goods Store at approximately 10:30 A.M.
   III. When the man heard Police Officer Chin, he stopped, dropped the knife, and began to cry.
   IV. As Police Officer Chin approached the man, he drew his gun and yelled, *Police, freeze.*
   V. After the man left the store, he began yelling, over and over, *I am going to kill myself!*

The MOST logical order for the above sentences to appear in the report is:

A. V, II, I, IV, III
B. II, V, I, IV, III
C. II, V, IV, I, III
D. II, I, V, IV, III

7. **Harassment** occurs when a person annoys or alarms another person, but does not intend or cause physical injury.
   Menacing occurs when a person threatens to cause serious physical injury to another person, but does not cause a serious physical injury.
   Assault occurs when a person causes physical injury to another person.
   After a softball game, team members from both the Tigers and Bombers go over to the local bar to drink a few beers. While there, Gardner, the third baseman for the losing Tigers, gets into a heated argument with Carter, the Bombers winning pitcher. Gardner threatens Carter, then picks up an empty beer bottle and smashes it over Carter's head, causing a serious head injury to Carter. Based on the definitions above, Gardner should be charged with

   A. Harassment
   B. Menacing
   C. Assault
   D. no crime

Questions 8-11.

DIRECTIONS: Questions 8 through 11 are to be answered SOLELY on the basis of the following passage.

Housing Police Officer Jones, Shield #691, assigned to foot patrol at Borinquen Plaza Housing Project and working a 4 P.M. to 12 P.M. tour on September 17, 2003, received a call from the Police Radio Dispatcher at 6:10 P.M. to respond to 60 Moore Street, Apartment 7E, on a case involving an elderly woman in need of medical assistance.

Police Officer Jones stated to the Dispatcher that he would respond but on two previous occasions he was called to that same location and the woman refused medical treatment.

Police Officer Jones arrived at 60 Moore Street at 6:15 P.M., took the elevator to the 7th floor, and walked over to Apartment 7E. The Police Officer found the apartment door open, and inside he found the woman, her daughter, and two paramedics. The paramedics had arrived five minutes before the Police Officer. Paramedics Smith #2634 and Hanson #1640 stated to Police Officer Jones that the woman identified as Maria Rivera, age 64, date of birth 5/29/39, who was lying on a dirty mattress in her bedroom, was in shock and in need of medical treatment, but she was refusing medical aid.

Police Officer Jones could not convince Mrs. Rivera to go to the hospital to receive medical treatment. Mrs. Aida Soto, age 32, daughter of Mrs. Rivera, who resides at 869 Flushing Avenue, Apartment 11F, was also present, but she too was unable to convince her mother to go to the hospital.

Police Officer Jones called the Police Radio Dispatcher at 6:25 P.M. and requested the Housing Supervisor to respond to the location. The Housing Supervisor, Sergeant Cuevas, Shield #664, arrived at 6:40 P.M., and Police Officer Jones informed him of the situation. Sergeant Cuevas spoke to Mrs. Rivera and her daughter in Spanish but could not get either to agree that Mrs. Rivera needed urgent medical treatment. Sergeant Cuevas directed paramedics Smith and Hanson to take Mrs. Rivera to the hospital.

Mrs. Rivera was removed from the apartment at 7:00 P.M. and was put in ambulance #1669 and taken to Greenwood Hospital. The ambulance arrived at the hospital at 7:10 P.M., and Mrs. Rivera received the medical treatment she so urgently needed.

Police Officer Jones and Sergeant Cuevas resumed normal patrol at 7:12 P.M. Police Officer Jones prepared Field Report #8964 before the end of his tour.

8. Which one of the following is the CORRECT time that Police Officer Jones arrived at 60 Moore Street?
   _____ P.M.

   A. 6:10   B. 6:15   C. 6:45   D. 7:15

9. Which one of the following is the CORRECT apartment to which Police Officer Jones responded?

   A. 11F   B. 7F   C. 11E   D. 7E

10. Which one of the following is the CORRECT birthdate of Mrs. Rivera?

    A. 5/19/39   B. 5/29/39   C. 7/30/42   D. 8/5/39

11. Which one of the following is the CORRECT name of the sick woman's daughter?

    A. Aida Soto   B. Aida Rivera
    C. Maria Rivera   D. Anna Soto

Questions 12-13.

DIRECTIONS: Questions 12 and 13 are to be answered SOLELY on the basis of the following information.

Police Officers while on patrol may observe a recently vacated building which can create a safety hazard. In such situations, Police Officers should follow these procedures in the order given:
- I. Walk through the vacated building to determine if a safety hazard exists.
- II. If a safety hazard exists, notify the Supervisor on patrol.
- III. Write an entry in the Activity Log.
- IV. Report the facts concerning the safety hazard in the vacant building to the Telephone Switchboard Operator.
- V. Place barriers in front of the vacated building if directed by the Patrol Supervisor.

12. While on patrol, Police Officer Edwards observes a recently vacated building. What action should Police Officer Edwards take NEXT?

    A. Report the safety hazard in the vacant building to the Telephone Switchboard Operator.
    B. Notify the Supervisor on patrol.
    C. Write an entry in the Memo Log.
    D. Determine if a safety hazard exists in the vacated building.

13. Police Officer Henshaw, who has observed a safety hazard in a vacated building while on motor patrol, has already completed all appropriate actions through writing an entry in the Activity Log.
    Police Officer Henshaw should NEXT

    A. determine if a safety hazard exists in other buildings on the block

B. report the facts concerning the safety hazard to the Telephone Switchboard Operator
C. notify the Supervisor on patrol
D. place barriers in front of the vacated building if directed by the Patrol Supervisor

14. Police Officer Miller is preparing a Complaint Report which will include the following five sentences:
    I. From across the lot, he yelled to the boys to get away from his car.
    II. When he came out of the store, he noticed two teenage boys trying to break into his car.
    III. The boys fled as Mr. Johnson ran to his car.
    IV. Mr. Johnson stated that he parked his car in the municipal lot behind Tams Department Store.
    V. Mr. Johnson saw that the door lock had been broken, but nothing was missing from inside the auto.

    The MOST logical order for the above sentences to appear in the report is:

    A. IV, I, II, V, III
    B. II, III, I, V, IV
    C. IV, II, I, III, V
    D. I, II, III, V, IV

15. Police Officer O'Hara completes a Universal Summons for a motorist who has just passed a red traffic light. The Universal Summons includes the following five sentences:
    I. As the car passed the light, I followed in the patrol car.
    II. After the driver stopped the car, he stated that the light was yellow, not red.
    III. A blue Cadillac sedan passed the red light on the corner of 79th Street and 3rd Avenue at 11:25 P.M.
    IV. As a result, the driver was informed that he did pass a red light and that his brake lights were not working.
    V. The driver in the Cadillac stopped his car as soon as he saw the patrol car, and I noticed that the brake lights were not working.

    The MOST logical order for the above sentences to appear in the Universal Summons is:

    A. I, III, V, II, IV
    B. III, I, V, II, IV
    C. III, I, V, IV, II
    D. I, III, IV, II, V

16. Detective Egan is preparing a follow-up report regarding a homicide on 170th Street and College Avenue. An unknown male was found at the scene. The report will contain the following five sentences:
    I. Police Officer Gregory wrote down the names, addresses, and phone numbers of the witnesses.
    II. A 911 operator received a call of a man shot and dispatched Police Officers Worth and Gregory to the scene.
    III. They discovered an unidentified male dead on the street.
    IV. Police Officer Worth notified the Precinct Detective Unit immediately.
    V. At approximately 9:00 A.M., an unidentified male shot another male in the chest during an argument.

    The MOST logical order for the above sentences to appear in the report is:

    A. V, II, III, IV, I;
    B. II, III, V, IV, I
    C. IV, I, V, II, III
    D. V, III, II, IV, I

17. A Police Officer normally does not issue summonses to cars with Diplomatic Credentials, that is, cars with *DPL* or *FC* license plates. However, when a car with *DPL* or *FC* license plates is observed creating a safety hazard, a Police Officer is allowed to issue a summons. In which one of the following situations should a Police Officer issue a summons? A car with

    A. *FC* plates parked at a fire hydrant
    B. *DPL* plates parked at an expired meter
    C. *FC* plates parked in a school zone
    D. *DPL* plates parked in a loading zone

17.____

18. Police Officer Tracey is preparing a Robbery Report which will include the following five sentences:
    I. I ran around the corner and observed a man pointing a gun at a taxidriver.
    II. I informed the man I was a Police Officer and that he should not move.
    III. I was on the corner of 125th Street and Park Avenue when I heard a scream coming from around the corner.
    IV. The man turned around and fired one shot at me.
    V. I fired once, shooting him in the arm and causing him to fall to the ground.

    The MOST logical order for the above sentences to appear in the report is:

    A. I, III, IV, II, V
    B. IV, V, II, I, III
    C. III, I, II, IV, V
    D. III, I, V, II, IV

18.____

19. Police Officer Lee is told by her Patrol Supervisor that the sector to which she is assigned has a high incidence of drug dealing, homicides, assaults, robberies, and burglaries. Police Officer Lee familiarizes herself with the crime statistics of the sector and finds that all the drug dealing takes place on Martin Street, all the homicides take place on Edward Street, all the assaults occur on Charles Street, all the robberies happen on Bruce Street, and all the burglaries are committed on Henry Street. The drug dealing occurs between 1 A.M. and 3 A.M.; the homicides take place between 2 A.M. and 4 P.M.; the assaults happen between 12 A.M. and 2 A.M.; the robberies occur between 3 A.M. and 7 A.M.; and the burglaries happen between 4 A.M. and 6 A.M. The drug dealing takes place on Mondays, the homicides take place on Tuesdays, the assaults happen on Thursdays, the robberies happen on Mondays, and the burglaries happen on Tuesdays. Police Officer Lee would MOST likely be able to reduce the incidence of assaults by patrolling

    A. Charles Street on Thursdays between 12 A.M. and 2 A.M.
    B. Bruce Street on Mondays between 3 A.M. and 7 A.M.
    C. Henry Street on Tuesdays between 4 A.M. and 6 A.M.
    D. Edward Street on Tuesdays between 2 A.M. and 4 A.M.

19.____

20. According to City Police Department procedure, a notification will NOT be made to the relatives of a prisoner who dies in a Department of Correction facility unless a request is made by the Correction Supervisor in charge of the facility.
    Prisoner Richard Jones dies at Rikers Island Correctional Facility where he had been serving a five-year prison term for robbery. Unable to notify the family of the deceased, Correction Supervisor Whitney requests the Police Department to make the notification.

20.____

Police Officer Barry goes to the Jones residence to inform Mrs. Jones of her son's death.

The action of Police Officer Barry in this case is

- A. *proper* because it follows Police Department procedure regarding notifications
- B. *improper* because the Department of Correction should have made its own notification
- C. *proper* because the Police Department is required to make a notification whenever a prisoner dies
- D. *improper* because the Sergeant should have made the notification by telephone

---

KEY (CORRECT ANSWERS)

1.	B		11.	A
2.	D		12.	D
3.	C		13.	B
4.	C		14.	C
5.	B		15.	B
6.	B		16.	A
7.	C		17.	A
8.	B		18.	C
9.	D		19.	A
10.	B		20.	A

EXAMINATION SECTION
TEST 1

DIRECTIONS: Each question or incomplete statement is followed by several suggested answers or completions. Select the one that BEST answers the question or completes the statement. *PRINT THE LETTER OF THE CORRECT ANSWER IN THE SPACE AT THE RIGHT.*

Questions 1-5.

DIRECTIONS: Questions 1 through 5 are to be answered SOLELY on the basis of the following passage.

Police Officers Murphy, Shield No. 7348, and Dunkin, Shield No. 3329, were assigned to patrol sector E in the 90th Precinct at 3:30 A.M. in patrol car 1749 on October 2, 1989.

Sector E is a residential area of rundown dilapidated houses where most of the city's poor live. Police Officers Murphy and Dunkin were traveling south on Jersey Street having a fairly quiet tour when they heard a woman's scream coming from an alley about two blocks south on Jersey Street. Police Officer Dunkin looked at his watch and saw that it was 3:33 M. The Police Officers sped to the area where they believed the scream came from and stopped in front of 998 Jersey Street, which was an abandoned building commonly frequented by junkies and derelicts. Police Officer Murphy called the Police Dispatcher at 3:35 M. to inform him that the Police Officers were investigating screams and requested back-up assistance. The Police Officers then walked to the side of the building which forms an alleyway with 994 Jersey Street. Using flashlights, the Police Officers entered into an alley until they came upon a woman lying on her stomach. Police Officer Dunkin touched her arm, feeling for a pulse, when the woman started moaning. At 3:38 A.M., Police Officer Murphy radioed for an ambulance, while Police Officer Dunkin aided and gathered information from the victim. The woman told the Police Officer that her name is Gloria Vargas, age 21, born on 5/15/68 and that she lives at 1023 Jersey Avenue, Apartment 3H, with her mother and father, Anna and Joseph Vargas, telephone number 784-3942. Ms. Vargas stated that she had been attending a birthday party for her friend, Jane Colon at 694 Jersey Street, Apartment 61, when she decided to leave at around 3:20 A.M. Since she didn't live far and the night was warm, she decided to walk home against the wishes of her friends.

She further stated to Police Officer Dunkin that she did not remember much after that. All she could recall was that she was four blocks from home when she was hit on the head and then woke up in the alley with two cops looking down on her and her purse missing. At 3:45 A.M., Police Officers Vasquez, Shield Number 473, and Booker, Shield Number 498, arrived in patrol car 1754 and were informed by Police Officer Dunkin to search the area for any suspicious person carrying a lady's purple purse. At 3:47 A.M., an ambulance arrived and Paramedics Anders, Shield Number 561, and Hargrove, Shield Number 623, administered first aid and prepared to take Ms. Vargas to Richmond County Hospital. Ms. Vargas refused to go to the hospital and stated that she wanted to go home so that her parents would not worry. After their attempts to convince Ms. Vargas to go to the hospital failed, Police Officers Murphy and Dunkin called the Dispatcher at 4:02 A.M. to report they were escorting Ms. Vargas home. After a search of the area for suspects proved negative, Police Officers Vasquez and Booker reported to the Dispatcher that they were resuming patrol at 4:05 A.M.

Police Officers Murphy and Dunkin arrived at the home of Ms. Vargas and saw that she was safely inside before calling the Dispatcher at 4:10 A.M. to indicate that they were resuming patrol. The Police Officers completed Crime Report Number 6395 and Aided Report Number 523 at 4:30 A.M.

1. Of the following, what kind of area is Sector E described as?

    A. Industrial
    B. Suburban
    C. Commercial
    D. Residential

2. Of the following, what is the number of the radio car used by Police Officers Vasquez and Booker?

    A. 1745   B. 1754   C. 1574   D. 5417

3. What is the date of birth of Ms. Vargas?

    A. 5/11/68   B. 5/15/68   C. 5/11/70   D. 5/15/70

4. What other building helped form an alleyway with 998 Jersey Street? _____ Jersey Street.

    A. 994   B. 1023   C. 694   D. 949

5. In what direction were Police Officers Murphy and Dunkin traveling on Jersey Street?

    A. North   B. East   C. South   D. West

6. An extra Police Officer is assigned to guard prisoners being transported to detention facilities in each of the following situations:
    I. More than two prisoners are being guarded and transport chains are not available, or
    II. More than nine prisoners are being transported by transport chains, or
    III. Several detention stops are involved, or
    IV. More than one prisoner is transported with different destinations.

    In which one of the following cases should an additional escort Police Officer be assigned?

    A. Nine prisoners are being guarded and transport chains are available.
    B. Two prisoners are being guarded and transport chains are available.
    C. Nine prisoners are being transported by transport chains to the same destination.
    D. Five prisoners are being transported by transport chains to separate locations.

7. During the month of November, three assaults occurred in the early evening near the Westville Movie Theatre on Concord Street. The description of each of the suspects is as follows:
    Suspect No. 1 - Male, Hispanic, early 30's, 5'6", 130 lbs., short curly hair, 3 inch scar under left ear, black jacket, dark green pants, black boots.
    Suspect No. 2 - Male, Hispanic, 30 to 35, 5'6", 170 lbs., dark hair, dark green jacket, black pants, black boots.
    Suspect No. 3 - Male, Hispanic, about 35, 5'6", 132 lbs., short curly hair, black turtleneck sweater, green pants, running shoes.

On December 2nd, a fourth assault occurs. However, this time the suspect is arrested by a plainclothes Police Officer. The description of this suspect is as follows:
Suspect No. 4 - Male, Hispanic, 30 to 35, 5'6", 135 lbs., short curly hair, scar on left side of neck, blue ski cap, black jacket, black denim pants, black boots.
Based upon the above descriptions of the suspects in the first three assaults, the suspect in the fourth assault should also be considered a suspect in Assault Number(s)

A. 1 *only* B. 1 and 3 C. 2 *only* D. 1, 2, and 3

8. Police Officer Dunn is patrolling his post and is told to report all hazardous conditions. Which one of the following should the Police Officer report?

    A. Derelicts burning wood in a barrel in front of a vacant building to keep warm
    B. Youths playing in a garbage-strewn lot
    C. A large amount of oil spilled on a busy street
    D. Cars double-parked on a one-way street

Questions 9-10.

DIRECTIONS: Questions 9 and 10 are to be answered SOLELY on the basis of the following passage.

On Thursday, September 13, at approximately 9:55 P.M., Detective George Smith, Shield #796, was off-duty and visiting his mother at 415 East 106th Street. While looking out of the first floor window of his mother's apartment, he notices a suspicious black male sitting in a car with the motor running in front of Joe's Pharmacy, located at 430 East 106th Street between Third and Second Avenue. The car was a blue Chevy Vega with New York license plate number L-77985. Detective Smith leaves the apartment and approaches from the opposite side of the street where he observes two men, both Caucasian, in Joe's Pharmacy. One of the men was standing in front of the cash register, while the other man was pointing a gun at the proprietor, who was pinned against the wall. Detective Smith proceeds to a phone booth on the corner of 106th Street and Second Avenue and dials 911 at 10:00 P.M. He informs 911 operator number 372 of the robbery, gives the address of Joe's Pharmacy, and gives the following description of the perpetrators. The first is a male Caucasian, 5'9", 155 lbs., blonde hair, wearing a brown jacket and black pants. The second is a male Caucasian, 6'3", 175 lbs., bald head, wearing a blue navy coat, black pants, and armed with a gun. The third is a black male, wearing dark clothing and sitting in a blue Chevy Vega, New York license plate number L-77985. Because Detective Smith is not in uniform, he informs the 911 operator that he is wearing a black leather coat and grey pants. Detective Smith requests a back-up unit to respond without lights or siren. He then proceeds to position himself behind a green vehicle parked in front of a closed liquor store opposite Joe's Pharmacy.

Police Officers Brown and Simms respond in Radio Patrol Car #1186 at 10:03 P.M. and park their vehicle on the northwest side of 106th Street on Second Avenue. Approximately at 10:05 P.M., both perpetrators exit from Joe's Pharmacy and run directly to the waiting vehicle which was blocked by a gypsy cab whose owner entered a grocery store. Detective Smith approaches the suspects' vehicle from the rear, and Police Officers Brown and Simms position themselves in view of the suspects and their vehicle, blocking all means of escape. The perpetrators are apprehended, and the property recovered amounts to $1200 in cash and a hand gun. Police Officers Brown and Simms take the perpetrators to the 23rd Precinct for Detective Smith.

4 (#1)

Detective Smith enters Joe's Pharmacy, questions Mr. Velez, the proprietor, informs him of the arrest procedure, and explains to him that he is required to appear at the courthouse the following day to press charges.

Detective Smith, the arresting Police Officer, arrives at the 23rd Precinct at 10:55 P.M., finishes his Police Complaint Report at 11:09 P.M., and removes the perpetrators to Central Booking at 11:20 P.M.

9. Where did Police Officers Brown and Simms park their radio patrol car?

   A. Southwest side of 105th Street on Second Avenue
   B. Southwest side of 105th Street on Third Avenue
   C. Northwest side of 106th Street on Second Avenue
   D. Northwest side of 106th Street on Third Avenue

10. Which one of the following is the BEST description of the second perpetrator?

    A. 5'9", 155 lbs., male, white, blond hair
    B. 5'9", 175 lbs., male, white, bald head
    C. 6'3", 155 lbs., male, white, blond hair
    D. 6'3", 175 lbs., male, white, bald head

11. Police Officer Ginzberg is told that she may have to decide when to help settle disputes. Which one of the following situations should Police Officer Ginzberg help settle?

    A. A group of young men talking about the score of a neighborhood softball game
    B. Four men talking about the feature article in a popular magazine
    C. Two women discussing the abilities of a national tennis star
    D. A man demanding a refund for his ticket from a theater cashier

12. Police Officer Peake is completing an entry in his Activity Log. The entry contains the following five sentences:
    I. He went to his parked car only to find he was blocked in.
    II. The owner of the vehicle refused to move the van until he had finished his lunch.
    III. Approximately 30 minutes later, I arrived on the scene and ordered the owner of the van to remove the vehicle.
    IV. Mr. O'Neil had an appointment and was in a hurry to keep it.
    V. Mr. O'Neil entered a nearby delicatessen and asked if anyone in there drove a dark blue van, license plate number BUS 265.

    The MOST logical order for the above sentences to appear in the Activity Log is:

    A. II, III, I, IV, V
    B. IV, I, V, II, III
    C. V, IV, I, III, II
    D. II, I, III, IV, V

13. Upon arrival at the scene of a person needing medical aid, a Police Officer should do the following in the order given:
    I. Render reasonable aid to the sick or injured person.
    II. Request an ambulance or doctor, if necessary.
    III. Notify the Radio Dispatcher if the person is wearing a Medic-Alert emblem, indicating that the person suffers from diabetes, heart disease, or other serious medical problems.

IV. Wait to direct the ambulance to the scene or have some responsible person do so.
V. Make a second call in 20 minutes if the ambulance does not arrive.
VI. Make an Activity Log entry, including the name of the person notified regarding the Medic-Alert emblem.

While on foot patrol, Police Officer Grayson is approached by a woman who informs the Police Officer that an elderly man has just collapsed on the sidewalk around the corner. Police Officer Grayson, while offering aid, notices that the man is wearing a Medic-Alert emblem indicating heart disease. Police Officer Grayson now requests an ambulance to respond. The NEXT step the Police Officer should take is

A. wait for the ambulance to arrive
B. have a responsible person direct the ambulance to the scene
C. inform the Radio Dispatcher of the Medic-Alert emblem
D. place a second call for the ambulance after 20 minutes

14. Police Officer Harrison is preparing a report regarding a 10-year-old who was sexually abused at school. The report will include the following five sentences:
    I. The child described the perpetrator as a white male with a mustache, six feet tall, wearing a green uniform.
    II. On September 10, 1989, I responded to General Hospital to interview a child who was sexually abused.
    III. He later confessed at the station house.
    IV. After I interviewed the child, I responded to the school and found a janitor who fit the description.
    V. I interviewed the janitor and took him to the station house for further investigation.

The MOST logical order for the above sentences to appear in the report is:

A. II, IV, I, V, III
B. I, IV, V, II, III
C. II, I, IV, V, III
D. V, III, II, I, IV

15. Police Officer Madden is completing a report of a theft. The report will include the following five sentences:
    I. I followed behind the suspect for two blocks.
    II. I saw a man pass by the radio car, carrying a shopping bag.
    III. I looked back in the direction he had just come from and noticed that the top of a parking meter was missing.
    IV. As he saw me, he started to walk faster, and I noticed a red piece of metal with the word *violation* drop out of the shopping bag.
    V. When I saw a parking meter in the shopping bag, I apprehended the suspect and placed him under arrest.

The MOST logical order for the above sentences to appear in the report is:

A. I, IV, II, III, V
B. II, I, IV, V, III
C. II, IV, III, I, V
D. III, II, IV, I, V

16. Transit Police Officer Crawford received a series of reports from several people who were mugged in the early evening as they were exiting from the Spruce Street subway station. The description of each suspect is as follows:

    Report No. 1 (November 16) - Male, white, early 30's, 5'10", 180 lbs., dark hair, moustache, one gold earring, blue jeans, black jacket, running shoes.
    Report No. 2 (November 20) - Male, white, 25-30, 5'6", 120 lbs., dark hair, dark glasses, one gold earring, blue jeans, green sweat shirt, running shoes.
    Report No. 3 (November 21) - Male, white, 40-45, 5'10", 130-140 lbs., dark hair, moustache, one gold earring, blue jeans, black jacket, running shoes.

    On November 23rd, another person was mugged by a male who was loitering near the subway station exit. However, the token clerk witnessed the mugging, called 911, and the male was apprehended two blocks away. The description of the suspect is as follows:

    Report No. 4 (November 23) - Male, white, 25-30, 5'10", 175 lbs., dark hair, moustache, blue jeans, black jacket, green ski cap, boots.

    Based on the above description of the suspects in the first three reports, the suspect in Report No. 4 should also be considered a suspect in Report Number(s)

    A. 1 *only*   B. 1 and 2   C. 2 and 3   D. 1, 2, and 3

17. Crime Reports are completed by Police Officers. One section of a report contains the following five sentences:

    I. The man, seeing that the woman had the watch, pushed Mr. Lugano to the ground.
    II. Frank Lugano was walking into the Flame Diner on Queens Boulevard when he was jostled by a man in front of him.
    III. A few minutes later, Mr. Lugano told a Police Officer on foot patrol about a man and a woman taking his watch.
    IV. As soon as he was jostled, a woman reached toward Mr. Lugano's wrist and removed his expensive watch.
    V. The man and woman, after taking Mr. Lugano's watch, ran around the corner.

    The MOST logical order for the above sentences to appear in the report is:

    A. II, IV, I, III, V
    B. II, IV, I, V, III
    C. IV, I, III, II, V
    D. IV, II, I, V, III

18. Murder - The crime of murder is committed when a person intends to cause the death of another person and he causes the person's death, or he causes a death because of a complete disregard for life by creating a great risk of immediate danger that someone may be killed. The person must be aware that such a risk exists.
    Which one of the following situations is the BEST example of murder?

    A. A construction worker is operating a crane in mid-town when the cable breaks. Three tons of steel fall to the sidewalk and kill three persons.
    B. Kevin Malloy is playing on the subway tracks with his friend John Wilson. Kevin is helping John off the tracks when he slips and lets go of his hand. A train comes and kills John.
    C. A nurse at Midtown Hospital gives a patient the wrong medication. The result is that the patient has an adverse reaction to the medication and dies.
    D. Billy Watson is a security guard at City Federal Bank. He goes out one afternoon and gets angry because his bus is late. He takes out a gun and starts firing wildly

into a crowded bus stop. Billy Watson is fully aware of his actions but fires the gun anyway. One person dies as a result.

19. When a Police Officer comes across an apparently lost child, the Police Officer should do the following in the order given:
    I. Notify the Desk Officer and the Radio Dispatcher.
    II. Ask the people in the vicinity of the place where the child was found what they might know concerning the child.
    III. Bring the child to the station house if a relative of the child is not located.
    IV. Prepare an Aided Report.
    Police Officer Dennis and his partner, Police Officer Mills, are patroling a residential area of the precinct when they notice a young child wandering about the street. When approached by the Police Officers, the child begins crying and says she is lost. Police Officer Dennis telephones Lieutenant Bennett, the Desk Officer, while Police Officer Mills alerts the Radio Dispatcher. The NEXT step the Police Officers should take is to

    A. take the child to the station house and explain the situation to the Desk Officer
    B. gather information and complete the Aided Report
    C. bring the relative to the station house when located
    D. question people in the area near where the child was found

20. When a Police Officer has an article of uniform or equipment that is lost or damaged, the Police Officer should do the following in the order given:
    I. Prepare two copies of the proper report and address it to the Deputy Commissioner of Management and Budget, stating:
       a. How the damage or loss occurred
       b. Date the article was purchased and the cost of the article
    II. Attach the statement of any witnesses.
    III. Show the damaged article to the Commanding Officer.
    Police Officer Gonder has ripped his pants while pursuing a criminal. Two people witnessed the chase. He has prepared two copies of the proper report and sent it to the proper office. On the report, he has stated the circumstances surrounding the cause of the damage and when it occurred. He has listed the date that the pants were purchased and how much they cost. The NEXT step Police Officer Gonder should take is to

    A. attach the statement of witnesses
    B. address and send the report to the Deputy Commissioner of Management and Budget
    C. list on the report the date the damage occurred
    D. show the damaged pants to the Commanding Officer

21. Police Officer McCaslin is preparing a report of disorderly conduct which will include the following five sentences:
    I. Police Officer Kenny and I were on patrol in a radio car when we received a dispatch to go to the Hard Rock Disco on Third Avenue.

II. We arrived at the scene and found three men arguing loudly and obviously intoxicated.
III. The Dispatcher had received a call from a bartender regarding a dispute.
IV. Two of the men left the disco shortly before we did.
V. We calmed the men down after managing to separate them.

The MOST logical order for the above sentences to appear in the report is:

A. I, II, V, III, IV
B. III, I, IV, II, V
C. II, I, III, IV, V
D. I, III, II, V, IV

22. Police Officer Langhorne is completing a report of a murder. The report will contain the following five statements made by a witness:
   I. The noise created by the roar of a motorcycle caused me to look out of my window.
   II. I ran out of the house and realized the man was dead, which is when I called the Police.
   III. I saw a man driving at high speed down the dead-end street on a motorcycle, closely followed by a green BMW.
   IV. The motorcyclist then parked the bike and approached the car, which was occupied by two males.
   V. Two shots were fired and the cyclist fell to the ground; then the car made a U-turn and sped down the street.

The MOST logical order for the above sentences to appear in the report is:

A. I, II, IV, III, V
B. V, II, I, IV, III
C. I, III, IV, V, II
D. III, IV, I, II, V

23. Police Officer Murphy is preparing a report of a person who was assaulted. The report will include the following five sentences:
   I. I responded to the scene, but Mr. Jones had already fled.
   II. She was bleeding profusely from a cut above her right eye.
   III. Mr. and Mrs. Jones apparently were fighting in the street when Mr. Jones punched his wife in the face.
   IV. I then applied pressure to the cut to control the bleeding.
   V. I called the Dispatcher on the radio to send an ambulance to respond to the scene.

The MOST logical order for the above sentences to appear in the report is:

A. III, II, IV, I, V
B. III, I, II, IV, V
C. I, V, II, III, IV
D. II, V, IV, III, I

24. Within a seven-day period, a local precinct received three reports of stolen bicycles. All of the incidents occurred within a five block radius of Briarwood Park. In each incident, the bicycle rider, who was stopped at an intersection waiting for a red light to change, was forced to the ground by an adolescent male who was standing in the crosswalk. After wrestling the bicycle away from the rider, the adolescent then rode off. The description of each of the suspects is as follows:

Incident No. 1 - Male, white, adolescent, blond curly hair, blue eyes, 5'4", 120 lbs., sunglasses, white Tshirt, scar on upper right arm, grey sweat pants, high-top sneakers.

Incident No. 2 - Male, white, adolescent, light curly hair, blue eyes, 5'5", 125 lbs., grey long-sleeved sweat shirt, running shorts, green socks, high-top sneakers.
Incident No. 3 - Male, white, adolescent, brown curly hair, blue eyes, 5'4", 120 to 130 lbs., tattoo on left arm, white tank top, blue sweat pants, running shoes.
In the following week, a fourth bicycle is stolen. However, this time the suspect is arrested by a Police Officer who observes the incident. The description of this suspect is as follows:
Incident No. 4 - Male, white, adolescent, light curly hair, blue eyes, 5'5", 124 lbs., scar on upper right arm, grey tank top, blue sweat pants, running shoes.
Based upon the descriptions of the suspects in the first three incidents, the suspect in the fourth incident should also be considered a suspect in Incident Number(s)

A. 1 *only* B. 1 and 2 C. 2 and 3 D. 1, 2, and 3

25. Detective Adams completed a Crime Report which includes the following five sentences:
   I. I arrived at the scene of the crime at 10:20 A.M. and began to question Mr. Sands about the security devices he had installed.
   II. Several clearly identifiable fingerprints were found.
   III. A Fingerprint Unit specialist arrived at the scene and immediately began to dust for fingerprints.
   IV. After questioning Mr. Sands, I called the Fingerprint Unit.
   V. On Friday morning at 10 A.M., Mr. Sands, the owner of the High Fashion Fur Store on Fifth Avenue, called the Precinct to report that his safe had been broken into.

The MOST logical order for the above sentences to appear in the Crime Report is:

A. I, V, IV, III, II B. I, V, III, IV, II
C. V, I, IV, II, III D. V, I, IV, III, II

KEY (CORRECT ANSWERS)

1.	D	11.	D
2.	B	12.	B
3.	B	13.	C
4.	A	14.	C
5.	C	15.	C
6.	D	16.	A
7.	B	17.	B
8.	C	18.	D
9.	C	19.	D
10.	D	20.	A

21. D
22. C
23. B
24. B
25. D

TEST 2

DIRECTIONS: Each question or incomplete statement is followed by several suggested answers or completions. Select the one that BEST answers the question or completes the statement. *PRINT THE LETTER OF THE CORRECT ANSWER IN THE SPACE AT THE RIGHT.*

Questions 1-2.

DIRECTIONS: Questions 1 and 2 are to be answered SOLELY on the basis of the following map. The flow of traffic is indicated by the arrows. If there is only one arrow shown, then traffic flows only in the direction indicated by the arrow. If there are two arrows shown, then traffic flows in both directions. You must follow the flow of traffic.

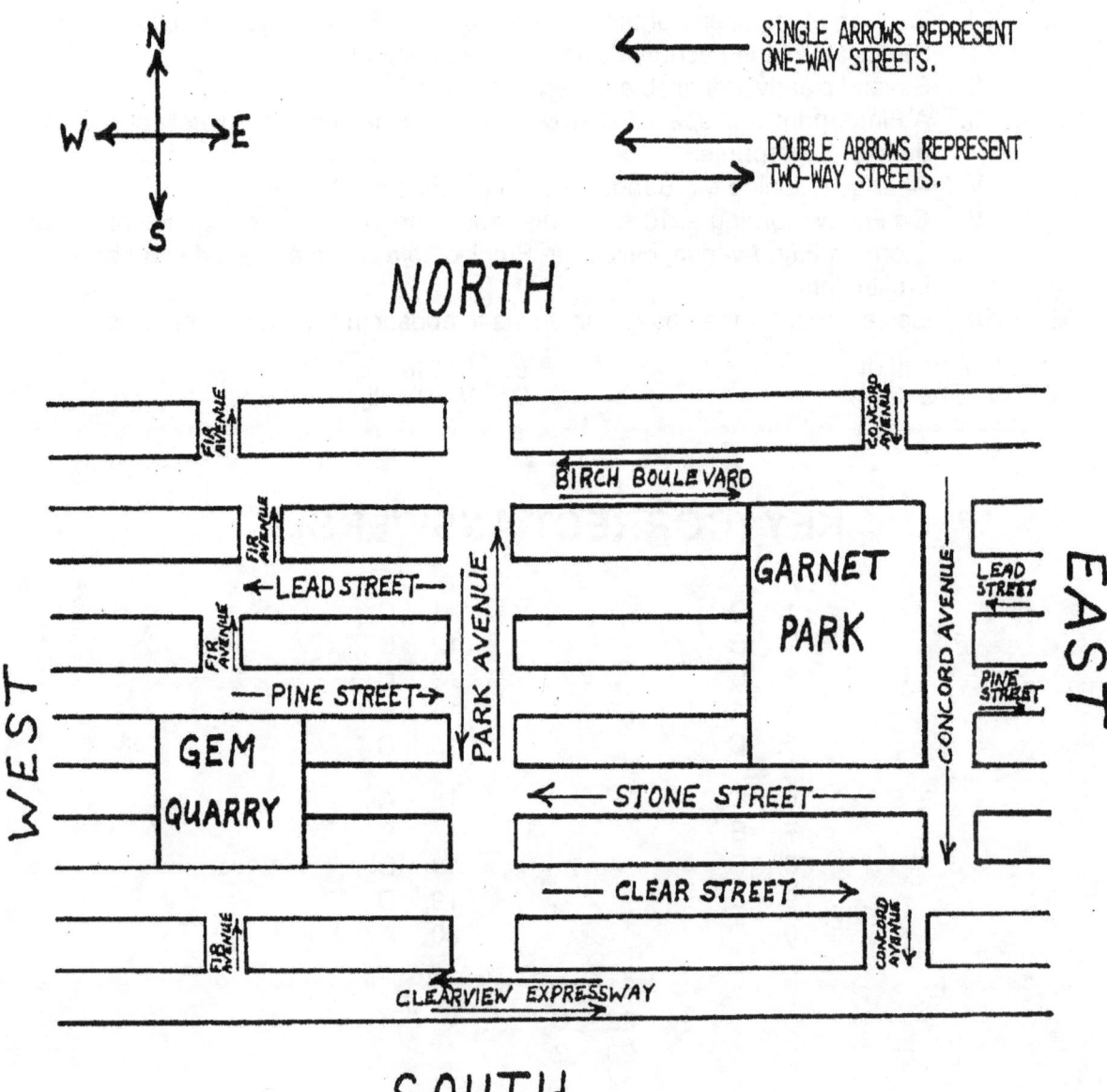

1. You are located at Fir Avenue and Birch Boulevard and receive a request to respond to a disturbance at Fir Avenue and Clear Street.
   Which one of the following is the MOST direct route for you to take in your patrol car, making sure to obey all traffic regulations?
   Travel

   A. one block east on Birch Boulevard, then four blocks south on Park Avenue, then one block east on Clear Street
   B. two blocks east on Birch Boulevard, then three blocks south on Concord Avenue, then two blocks west on Stone Street, then one block south on Park Avenue, then one block west on Clear Street
   C. one block east on Birch Boulevard, then five blocks south on Park Avenue, then one block west on the Clearview Expressway, then one block north on Fir Avenue
   D. two blocks south on Fir Avenue, then one block east on Pine Street, then three blocks south on Park Avenue, then one block east on the Clearview Expressway, then one block north on Fir Avenue

2. You are located at the Clearview Expressway and Concord Avenue and receive a call to respond to a crime in progress at Concord Avenue and Pine Street.
   Which one of the following is the MOST direct route for you to take in your patrol car, making sure to obey all traffic regulations?
   Travel

   A. two blocks west on the Clearview Expressway, then one block north on Fir Avenue, then one block east on Clear Street, then four blocks north on Park Avenue, then one block east on Birch Boulevard, then two blocks south on Concord Avenue
   B. one block north on Concord Avenue, then one block west on Clear Street, then one block north on Park Avenue, then one block east on Stone Street, then one block north on Concord Avenue
   C. one block west on the Clearview Expressway, then four blocks north on Park Avenue, then one block west on Lead Street, then one block south on Fir Avenue
   D. one block west on the Clearview Expressway, then five blocks north on Park Avenue, then one block east on Birch Boulevard, then two blocks south on Concord Avenue

3. Police Officer Ling is preparing a Complaint Report of a missing person. His report will contain the following five sentences:
   I. I was greeted by Mrs. Miah Ali, who stated her daughter Lisa, age 17, did not return from school.
   II. I questioned Mrs. Ali as to what time her daughter left for school and what type of clothing she was wearing.
   III. I notified the Patrol Sergeant, searched the building and area, and prepared a Missing Person Complaint Report.
   IV. I received a call from the Radio Dispatcher to respond to 9 Maple Street, Apartment 1H, on a missing person complaint.
   V. Mrs. Ali informed me that Lisa was wearing a grey suit and black shoes, and departed for school at 7:30 A.M.

   The MOST logical order for the above sentences to appear in the report is:

   A. IV, I, V, II, III
   B. I, IV, V, III, II
   C. IV, I, II, V, III
   D. III, I, IV, II, V

Questions 4-7.

DIRECTIONS: Questions 4 through 7 are to be answered SOLELY on the basis of the following passage.

Police Officers Larson and Kelly were on patrol in their radio car in the area of the 13th Precinct when they received a dispatch to go to the scene of a robbery in progress. The Dispatcher had received a call from a Mr. Morris, the owner of a liquor store located at 1341 3rd Avenue in Manhattan at 8 P.M.

As the Police Officers arrived at the scene approximately five minutes later, a red Buick was pulling away from the liquor store, and Police Officer Kelly made a note of the license plate number, 346-BY They entered the store to find Mr. Morris standing beside an empty cash register. He said that one of the robbers was a white male about 5'10" tall, approximately 180 lbs., blond hair, cleanshaven, wearing a plaid shirt, blue dungarees, and sunglasses. He described the other person as a black female about 5"6" tall, about 140 lbs., black hair, also wearing dark glasses. She was dressed in a red T-shirt and blue dungarees. The Police Officers asked Mr. Morris to describe what had happened. He stated that a female customer, someone he had never seen before, had just purchased some liquor. The woman asked him where the Peter Cooper apartment complex was located. Mr. Morris gave her directions, and the woman left the store at approximately 7:50 P.M. Almost immediately, the robbers entered the store, and the male drew a gun and demanded all the money in the cash register. Mr. Morris opened the register, and the female took all the money, placed it in a large brown bag, and backed toward the door. The male followed closely while holding a light blue bag over the gun. It was then about 7:58 P.M. Mr. Morris ran to the door and saw the robbers get into a blue Chevy Vega, license plate number 574-KJL.

Police Officer Larson asked for a description of the female who had purchased the liquor immediately prior to the hold-up, and Mr. Morris said she was white, about 5'2" tall, 120 lbs., wearing a straw hat, a smock-type of dress, and carrying a large black bag.

4. When did Mr. Morris report the robbery?
   _____ P.M.

   A. 7:50   B. 7:58   C. 8:00   D. 8:05

5. The person who drew the gun on the store owner was a

   A. white male   B. black female
   C. white female   D. black male

6. Which one of the following BEST describes the clothing worn by the female robber?

   A. Plaid shirt, blue dungarees
   B. Blue dungarees, blue T-shirt
   C. Smock-type dress and straw hat
   D. Red T-shirt, blue dungarees

7. Which one of the following is the CORRECT license plate number of the car that the Police Officers saw pulling away from the liquor store?

   A. 346-BIY   B. 574-KJL   C. 346-BYI   D. 574-KLJ

8. Police Officer Carson is told to place barricades or signals on a roadway when it is necessary to warn motorists of hazardous conditions.
   For which one of the following conditions should Police Officer Carson place a barricade on the roadway?
   A

   A. road with a broken overhead street lamp
   B. street with garbage piled four feet high on the sidewalk
   C. road with a tree fallen across one lane
   D. street with a filled-in pothole

9. Police Officer Dunn is preparing a Complaint Report which will include the following five sentences:
   I. Mrs. Field screamed and fought with the man.
   II. A man wearing a blue ski mask grabbed Mrs. Field's purse.
   III. Mrs. Fields was shopping on 34th Street and Broadway at 1 o'clock in the afternoon.
   IV. The man then ran around the corner.
   V. The man was white, five feet six inches tall with a medium build.
   The MOST logical order for the above sentences to appear in the report is:

   A. I, V, II, IV, III
   B. III, II, I, IV, V
   C. III, IV, V, I, II
   D. V, IV, III, I, II

Questions 10-11.

DIRECTIONS: Questions 10 and 11 are to be answered SOLELY on the basis of the following information.

Police Officer Winter reads a report concerning robberies, burglaries, and assaults which occur in his sector. From the report, Police Officer Winter notices that all the robberies take place on Martin Street, all the burglaries take place on Adam Street and on William Street, and all the assaults take place on Eddy Street.

Most of the robberies occur on Thursdays and Fridays, most of the burglaries occur on Thursdays, and most of the assaults occur on Saturdays.

Most of the robberies happen between 5 P.M. and 11 P.M., most of the burglaries happen between 7 P.M. and 12 A.M., and most of the assaults happen between 9 P.M. and 2 A.M.

10. Police Officer Winter would MOST likely be able to decrease the number of burglaries if he were to patrol

    A. Adam Street on Thursdays from 7 P.M. to 12 A.M.
    B. William Street on Fridays from 5 P.M. to 11 P.M.
    C. Eddy Street on Thursdays from 7 P.M. to 12 P.M.
    D. Martin Street on Fridays from 5 P.M. to 11 P.M.

11. Police Officer Winter would MOST likely be able to decrease the number of assaults if he were to patrol on

    A. Fridays from 5 P.M. to 11 P.M.
    B. Fridays from 9 A.M. to 2 A.M.

C. Saturdays from 7 P.M. to 12 A.M.
D. Saturdays from 9 P.M. to 2 A.M.

Questions 12-14.

DIRECTIONS: Questions 12 through 14 are to be answered SOLELY on the basis of the following information.

A Police Officer is told to notify the station house when he observes dangerous conditions.

12. For which one of the following should a Police Officer notify the station house? A(n)

    A. male sleeping in the staircase of a building
    B. missing glass panel at the entrance of a building
    C. elevator door which has opened between floors
    D. broken bottle in the lobby of a building

13. For which one of the following should a Police Officer notify the station house?

    A. A female dumping water out of a window
    B. Smoke coming out of the fifth floor windows of a housing project
    C. A fire hydrant opened in front of a building
    D. A locked entrance door

14. For which one of the following should a Police Officer notify the station house?

    A. Bricks falling from a tall building
    B. A nude male in the lobby of a building
    C. Two females arguing in front of a building entrance
    D. An intoxicated male sleeping on the sidewalk

15. Police Officer Jackson is told that he will sometimes be required to use his patrol car to transport seriously injured people to a hospital. However, the Police Officer should call an ambulance for people who are NOT seriously injured.
    For which one of the following people should Police Officer Jackson call an ambulance rather than use his patrol car? A person

    A. who is unconscious
    B. who is bleeding from the chest
    C. whose face is burned
    D. who has a sprained wrist

16. When a Police Officer recovers a loaded gun, the Police Officer should do the following in the order given:
    I. Unload the bullets from the gun.
    II. Scratch an identifying mark on the side of the bullets.
    III. Place the bullets in an envelope and seal the envelope.
    IV. Mark *Ammunition Removed from Firearm* across the face of the envelope and record the serial number of the gun.
    V. Deliver the gun and the ammunition to the Desk Officer of the Precinct.

    Police Officer Parrish arrests a burglary suspect and discovers a loaded gun tucked in the jacket pocket of the suspect. At the Precinct, the Police Officer unloads the gun and marks his initials on the side of each of the three bullets removed. The NEXT step the Police Officer should take is to

    A. present the bullets to the Precinct Desk Officer
    B. place the gun in an envelope and seal it
    C. mark the envelope across the face and record the serial number
    D. place the bullets in an envelope and seal it

16.____

17. Missing persons are often reported to the City Police Department. When the report involves people who are not able to fully care for themselves, then a search of the area is required. A search is required when the missing person is a child under ten years of age, a possible drowning victim, a retarded or handicapped person, or an elderly person suffering from senility.
    In which one of the following situations is a search required?

    A. Mrs. Johnson waits until 5:30 P.M. for John to come home from school. John is 11 years old and plays basketball after school every day, but today he didn't leave a note to that effect.
    B. Mrs. Smith waits until 3:45 P.M., but Bill, her 8-year-old son, hasn't come home from school. He has never been late before.
    C. Alexander Saunders is 25 years old and had a fight with his mother. He left and hasn't called in two days.
    D. Loraine Smith is a 17-year-old girl who wants to quit high school, but her mother won't let her. She left home and has not been heard from in three days.

17.____

Questions 18-20.

DIRECTIONS: Questions 18 through 20 are to be answered SOLELY on the basis of the following passage.

On Monday evening, February 6, 1990, while I was on duty in the guard box outside the Liberian Embassy on Lexington Avenue and 38th Street, I noticed a grey Volvo, New York license plate number 846 DSB, parked across the street on the northeast corner of 38th Street at approximately 5:15 P.M. There were two occupants in the car. One was a white male who had grey hair and was wearing a pale blue jacket; the other was a young male with a dark complexion who was wearing a hat, sunglasses, and a dark grey jacket.

After about 20 minutes, the man wearing the dark grey jacket got out of the car and read the traffic sign which described the parking regulations. He then spoke to the driver of the car, the man wearing the blue jacket, and walked up 38th Street toward Park Avenue. Because I know the parking rules of this area and since the car was not in violation, I ceased to observe it. However, approximately five minutes later, my attention was drawn to the sight of the male passenger who had previously left the car to walk up 38th Street. He now appeared on Lexington Avenue from the southeast corner of 39th Street and entered a high-rise building located directly opposite the Embassy. Almost simultaneously, a blue Ford bearing a New Jersey license plate number 691 ASD, pulled up to the curb in front of the building, and the driver, a tall white male with blonde hair, who was wearing a dark blue suit and carrying a briefcase, got out and entered the lobby.

   I walked across the street from the guard box and went into the lobby of the high-rise building where the doorman hurried over to ask if he could assist me. There was no sign of either of the men. After describing them, I asked the doorman if he knew whether they were tenants or visitors to the building. He said the tall blonde man was a tenant by the name of George Altman who lived in Apartment 19G. The other young, dark complexioned man announced himself as Mr. Donabuto and entered the elevator with Mr. Altman, whom he had come to visit. The doorman also added that Mr. Donabuto had visited the building at least twice the previous week. On one occasion, he visited Mr. Ehrenwald, a tenant who lives in Apartment 19C. On the other occasion, he visited Mr. Escobar, who lives in Apartment 19D. In addition, the doorman said that he had observed Mr. Yepes, the driver of the grey Volvo, visit Mr. Altman the day before.

   After investigating the layout of the building, I decided to make an entry in the Activity Log and report the incident as suspicious due to the fact that Apartment 19G directly overlooks the room occupied by the Consul General in the Liberian Embassy.

18. Which one of the following BEST describes the driver of the Volvo? A _____ man.

   A. dark-complexioned
   B. white, grey-haired
   C. tall blonde
   D. dark middle-aged

19. At approximately what time did the young male wearing a hat and sunglasses enter the building on Lexington Avenue? _____ P.M.

   A. 5:15
   B. 5:20
   C. 5:40
   D. 6:00

20. At which one of the following locations was the grey Volvo parked? _____ corner of _____ Street.

   A. Southeast; 39th
   B. Northwest; 39th
   C. Southwest; 38th
   D. Northeast; 38th

21. *According to State law, it is unlawful for a person to possess a loaded gun outside his home or place of business.* Based on this statement, which one of the following persons is violating the law?

   A. Joel Roberts manages a grocery store and keeps a loaded gun near the cash register of his store.
   B. Marcia Cohen works as a security guard and keeps her loaded gun in her apartment.
   C. Ken Caldwell owns a jewelry store and carries a loaded gun when he visits his brother's house in the Bronx.
   D. Steve Davis sells real estate and keeps his unloaded gun in his summer house upstate.

22. Police Officer Durant is completing a report of a robbery and assault. The report will contain the following five sentences:
    I. I went to Mount Snow Hospital to interview a man who was attacked and robbed of his wallet earlier that night.
    II. An ambulance arrived at 82nd Street and 3rd Avenue and took an intoxicated, wounded man to Mount Snow Hospital.
    III. Two youths attacked the man and stole his wallet.
    IV. A well-dressed man left Hanratty@s Bar very drunk, with his wallet hanging out of his back pocket.
    V. A passerby dialed 911 and requested police and ambulance assistance.
    The MOST logical order for the above sentences to appear in the report is:

    A. I, II, IV, III, V   B. IV, III, V, II, I
    C. IV, V, II, III, I   D. V, IV, III, II, I

23. Police Officer Boswell is preparing a report of an armed robbery and assault which will contain the following five sentences:
    I. Both men approached the bartender and one of them drew a gun.
    II. The bartender immediately went to grab the phone at the bar.
    III. One of the men leaped over the counter and smashed a bottle over the bartender's head.
    IV. Two men in a blue Buick drove up to the bar and went inside.
    V. I found the cash register empty and the bartender unconscious on the floor, with the phone still dangling off the hook.
    The MOST logical order for the above sentences to appear in the report is:

    A. IV, I, II, III, V   B. V, IV, III, I, II
    C. IV, III, II, V, I   D. II, I, III, IV, V

24. Police Officer Mitzler is preparing a report of a bank robbery, which will contain the following five sentences:
    I. The teller complied with the instructions on the note, but also hit the silent alarm.
    II. The perpetrator then fled south on Broadway.
    III. A suspicious male entered the bank at approximately
    IV. 10:45 A.M. At this time, an undetermined amount of money has been taken.
    V. He approached the teller on the far right side and handed her a note.
    The MOST logical order for the above sentences to appear in the report is:

    A. III, V, I, II, IV   B. I, III, V, II, IV
    C. III, V, IV, I, II   D. III, V, II, IV, I

25. A Police Officer is preparing an Accident Report for an accident which occurred at the intersection of East 119th Street and Lexington Avenue. The report will include the following five sentences:
    I. On September 18, 1990, while driving ten children to school, a school bus driver passed out.
    II. Upon arriving at the scene, I notified the Dispatcher to send an ambulance.
    III. I notified the parents of each child once I got to the station house.
    IV. He said the school bus, while traveling west on East 119th Street, struck a parked Ford which was on the southwest corner of East 119th Street.
    V. A witness by the name of John Ramos came up to me to describe what happened.

    The MOST logical order for the above sentences to appear in the Accident Report is:

    A. I, II, V, III, IV
    B. I, II, V, IV, III
    C. II, V, I, III, IV
    D. II, V, I, IV, III

25.____

KEY (CORRECT ANSWERS)

1.	C	11.	D
2.	D	12.	C
3.	C	13.	B
4.	C	14.	A
5.	A	15.	D
6.	D	16.	D
7.	C	17.	B
8.	C	18.	B
9.	B	19.	C
10.	A	20.	D

21.	C
22.	B
23.	A
24.	A
25.	B

TEST 3

DIRECTIONS: Each question or incomplete statement is followed by several suggested answers or completions. Select the one that BEST answers the question or completes the statement. *PRINT THE LETTER OF THE CORRECT ANSWER IN THE SPACE AT THE RIGHT.*

1. A Police Officer is preparing a report concerning a dispute. The report will contain the following five sentences:
    I. The passenger got out of the back of the taxi and leaned through the front window to complain to the driver about the fare.
    II. The driver of the taxi caught up with the passenger and knocked him to the ground; the passenger then kicked the driver and a scuffle ensued.
    III. The taxi drew up in front of the high-rise building and stopped.
    IV. The driver got out of the taxi and followed the passenger into the lobby of the apartment building.
    V. The doorman tried but was unable to break up the fight, at which point he called the Precinct.

    The MOST logical order for the above sentences to appear in the report is:

    A. III, I, IV, II, V
    B. III, IV, I, II, V
    C. III, IV, II, V, I
    D. V, I, III, IV, II

1.____

Questions 2-3.

DIRECTIONS: Questions 2 and 3 are to be answered SOLELY on the basis of the following information.

Police Officer Forster notices that in his sector all the robberies take place on Eaton Street, all the traffic accidents occur on Country Club Road, and all the assaults happen on Monmouth Street.

Most of the assaults take place between 8 A.M. and 11 A.M. and between 2 P.M. and 7 P.M. Most of the traffic accidents occur between 11 A.M. and 4 P.M. Most of the robberies take place between 7 P.M. and 11 P.M.

Most of the traffic accidents happen on Mondays, most of the robberies take place on Wednesdays and Saturdays, and most of the assaults occur on Thursdays.

2. Police Officer Forster would MOST likely be able to reduce the incidence of robberies by patrolling

    A. Monmouth Street on Thursdays from 8 P.M. to 11 P.M.
    B. Eaton Street on Wednesdays from 7 A.M. to 11 A.M.
    C. Eaton Street on Saturdays from 6 P.M. to 10 P.M.
    D. Eaton Street on Thursdays from Noon to 4 P.M.

2.____

3. Due to his knowledge of the crime patterns in his sector, Police Officer Forster's superiors want him to work a steady tour each week that would allow him to concentrate on assaults and robberies within his sector.
    For this purpose, it would be MOST appropriate for Police Officer Forster to work

3.____

257

A. Monday through Friday, 4 P.M. to Midnight
B. Tuesday through Saturday, 4 P.M. to Midnight
C. Tuesday through Saturday, 2 P.M. to 10 P.M.
D. Monday through Friday, 8 A.M. to 4 P.M.

4. Police Officer Morrow is writing an Incident Report. The report will include the following four sentences:
    I. The man reached into his pocket and pulled out a gun.
    II. While on foot patrol, I identified a suspect, who was wanted for six robberies in the area, from a wanted picture I was carrying.
    III. I drew my weapon and fired six rounds at the suspect, killing him instantly.
    IV. I called for back-up assistance and told the man to put his hands up.
The MOST logical order for the above sentences to appear in the report is:

A. II, III, IV, I
B. IV, I, III, II
C. IV, I, II, III
D. II, IV, I, III

Questions 5-9.

DIRECTIONS: Questions. 5 through 9 are to be answered SOLELY on the basis of the following passage.

Police Officer Davies, Shield Number 3935, patrolling Sector D in the 79th Precinct on Scooter Number 569, was dispatched at 9:26 A.M. on November 12, 1989 to Roosevelt Houses, 928 Dekalb Avenue, Apartment 15J, on a family dispute. Police Officer Davies requested back-up units to meet him in front of the building.

Police Officer Davies arrived on the scene at 9:30 A.M. A back-up unit consisting of Police Officers Mark #2310 and Harris #1542 arrived at the same time in Patrol Car #9843. The Police Officers were assigned to the same precinct and sector. The Police Officers took the elevator to the 15th floor and proceeded to Apartment 15J.

The Police Officers rang the apartment bell and were met by a black female who told them that she had a court Order of Protection against her husband. She further stated that her husband was trying to force his way into the apartment but fled the scene when she called the Police. She gave the following description of her husband: male, black, age 38, date of birth 8/14/51, named Carl Tyler, 6'1" tall, about 185 pounds, clean-shaven, wearing a dark blue long sleeve shirt, black pants, and black shoes. She further stated that he resides at 89-27 Bellmore Avenue in Queens, Apartment 2A.

At 9:35 A.M., Police Officers Mark and Harris searched the building and the surrounding area for Mr. Tyler or for someone fitting the description given by the woman, while Police Officer Davies obtained further information for his report.

The woman stated her name as Betty Tyler, 37-years-old, born 4/10/52, home telephone number 387-3038. She gave Police Officer Davies her copy of the Order of Protection, and he recorded the information in his Memo Book.

The Order of Protection was dated 11/5/89, issued at Brooklyn Criminal Court, 120 Schermerhorn Street, by Judge Harry Cohn, Docket Number APG482/89 and in effect until 1/19/90.

Police Officers Mark and Harris returned to Apartment 5J at 9:45 A.M. after a search for Mr. Tyler proved negative. The Police Officers advised Mrs. Tyler to call the Police again if her husband returned.

Police Officers Mark and Harris notified the Radio Dispatcher that they were resuming patrol at 9:52 A.M. Police Officer Davies proceeded to the station house to prepare two Complaint Reports and to refer the matter to the Detective Unit for follow-up.

5. In which precinct and sector do Police Officer Davies and the back-up Police Officers work?
   _____ Precinct, Sector _____ .
   A. 79th; D
   B. 79th; B
   C. 97th; D
   D. 97th; B

6. What is the TOTAL number of Police Officers who responded to assist Police Officer Davies on the family dispute?
   A. 1
   B. 2
   C. 3
   D. 4

7. Which docket number did Police Officer Davies record in his Memo Book?
   A. AFG482/89
   B. APG428/89
   C. APG482/89
   D. AFG428/89

8. Which one of the following is the APPROXIMATE time that Police Officers Mark and Harris arrived at the location? _____ A.M.
   A. 9:30
   B. 9:35
   C. 9:45
   D. 9:52

9. Which one of the following is the BEST description of Mr. Tyler?
   Black, 6 ft.
   A. 1 in. tall, 185 pounds
   B. 1 in. tall, 160 pounds
   C. 6 in. tall, 185 pounds
   D. 6 in. tall, 160 pounds

10. Sergeant Allen responds to a call at 16 Grove Street regarding a missing child. At the scene, the Sergeant is met by Police Officer Samuels, who gives a brief account of the incident consisting of the following five sentences:
    I. I transmitted the description and waited for you to arrive before I began searching the area.
    II. Mrs. Banks, the mother, reports that she last saw her daughter Julie about 7:30 A.M. when she took her to school.
    III. About 6 P.M., my partner and I arrived at this location to investigate a report of a missing 8-year-old girl.
    IV. When Mrs. Banks left her, Julie was wearing a red and white striped T-shirt, blue jeans, and white sneakers.
    V. Mrs. Banks dropped her off in front of the playground of P.S. 11.
    The MOST logical order for the above sentences to appear in the report is:
    A. III, V, IV, II, I
    B. III, II, V, IV, I
    C. III, IV, I, II, V
    D. III, II, IV, I, V

11. Police Officer Franco is completing a report of an assault. The report will contain the following five sentences:
    I. In the park I observed an elderly man lying on the ground, bleeding from a back wound.

II. I applied first aid to control the bleeding and radioed for an ambulance to respond.
III. The elderly man stated that he was sitting on the park bench when he was attacked from behind by two males.
IV. I received a report of a man's screams coming from inside the park, and I went to investigate.
V. The old man could not give a description of his attackers.

The MOST logical order for the above sentences to appear in the report is:

A. IV, I, II, III, V
B. V, III, I, IV, II
C. IV, III, V, II, I
D. II, I, V, IV, III

12. Police Officer Williams is completing a Crime Report. The report contains the following five sentences:

I. As Police Officer Hanson and I approached the store, we noticed that the front door was broken.
II. After determining that the burglars had fled, we notified the Precinct of the burglary.
III. I walked through the front door as Police Officer Hanson walked around to the back.
IV. At approximately Midnight, an alarm was heard at the Apex Jewelry Store.
V. We searched the store and found no one.

The MOST logical order for the above sentences to appear in the report is:

A. I, IV, II, III, V
B. I, IV, III, V, II
C. IV, I, III, II, V
D. IV, I, III, V, II

Questions 13-20.

DIRECTIONS: Questions 13 through 20 are to be answered SOLELY on the basis of the following sketches. The first face, on the left, is a sketch of an alleged criminal based on witnesses' descriptions at the crime scene. One of the four sketches to the right is the way the suspect looked *after* changing appearance. Assume that NO surgery has been done on the suspect. Select the face which is MOST likely that of the suspect.

13.

A.   B.   C.   D.

6 (#3)

18. 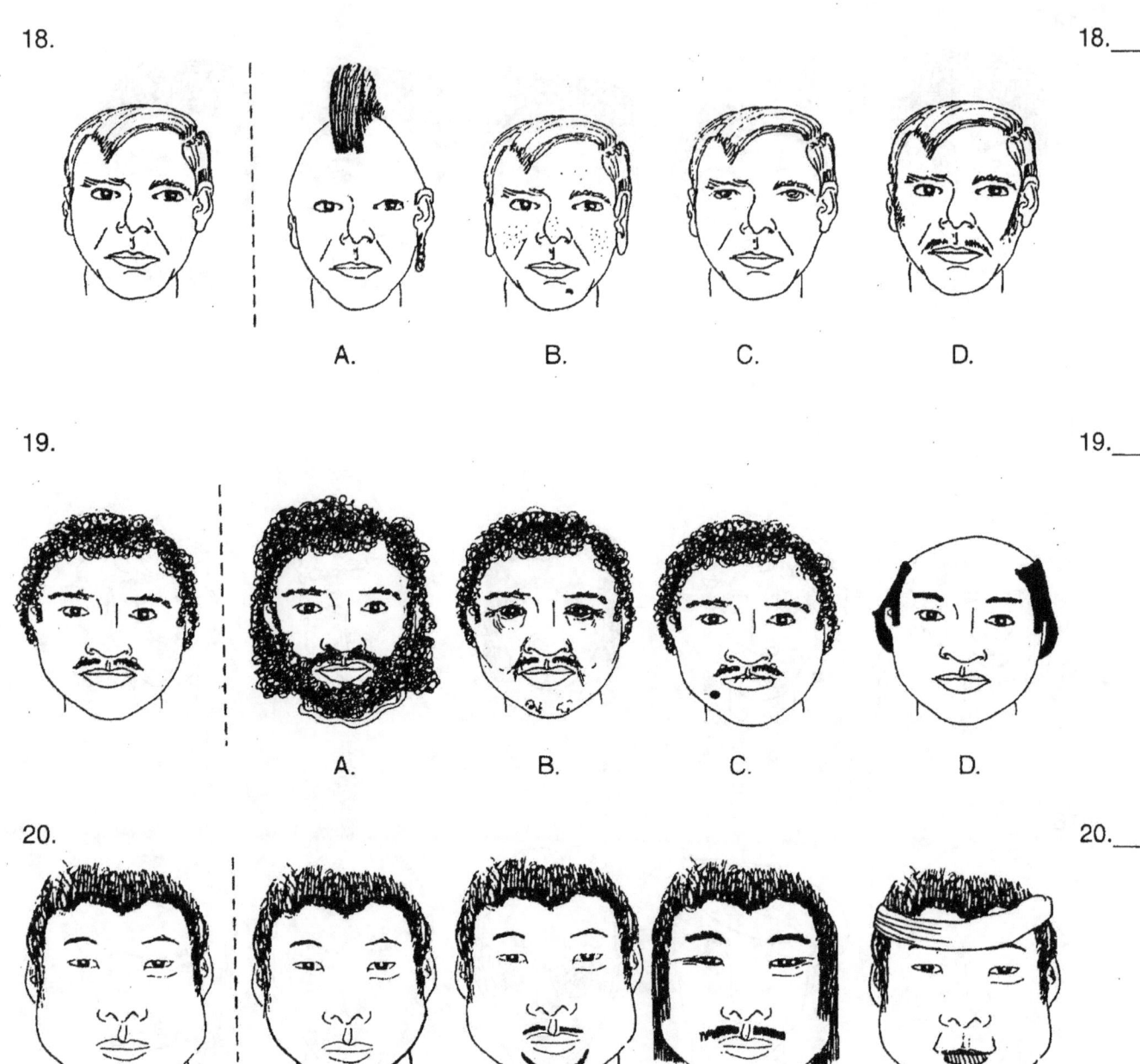 18.____

19.

20.

KEY (CORRECT ANSWERS)

1.	A	11.	A
2.	C	12.	D
3.	B	13.	B
4.	D	14.	D
5.	A	15.	A
6.	B	16.	B
7.	C	17.	C
8.	A	18.	D
9.	A	19.	A
10.	B	20.	B

EXAMINATION SECTION
TEST 1

DIRECTIONS: Each question or incomplete statement is followed by several suggested answers or completions. Select the one that BEST answers the question or completes the statement. *PRINT THE LETTER OF THE CORRECT ANSWER IN THE SPACE AT THE RIGHT.*

MEMORY PAGES

Memory Sketch 1 is on Pages 2 and 3. Memory Sketch 2 is on Pages 4 and 5. You are to study Scene 1 carefully and try to remember as many details in the scene as you can. You should pay equal attention both to objects and to people shown in the scene. Then turn to Questions 1 through 7 which follow and answer these questions based upon what you remember from Scene 1. Do not turn back to Sketch 1 while answering. After you complete Questions 1 through 7, study Memory Sketch 2. Then turn to Questions 8 through 14 and answer them based on Sketch 2.

4 (#1)

5 (#1)

Questions 1-7.

DIRECTIONS: Questions 1 through 7 are to be answered SOLELY on the basis of Sketch 1.

1. The scaffold is located on the

    A. McManus Iron Works building
    B. bridge
    C. Tarrago Bag Company building
    D. gas storage tank

2. The woman with the long pants and boots is standing closest to the

    A. Tarrago Bag Company
    B. diner
    C. gas storage tank
    D. McManus Iron Works building

3. The garbage truck (Weber's Collection Truck) is located closest to the

    A. Yate truck
    B. gas storage tank
    C. bridge
    D. Tarrago Bag Company building

4. The man using the hand truck is closest to the

    A. garbage truck   B. automobile
    C. railroad cars   D. oil drums

5. The license plate number of the car is

    A. MM-12   B. MOM-1   C. M731   D. MOM-2

6. The trailer truck without the cab which is near McManus Iron Works has which one of the following names on it?

    A. Jet Transport   B. Yate
    C. Steels   D. Weber's Collection

7. The person just inside the door of the diner is BEST described as having a

    A. cap on his head and a cigarette in his mouth
    B. bald head and a mustache
    C. cap on his head with a patch over his right eye
    D. pair of sunglasses covering his eyes and a scarf around his neck

Questions 8-14.

DIRECTIONS: Questions 8 through 14 are to be answered SOLELY on the basis of Sketch 2.

8. The group of four teenagers is standing closest to a

    A. fire hydrant
    B. street which is closed by a barricade

C. car
D. no parking sign

9. The fire alarm box (marked FD) is located at the corner of

    A. Graham Street and Devoe Avenue
    B. Grand Street and Devoe Avenue
    C. Graham Street and Beekman Avenue
    D. Graham Street and Frost Avenue

10. The group of three young boys is standing near the corner of

    A. Grand Street and Beekman Avenue
    B. Graham Street and Devoe Avenue
    C. Graham Street and Frost Avenue
    D. Grand Street and Devoe Avenue

11. At 52 Graham Street, there is _____ on the roof and _____ at a window.

    A. a woman; a man
    B. a man; a man
    C. a man; a woman
    D. no one; no one

12. A fire hydrant is located on

    A. Grand Street
    B. Devoe Avenue
    C. Frost Avenue
    D. Graham Street

13. The car that appears to be abandoned is located on

    A. Graham Street
    B. Devoe Avenue
    C. Beekman Avenue
    D. Frost Avenue

14. Which one of the following stores is NOT shown in the sketch?
    A

    A. bake shop
    B. fish store
    C. liquor store
    D. boutique

15. A Police Officer is completing a report concerning the response to a crime in progress. The report will include the following five sentences:
    I. The Officers saw two armed men run out of the liquor store and into a waiting car.
    II. Police Officers Lunty and Duren received the call and responded to the liquor store.
    III. The robbers gave up without a struggle.
    IV. Lunty and Duren blocked the getaway car with their patrol car.
    V. A call came into the precinct concerning a robbery in progress at Jane's Liquor Store.

    The MOST logical order for the above sentences to appear in the report is:

    A. V, II, I, IV, III
    B. II, V, I, III, IV
    C. V, I, IV, II, III
    D. I, V, II, III, IV

16. The following five sentences are part of an Activity Log entry Police Officer Rogers made regarding an explosion:
    I. I quickly treated the pedestrian for the injury.
    II. The explosion caused a glass window in an office building to shatter.
    III. After the pedestrian was treated, a call was placed to the precinct requesting additional Police Officers to evacuate the area.
    IV. After all the glass settled to the ground, I saw a pedestrian who was bleeding from the arm.
    V. While on foot patrol near 5th Avenue and 53rd Street, I heard a loud explosion.

    The MOST logical order for the above sentences to appear in the report is:

    A. II, V, IV, I, III
    B. V, II, IV, III, I
    C. V, II, I, IV, III
    D. V, II, IV, I, III

17. Police Officer David is completing a report regarding illegal activity near the entrance to Madison Square Garden during a recent rock concert. The report will contain the following five sentences:
    I. As I came closer to the man, he placed what appeared to be tickets in his pocket and began to walk away.
    II. After the man stopped, I questioned him about *scalping* tickets.
    III. While on assignment near the Madison Square Garden entrance, I observed a man apparently selling tickets.
    IV. I stopped the man by stating that I was a Police Officer.
    V. The man was then given a summons and he left the area.

    The MOST logical order for the above sentences to appear in the report is:

    A. I, III, IV, II, V
    B. III, I, IV, V, II
    C. III, IV, I, II, V
    D. III, I, IV, II, V

18. Police Officer Sampson is preparing a report concerning a dispute in a bar. The report will contain the following five sentences:
    I. John Evans, the bartender, ordered the two men out of the bar.
    II. Two men dressed in dungarees entered the C and D Bar at 5:30 P.M.
    III. The two men refused to leave and began to beat up Evans.
    IV. A customer in the bar saw me on patrol and yelled to me to come separate the three men.
    V. The two men became very drunk and loud within a short time.

    The MOST logical order for the above sentences to appear in the report is:

    A. II, I, V, III, IV
    B. II, III, IV, V, I
    C. III, I, II, V, IV
    D. II, V, I, III, IV

19. Police Officer Jenkins is preparing a Crime Report which will consist of the following five sentences:

    I. After making inquiries in the vicinity, Smith found out that his next door neighbor, Viola Jones, had seen two local teenagers, Michael Heinz and Vincent Gaynor, smash his car's windshields with a crowbar.
    II. Jones told Smith that the teenagers live at 8700 19th Avenue.
    III. Mr. Smith heard a loud crash at approximately 11:00 P.M., looked out his apartment window, and saw two white males running away from his car.
    IV. Smith then reported the incident to the precinct, and Heinz and Gaynor were arrested at the address given.
    V. Leaving his apartment to investigate further, Smith discovered that his car's front and rear windshields had been smashed.

The MOST logical order for the above sentences to appear in the report is:

  A. III, IV, V, I, II
  B. III, V, I, II, IV
  C. III, I, V, II, IV
  D. V, III, I, II, IV

Questions 20-21.

DIRECTIONS: Questions 20 and 21 are to be answered SOLELY on the basis of the following information.

Police Officers may be required to respond to vehicular accidents. The following procedure should be used, in the order given, when inspecting vehicles involved in a traffic accident:

    I. Inspect tires for wear. Check tires to determine if they have less than allowed tread.
    II. Inspect side view and rear view mirrors. Check mirrors to determine if any are missing or damaged to the point where vision is not adequate.
    III. At night only, turn on headlights to ensure that both are working properly.
    IV. Only if one of the above defects is found should entries be made in the Officer's Activity Log.
    V. Return to precinct to complete Vehicular Accident Inspection Report in duplicate.
    VI. Give original copy to Sergeant.
    VII. Duplicate copy should be given to Station House Supervisor.

20. On December 6 at 9:05 P.M., Police Officer William Hart begins inspecting vehicles which had just been involved in an accident. He examines the tires and mirrors of each car and finds no defects.
Which one of the following actions should Police Officer Hart take NEXT?

  A. Complete Vehicular Accident Inspection Report in duplicate.
  B. Turn on headlights to ensure that both are working properly.
  C. Make appropriate entries in Activity Log.
  D. Give duplicate of Vehicular Accident Inspection Report to Station House Supervisor.

21. Police Officer Robert Burns, while on foot patrol on December 17 at 1:35 P.M., observes a traffic accident on the corner of Madison Avenue and 25th Street. He checks the tires and then the mirrors of each car and notices that one car has a side view mirror cracked to the point where side view vision is not adequate. Which one of the following actions should Police Officer Robert Burns take NEXT?

   A. Give one copy of Vehicular Accident Inspection Report to Sergeant.
   B. Give one copy of Vehicular Accident Inspection Report to Station House Supervisor.
   C. Make appropriate entries in his Activity Log.
   D. Complete Vehicular Accident Inspection Report in duplicate.

22. A Police Officer is prohibited from either accepting awards, gifts, loans, or things of value to defray or reimburse any fine or penalty, or accepting a reward for the performance of police service except:
   I. Awards from the City Employees' Suggestion Board
   II. Official awards of Departmental recognition
   III. Awards to a member of an Officer's family for a brave or meritorious act, from a metropolitan newspaper

   Police Officer Gold captures a bank robber in the act of holding up a bank. to show appreciation, the bank manager gives the Officer a check for $100.00. Officer Gold accepts the check. Officer Gold's action in accepting the $100.00 is

   A. *proper* because the money was given for performance of a brave act
   B. *improper* because the capture of the bank robber was not a meritorious act deserving of a reward
   C. *proper* because the money was given as a substitute for Departmental recognition
   D. *improper* because a Police Officer is not allowed to accept a reward from a bank for performance of his duties

23. Rape - The crime of rape is committed when
   I. a male, being 21 years of age or more, engages in sexual intercourse with a female under 17 years of age; or
   II. a male, being 18 years of age or more, engages in sexual intercourse with a female under 14 years of age; or
   III. a male, being 16 years of age or more, engages in sexual intercourse with a female under 11 years of age.

   According to the definition given, which one of the following is the BEST example of rape?

   A. Ricky, a 17-year-old male, engages in sexual intercourse with a 12-year-old female.
   B. Gil, a 15-year-old male, engages in sexual intercourse with a 10-year-old female.
   C. Kim, a 20-year-old male, engages in sexual intercourse with a 15-year-old female.
   D. Tony, a 17-year-old male, engages in sexual intercourse with a 10-year-old female.

24. **Missing Person** - The City Police Department classifies as a missing person any person missing from a City residence who is:
    I. Under 18 years of age, or
    II. Likely to commit suicide, or
    III. Mentally or physically handicapped, or
    IV. Absent under suspicious circumstances, or
    V. A possible victim of drowning.

    According to this definition, which one of the following should NOT be classified as a missing person?

    A. Glen Greber, an 18-year-old male, is reported missing from his home in lower Manhattan. He had just returned home from vacation.
    B. Bobby Brody, a 22-year-old man, is reported missing from his Queens home. He was last seen swimming at a Coney Island beach in very choppy water.
    C. George Gilliam, a 17-year-old boy, is reported missing from his Brooklyn home by his parents. He had an argument with his mother and walked out of the house 4 days earlier.
    D. Sally Sanders, a 15-year-old girl who is mentally retarded, is reported missing after she wandered away from her Bronx home.

25. **Reckless Endangerment** - The crime of reckless endanger-ment is committed when a person performs an act, realizing that he is unjustifiably creating a great risk that another person may be seriously injured or killed, and disregards the risk.

    According to the definition given, which one of the following is the BEST example of reckless endangerment?

    A. Al Green, an exterminator, sprays Bob Boyd's house with a powerful chemical insecticide as Boyd requested. Nobody is supposed to be in the house since inhaling the chemical could cause death. Unknown to Green, one of Boyd's children is sleeping upstairs during the spraying.
    B. Joe Brown, a trapeze artist, performs for a circus. As part of his act. he dangles from a rope 250 feet in the air without a safety net beneath him. There are no spectators seated nearby.
    C. Bill White, a construction worker, is removing bricks from a footbridge 30 feet above a highway. Since he has nothing in which to cart the bricks away, he decides to drop them down onto the highway, where he sees many autos passing below.
    D. Jimmy Ocher, a teenager, receives a set of darts as a present. Because he has no dartboard, he throws his darts at the wall in his bedroom when no one else is home, realizing he could be causing serious damage to the property.

KEY (CORRECT ANSWERS)

1. C
2. B
3. B
4. D
5. B

6. C
7. A
8. A
9. A
10. D

11. C
12. D
13. B
14. C
15. A

16. D
17. D
18. D
19. B
20. B

21. C
22. D
23. D
24. A
25. C

TEST 2

DIRECTIONS: Each question or incomplete statement is followed by several suggested answers or completions. Select the one that BEST answers the question or completes the statement. *PRINT THE LETTER OF THE CORRECT ANSWER IN THE SPACE AT THE RIGHT.*

Questions 1-12.

DIRECTIONS: Questions 1 through 12 are to be answered SOLELY on the basis of the following passage.

Police Officers Bret Clemens and Sam Harte are dispatched to 83-67 Richardson Boulevard, Apt. 23F, at 8:53 P.M., on November 18 in response to a burglary reported by a Mr. Kegler. They arrive at the apartment at 8:58 P.M., ting the doorbell, and are greeted by Mr. and Mrs. Kegler. Mr. Kegler tells the Officers that he left for his foreman's job at the telephone company at 7:00 A.M. and that his wife left for her secretary's job 10 minutes later. After work, Mr. Kegler picked up his wife, and they returned to their apartment at 8:40 P.M., having eaten dinner out. When Mrs. Kegler entered the bedroom, she noticed her jewelry box on the floor. She told her husband, who then called the police. While the Keglers waited for the Police to arrive, they discovered that all of Mrs. Kegler's jewelry and Mr. Kegler's coin collection, as well as approximately $175.00 in cash, were missing.

While Officer Harte begins to fill out a crime report, Officer Clemens goes to other apartments on the same floor to interview neighbors who might have additional information about the burglary.

Mrs. Johnston, age 35, a housewife, who lives in Apt. 23C located directly opposite the elevator, tells Officer Clemens that she heard voices in the hallway outside her apartment door at 4:30 P.M. She thought that the voices were those of a neighbor's children who sometimes play in the hallway. She opened her door to chase them away but, instead, saw two strange males standing by the elevator. They wore green work clothes. She noticed that the taller man was white, about 28 years old, 5'11", 165 lbs., with brown hair and was carrying a square leather case. The other man was Hispanic, about 21 years old, 5'7", 150 lbs., with black hair and a scar on the left side of his face.

Officer Clemens then contacts other residents at Apartments 23D, 23E, and 23G. All of them tell the Officer that they did not see or hear anything unusual. Officer Clemens then returns to the Keglers' apartment to tell his partner what he learned. In the meantime, Officer Harte had been told by Mr. Kegler that his coin collection was in a square brown leather carrying case.

Officer Harte was also told that Mr. Kegler is 42 years old. His telephone number at work is 827-6138, and his work address is 273 Eastern Avenue. Mrs. Kegler's telephone number at work is 746-3279, and her work address is 131 South Moore Street. The Keglers' home telephone number is 653-3946. Mrs. Johnston's telephone number at home is 6353-2714.

Officers Harte and Clemens finish their investigation and complete the crime report.

277

1. Which one of the following is the APPROXIMATE time that the two strange men were seen in the hallway?

   A. 7:00 A.M.   B. 4:30 P.M.   C. 8:40 P.M.   D. 8:53 P.M.

2. Which one of the following apartments is directly opposite the elevator?

   A. 23B   B. 23C   C. 23F   D. 23G

3. Which one of the following is Mrs. Kegler's work address?

   A. 273 Eastern Avenue
   B. 653 Eastern Avenue
   C. 131 South Moore Street
   D. 746 South Moore Street

4. Which one of the following was NOT stolen during the burglary of the Keglers' apartment?

   A. $175.00
   B. Mrs. Kegler's jewelry
   C. Mr. Kegler's coin Collection
   D. Credit cards

5. When did the Keglers return to their apartment? _____ P.M.

   A. 8:40   B. 8:45   C. 8:53   D. 8:58

6. What is Mrs. Kegler's occupation?

   A. Housewife   B. Supervisor
   C. Secretary   D. Unknown

7. What is Mr. Kegler's telephone number at work?

   A. 653-2714   B. 746-3279   C. 653-3946   D. 827-6138

8. What is the approximate age of the TALLER of the two strangers seen standing inear the elevator?

   A. 21   B. 28   C. 42   D. 57

9. Which one of the following is the MOST accurate description of the male stranger who was seen near the elevator carrying the leather case?

   A. 5'7" and 165 lbs., Hispanic, brown hair
   B. 5'11" and 150 lbs., White, black hair
   C. 5'7" and 150 lbs., Hispanic, black hair
   D. 5'11" and 165 lbs., White, brown hair

10. Which one of the following identifying marks is part of the description of the shorter male stranger seen standing near the elevator?

    A. Scar   B. Tattoo   C. Birthmark   D. Mole

11. Mr. Kegler's employer is the _____ company.

    A. electric   B. jewelry   C. gas   D. telephone

12. At what time did Mrs. Kegler leave for work? _____ A.M.

    A. 7:00   B. 7:10   C. 7:30   D. 8:40

13. In certain circumstances, Police Officers should warn an offender instead of making an arrest or issuing a summons. Some of the circumstances would be:
    I. Lack of intent to commit a crime on the part of the offender for minor offenses such as traffic violations.
    II. Lack of knowledge by the offender that an offense is a crime
    III. Lack of perception by the offender that an action would result in a criminal offense.

    Police Officer Boggs stops a woman who has made a right turn through a red traffic light. The woman tells the Officer that she is in New York City on vacation from Los Angeles where right turns on a red traffic light are permitted. Police Officer Boggs should

    A. warn the woman, explaining to her that in New York City this is not permitted
    B. issue a summons to the woman because she intentionally went through a red traffic light
    C. warn the woman only if she further states that she never received a traffic summons
    D. issue a summons to the woman because she may have done this many times in the past

Questions 14-15.

DIRECTIONS: Questions 14 and 15 are to be answered SOLELY on the basis of the following information.

While making an arrest, a Police Officer may find that the prisoner has a substance which the Officer suspects to be narcotics. After the arrest has been made, the following procedures concerning the suspected narcotics should be used in the order given:
   I. The arresting Police Officer should notify a superior Officer that the suspected narcotics will be taken to the Police Laboratory for analysis.
   II. The Police Officer must record such notification in his Activity Log.
   III. Superior Officer must sign Activity Log under Police Officer's name.
   IV. At Police Laboratory, Police Officer will complete a Narcotics Analysis Request Form in duplicate.
       a. Original copy should be given to Police Laboratory personnel.
       b. Duplicate should be retained by arresting Police Officer and given to Superior Officer upon return to precinct.

14. Police Officer Ferris, while making an arrest, found a substance that he suspected to be narcotics. Ferris has already notified a Superior Officer that he intends to take the substance to the Police Laboratory for analysis. Which one of the following actions should Police Officer Ferris take NEXT?

    A. Complete Narcotics Analysis Request Form in duplicate.
    B. Record notification in his Activity Log.
    C. Ask Superior Officer to sign Activity Log.
    D. Have copy of Narcotics Analysis Request Form forwarded to Superior Officer.

15. Police Officer Johnson suspects that a substance he found in the pocket of a man he has arrested may be cocaine. Johnson has already completed all the appropriate actions through completion of Narcotics Analysis Request Form in duplicate at the Police Laboratory.
    Which one of the following actions should Police Officer Johnson take NEXT?

    A. Give duplicate copy of Narcotics Analysis Request Form to Superior Officer,
    B. Give original copy of Narcotics Analysis Request Form to Police Laboratory personnel.
    C. Notify a Superior Officer.
    D. Record notification in Activity Log.

16. In order to prevent injury to children, a Police Officer who finds a refrigerator, freezer, or similar device in a public area should do the following in the order given:
    I. If possible, determine who owns the refrigerator, freezer, or similar device.
    II. If the determination above has been made and the person is able, direct such person to remove the door.
        a. If the owner is known and refuses to remove the door, make arrest.
    III. Remove the door if owner is unknown or unavailable.
    IV. Summon Radio Emergency Patrol Car if the Officer is unable to make the device safe.

    Police Officer Santiago, while on patrol, observes a refrigerator with the door still on in front of 45 Bushwick Avenue. Police Officer Santiago questions residents of the building and learns that the refrigerator belongs to a Mrs. Gomez, who has gone away on vacation.
    Which one of the following actions should Police Officer Santiago take NEXT?

    A. Direct owner of refrigerator to remove the door.
    B. Attempt to remove the door.
    C. Wait until Mrs. Gomez returns from vacation.
    D. Ask owner to call Radio Emergency Patrol Car.

Questions 17-18.

DIRECTIONS: Questions 17 and 18 are to be answered SOLELY on the basis of the following information.

Police Officers may find it necessary to stop the driver of a vehicle in order to give the driver a summons, or to arrest or question the occupants. In such situations, Police Officers should follow the following procedures in the order given:
I. Inform Radio Dispatcher of location, reason for stopping the vehicle, and description of vehicle and its occupants.
II. Position the Police vehicle six to ten feet behind the stopped vehicle.
III. Each Police Officer is to watch for any suspicious actions by the stopped vehicle's driver or passengers before approaching the vehicle.
IV. Determine whether driver is to be summoned or arrested.
V. If driver is to be given a summons, one Police Officer is to write the summons while the other observes the driver and passengers for any suspicious action.
VI. If arrest is necessary, and additional Police Officers are required, the additional Officers should be summoned by informing the Radio Dispatcher.

17. Police Officers Fenster and Dickens stop the driver of a 1991 Dodge in order to issue a summons for a traffic violation. There are two passengers in the car.
    If all appropriate steps have been taken prior to the issuing of the summons, while Police Officer Dickens is writing a summons for the driver, Fenster should be

    A. checking to ensure that Police vehicle is six to ten feet behind stopped vehicle
    B. summoning Radio Dispatcher for additional Police Officers
    C. watching the driver and passengers for any suspicious action
    D. informing the Radio Dispatcher of their location, reason for stopping vehicle, description of vehicle, and description of occupants

17.____

18. Police Officers Benson and Jenson stopped a vehicle in order to question the driver and three occupants. The Officers have already completed all appropriate actions through determining that the driver and other occupants should be arrested and that additional Police Officers are needed.
    Which one of the following actions should the Officers take NEXT?

    A. Inform Radio Dispatcher that additional Police Officers are to be summoned.
    B. Inform Radio Dispatcher of location and reason for stopping vehicle.
    C. Write out summons and give it to driver.
    D. Position Police vehicle six to ten feet behind stopped vehicle.

18.____

19. *Murder - The crime of murder is committed when a person intends to cause the death of another person and he causes that person's death, or when he causes another person's death because he acted with complete disregard for human life even though he knew he was creating a great risk that another person might be killed.*
    According to the definition given, which one of the following is the BEST example of a murder?

    A. Fred Bandy is arguing with his wife. He slaps her in the face to make her stop screaming, accidentally knocking her down. As she falls, she hits her head on the floor, and later dies as a result of the head injury.
    B. An old man suffering from an incurable disease cannot stand the pain anymore and asks his nurse to give him a deadly dose of sleeping pills. The nurse, feeling great pity for him, gives him the pills, and he dies as a result.
    C. Phil Brady is driving his car down a crowded highway at 95 miles an hour. Because he is driving so recklessly, he loses control of the car and crashes, causing his own death.
    D. Ted Ryan, a zookeeper, is cleaning the gorilla's cage at the zoo. When he finishes cleaning the cage, he forgets to lock it. As a result, the gorilla escapes from the cage and kills one of the visitors to the zoo.

19.____

20. According to the regulations of the City Police Department, a notification will not be made by a Police Officer to the relatives of a fireman who is killed or injured while on duty without the permission of the fire officer in charge.
    An on-duty fireman is injured seriously in an auto accident, and the first Police Officer on the scene immediately calls the injured fireman's wife to inform her which hospital her husband was; being taken to. The action of the Officer in this case is

    A. *proper* because it conforms to the notification policy
    B. *improper* because the Officer does not have the authority to make the notification

20.____

C. *proper* because the next of kin should always be notified in hospital cases
D. *improper* because the Officer should make an in-person notification

21. Police Officers must sometimes record and process lost property that has been found by civilians. Upon coming into possession of found property, Police Officers should use the following procedures in the order given:
    I. Give a receipt to the person who found the property if the person is not a member of the Police Department.
    II. Turn in property at precinct.
    III. Enter facts in Activity Log.
    IV. Complete Property clerk's Invoice.
    V. Check accuracy of property Clerk's Invoice.
    VI. Make Command Log entry.

    Police Officer Dexter is given a pocketbook by a pedestrian who stated that she found it on the bus. After issuing a receipt to the pedestrian, Police Officer Dexter turns in the pocketbook at the precinct.
    Which one of the following actions should Police Officer Dexter take NEXT?

    A. Make Command Log entry.
    B. Enter facts in Activity Log.
    C. Complete Property Clerk's Invoice.
    D. Check accuracy of property Clerk's Invoice.

Questions 22-23.

DIRECTIONS: Questions 22 and 23 are to be answered SOLELY on the basis of the following information.

A Police Officer should complete a Universal Summons for a parking violation when the vehicle is unoccupied. When issuing a Universal Summons in this case, the Police Officer should use the following procedures in the order given:
   I. Check with Stolen Vehicle Desk if it appears that vehicle may be stolen or abandoned.
   II. Take out Universal Summons Book.
      a. Use ballpoint !pen to print information.
      b. Enter all available information required on Universal Summons.
      c. Enter only one offense on each Universal Summons.
   III. Place parking violation part of Universal Summons on windshield of vehicle.
      a. Fold Universal Summons if it is raining in order to be certain that form remains legible.
   IV. Detach and hold last copy of Universal Summons.
   V. Deliver remaining two parts of Universal Summons to precinct of occurrence at end of tour or as directed by Commanding Officer.
   VI. Place Universal Summons in appropriate basket on desk in precinct.

22. Police Officer Dyan, whale on foot patrol, observes an illegally parked vehicle which is unoccupied. The hood and trunk are open, and one tire is missing.
    Police Officer Dyan's FIRST action should be to

    A. question shop owners as to the whereabouts of owner of vehicle
    B. close hood and trunk and wait for owner of vehicle to arrive

C. take out Universal Summons Book
D. check with Stolen Vehicle Desk

23. On a rainy night, Police Officer Brown has already completed all the appropriate actions through writing out a Universal Summons for an illegally parked, unoccupied vehicle. The NEXT step that Police Officer Brown should take is to

   A. detach and hold last copy of Universal Summons
   B. place Universal Summons in appropriate basket on desk in precinct
   C. fold parking violation part of summons and place it on windshield of vehicle
   D. deliver remaining two parts of Universal Summons to precinct of occurrence

Questions 24-25.

DIRECTIONS: Questions 24 and 25 are to be answered SOLELY on the basis of the following information.

Police Officers must occasionally transport prisoners in a radio patrol car for booking. In such situations, Police Officers must follow these procedures in the order given:
   I. Obtain permission from the Patrol Supervisor or Station House Supervisor to transport the prisoner in a radio patrol car.
   II. Notify the Radio Dispatcher at the start of the trip. Search prisoner area of car for weapons, drugs, or other
   III. property when trip is over.
   IV. Record all details of trip in Activity Log.
   V. Inform Police Telephone Switchboard Operator of the details of the trip.

24. Police Officer Westcott must transport a prisoner he has just arrested for robbing a liquor store. Westcott has already obtained permission from the Station House Supervisor to transport the prisoner in the radio patrol car. Which one of the following actions should Police Officer Westcott take NEXT?

   A. Notify Radio Dispatcher.
   B. Search prisoner area of car for weapons, drugs, or other property.
   C. Record all details of trip in Activity Log.
   D. Give Patrol Supervisor all details of trip.

25. Police Officers Hill and Blue are transporting a prisoner in their radio patrol car for booking. They have already completed all appropriate actions through notifying the Radio Dispatcher at the start of the trip. After arriving at their destination, which one of the following actions should the Police Officers take NEXT?

   A. Record all details of trip in Activity Log.
   B. Search prisoner area of car for weapons, drugs, or other property.
   C. Inform Police Telephone Switchboard Operator of the details of the trip.
   D. Notify Radio Dispatcher.

KEY (CORRECT ANSWERS)

1.	B	11.	D
2.	B	12.	B
3.	C	13.	A
4.	D	14.	B
5.	A	15.	B
6.	C	16.	B
7.	D	17.	C
8.	B	18.	A
9.	D	19.	B
10.	A	20.	B

21. B
22. D
23. C
24. A
25. B

TEST 3

DIRECTIONS: Each question of incomplete statement is followed by several suggested answers or completions. Select the one that BEST answers the question or completes the statement. *PRINT THE LETTER OF THE CORRECT ANSWER IN THE SPACE AT THE RIGHT.*

1. Police Officers assigned to transport prisoners to court should follow these procedures in the order given:
    I. Make certain that the prisoners placed in chains are the same as those listed on the Prisoner List Form and take a head count.
    II. Ride in transporting vehicle so that the prisoners can be constantly watched.
    III. Make certain that prisoners are taken to holding area at destination.
    IV. Return to precinct for assignment or proceed to original destination, as directed by the Station House Supervisor.

    Police Officers Gray and Smith have been assigned by the Station House Supervisor to take prisoners to court. While Police Officer Gray is taking the head count, Police Officer Smith should

    A. recount the prisoners
    B. make certain that the prisoners placed in chains are the same as those listed on the Prisoner List Form
    C. make certain that prisoners are taken to holding area at destination
    D. constantly watch the prisoners while riding in the vehicle transporting prisoners

2. Sergeant Nancy Winston is reviewing a Gun Control Report which will contain the following five sentences:
    I. The man fell to the floor when hit in the chest with three bullets from the .22 caliber gun.
    II. Merriam's .22 caliber gun was seized, and he was given a summons for not having a pistol permit.
    III. Christopher Merrian, the owner of A-Z Grocery, shot a man who attemptec. to rob him.
    IV. Police Officer Frarks responded and asked Merriam for his pistol permit, which he could not produce.
    V. Merriam phoned the Police to report he had just shot a man who had attempted to rob him.

    The MOST logical order for the above sentences to appear in the report is:

    A. III, I, V, IV, II
    B. I, III, V, IV, II
    C. III, I, V, II, IV
    D. I, III, II, V, IV

3. Detective John Manville is completing a report for his superior regarding the murder of an unknown male who was shot in Central Park. The report will contain the following five sentences:
    I. Police Officers Langston and Cavers responded to the scene.
    II. I received the assignment to investigate the murder in Central Park from Detective Sergeant Rogers.
    III. Langston notified the Detective Bureau after questioning Jason.
    IV. An unknown male, apparently murdered, was discovered in Central Park by Howard Jason, a park employee, who immediately called the Police.
    V. Langston and Cavers questioned Jason.

    The MOST logical order for the above sentences to appear in the report is:

    A. I, IV, V, III, II
    B. IV, I, V, II, III
    C. IV, I, V, III, II
    D. IV, V, I, III, II

4. A Police Officer is completing a report concerning the arrest of a juvenile. The report will contain the following five sentences:
   I. Sanders then telephoned Jay's parents from the precinct to inform them of their son's arrest.
   II. The store owner resisted, and Jay then shot him and ran from the store.
   III. Jay was transported directly to the precinct by Officer Sanders.
   IV. James Jay, a juvenile, walked into a candy store and announced a hold-up.
   V. Police Officer Sanders, while on patrol, arrested Jay a block from the candy store.

   The MOST logical order for the above sentences to appear in the report is:

   A. IV, V, II, I, III
   B. IV, II, V, III, I
   C. II, IV, V, III, I
   D. V, IV, II, I, III

5. Police Officer Olsen prepared a crime report for a robbery which contained the following five sentences:
   I. Mr. Gordon was approached by this individual who then produced a gun and demanded the money from the cash register.
   II. The man then fled from the scene on foot, southbound on 5th Avenue.
   III. Mr. Gordon was working at the deli counter when a white male, 5'6", 150-160 lbs., wearing a green jacket and blue parts, entered the store.
   IV. Mr. Gordon complied with the man's demands and handed him the daily receipts.
   V. Further investigation has determined there are no other witnesses to this robbery.

   The MOST logical order for the above sentences to appear in the report is:

   A. I, III, IV, V, II
   B. I, IV, II, III, V
   C. III, IV, I, V, II
   D. III, I, IV, II, V

6. Police Officer Bryant responded to 285 E. 31st Street to take a crime report of a burglary of Mr. Bond's home. The report will contain a brief description of the incident, consisting of the following five sentences:

   I. When Mr. Bond attempted to stop the burglar by grabbing him, he was pushed to the floor.
   II. The burglar had apparently gained access to the home by forcing open the 2nd floor bedroom window facing the fire escape.
   III. Mr. Bond sustained a head injury in the scuffle, and the burglar exited the home through the front door.
   IV. Finding nothing in the dresser, the burglar proceeded downstairs to the first floor, where he was confronted by Mr. Bond who was reading in the dining room.
   V. Once inside, he searched the drawers of the bedroom dresser.

   The MOST logical order for the above sentences to appear in the report is:

   A. V, IV, I, II, III
   B. II, V, IV, I, III
   C. II, IV, V, III, I
   D. III, II, I, V, IV

7. Police Officer Derringer responded to a call of a rape-homicide case in his patrol area and was ordered to prepare an incident report, which will contain the following five sentences:

   I. He pushed Miss Scott to the ground and forcibly raped her.
   II. Mary Scott was approached from behind by a white male, 5"7", 150-160 lbs., wearing dark pants and a white jacket.
   III. As Robinson approached the male, he ordered him to stop.
   IV. Screaming for help, Miss Scott alerted one John Robinson, a local grocer, who chased her assailant as he fled the scene.
   V. The male turned and fired two shots at Robinson, who fell to the ground mortally wounded.

   The MOST logical order for the above sentences to appear in the report is:

   A. IV, III, I, II, V
   B. II, IV, III, V, I
   C. II, IV, I, V, III
   D. II, I, IV, III, V

Questions 8-18.

DIRECTIONS: Questions 8 through 18 are to be answered SOLELY on the basis of the following passage.

Police Officers Tom Riggins and John Landry were patrolling in their police car in the 65th Precinct at 10:15 A.M. on December 3. They came upon the scene of a traffic accident at Avenue C and 30th Street, which had occurred five minutes earlier. Officer Landry called the Police Radio Dispatcher at 10:20 A.M. and reported that he and his partner in Police Car #65B were handling a traffic accident involving a van and an auto at that location. Officer Landry further reported to the Dispatcher that there were no personal injuries to the van driver or to the driver of the auto or her two children. However, the two Vehicles were damaged.

The Officers checked each driver's license, vehicle registration certificate, and vehicle insurance identification card. The van driver was John Hudson, age 36, residing at 1102 South Elliot Boulevard, Cranford, N.J. He was driving a white 1992 GMC van, N.Y. license plate #9723GH, owned by his employer, Zenith Trucking Corp. of 257 West 63rd Street, N.Y., N.Y. Mr. Hudson's N.J. driver's license identification number is H138569, and the expiration date is December 31, 2010.

The driver of the auto was Mrs. Anne Cloris, age 38, residing at 49 Christopher Avenue, Queens, N.Y. She had two children with her, Charles Cloris, Jr., ago 10, and Anita Cloris, age 8. Mrs. Cloris' auto was a red 1994 Chevrolet 4-door station wagon, N.Y. license plate #319GAZ. Mrs.Cloris' N.Y. driver's license identification number is C12192-16619, and the expiration date is May 31, 2010.

The Officers examined both vehicles for damage from the accident and found that the van had a dented rear panel on its left side and that the auto had a dented right front fender.

The Officers completed a vehicle accident report at 10:45 A.M. The report number was V4359.

8. Which one of the following is the CORRECT description of the vehicles involved in the traffic accident?

   A. One van and one 4-door station wagon
   B. One 4-door station wagon and one trailer truck
   C. One 2-door station wagon and one van
   D. One van and one 4-door sedan

9. Which one of the following is the CORRECT license plate number and description of Mrs. Cloris' vehicle?
   N.Y. Plate #

   A. 319GAZ, white 1992 Chevrolet van
   B. 319GZA, red 1994 GMC station wagon
   C. 319GAZ, red 1994 Chevrolet station wagon
   D. 318GAZ, white 1992 Chevrolet van

10. At what time did the traffic accident occur?
    _____ A.M.

    A. Before 10:00   B. 10:10
    C. 10:15   D. 10:20

11. How many personal injuries resulted from the traffic accident?

    A. 0   B. 1   C. 2   D. 3

12. Which one of the following is the age of Charles Cloris, Jr.?

    A. 8   B. 10   C. 12   D. Unknown

13. Which one of the following is Mrs. Cloris' N.Y. driver's license identification number?

    A. H315869   B. H138569
    C. C12291-16619   D. C12192-16619

14. Which one of the following is the license plate number of Mr. Hudson's vehicle?

    A. 9724GH   B. 9723GH   C. 9724HG   D. 9723HG

15. Which one of the following is the expiration date of Mr. Hudson's driver's license?

    A. December 30, 2010   B. December 31, 2010
    C. May 30, 2010   D. May 31, 2010

16. Which one of the following is the address of Mr. Hudson's residence?

    A. 1201 South Elliot Boulevard, Cranford, N.J.
    B. 1102 South Elliot Avenue, Cranford, N.Y.
    C. 1102 South Elliot Boulevard, Cranford, N.J.
    D. 1102 North Elliot Boulevard, Cranford, N.Y.

17. Which one of the following is the address of Mr. Hudson's employer? 17.____

   A. 257 West 63rd Street, N.Y., N.Y.
   B. 49 Christopher Avenue, Queens, N.Y.
   C. 263 West 57th Street, N.Y., N.Y.
   D. 94 Christopher Street, Queens, N.Y.

18. Which one of the following is the CORRECT description of the damage to Mr. Hudson's 18.____
    vehicle from the accident?
    A dented

   A. right front fender   B. left rear panel
   C. left rear fender   D. right front panel

Questions 19-20.

DIRECTIONS: Questions 19 and 20 are to be answered SOLELY on the basis of the guidelines below concerning the use of firearms and the following incident.

Police Officers must follow these guidelines concerning the use of firearms:
   I. Use all reasonable means before using a firearm when making an arrest, preventing a felony, or defending yourself or another person.
   II. Do not fire warning shots.
   III. Do not discharge a firearm to call for help unless your safety is endangered.
   IV. Do not discharge a firearm at a moving vehicle unless occupants are using deadly physical force, by means other than the vehicle.
   V. Do not discharge a firearm at an animal unless there is no other way to control the animal.

Police Officer Rodgers is patrolling near an alley-way when he observes several youths drag-racing down the street. One vehicle goes out of control and is headed toward him at a very fast speed. Police Officer Rodgers fires one shot at the tires of the vehicle and it slows to a halt. The Officer approaches the vehicle to issue the driver a traffic violation summons. A large dog is also in the vehicle, apparently injured and unable to escape. The dog sees the Officer and attempts to bite the Officer. He fires one shot at the dog to bring it under control and notifies the A.S.P.C.A. It is later determined that the dog has rabies.

19. Police Officer Rodgers' action in shooting at the tires was 19.____

   A. *proper* because the fast speed of the vehicle justified quick and thorough action
   B. *improper* because the occupants did not use deadly force, other than the vehicle
   C. *proper* because drag-racing is a crime which requires Police action
   D. *improper* because the Officer should have fired at the driver to insure direct results

20. Police Officer Rodgers action in shooting the dog was 20.____

   A. *proper* because the animal was a danger to the Officer's safety
   B. *improper* because the dog was contained in the vehicle and the Officer was in no immediate danger
   C. *proper* because the dog had rabies and could have contaminated others
   D. *improper* because a dog with rabies must be kept under Police observation

KEY (CORRECT ANSWERS)

1.	B	11.	A
2.	A	12.	B
3.	C	13.	D
4.	B	14.	B
5.	D	15.	B
6.	B	16.	C
7.	D	17.	A
8.	A	18.	B
9.	C	19.	B
10.	B	20.	B

EXAMINATION SECTION
TEST 1

DIRECTIONS: Each question ojr incomplete statement is followed by several suggested answers or completions. Select the one that BEST answers the question or completes the statement. *PRINT THE LETTER OF THE CORRECT ANSWER IN THE SPACE AT THE RIGHT.*

Questions 1-6.

DIRECTIONS: Questions 1 through 6 are to be answered SOLELY on the basis of the following map. The flow of traffic is indicated by the arrows. You must follow the flow of traffic.

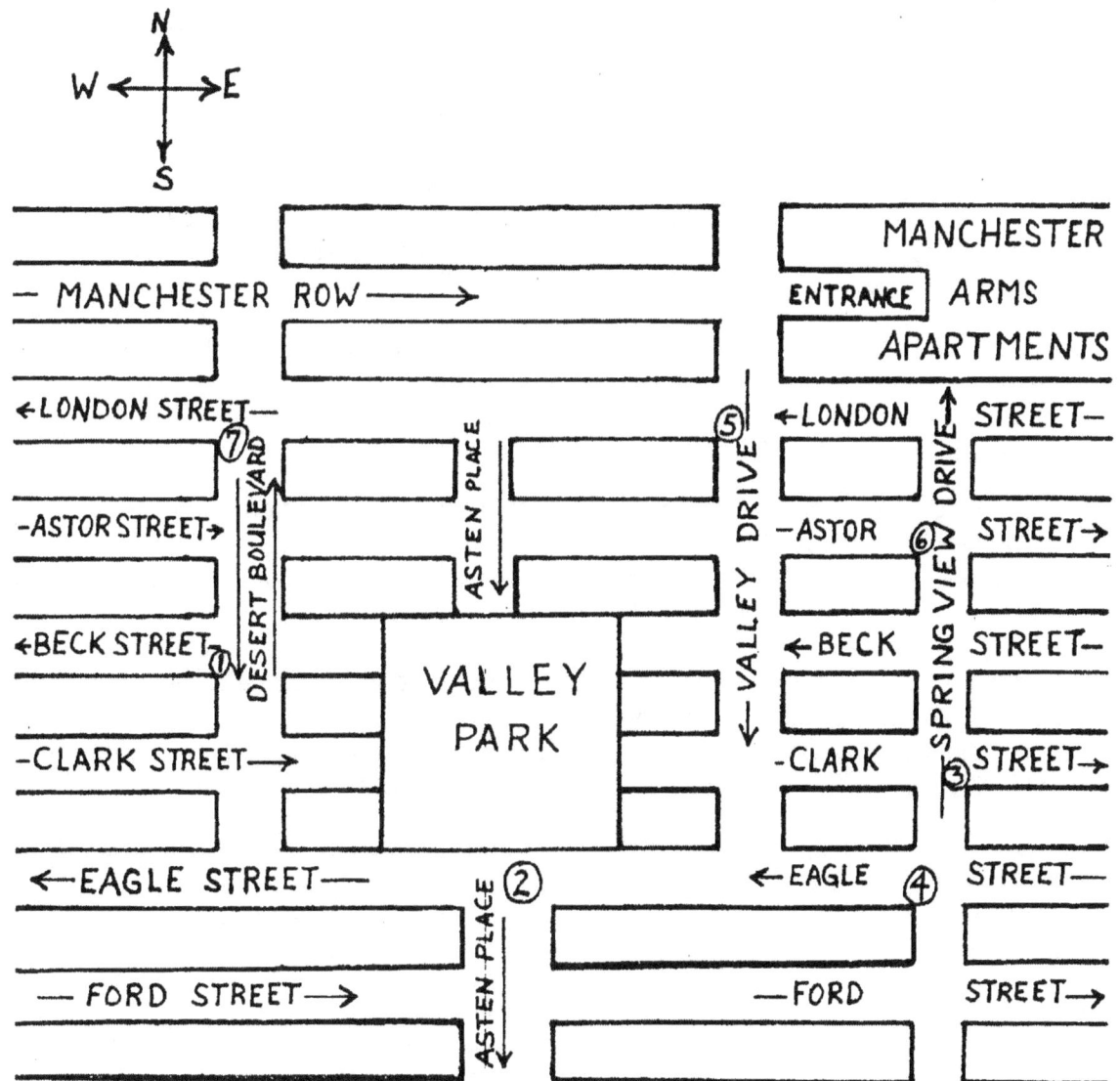

1. If you are located at Point (7) and travel south for one block, then turn east and travel two blocks, then turn south and travel two blocks, then turn east and travel one block, you will be CLOSEST to Point

    A. 2 B. 3 C. 4 D. 6

2. If you are located at Point (3) and travel north for one block, and then turn west and travel one block, and then turn south and travel two blocks, and then turn west and travel one block, you will be CLOSEST to Point

    A. 1 B. 2 C. 4 D. 6

3. You are located at Astor Street and Spring View Drive. You receive a call of a crime in progress at the intersection of Beck Street and Desert Boulevard.
   Which one of the following is the MOST direct route for you to take in your patrol car, making sure to obey all traffic regulations? Travel

    A. one block north on Spring View Drive, then three blocks west on London Street, then two blocks south on Desert Boulevard
    B. three blocks west on Astor Street, then one block south on Desert Boulevard
    C. one block south on Spring View Drive, then three blocks west on Beck Street
    D. three blocks south on Spring View Drive, then three blocks west on Eagle Street, then two blocks north on Desert Boulevard

4. You are located on Clark Street and Desert Boulevard and must respond to a disturbance at Clark Street and Spring View Drive.
   Which one of the following is the MOST direct route for you to take in your patrol car, making sure to obey all traffic regulations? Travel

    A. two blocks north on Desert Boulevard, then three blocks east on Astor Street, then two blocks south on Spring View Drive
    B. one block south on Desert Boulevard, then three blocks east on Eagle Street, then one block north on Spring View Drive
    C. two blocks north on Desert Boulevard, then two blocks east on Astor Street, then three blocks south on Valley Drive, then one block east on Eagle Street, then one block north on Spring View Drive
    D. two blocks north On Desert Boulevard, then two blocks east on Astor Street, then two blocks south on Valley Drive, then one block east on Clark Street

5. You are located at Valley Drive and Beck Street and receive a call to respond to the corner of Asten Place and Astor Street.
   Which one of the following is the MOST direct route for you to take in your patrol car, making sure to obey all traffic regulations? Travel _____ on Astor Street.

    A. one block north on Valley Drive, then one block west
    B. two blocks south on Valley Drive, then one block east on Eagle Street, then three blocks north on Spring View Drive, then two blocks west
    C. two blocks south on Valley Drive, then two blocks west on Eagle Street, then three blocks north on Desert Boulevard, then one block east
    D. one block south on Valley Drive, then one block east on Clark Street, then two blocks north on Spring View Drive, then two blocks west

6. You are in your patrol car on Manchester Row at the entrance to the Manchester Arms Apartments. You receive a call to respond to the intersection of Eagle Street and Spring View Drive.
   Which one of the following is the MOST direct route for you to take in your patrol car, making sure to obey all traffic regulations? Travel

   A. five blocks south on Valley Drive, then one block east on Eagle Street
   B. two blocks south on Valley Drive, then one block east on Astor Street, then three blocks south on Spring View Drive
   C. five blocks south on Valley Drive, then one block west on Eagle Street, then one block south on Asten Place, then one block east on Ford Street, then one block north on Spring View Drive
   D. one block south on Valley Drive, then two blocks west on London Street, then four blocks south on Desert Boulevard, then three blocks east on Eagle Street

Questions 7-8.

DIRECTIONS: Questions 7 and 8 are to be answered SOLELY on the basis of the following information.

A person who is driving his own personal auto in New York City must have in his possession a valid driver's license, the auto's valid registration certificate, and, if a New York State resident, a valid insurance identification card. If such driver is stopped by a Police Officer and does not have with him any of these documents, the Police Officer should issue the driver a summons for each violation of these requirements.

7. Alice Broderick drives her station wagon into New York City from her home in Rutherford, N.J. She is stopped by a New York City Police Officer for making an illegal turn. She gives the Officer her valid driver's license but has left the auto registration certificate at home. She does not have an insurance identification card.
   In addition to a summons for the illegal turn, the Police Officer should issue to Ms. Broderick a summons for driving without a valid

   A. auto registration certificate *only*
   B. insurance identification card *only*
   C. auto registration certificate and a summons for driving without a valid insurance identification card
   D. driver's license and a summons for driving without a valid auto registration certificate

8. Peter Lanceworth, a New York State resident, is driving his own 1991 BMW sedan through New York City when he is pulled over by Police officer Hardy for going through a stop sign. Mr. Lanceworth gives Officer Hardy his expired driver's license, his auto's valid registration certificate, and the auto's insurance identification card, which is no longer in effect.
   In addition to a summons for the stop sign violation, Officer Hardy should issue to Mr. Lanceworth a summons for driving without a Valid

   A. driver's license *only*
   B. insurance identification card *only*
   C. driver's license and a summons for driving without a valid insurance identification card
   D. driver's license and a summons for driving without a valid auto registration certificate

Questions 9-11.

DIRECTIONS: Questions 9 through 11 are to be answered SOLELY on the basis of the guidelines below concerning treatment of foreign diplomats and the following incident.

Foreign diplomats cannot be arrested or personally served with a summons. When a Police Officer arrives at the scene of an incident involving a diplomat, he should take necessary action to protect life and property, and obtain the name and title of the diplomat and his government. If the person claiming to be a diplomat does not have an identification card, the Officer should telephone the Operations Unit. A diplomat should not be detained after his identity is verified. A Police Officer should place a parking summons on a vehicle with *DPL* license plates which is unoccupied, illegally parked, and creating a safety hazard. These violations create a safety hazard: double-parking, fire hydrant, and bus stop. The issuing of such a parking summons is NOT considered a diplomatic incident.

Police Officer Sharkey arrives at the scene of a shooting. The victim, Ray Andrews, tells Sharkey that he was about to drive his car out of a parking space when another car pulled up and double-parked right next to him, blocking his way. The driver and the passenger of the other car both got out and ran into a restaurant. Andrews ran after them and asked the driver to move his car, but he refused. A fight started, and the passenger took out a small gun and shot at Andrews, grazing his shoulder. Andrews points out both men, who are standing on the sidewalk, to Sharkey. Their car, still double-parked next to Andrews' car, has *DPL* license plates. Sharkey asks the two men for identification. The driver produces a proper I.D., showing he is a foreign diplomat named Rene Pompe. The passenger claims he is also a foreign diplomat named Pierre Tragere, but cannot produce an appropriate I.D. Sharkey, after making sure that Andrews receives proper medical aid, hands Pompe a parking summons for double-parking and arrests Tragere for shooting Andrews. Sharkey asks Pompe to accompany him to the station house to answer some questions about the incident, but Pompe refuses to go willingly and Sharkey lets him leave.

9. Police Officer Sharkey's action in handing a parking summons to Pompe is

   A. *appropriate* because Pompe, the driver, created a safety hazard by double-parking
   B. *inappropriate* because Pompe, as a foreign diplomat, cannot be handed a summons of any kind
   C. *appropriate* because Pompe's car was left unoccupied and double-parked for several minutes
   D. *inappropriate* because issuing a parking summons to a car with *DPL* license plates creates a diplomatic incident

10. Police Officer Sharkey's action in arresting Tragere is

    A. *appropriate* because Andrews identified Tragere as the man who shot him
    B. *inappropriate* because Tragere, as a foreign diplomat, cannot be arrested
    C. *appropriate* because Tragere could not prove his identity as a foreign diplomat
    D. *inappropriate* because Sharkey should have first checked with the Operations Unit

11. Police Officer Sharkey's action in allowing Pompe to leave is   11.____
    A. *appropriate* because Pompe did not shoot Andrews so Sharkey had no reason to detain him
    B. *inappropriate* because Pompe was a witness to the shooting and should have been questioned further
    C. *appropriate* because once Pompe produced his identification card showing he is a foreign diplomat, he could no longer be detained
    D. *inappropriate* because Sharkey should have received permission from the Operations Unit before allowing Pompe to leave the scene of a crime

12. Police Officer Weiker is completing a Complaint Report which will contain the following five sentences: 12.____
    I. Mr. Texlor was informed that the owner of the van would receive a parking ticket and that the van would be towed away.
    II. The Police tow truck arrived approximately one half hour after Mr. Texlor complained.
    III. While on foot patrol on West End Avenue, I saw the owner of Rand's Restaurant arrive to open his business.
    IV. Mr. Texlor, the owner, called to me and complained that he could not receive deliveries because a van was blocking his driveway.
    V. The van's owner later reported to the precinct that his van had been stolen, and he was then informed that it had been towed.
    The MOST logical order for the above sentences to appear in the report is:
    A. III, V, I, II, IV   B. III, IV, I, II, V
    C. IV, III, I, II, V   D. IV, III, II, I, V

13. Police Officer Ames is completing an entry in his Activity Log. The entry contains the following five sentences: 13.____
    I. Mr. Sands gave me a complete description of the robber.
    II. Alvin Sands, owner of the Star Delicatessen, called the precinct to report he had just been robbed.
    III. I then notified all Police patrol vehicles to look for a white male in his early twenties wearing brown pants and shirt, a black leather jacket, and black and white sneakers.
    IV. I arrived on the scene after being notified by the precinct that a robbery had just occurred at the Star Delicatessen.
    V. Twenty minutes later, a man fitting the description was arrested by a Police Officer on patrol six blocks from the delicatessen.
    The MOST logical order for the above sentences to appear in the Activity Log is:
    A. II, I, IV, III, V   B. II, IV, III, I, V
    C. II, IV, I, III, V   D. II, IV, I, V, III

Questions 14-15.

DIRECTIONS: Questions 14 and 15 are to be answered SOLELY on the basis of the guidelines below concerning *Miranda Warnings* and the following incident.

When questioning persons concerning the facts of a criminal incident, it is not ordinarily necessary for a Police Officer to give *Miranda Warnings*. Such warnings are required only when the investigation has focused on the individual being questioned or the Officer intends to arrest the individual, regardless of the person's responses during the general questioning. When the investigation is no longer a general inquiry into an unsolved crime, but begins to focus on a particular suspect, or when the suspect has in fact been taken into custody, the suspect must be given what are generally referred to as *Miranda Warnings*. These include a notice that any incriminating statements by the suspect may be used against him and that he is entitled to legal counsel before and during any questioning by the Police.

Police Officer Harrington arrives at the scene of a shooting. The victim is lying in the street, but is not badly hurt. In an effort to learn the facts of the shooting, the Officer questions possible witnesses. As he prepares to question one particular female, she quickly walks away. The Officer pursues the woman and proceeds to ask her general questions about the incident. He does not give her *Miranda Warnings* at this time. The woman answers all of the questions asked of her. Officer Harrington, satisfied with her responses, returns to the victim, who observes the departing woman and identifies her as the person who shot him. Officer Harrington, who now intends to arrest the female, gives her the *Miranda Warnings* before briefly questioning her again.

14. The Officer's action in not giving the *Miranda Warnings* at the initial questioning of the woman was

    A. *appropriate* because the woman answered the Officer's questions, and, therefore, *Miranda Warnings* were not required
    B. *inappropriate* because the woman's action was suspicious and she should have been given *Miranda Warnings*
    C. *appropriate* since he did not intend to arrest her then
    D. *inappropriate* because *Miranda Warnings* should always be given as a safety measure

15. The Officer's action in giving the *Miranda Warnings* at the second questioning of the woman was

    A. *appropriate* because the Officer's intention to arrest the woman required *Miranda Warnings*
    B. *inappropriate* because the victim could probably not make an accurate identification
    C. *appropriate* because the woman's suspicious behavior indicated her guilt, making *Miranda Warnings* necessary
    D. *inappropriate* because a cooperative suspect should not be intimidated with *Miranda Warnings*

16. Police Officer Benson is completing a Complaint Report concerning a stolen taxicab, which will include the following five sentences:
    I. Police Officer Benson noticed that a cab was parked next to a fire hydrant.
    II. Dawson *borrowed* the cab for transportation purposes since he was in a hurry.
    III. Ed Dawson got into his car and tried to start it, but the battery was dead.
    IV. When he reached his destination, he parked the cab by a fire hydrant and placed the keys under the seat.
    VI. He looked around and saw an empty cab with the engine running.

The MOST logical order for the above sentences to appear in the report is:

A. I, III, II, IV, V
B. III, I, II, V, IV
C. III, V, II, IV, I
D. V, II, IV, III, I

17. Police Officer Hatfield is reviewing his Activity Log entry prior to completing a report. The entry contains the following five sentences:

    I. When I arrived at Zand's Jewelry Store, I noticed that the door was slightly open.
    II. I told the burglar I was a Police Officer and that he should stand still or he would be shot.
    III. As I entered the store, I saw a man wearing a ski mask attempting to open the safe in the back of the store.
    IV. On December 16, 1990, at 1:38 A.M., I was informed that a burglary was in progress at Zand's Jewelry Store on East 59th street.
    V. The burglar quickly pulled a knife from his pocket when he saw me.

The MOST logical order for the above sentences to appear in the report is:

A. IV, I, III, V, II
B. I, IV, III, V, II
C. IV, III, II, V, I
D. I, III, IV, V, II

Questions 18-20.

DIRECTIONS: Questions 18 through 20 are to be answered SOLELY on the basis of the following passage.

At 10:30 P.M., Officers Gaines and Palmer respond to a call of shots fired on the fifth floor of a large apartment building. When they arrive on the floor, they are taken to a body of a dead man lying near the stairwell. The man appears to have been shot twice in the head. Officer Gaines remains with the body while Officer Palmer begins interviewing the people standing around the body. The dead man is identified as Charles Morton of Apartment 5C. The interviews reveal the following information:

Mrs. C: About 9:30 P.M., I heard the sounds of an argument coming from next door, Apartment 5C. I recognized one voice as belonging to Mr. Morton. I didn't recognize the other voices, but there were clearly two other men and a woman. I couldn't hear what they were arguing about. At 10:15 P.M., I heard what sounded like two shots coming from that apartment. Then I heard the door slam and people running down the hall. My apartment faces the street so I looked out and about a minute or so later saw two people running out of the building and into a yellow Chevrolet parked in front of this building. Their license plate had all letters on it. I couldn't read the plate numbers. Then I heard someone moaning out in the hall. I opened the door and saw Mr. Morton lying near the steps. Blood was coming from his head. When I got to him, he was dead. Mr. H was standing near him. I then went to my apartment and called the Police.

Mr. G: I went to the seven o'clock show at the movies tonight and came back home after the movie. While I was waiting for the elevator, which was on the fifth floor, I noticed that the hall clock said 10:15 P.M. When the elevator arrived, a young man and woman ran out. They seemed to be very excited and nervous. I was curious so I followed them a little and saw them get into a yellow Chevrolet parked in front of this building. I couldn't see the plate that clearly, but it was one of those new plates with all letters on it. They drove up the block and made a right turn at the corner. Then I saw Mr. p arrive from the left with a girl. I went upstairs and saw Mr. Morton's body lying near the fifth floor stairwell. Mr. H was standing next to it.

Mr. P: At 10:30 P.M., my girlfriend and I arrived at this building. I noticed a woman, whom I didn't recognize, quickly getting into a red Chevrolet parked in front of this building. The plate had all letters. The car took off in a real hurry. When we got off at the fifth floor, we saw Mr. Morton lying on the floor with blood pouring from his head. Mr. H and Mrs. S were standing next to the body.

Mr. H: Tonight at 10:00 P.M., after I turned off the TV, I heard noise coming from Mr. Morton's apartment next door. He was arguing with two men, and I heard the word money come up a few times. Anyway, at a quarter after ten, I heard the sound of two gunshots coming from Mr. Morton's apartment. Then the door slammed, and I heard people running down the hall. I heard sounds coming from Mr. Morton's apartment and then from the hall. I opened the door a crack and saw Mr. Morton lying on the floor and pushing himself along. I went out to help him, but I was too late. He said something I couldn't make out, closed his eyes, and died. Mrs. C then came down the hall to the body. She said she was going to call the Police.

Mrs. S: I live near the elevator and the stairwell. I heard people running down the hall to the elevator and peeked out of my keyhole. I saw two young men and a woman waiting for the elevator. They seemed nervous. One of the men then took the stairs. About two minutes after the elevator came, I heard moans coming from the hall. I opened my door a crack and saw poor Mr. Morton lying on the carpet dragging himself down the hall. I went to get my keys, locked the door, and went out to see if he needed help. Mr. H was already with him. I just happened to look at my watch and noticed that it was 10:20 P.M.

Mrs. W: About 9:45 P.M., I left my apartment to visit Mrs. L on the second floor and heard a woman and another man arguing with Mr. Morton. Anyway, at 10:15 P.M. when I came back from visiting Mrs. L, I heard three shots ring out. I ran back to my apartment and called the Police.

18. Which one of the above people's statements has no bearing on the murder?

    A. Mr. G B. Mrs. S C. Mr. P D. Mrs. W

19. Based on the above information, the Officer should report that there is a conflict in which one of the following elements?
    The

    A. identity of the first person to reach the body
    B. location of the murder
    C. location of the get-away car
    D. number of shots fired

20. Based on the above information, the Officer should report that there is a conflict in which one of the following elements?
    The

    A. time the shots were fired
    B. number of people heard arguing with Mr. Morton
    C. description of the license plate on the get-away car
    D. location of the body

21. Police Officer Lorenz is completing a report of a murder. The report will contain the following five statements made by a witness:
    I. I was awakened by the sound of a gunshot coming from the apartment next door, and I decided to check.
    II. I entered the apartment and looked into the kitchen and the bathroom.
    III. I found Mr. Hubbard's body slumped in the bathtub.
    IV. The door to the apartment was open, but I didn't see anyone.
    V. He had been shot in the head.

    The MOST logical order for the above sentences to appear in the report is:

    A. I, III, II, IV, V
    B. I, IV, II, III, V
    C. IV, II, I, III, V
    D. III, I, II, IV, V

22. Police Officer Baldwin is preparing an accident report which will include the following five sentences:
    I. The old man lay on the ground for a few minutes, but was not physically hurt.
    II. Charlie Watson, a construction worker, was repairing some brick work at the top of a building at 54th Street and Madison Avenue.
    III. Steven Green, his partner, warned him that this could be dangerous, but Watson ignored him.
    IV. A few minutes later, one of the bricks thrown by Watson smashed to the ground in front of an old man, who fainted out of fright.
    V. Mr. Watson began throwing some of the bricks over the side of the building.

    The MOST logical order for the above sentences to appear in the report is:

    A. II, V, III, IV, I
    B. I, IV, II, V, III
    C. III, II, IV, V, I
    D. II, III, I, IV, V

23. Police Officer Porter is completing an incident report concerning her rescue of a woman being held hostage by a former boyfriend. Her report will contain the following five sentences:
    I. I saw a man holding a .25 caliber gun to a woman's head, but he did not see me.
    II. I then broke a window and gained access to the house.
    III. As I approached the house on foot, a gunshot rang out and I heard a woman scream.
    IV. A decoy van brought me as close as possible to the house where the woman was being held hostage.
    V. I ordered the man to drop his gun, and he released the woman and was taken into custody.

    The MOST logical order for the above sentences to appear in the report is:

    A. I, III, II, IV, V
    B. IV, III, II, I, V
    C. III, II, I, IV, V
    D. V, I, II, III, IV

24. Police Officer Byrnes is preparing a crime report concerning a robbery. The report will consist of the following five sentences:
    I. Mr. White, following the man's instructions, opened the car's hood, at which time the man got out of the auto, drew a revolver, and ordered White to give him all the money in his pockets.
    II. Investigation has determined there were no witnesses to this incident.
    III. The man asked White to check the oil and fill the tank.
    IV. Mr. White, a gas attendant, states that he was working alone at the gas station when a male black pulled up to the gas pump in a white Mercury.
    V. White was then bound and gagged by the male and locked in the gas station's rest room.

    The MOST logical order for the above sentences to appear in the report is:

    A. IV, I, III, II, V
    B. III, I, II, V, IV
    C. IV, III, I, V, II
    D. I, III, IV, II, V

25. Police Officer Gale is preparing a report of a crime committed against Mr. Weston. The report will consist of the following five sentences:
    I. The man, who had a gun, told Mr. Weston not to scream for help and ordered him back into the apartment.
    II. With Mr. Weston disposed of in this fashion, the man proceeded to ransack the apartment.
    III. Opening the door to see who was there, Mr. Weston was confronted by a tall white male wearing a dark blue jacket and white pants.
    IV. Mr. Weston was at home alone in his living room when the doorbell rang.
    V. Once inside, the man bound and gagged Mr. Weston and locked him in the bathroom.

    The MOST logical order for the above sentences to appear in the report is:

    A. III, V, II, I, IV
    B. IV, III, I, V, II
    C. III, V, IV, II, I
    D. IV, III, V, I, II

KEY (CORRECT ANSWERS)

1. B
2. B
3. A
4. D
5. C

6. C
7. A
8. C
9. B
10. D

11. C
12. B
13. C
14. C
15. A

16. C
17. A
18. C
19. D
20. B

21. B
22. A
23. B
24. C
25. B

TEST 2

DIRECTIONS: Each question or incomplete statement is followed by several suggested answers or completions. Select the one that BEST answers the question or completes the statement. *PRINT THE LETTER OF THE CORRECT ANSWER IN THE SPACE AT THE RIGHT.*

Questions 1-10.

DIRECTIONS: Questions 1 through 10 are to be answered SOLELY on the basis of the following passage and Stolen Vehicle Report Form, which appears on the following page. The Form contains 43 numbered boxes. Read the passage and look at the Form before answering the questions.

Police Officers Walton and Wright, patrolling in their radio patrol car in the industrial area of the 29th Precinct, were dispatched to 523 Johnson Boulevard at 10:30 A.M. on October 30, 2003 by the Police Radio Dispatcher. The Dispatcher had received a telephone call from a Ms. Ann Graham at 10:28 A.M. that her friend's car was being stolen from in front of her house.

Officers Walton and Wright arrived at 523 Johnson Boulevard at 10:32 A.M. Ms. Graham was waiting outside and informed them that the car had already been stolen. She stated that her friend, Samantha Merlin, had gone on vacation to California three days before and had left her car in Ms. Graham's care. Ms. Graham had parked the car in front of her own house the night before.

Ms. Graham stated that she looked out of her window at 10:25 A.M. that day and saw a strange man breaking into the car using a wire coat hanger. The car's hood was raised. She ran to her telephone to call the Police. When she returned to her window, she saw the man doing something under the hood and, within a minute, he drove the car away. She had been too frightened to try to stop him, and there was no one else on the street.

Ms. Graham described the stolen car as a black 1990 Buick 2-door sedan, New York license plate number 113-ABT, Vehicle Identification Number 7641239877. She stated that her friend, Ms. Merlin, lives at 1905 Junis Road, her telephone number is 978-4123, she is unmarried, 30 years old, and will return from vacation on November 13, 2003. Until then, she can be reached by telephone at 213-804-9112. She is employed at the law firm of Adams and Adams, 360 Park Avenue, as an office manager.

Ms. Graham described the man who stole the car as white, in his early twenties, about 5'7", 155 lbs., and wearing blue pants, a black jacket, and an earring in his left ear. He had dark brown, short curly hair.

Ms. Graham gave her telephone number as 275-8722 and stated that she is divorced, employed as a securities analyst at F.G. Sutton and Company, 125 Wall Street, and is 32 years old. Her birth date is June 13, 1971. Her telephone number at work is 217-7273.

STOLEN VEHICLE REPORT FORM

COMPLAINT INFORMATION	Complaint Number (1)	Precinct (2)	Date Complaint Reported (3)	Time Reported (4)	Place Complaint Taken (5)
VEHICLE DESCRIPTION	Year (6)	Make (7)	Color (8)	License Number (9)	
	I.D. Number (10)		Type (11)	Location of Theft (12)	
OWNER INFORMATION	Name (13)		Address (14)	Home Telephone (15)	
	Age (16)		Marital Status (17)	Occupation (18)	
	Business Address (19)			Business Telephone (20)	
WITNESS INFORMATION	Name (21)		Address (22)	Home Telephone (23)	
	Age (24)		Marital Status (25)	Occupation (26)	
	Business Address (27)			Business Telephone (28)	
	Witness' Description of Incident (29)				
DESCRIPTION OF SUSPECT	Name (If Known) (30)	Age (31)	Race (32)	Sex (33)	Height (34)	Weight (35)	Hair (36)
	Eyes (37)	Clothing (38)		Distinctive Marks (39)			
	Other (40)						
OFFICER INFORMATION	Name (41)			Date (42)			
	Shield Number (43)						

1. Which one of the follotwing should be entered in Box 3?   1.____

   A. June 13, 2003   B. October 13, 2003
   C. October 30, 2003   D. November 13, 2003

2. Which one of the following should be entered in Box 31?   2.____

   A. Late teens   B. Early twenties
   C. 30   D. 32

3. Which one of the following should be entered in Box 12? In front of   3.____

   A. 1905 Junis Road   B. 523 Johnson Boulevard
   C. 125 Wall Street   D. 360 Park Avenue

4. Which one of the following should be entered in Box 8?   4.____

   A. Blue   B. Brown   C. Black   D. Red

5. Which one of the following should be entered in Box 11?   5.____

   A. 2-door sedan   B. 4-door sedan
   C. 4-door station wagon   D. 2-door sportscar

6. Which one of the following should be entered in Box 15?   6.____

   A. 804-9112   B. 217-7273   C. 275-8722   D. 978-4123

7. Which one of the follotwing should be entered in Box 17?   7.____

   A. Married   B. Legally separated
   C. Single   D. Divorced

8. Which one of the following should be entered in Box 21?   8.____

   A. Samantha Merlin   B. Samantha Graham
   C. Ann Merlin   D. Ann Graham

9. Which one of the following should be entered in Box 26?   9.____

   A. Securities analyst   B. Housewife
   C. Office manager   D. Secretary

10. Which one of the follotwing should be entered in Box 40?   10.____

    A. Scar on left cheek   B. Earring in left ear
    C. Short curly brown hair   D. Blue pants, black jacket

Questions 11-13.

DIRECTIONS: Questions 11 through 13 are to be answered SOLELY on the basis of the following:

Officer Pei is told to notify the station house when he spots dangerous conditions.

11. Which one of the following should the Officer report?   11.____
    A

A. car with a stuck horn parked on a side street
B. broken traffic light at a busy intersection
C. car, double-parked in front of a newspaper stand, with its flashers on
D. truck unloading vegetable crates into a supermarket

12. Which one of the following should the Officer report? 12._____
A

    A. scaffold on the sixteenth floor of an office building containing two men washing the windows
    B. crane moving girders to the ground floor of a building under construction
    C. man working on a chimney of a three-story house
    D. section of roof about to fall on the street from a two-story house

13. Which one of the following should the Officer report? A(n) 13._____

    A. open sewer, cover missing, just off the curb
    B. missing wire garbage bin at the corner of a busy street
    C. missing telephone in a phone booth on a busy corner
    D. parking meter with the entire top missing

Questions 14-15.

DIRECTIONS: Questions 14 and 15 are to be answered SOLELY on the basis of the following passage.

At 11 o'clock on Sunday morning, Police Officer Dempsey arrives on the scene of a vehicle accident that had happened approximately 30 minutes earlier involving a school bus carrying 20 children travelling north on Sumpter Ave.; a cement truck travelling south on Sumpter Ave.; a car travelling east on Swan Blvd.; and a motorcycle travelling west on Swan Blvd. The Officer asks the people standing around at the scene if any of them had seen the accident take place. The following is what each of those who claimed to have seen the accident take place said:

Mr. W: I was walking my dog at 10:30 when I saw a cement truck that was travelling on Sumpter Ave. swerve to miss a stalled car in the intersection of Sumpter and Swan, and hit a school bus travelling in the opposite direction. The bus in turn spun around and hit a car travelling on Swan, which in turn hit a motorcycle, also on Swan.

Miss X: At 10:30, I was on my way to work when I heard a loud screeching of brakes. I immediately looked around and saw a cement truck swerve, miss a stalled car in the intersection of Sumpter and Swan, hit a school bus, which in turn hit a car on Swan. The car then collided with a motorcycle on Swan. I saw a man jump out of the cement truck and run down Sumpter.

Mrs. Y: I was returning home after having bought a bottle of whiskey from the corner liquor store when I saw a cement truck going down Sumpter hit its brakes, swerve around a car that had stalled, and collide with a school bus. The school bus then hit into a car and motorcycle that were on Swan.

Mr. Z: I was in my house which is located on the corner of Sumpter and Swan when I heard a crash. I looked out and saw a cement truck and school bus that apparently had collided at the intersection of Sumpter and Swan. I then saw that a car and motorcycle on Swan had been involved in the accident as well. There was a stalled car in the intersection.

14. The Officer should report that there are errors in the statements made by one or more of the above four people concerning which one of the following elements?

    A. The number of vehicles involved in the accident
    B. The location of the accident
    C. Their activities prior to the accident
    D. The time the accident took place

15. Whose account of the accident includes a possibly important element NOT mentioned by the others?

    A. Mr. W   B. Miss X   C. Mrs. Y   D. Mr. Z

16. Police Officer Haines has received three complaints in a one-week period from elderly people who have been victimized while banking. Each incident was basically the same: a stranger would walk over to the elderly person and convince him or net to withdraw large amounts of money from a savings account. The description of each suspect is as follows:
    Incident No. 1 (January 5) - Female, white, late 20's, 5'5", 130 lbs., short curly dark hair, large mole on chin, pierced ears, blue jeais, grey jacket, grey boots.
    Incident No. 2 (January 7) - Female, white, 25-30, 5'4", 95 lbs., short curly dark hair, large mole on chin, pierced ears, black pants, grey jacket, boots.
    Incident No. 3 (January 8) - Female, white, 40-45, 5'5", 130-140 lbs., short curly dark hair, no visible distinguishing marks, blue jeans, grey jacket, boots.

    On January 9, a fourth incident occurs, but this time the elderly person informs a bank officer who calls the Police, and an arrest is made. The description of the suspect is as follows:
    Incident No. 4 (January 9) - Female, white, 25-30, 5'5", 130 lbs., short curly dark hair, large mole on chin, blue jeans, grey jacket, grey boots, ear muffs.

    Based upon the descriptions given above of the suspects in the first three incidents, the suspect in Incident No. 4 should also be considered a suspect in Incident Number(s)

    A. 1 only   B. 1 and 2   C. 1 and 3   D. 1, 2, and 3

Questions 17-18.

DIRECTIONS: Questions 17 and 18 are to be answered SOLELY on the basis of the following.

A Police Officer may have to place barricades or signals on a roadway to warn motorists of hazardous spots on the road.

17. For which one of the following should an Officer place a barricade on the roadway? 17.____
    A

    A. one-lane country road
    B. road with several sharp turns
    C. road with two filled-in potholes
    D. road with a broken water main

18. For which one of the following should an Officer place a barricade on the roadway? 18.____
    A

    A. 4-lane road with on emergency phone
    B. narrow 2-lane road with an obstruction in the middle
    C. road recently repaved
    D. road covered with dry leaves

19. A Police Officer may have to evacuate people from a dangerous area. 19.____
    From which one of the following areas should a Police Officer evacuate people?
    A

    A. crowded disco
    B. crowded subway station
    C. building where gas is leaking
    D. parking lot where a minor traffic accident has occurred

20. Police Officer White is preparing a crime report concerning the burglary of Mr. Smith's 20.____
    home. The report will contain the following five sentences:
    I. Upon entering the house, Mr. Smith noticed that the mortgage money, which had been left on the kitchen table, had been taken.
    II. An investigation by the reporting Officer determined that the burglar had left the house through the first floor rear door.
    III. Further investigation revealed that there were no witnesses to the burglary.
    IV. In addition, several pieces of jewelry were missing from a first floor bedroom.
    V. After arriving at home, Mr. Smith discovered that someone had broken into the house by jimmying the front door.
    The MOST logical order for the above sentences to appear in the report is:

    A. V, IV, II, III, I   B. V, I, III, IV, II
    C. V, I, IV, II, III   D. V, IV, II, I, III

21. A Police Officer is completing a report of a robbery, which will contain the following five 21.____
    sentences:
    I. Two Police Officers were about to enter the Red Rose Coffee Shop on 47th Street and 8th Avenue.
    II. They then noticed a male running up the street carrying a brown paper bag.
    III. They heard a woman standing outside the Broadway Boutique yelling that her store had just been robbed by a young man, and she was pointing up the street.
    IV. They caught up with him and made an arrest.
    V. The Police Officers pursued the male, who ran past them on 8th Avenute.
    The MOST logical order for the above sentences to appear in the report is:

    A. I, III, II, V, IV   B. III, I, II, V, IV
    C. IV, V, I, II, III   D. I, V, IV, III, II

22. Police Officer Capalbo is preparing a report of a bank robbery. The report will contain the following five statements made by a witness:
    I. Initially all I could see were two men, dressed in maintenance uniforms, sitting in the area reserved for bank officers.
    II. I was passing the bank at 8 P.M. and noticed that all the lights were out, except in the rear section.
    III. Then I noticed two other men in the bank, coming from the direction of the vault, carrying a large metal box.
    IV. At this point, I decided to call the Police.
    V. I knocked on the window to get the attention of the men in the maintenance uniforms, and they chased the two men carrying the box down a flight of steps.

    The MOST logical order for the above sentences to appear in the report is:

    A. IV, I, II, V, III
    B. I, III, II, V, IV
    C. II, I, III, V, IV
    D. II, III, I, V, IV

22.___

23. Police Officer Roberts is preparing a crime report concerning an assault and a stolen car. The report will contain the following five sentences:
    I. Upon leaving the store to return to his car, Winters noticed that a male unknown to him was sitting in his car.
    II. The man then re-entered Winters' car and drove away, fleeing north on 2nd Avenue.
    III. Mr. Winters stated that he parked his car in front of 235 East 25th Street and left the engine running while he went into the butcher shop at that location.
    IV. Mr. Robert Gering, a witness, stated that the male is known in the neighborhood as Bobby Rae and is believed to reside at 323 East 114th Street.
    V. When Winters approached the car and ordered the man to get out, the man got out of the auto and struck Winters with his fists, knocking him to the ground.

    The MOST logical order for the above sentences to appear in the report is:

    A. III, II, V, I, IV
    B. III, I, V, II, IV
    C. I, IV, V, II, III
    D. III, II, I, V, IV

23.___

24. Police Officer Robinson is preparing a crime report concerning the robbery of Mr. Edwards' store. The report will consist of the following five sentences:
    I. When the last customer left the store, the two men drew revolvers and ordered Mr. Edwards to give them all the money in the cash register.
    II. The men proceeded to the back of the store as if they were going to do some shopping.
    III. Janet Morley, a neighborhood resident, later reported that she saw the men enter a green Ford station wagon and flee northbound on Albany Avenue.
    IV. Edwards complied after which the gunmen ran from the store.
    V. Mr. Edwards states that he was stocking merchandise behind the store counter when two male whites entered the store.

    The MOST logical order for the above sentences to appear in the report is:

    A. V, II, III, I, IV
    B. V, II, I, IV, III
    C. II, I, V, IV, III
    D. III, V, II, I, IV

24.___

25. Police Officer Wendell is preparing an accident report for a 6-car accident that occurred at the intersection of Bath Avenue and Bay Parkway. The report will consist of the following five sentences:

   I. A 1994 Volkswagon Rabbit, travelling east on Bath Avenue, swerved to ;he left to avoid the Impala, and struck a 1992 Ford station wagon which was travelling west on Bath Avenue.
   II. The Seville then mounted the curb on the northeast corner of Bath Avenue and Bay Parkway and struck a light pole.
   III. A 1991 Buick Lesabre, travelling northbound on Bay Parkway directly behind the Impala, struck the Impala, pushing it into the intersection of Bath Avenue and Bay Parkway.
   IV. A 1993 Chevy Impala, travelling northbound on Bay Parkway, had stopped for a red light at Bath Avenue.
   V. A 1995 Toyota, travelling westbound on Bath Avenue, swerved to the right to avoid hitting the Ford station wagon, and struck a 1995 Cadillac Seville double-parked near the corner.

   The MOST logical order for the above sentences to appear in the report is:

   A. IV, III, V, II, I
   B. III, IV, V, II, I
   C. IV, III, I, V, II
   D. III, IV, V, I, II

KEY (CORRECT ANSWERS)

1.	C	11.	B
2.	B	12.	D
3.	B	13.	A
4.	C	14.	C
5.	A	15.	D
6.	D	16.	A
7.	C	17.	D
8.	D	18.	B
9.	A	19.	C
10.	B	20.	C

21. A
22. C
23. B
24. B
25. C

TEST 3

DIRECTIONS: Each question or incomplete statement is followed by several suggested answers or completions. Select the one that BEST answers the question or completes the statement. *PRINT THE LETTER OF THE CORRECT ANSWER IN THE SPACE AT THE RIGHT.*

1. A Police Officer may be called upon to help settle disputes.
Which one of the following situations should the Officer help settle?

    A. Two men talking about sports outside a bar
    B. A shopkeeper arguing with a customer over an unpaid bill
    C. Four teenagers discussing fashion with a shopkeeper
    D. A man and woman running for political office having a debate

    1.____

2. A Police Officer is required to check the condition of his patrol car and fill out a report for anything that is found to be unsafe.
For which one of the following conditions would the Police Officer have to fill out such a report?

    A. Two missing hubcaps in the rear
    B. A horn that does not work
    C. A small chip on the right side of the windshield
    D. Two dents on the hood of the car

    2.____

3. A Police Officer is required to inspect the driver's license of any driver he stops. The Officer must detain any driver whose description does not match the description on the license, while he checks to see if the driver is using someone else's license.
In which one of the following situations should the Police Officer detain the driver?
A(n) _____ whose date of birth on _____ license is _____

    A. young male; his; 12/20/82
    B. young female; her; 5/15/84
    C. middle-aged male; his; 4/3/78
    D. elderly female; her; 8/16/28

    3.____

4. Officers are sometimes required to use their patrol cars to transport seriously injured people to a hospital. Officers should call an ambulance for people who are NOT seriously injured.
Which one of the following people should the Officer transport in the patrol car? A person

    A. bleeding from the head
    B. with a sprained ankle
    C. with a badly skinned knee
    D. with a limp

    4.____

5. Three purse snatchings are reported during a three-week period near the Bay Housing Project. In each case, the victim provided a description of the suspect. The description of each suspect is as follows:
Purse Snatching #1 (September 8) - Male, white, teenager, 5"5", 175 lbs., cap, tattoo on upper left arm, short sleeve grey shirt, black pants, and black shoes.

    5.____

Purse Snatching #2 (September 14) - Male, white, teenager, 5'5", 145 lbs., white cowboy hat, large scar directly over right eyebrow, short sleeve shirt, blue pants, and black shoes.

Purse Snatching #3 (September 22) - Male, white, teenager, 5' 5", 140 lbs., short brown hair, large-sized sunglasses, short sleeve blue shirt, blue jeans, and black sneakers.

On September 24, a fourth purse snatching occurs near the Bay Housing Project. This time the suspect is observed by a Police Officer and is arrested. His description is as follows:

Purse Snatching #4 (September 24) - Male, white, teenager, 5'5",143 lbs.,short brown hair, large scar directly over right eyebrow, short sleeve grey shirt, black pants, and black shoes.

Based upon the description given above of the suspects in the first three purse snatchings, the suspect in Purse Snatching #4 should also be considered a suspect in

- A. Purse Snatching 1 *only*
- B. Purse Snatchings 2 and 3
- C. Purse Snatchings 1, 2, and 3
- D. none of the above

6. A Police Officer patrolling in a Police vehicle must sometimes use the vehicle's flashing lights and/or siren. When responding to a crime in progress in a Police vehicle, a Police Officer must use the following procedures in the order given:
    I. Determine, from the Radio Dispatcher, the nature of the crime and whether anyone is in immediate danger of serious injury.
        a. If someone is in immediate danger of serious injury, turn on flashing lights and use siren.
        b. If no one is in immediate danger of serious injury, use flashing lights only.
    II. Upon arrival at crime scene, turn off siren.

Police Officer Emerson receives a call to respond to a burglary in progress. He determines from the Radio Dispatcher that no one is in immediate danger of serious injury. Which one of the following actions should Emerson take NEXT? Turn

- A. on flashing lights *only*
- B. on siren
- C. on flashing lights and siren
- D. off siren

Questions 7-8.

DIRECTIONS: Questions 7 and 8 are to be answered SOLELY on the basis of the following information.

Housing Officer Duggan is assigned to the Evans Housing Project on West 259th Street and April Avenue. Duggan familiarizes himself with the crime statistics of the four buildings in the project for September. All the robberies took place at 20 West 259th Street. All the assaults took place at 5 April Avenue. Mail boxes were broken into only at 7 April Avenue. All the rapes took place at 22 West 259th Street. All off the assaults happened between 3 P.M.

and 4 P.M. Robberies occurred between 11 A.M. and 1 P.M. The mail boxes were broken into shortly after the mail delivery between 1:30 P.M. and 2:30 P.M. Rapes occurred early in the morning when women left for work from 8 A.M. to 9 A.M.

When Duggan is working an 8 A.M. to 4 P.M. tour, he must divide his time among the four buildings to prevent these crimes.

7. To reduce the number of rapes, he should patrol

   A. 20 West 259th Street from 11 A.M. to 1 P.M.
   B. 5 April Avenue from 1:30 to 2:30 P.M.
   C. 12 West 259th Street from 8 to 9 A.M.
   D. 22 West 259th Street from 8 to 9 A.M.

8. To reduce the number of assaults, he should patrol from

   A. 3 to 4 P.M. at 5 April Avenue
   B. 8 to 9 A.M. at 7 April Avenue
   C. 11 A.M. to 1 P.M. at 5 April Avenue
   D. 3 to 4 P.M. at 7 April Avenue

9. Three robberies occurred during a two-week period in the Diamond District. In each case, the owner of a jewelry store was robbed, and the description of each suspect is as follows:
   Robbery No. 1 (December 6) - Male, white, early 30's, 5 "9", 160 lbs., long blonde hair, mustache and beard, large scar on right hand, blue suit and black shoes.
   Robbery No. 2 (December 14) - Male, white, 35, 5'9", 165 lbs., short blonde hair, clean-shaven, large scar on right hand, grey suit and blaick shoes.
   Robbery No. 3 (December 16) - Male, white, 30, 5'9", 160 lbs., bald, clean-shaven, large scar on right hand, blue suit and black shoes.

   On December 17, a fourth robbery occurs, but this time a suspect is arrested during the robbery. The description of this suspect is as follows:
   Robbery No. 4 (December 17) - Male, white, 33, 5'9", 160 lbs., bald, clean-shaven, large scar on right hand, black suit and shoes.
   Based upon the descriptions given above of the suspects in the first three robberies, the suspect in Robbery No. 4 should also be considered a suspect in

   A. Robbery No. 1 *only*
   B. Robbery No. 3 *only*
   C. Robbery Nos. 1, 2, and 3
   D. none of the above

Questions 10-11.

DIRECTIONS: Questions 10 and 11 are to be answered SOLELY on the basis of the following information.

Police Officers are sometimes required to respond to the scene of a traffic accident involving two vehicles. In situations in which one of the drivers involved in the accident has driven away from the scene before the Officer arrives, the responding Police Officer must use the following procedures in the order given:

I. Ask the driver of the remaining vehicle if he noticed the license plate number of vehicle which fled.
   A. If license plate number is known, call Vehicle Inquiry Section to determine name and address of owner.
   B. Write down the name and the address of owner of vehicle which fled.
   C. Give name and address of owner of vehicle which fled to driver remaining at scene of accident.
II. Obtain from driver remaining at scene all details of the accident including description of vehicle which fled.
III. Call Stolen Vehicle Desk.
IV. Prepare Complaint Form in duplicate upon return to precinct.
V. Give original of Complaint Form to Sergeant.
VI. Place copy of Complaint Form in Vehicle Complaint Folder.

10. Police Officer Mica arrives at the scene of a traffic accident involving two cars. One of the drivers fled the scene five minutes before Mica arrived, but the driver of the remaining vehicle, Henry Bates, was able to see the fleeing vehicle's license plate number and reports it to Mica.
Which one of the following actions should Police Officer Mica take NEXT?

   A. Prepare Complaint Form in duplicate.
   B. Call Stolen Vehicle Desk.
   C. Give original of Complaint Form to Sergeant.
   D. Call Vehicle Inquiry Section.

11. Five minutes later, Police Officer Mica has already completed all the appropriate actions through obtaining from Bates all details of the accident and a description of the fleeing vehicle.
Which one of the following actions should Police Officer Mica take NEXT?

   A. Call Stolen Vehicle Desk.
   B. Call Vehicle Inquiry Section.
   C. Prepare Complaint Form in duplicate.
   D. Place copy of Complaint Form in Vehicle Complaint Folder.

Questions 12-13.

DIRECTIONS: Questions 12 and 13 are to be answered SOLELY on the basis of the following information.

Police Officer Gentry notices that in his sector all the robberies take place on Henry Street, all the burglaries occur on Thomas Street, and all the traffic accidents happen on John Street.

Most of the robberies take place between 5 P.M. and 11 P.M. Most of the traffic accidents occur during the hours of 3 P.M. to 7 P.M. Most of the burglaries happen from 6 P.M. to 2 A.M.

Most of the burglaries happen on Thursdays, most of the robberies occur on Thursdays, and most of the traffic accidents happen on Fridays.

12. Police Officer Gentry would MOST likely be able to reduce the incidents of burglary by patrolling

    A. Henry Street on Thursdays from 3 P.M. to 7 P.M.
    B. John Street on Thursdays from 6 P.M. to 2 A.M.
    C. Thomas Street on Thursdays from 6 P.M. to 2 A.M.
    D. Thomas Street on Fridays from 3 P.M. to 7 P.M.

13. Police Officer Gentry would MOST likely be able to reduce the number of traffic accidents by patrolling John Street on

    A. Fridays from 3 A.M. to 7 A.M.
    B. Fridays from 5 A.M. to 11 A.M.
    C. Thursdays from 3 P.M. to 7 P.M.
    D. Fridays from 3 P.M. to 7 P.M.

Questions 14-20.

DIRECTIONS: Questions 14 through 20 are to be answered SOLELY on the basis of the following sketches. The first face, on the left, is a sketch of an alleged criminal based on witnesses' descriptions at the crime scene. One of the four sketches to the right is the way the suspect looked after changing appearance. Assume that NO surgery has been done on the suspect. Select the face which is MOST likely that of the suspect.

14.

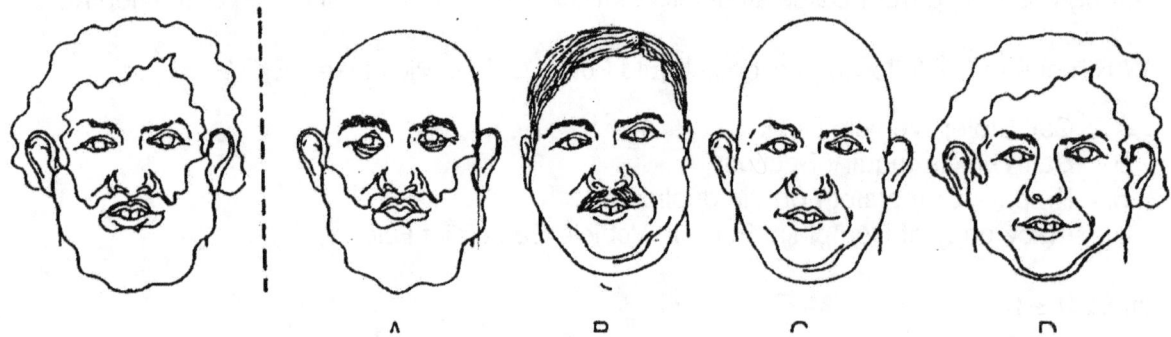

15.

A. B. C. D.

16.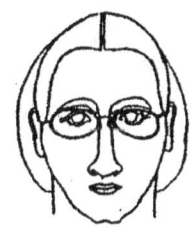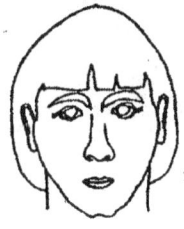
   A. B. C. D.

16.____

17.
   A. B. C. D.

17.____

18.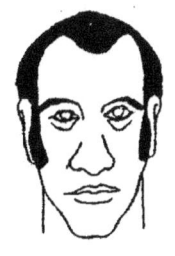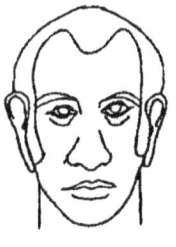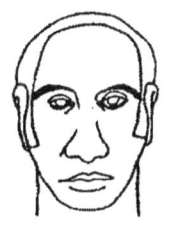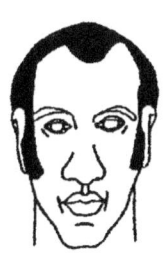
   A. B. C. D.

18.____

19.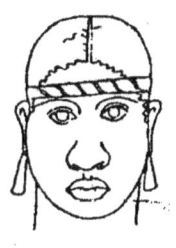
   A. B. C. D.

19.____

20.

                A.   B.   C.   D.

20. ____

KEY (CORRECT ANSWERS)

1.	B	11.	A
2.	B	12.	C
3.	C	13.	D
4.	A	14.	C
5.	B	15.	A
6.	A	16.	D
7.	D	17.	D
8.	A	18.	A
9.	C	19.	B
10.	D	20.	D

www.ingramcontent.com/pod-product-compliance
Lightning Source LLC
Chambersburg PA
CBHW081758300426
44116CB00014B/2164